# Doctors and Discoveries

## Lives That Created Today's Medicine

John Galbraith Simmons

Houghton Mifflin Company    Boston    New York

*Library of Congress Cataloging-in-Publication Data*

Simmons, John, 1949–
    Doctors and discoveries : lives that created today's medicine/
    John Galbraith Simmons.
       p.   cm.
    Includes index.
    ISBN 0–618–15276–8
      1. Physicians—Biography.  2. Medical scientists—Biography.
      3. Medicine—History.   I. Title.

R134.5 .S56 2002
610'.92'2—dc21
[B]                                  2001059353

Manufactured in the United States of America

QWF 10 9 8 7 6 5 4 3 2 1

*For my brother Gar*

But what, without the social thought of thee,
Would be the wonders of the sky and sea?
— KEATS

# Contents

## Part III Figures of Constant Reference

## Part IV Creating Modern Medicine

## Part V  Recent and Contemporary

## Part VI  Omnium-Gatherum

*Ars longa, vita brevis* — "Art is long, life is short"

—HIPPOCRATES, *Aphorisms*

# Acknowledgments

Several people whom I know only slightly helped me shape the contents of this book, perhaps more than they imagine. I would particularly like to thank Jacalyn Duffin, the Jason A. Hannah Professor of the History of Medicine at Queen's University, and Edward T. Morman, librarian and director of the Francis C. Wood Institute for the History of Medicine at the College of Physicians of Philadelphia. They evaluated early drafts of the table of contents and provided eminently useful suggestions; later they answered questions and offered welcome advice. My thanks also to Keith Benson, Lawrence Creshkoff, John Munder Ross, and Margaret A. Reilly. I am responsible for the final selection.

This book required the help of a host of historians of medicine, physicians, and scientists whose works investigate in depth the subjects here profiled briefly. Accuracy and balance were major aims, and wherever plausible I asked scholars to read individual chapters. With almost unfailing grace they consented. I thank Louis Acierno, Debra Jan Bibel, Jill V. Brazier, Charles S. Bryan, Jeffrey A. Cohlberg, Alfred W. Crosby, Allen G. Debus, Steven Epstein, Julie M. Fenster, Daniel Garrison, Sir Henry Harris, Katya Harvey, Malcolm H. Hast, Peter Hawkes, Ilse Hoffmann, Frederic Lawrence Holmes, Saul Jarcho, Hugh LaFollette, Lori A. Leipold, Kenneth M. Ludmerer, Maclyn McCarty, Jane Maienschein, Thomas Maier, Theodore I. Malinin, Sherwin B. Nuland, Janis Pallister, Nigel Paneth, Paul Potter, John Riddle, Roy Schafer, Hugh Small, James Strick, E. M. Tansey, Alfred I. Tauber, Byron H. Waksman, Dora B. Weiner, and Peter Wolbert.

Some of the individual physicians and scientists profiled in this volume are still alive, or were still living while the book was being written. I offered them the opportunity to read their respective chapters for factual errors. My thanks to Sir James Black, Raymond Damadian, Jean Dausset, Gerald M. Edelman, Walter Gilbert, Sir Godfrey Hounsfield, Willem J. Kolff, Arthur Kornberg, the late William Masters, Luc Montagnier, Solomon Snyder, Harold Varmus, and Bert Vogelstein.

At Houghton Mifflin, Margery S. Berube was the first to recognize the value of a project such as this, and I am grateful to her. My editor,

Hanna Schonthal, brought great sensitivity and intelligence to a difficult and time-consuming task, and I can't begin to express my gratitude. Diane Fredrick copyedited the manuscript with forbearance, and corrected numerous errors, as did proofreaders Ben Fortson and Wade Ostrowski. The flaws and faults that remain, in broad outline and in the details, are all mine. For production and for preparing the illustration program, I am grateful to Christopher Granniss and Margaret Anne Miles. My thanks also to literary agent Giles Anderson.

Finally, Jocelyne Barque and Clayton Simmons provided help and much-needed homeostasis. My good friend Bill Grantham provided crucial, indispensable guidance. My warmest thanks extend to science writer Ben Patrusky, to colleagues at the Writers Room in New York, and as always to Jim Ellison, Fred Korndorf, Mia Rublowska, and Donald Nicholson-Smith.

# Introduction

## A Human Dimension to the History of Medicine

It did not become a juggernaut overnight. The power and authority that medicine today enjoys in the Western world took about 2500 years to acquire. Doctors and surgeons, not to mention healers and mountebanks, long worked with ingenious but often ineffective theories. They followed wrong ideas and dispensed bad medicine all their lives. Yet, long before medicine was allied to science and technology, some among them also cultivated insights and developed techniques that made their medicine work. They accumulated and created knowledge that served patients with rational explanations for all that ailed. For that alone, the great historical figures of medicine, from Hippocrates on, merit recollection and reflection. But they should not be treated as icons. They wrestled with baffling diseases and strange conditions, as well as with the labyrinthine architecture of the human body. They brought to bear, and were often brought down by, their own preconceptions and ideas.

Elie Metchnikoff, for example, was one of the vital figures in modern medicine. He discovered the large white blood cells known as phagocytes, and in the late nineteenth century developed an early theory of immunity. Temperamental, of unkempt appearance and long flowing beard, Metchnikoff could not keep an academic post in spite of his fame. He moved from place to place, finally becoming successor to Pasteur himself at the Institut Pasteur in Paris. Metchnikoff hoped to live to a ripe old age, possibly even to 130 years. To that end he ate a great deal of yogurt. For decades afterward his name, as an endorsement, was found on yogurt packages in French groceries. But longevity is more than sour milk. Metchnikoff's heart began to fail in 1913. In 1916 he fell gravely ill. It is poignant to record that, as he lay dying, he made one final stab at discovery. To his friend Dr. Salimbeni he said, "You will do my post-mortem? Look at the intestines carefully, for I think there is something there now."

Well, there wasn't. But much discovery in medicine is driven not just by curiosity but by felt frustration and emotional distress. In 1537 Ambroise Paré couldn't sleep because he hadn't cauterized his soldier-patients with boiling oil—only to learn from experience when they healed without that agonizing treatment. Centuries later, tragedy in the family tended to serve as a modern inspiration. Raymond Damadian, for example, recalls his grandmother's painful death from breast cancer when he was a child. "Grandma was gone, but the moaning wouldn't seem to go away. I'd keep hearing it night after night after night." Cancer was on his mind when he conceived magnetic resonance imaging (MRI). From cautery to soft tissue visualization, medicine has often moved forward with this combination of empathy and scrutiny.

But not to devalue pure intellectual genius. It intercedes on behalf of great advances in medicine, though often enough in conjunction with rife narcissism, grandiose fantasy, identification with heroes, and ambition and competitiveness beyond measure. Robert Koch and Louis Pasteur are both among the most renowned scientists in history. Koch, anxious to discover a treatment for the scourge of tuberculosis, impulsively announced a cure in 1890. But "tuberculin" was nothing much more than bacteria in aspic, and caused more harm than good. His rival Pasteur had better luck. Distressed by the appearance of a young boy bitten by a rabid dog, he decided to try a vaccine he had used until then only on animals. We don't know to this day if the boy had rabies, but young Joseph Meister did not fall sick, and Pasteur was covered in glory. Koch and Pasteur were two of the thirteen greatest "Microbe Hunters" whom Paul de Kruif profiled in a famous book by that title that has been reprinted dozens of times up to the present. Many boys and girls devoured its purple prose, and several among them went on to win the Nobel Prize. One of them, Carleton Gajdusek, affixed the names of de Kruif's great men to the steps leading to his attic laboratory.

Biographies in the history of medicine in recent years have a more nuanced human dimension, both for professional and popular consumption. Medical history used to be in large part hagiographic, intent on celebrating the triumphs of great doctors, misleading educated readers while boring medical students to distraction. In the classroom it was a slideshow procession of gray faces from the past, from which you could conclude "that one old gentleman with a beard," as Lester S. King once wrote, "looked very much like any other old gentleman with a beard." It was a "dry faded herbarium." Whole symposia would be launched with wooden titles like "On the Utility of Medical History."

This began to change as early as the 1930s, however, with the writings of such historians as Henry Sigerist—brilliant scholar, left-wing socialist and fighter for universal health care, and author of *Great Doctors*. It continues today, sustained by tremendous growth in medical knowledge and by historians who combine a grasp of medicine with larger issues of social history and culture. They know that to denigrate or misunderstand the past is the best way to misperceive the future. The task of the history of medicine is not to celebrate, but, wrote Sigerist, "to resuscitate what was, and to bring it back to life, so that the past may become an experience in the present, and so that we may be aware of where we came from, where we stand today, and in what direction we are moving."

## Western Medicine: A Brief Historical Sketch

The history of Western medicine, reprised by the profiles in this volume in eighty-six doses, is not hard to encapsule. For over two thousand years, with limited tools, physicians nurtured the ideas of rational (as opposed to magical) medicine. From Hippocrates in Ancient Greece, to Galen during the Roman Empire, to Ibn Sina (Avicenna) during the Middle Ages, a basic canon was developed that provided a framework for understanding how the body worked, described what happened when a person fell ill, and prescribed things that might be done to help. Surgery was limited to the body's surface, or else was a drastic, last-ditch intervention.

The limits of this medicine, in retrospect, are fairly plain. But life itself was brief, physical pain and cruelty were not uncommon, and the relations between self and others were not always subtle and refined. The famous Hippocratic dictum possessed the wisdom of realistic pessimism: "Art is long and life is short, the occasion fleeting, experience fallacious, and judgment difficult." This was a durable aphorism, as true in 1700 as in the fifth century B.C. The coming of the Scientific Revolution, whether we date it to the "Long Renaissance" or to the seventeenth century, did not change much for medicine. The writings of Paracelsus might have realigned the theoretical mindset of some physicians, but in the end they did not mean a great deal to patients, much less to surgeons or to the innumerable healers who treated the rural masses. Anton van Leeuwenhoek, the Dutch draper, could see "little animalcules" with his simple microscopes, but he had no context to understand their significance. William Harvey could demonstrate that the blood circulates through the body, and could characterize the heart as its pump. Anatomist Marcello Malpighi was able to discover the minute capillaries that link veins and arteries — as Harvey had predicted. But how the body works in subtler ways remained mysterious. For a time scientists conceived it to be much like a hydraulic machine, comprised of humors within solids, with fluids pumped into fibers through tubes. To call Thomas Sydenham, of the seventeenth century, the "English Hippocrates" was to honor him, but also to express the limits of his craft.

Not until the beginning of the nineteenth century did scientific medicine begin to acquire substance and a new foundation — though even then, for many years its role in ameliorating disease had strict limits. The onset of this new scientific medicine is usually traced to the aftermath of the French Revolution, when unique conditions in France permitted a marriage, consummated largely on the dissection table, between clinical medicine and pathology. For the first time, with magnifying lens and such tools as the stethoscope, symptoms and manifestations of various diseases were directly linked to changes in the body, usually as discovered at autopsy. A whole succession of key figures—Xavier Bichat, René Laennec, François Magendie, and others—laid the groundwork for a new physiology, at whose head, a generation later, came Claude Bernard. Modern clinical medicine was in gestation.

Physiology also flourished in Germany beginning in the 1820s, and it established a solid base of knowledge in medical science. Its first important school was headed by Johannes Müller. One of his students, Jacob Henle, used the recently improved microscope to yield an impressive new histology that described and reclassified the various tissues, pretty much as they are understood today. Even more significant was cell theory. It was first glimpsed by botanists, but soon acquired prominence in medicine, where it became the instrument of inquiry into pathology. Attention to the cell as the self-replicating unit of life is owed to Rudolf Virchow and dates to 1858, just a year before Charles Darwin published *On the Origin of Species.* In general, it is difficult to overestimate the overarching importance of cell theory and a modern biology on the subsequent development of medicine.

In spite of all these advances, well into the nineteenth century new medical knowledge did not generate much in the way of therapy. When epidemics struck, sometimes medicine seemed scarcely more effective than during the Black Death in the fourteenth century, when Europe lost a quarter of its population. Disease still frequently carried off people in every decade of life. Infant mortality remained high, complicated by a growing urban society and little attention to public health. Although smallpox came under partial control with the vaccine developed by Edward Jenner, among the diseases that menaced young and old were diphtheria, typhus, influenza, and cholera. The cause of a chronic disease such as pellagra was malnutrition, but this remained unknown, and for many victims its multiple symptoms, from diarrhea to dementia, ended with death. Similar problems applied to other illnesses.

Nevertheless, it is fair to say, in retrospect, that beginning about 1850, medicine began a century-long transformation. Advances in public health and hygiene came first in England, the most advanced of the industrializing countries. In London in 1854, John Snow traced an epidemic outbreak of cholera to the Broad Street pump. Nursing, most prominently represented by Florence Nightingale, is usually dated from her work during and after the 1854 Crimean War. The importance of aseptic measures was recognized, first with little influence by the Viennese physician Ignaz Semmelweis, and somewhat later, independently and more prominently, by the British surgeon Joseph Lister. The modern hospital would be born of these advances, together with anesthesia, which also dates from midcentury. For the first time, surgeons could open the body to perform what soon became a variety of extended interventions with scalpel and suture.

The rise of microbiology, with the famous experiments on anthrax and rabies by Louis Pasteur, and identification of the bacterium that causes tuberculosis by Robert Koch, gave birth to the "germ theory of disease" in the 1880s. In 1894 the first of the great killer diseases was dealt a severe blow — or so it seems — when Emil von Behring and others developed a blood-serum treatment (a vaccine came later) to combat diphtheria. "Protect us, oh God, from diphtheria!" parents used to cry, for the disease could strangle their children, one after another, when it struck. Although success with diphtheria did not lead to hoped-for wonder drugs, it was arguably the first of a number of triumphs of modern medicine to touch the broadest possible public.

The prestige of medicine grew with the eventual achievements of the germ theory of disease, and also greatly benefited from institutional reforms such as improvements in public health. But medicine's real sophistication, power, and promise came only with advances in understanding basic biological and chemical processes. The first half of the twentieth century witnessed the gradual discovery of vitamins as necessary nutrients, of hormones as chemical messengers, of enzymes as molecular machines. The cell's innards spilled out in great complexity. Techniques in medicine advanced in conspiracy with the twentieth-century revolution in physics, making the discovery of X rays, in 1895, a fitting place to start. A new pharmacology emerged with the discovery of antibiotics. Some of the older bacterial diseases succumbed to vaccines, one of which — the Salk vaccine developed in 1954 — helped eventually vanquish the crippling and sometimes lethal viral disease of polio.

At this point in chronological time, one revolution ends and another begins. For in 1953 came the discovery of the structure of deoxyribonucleic acid (DNA), the molecule found in every nucleated cell. DNA, the "ultimate molecule of life," encodes genetic information that directs an organism's growth and maintenance — and, when instructions go awry, can give rise to disease.

The transformations in medicine that commenced or were predicted in the second half of the twentieth century were based on what was discovered during the first half. The central feature was the development of life sciences at the molecular level, essentially combining the tools of biochemistry with the insights of molecular biology. As was the case with the germ theory of disease, some years passed before basic research in these domains had serious clinical value for doctors and patients. In the developed countries, the institutional scope and perceived success of medicine were magnified by other scientific and technological advances, from lasers to computers.

Today it is possible to say that Western medicine has a long reach into the human body. Doctors have recourse to powerful drugs that can stave off death and sometimes modify the ravages of chronic illnesses. For diagnosis and treatment, they can render visible and sometimes manipulate the microscopic structures that comprise, control, and define the physical structure of human beings. Even greater accomplishments are promised with yet another long-awaited revolution. A large number of diseases may be controlled, if not cured, through intervention on the level of the genome—perhaps even before birth. To what extent and just how genetic manipulation may constitute the future of medicine remain large and controversial issues. But a fully decoded human genome was drafted—in two versions—in the year 2000, and the twenty-first century opened with a new focus on efforts to discover the genetics—and proteomics—of disease processes, to forge new diagnostic tools from this information, and to develop new drugs.

For all these many recent accomplishments, there is no place in the history of medicine for a return to the old triumphalism. Medicine faces a troublesome agenda, ever on display in a media-driven information age. The epic pandemic of AIDS is the greatest of contemporary health crises; still others may be expected. The robust treatments for infectious illnesses today may be flawed tomorrow: antibiotics have limits, and for all we know, so will some of the medicines, so slow to come to fruition, to prevent or treat viral diseases. The prospect of biological terrorism is, in part, a sorry artifact of progress in medicine.

Too much progress? A generation ago, few would have guessed that, in the pages of the journal *Science,* a philosopher and bioethicist, John Harris, would be invited in the year 2000 to grapple with the prospect of human immortality. Today, some would not be surprised if the day came when people were commonly thought to live too long. In wealthy countries, writes Roy Porter in a recent history, medicine "has become the prisoner of its success."

It has also become hugely expensive in the developed world. Some system of socialized medicine is in place in most countries, but everywhere resources are strained. In the year 2000 the North American continent was a pyramidal microcosm: Canada, with a functioning national health system; the United States, with upwards of 40 million people lacking any health insurance whatever; and Mexico, with an infant mortality rate of 40 per thousand.

In short, the problems medicine faces at present are as complex as the ones it has overcome in the past—and they are global. Western medicine has become powerful, with its influence felt worldwide—but its more modest history has much to teach the future. "We must strive to enhance and hand on the noble legacy that has come down to us," wrote George Rosen in 1958, concluding his classic history of public health on a note that breathes a trifle ironic today: "And may the outcome be a happy one!"

This volume is meant to engage anyone interested in knowing something about the people who created the medical universe with which most of us are familiar. Chapters are arranged to provide a weave of historical context, with contemporary relevance as a guide. Part I profiles seven figures who represent the scope and trajectory of Western medicine. Individuals associated with the major transformations in medical thinking come next in Part II, from Vesalius to the dawn of the discovery of DNA. Part III includes the foundational figures who are constantly alluded to, wherever medicine is taught. Some whose discoveries laid the basis for modern medicine comprise Part IV, while Part V brings the story close to the present, with a sampling of contemporary researchers—molecular biologists, immunologists, neuroscientists, pharmacologists, enzyme hunters, and prominent names in the current efforts to fight cancer and AIDS. The final section, Part VI, is a miscellany of figures both inside and outside the medical mainstream.

Some of the individuals profiled in this volume are controversial, while others are customarily treated with respect and even reverence. Recent biographies and historical investigations have often rectified the balance, resolving old disputes and challenging the old hagiography. Scholars have raised fascinating questions about the historical record, investigating diverse aspects of medical discovery and practice in social, economic, and political context. To the extent that brief biographies allow, every effort has been made to take such studies into account, although their sheer number insures some have been overlooked. The larger point is that the legacies of many complex and contentious figures in the history of medicine are under constant reappraisal. Verdicts in the history of medicine sometimes withstand scrutiny, but they are rarely simple or unanimous.

Finally, it is scarcely worth saying that the choices that comprise this book cannot be comprehensive—there isn't room or time. The great number left out don't require apology but rather serve to remind that the history of medicine cannot be a registry of kings and prime ministers, that doctors are many because the focus of their work, in the last analysis, is on the individuals they try to help. The mix chosen here is meant to be stimulating, to encourage readers to envision other inclusions and omissions. Eighty-six is a small number, but those included enlarge it themselves—by their works, their influence, and often enough, their visionary and sometimes iconoclastic views of pain and suffering, the human body and mind, and nature itself.

# Part I  Compass of Western Medicine

# Charles Darwin [1809–1882]

## Biology and Medicine

The incalculable debt of medicine to science, acquired over a little more than a century, is owed in the first instance to disciplines associated with biology. Technologies created around the twentieth-century revolution in physics and chemistry play key contextual and instrumental roles; but to talk of influence, the real fabric of advances in medicine has been woven from basic insights into how organisms live and interact, grow and reproduce. Microbiology and biochemistry, genetics, embryology, and other life sciences underlie contemporary views of disease as well as the powerful therapeutics for treating it. Although a host of pivotal figures brought these disciplines to their present state of sophistication, the person who put forth the fundamental concepts that underlie them all should be given pride of place. That is Charles Darwin.

Placing Darwin at the entrance to a pantheon of the history of medicine invites discussion and dispute. He was not a physician, nor did he perform medical research—and one may argue he doesn't belong in this book at all. This line of reasoning would be forceful if any of the other prepotent influences on modern medicine—Rudolf Virchow (p. 8), Claude Bernard (p. 14), Louis Pasteur (p. 18), or Robert Koch (p. 24)—had paid much attention to evolutionary principles or to the concept of natural selection. But, for historical and various other reasons, they did not. To bring forth these individuals—by loose consensus the founders of medicine as we know and experience it—*without* Darwin, becomes finally a major negligence.

If not a physician himself, Charles Darwin could look to his father and grandfather. He was born on February 12, 1809, to the prosperous family of Robert Waring Darwin, a doctor, and Susannah Wedgwood. His paternal grandfather was Erasmus Darwin, a famous physician, poet, philosopher, and inventor. After Charles's mother died, probably from cancer, when he was eight years old, his grief-stricken sisters forbade him to discuss her. At school he was little interested by the classics but developed an early ardor for nature. "The passion for collecting," wrote Darwin in his *Autobiography,* "which leads a man to be a systematic naturalist, a virtuoso or a miser, was

very strong in me, and was clearly innate, as none of my sisters or brother ever had this taste."

Although Darwin intended to follow his father and enter medicine when he began Edinburgh University in 1825, he found it a drudgery. Anatomy would have been a useful skill, but because he disliked the curriculum, he never learned to dissect. Most of all, Darwin was sensitive to suffering. He had a morbid fear of blood and could not bear the operating theater. In 1827 he changed course, moving to Christ's College, Cambridge, with a view to becoming a minister. But his friends and mentors were botanists and geologists, and Darwin's interest in nature abided and grew.

The turning point in Darwin's life was his appointment, on recommendation of botany professor John Stevens Henslow, as unpaid naturalist for the voyage of the HMS *Beagle*. The primary mission was to survey exotic Patagonia, Tierra del Fuego, Chile, Peru, and some of the Pacific Islands. On the advice of his father, Darwin initially declined. But desire overcame parental injunction. He was aboard on December 27, 1831, when the *Beagle* left England, not to return for five years.

The great significance of this long, exotic voyage was to expose Darwin to the teeming forms of life amidst landscapes untouched by civilization. He kept a series of notebooks, puzzling over basic issues embodied by the architecture and behavior of living things. He collected flora and fauna. In the Galápagos, for example, he noticed slight variations among various populations of birds on neighboring islands. While aboard ship Darwin read and studied the just-published work by Charles Lyell, *Principles of Geology*. A challenge to the older theory of catastrophism that ascribed the physical characteristics of the Earth to flood or fire, Lyell's theory of gradualism — significant change accumulates over long periods of time — became the basis for all modern geological research. It also organized Darwin's view of the exotic world he encountered, and so became one of the chief underpinnings for his theory of evolution.

The gestation of that theory, which famously lasted two decades, began after Darwin returned to England in late 1836. It was long common wisdom that Thomas Malthus's dour ideas concerning population were central to Darwin's evolving theory and the concept of a "struggle for existence." Today other influences are understood also to have been at work. Adam Smith's economic ideas stressed for Darwin the centrality of the individual. He also took note of philosopher Auguste Comte's idea that a scientific theory ought to be predictive and quantifiable, at least in principle. And, like Florence Nightingale (p. 88), Darwin read the controversial early statistician, the Belgian Adolphe Quételet. He soon began parsing all such ideas for their relevance to the natural world of plants and animals. By 1842 he had made the first sketch of evolutionary theory and the concept of the descent of species, employing the term "natural selection."

Darwin was well aware that his theory was potentially subversive to religion. Indeed, his willingness to overcome theological objections was one of his strengths as a scientist. But it also was a consideration in his careful approach to—indeed, reticence in—promulgating his ideas. Darwin continually refined his theory and would complete a third sketch of it in 1856.

Darwin spent his middle years accumulating the mass of circumstantial evidence upon which his theory of evolution, when first publicly proposed, would depend. In 1842 he married and moved to a manor outside London, Down House, where he would spend the rest of his life. He published an account of his voyage on the *Beagle* and, in 1842, *The Structure and Distribution of Coral Reefs*. These and other works brought him a considerable reputation as a naturalist. Darwin also continued to collect specimens, specializing in barnacles, and amassed and classified a huge assortment.

Darwin's persistent refusals to publish his theory, despite the encouragement of Charles Lyell, came to an end in 1858, after he received a long letter from Alfred Wallace, an amateur naturalist. Wallace had also traveled to exotic lands and had developed a theory of evolution which in many ways was Darwin's own. This potential priority dispute was resolved with aplomb and decorum. Wallace and Darwin read joint papers to the Linnean Society on July 1, 1859. Having made his theory public in this way, Darwin now hastened to prepare his longer work for what turned out to be a waiting public. When *On the Origin of Species by Means of Natural Selection, or the Preservation of Favoured Races in the Struggle for Life* was published in 1859, the first edition of 1,250 copies all but sold out in a single day.

Darwinism became much discussed, acquired scientific status, and had its adherents and opponents. As tightlipped as he had been about evolution before publication of the *Origin*, Darwin became exceptionally prolific soon after. Among other works, he published *Variations of Animals and Plants Under Domestication* in 1868, and some six books during the

1870s, including the influential *The Expression of the Emotions in Man and Animals,* from 1872, and *The Formation of Vegetable Mould through the Action of Worms,* from 1881. But the most famous of these later works was the controversial *The Descent of Man,* from 1871. Here Darwin put forth his "main conclusion" that "man is descended from some less highly organized form." The grounds, beyond dispute, are: "the close similarity between man and the lower animals in embryonic development, as well as in innumerable points of structure and constitution, both of high and of the most trifling importance. . . ." Consonant with the trajectory of much science since the sixteenth century, Darwin's concept of human evolution represented a distinct movement away from viewing human beings as privileged in the scheme of nature.

Darwin's complex personality resists capsulization, all the more since it has often been romanticized. As a child he was mischievous and could be rowdy; as an adult he loved solitude—a result, he said, of his voyage on the *Beagle.* He was affable but insecure, and prone to illnesses, some of which were perhaps psychosomatic. In any event, Darwin enjoyed being taken care of as much as he liked caring for his children. His marriage to his first cousin, Emma Wedgwood, was a success. Of the couple's ten children, seven lived to adulthood. In religion, Darwin was originally a theist, but by the end of his life he had become an agnostic. Darwin died on April 19, 1882. He was buried in Westminster Abbey, not far from Isaac Newton.

Darwin's influence on all of biology is today beyond question. His reputation was eventually consolidated, and the range of his thought extended, some years after the rediscovery of Mendel's laws of heredity in 1900. Although it was not initially clear if Darwin's concept of natural selection and the idea of change through mutation were compatible, by 1930 this issue was definitively resolved. Darwinian selection and Mendelian genetics became "mutually indispensable," writes Anthony Flew, "and between them [provided] exactly the mechanism needed for evolution by natural selection." Classical genetics arising from Mendelian laws of inheritance intersected population genetics at the crossroads provided by natural selection.

Darwin's renewed influence continued to dominate biology, combining evidence from genetics (with the help of fruit flies) and paleontology (an encouraging grasp of the fossil record), so that there emerged a "neo-Darwinian" point of view that matured into a theory often called the "modern synthesis." Many of Darwin's ideas have been modified and extended, as expected; various aspects of evolutionary biology remain in healthy flux. The neo-Darwinian paradigm is at the root of nearly all contemporary biological thought.

What of medicine? "What have the doctors got from Darwin?" asks historian of medicine W. F. Bynum. "The short answer is, that, like so many life scientists of the past century, a great deal." Physicians were generally receptive to Darwinian thought as it acquired explanatory power in comparative anatomy and physiology, bacteriology, and pharmacology. Over the past hundred years and more, major discoveries in these and other fields were made with evolutionary thought as a formative influence and a necessary condition.

That is to say, Darwin's influence on medical thinking is not merely diffuse but in many cases specific and constantly expanding. Evolutionary concepts were frequently on the minds of scientists and physicians who devised the experiments that shaped medical research. As simple ideas, evolution and the concept of diathesis, or hereditary predisposition to disease, preceded Darwin. But evolutionary theory organized what had been speculation and observation. John Hughlings Jackson, via Herbert Spencer, made basic contributions to neurology based on evolutionary ideas. In 1882 Sir James Paget suggested that various "new" diseases, such as osteitis deformans (Paget's disease), should be studied "as Darwin studied the variations of species." Archibald Garrod (p. 214), at the end of the nineteenth century, brought forth evidence for inherited disorders and linked them directly to Mendelian laws within months after they were rediscovered, in essence applying to medical thought Darwin's idea of individual variation. Garrod himself called it "a little explored but promising field in relation to natural selection." Initially ignored, its importance has continued to grow; recently the term "evolutionary medicine" has acquired a clinical connotation.

But that is not all. In the twentieth century, Darwin's concepts turned out to have great value as medical knowledge became molecular. In the 1930s, when Hans Krebs (p. 240) discovered the famous "citric acid cycle"—the key to intermediate metabolism—he recalled that among his considerations was his "conviction, based on evolutionary principles," that oxidizability was related to combustion of foodstuffs—in animals, plants, and even bacteria. In 1954 Macfarlane Burnet (p. 280) formulated clonal selection theory, the root of all of contemporary immunology, with Darwinian concepts in mind. The list could go on. But, in brief, Charles Darwin shaped the biology that underlies contemporary medicine. His influence ought not go unstated, for Darwin, as much as Isaac Newton or Albert Einstein, is responsible for a new relationship between humans and nature in the Western world. His great significance for medicine should be apparent, time and again, in many ways, in the chapters that follow.

# Rudolf Virchow [1821–1902]

## The Scope of Modern Medicine: Cellular and Social

Rudolf Virchow was a gifted experimental investigator, an adept microscopist, anatomist, pathologist, and physician. He is perhaps best remembered for crystallizing the theory—fundamental for scientific medicine—that cells, the basic units of life, arise from other cells and represent the ultimate seat of disease. Virchow, Levi C. Lane could write by 1893, "has made the whole medical profession heir of his doctrine." A century on, one could say the same.

But additionally, Virchow was a major activist on behalf of public health, epidemiology, and medical reform. A proponent of medical statistics, he was also acutely aware of the social and political dimensions of disease and epidemic. As early as 1848 Virchow charted the significance of decent sanitation and championed the right of citizens to good health as an issue for government regulation. In a rhetorical question, deservedly famous, he asked, "Are the triumphs of human genius to lead only to this, that the human race shall become more miserable?" Virchow's awareness of, and contributions to, public health and medical reform remain central to his enduring reputation.

Rudolf Ludwig Carl Virchow was born on October 13, 1821. His birthplace was Schivelbein, a small town (now Świdwin, Poland) in eastern Pomerania, a backward, politically conservative region of Prussia. His father, intelligent but eccentric and not prosperous, was Carl Christian Siegfried Virchow; his mother was the querulous Johanna Maria Hesse. The family background was not illustrious, and little in Rudolf's childhood environment was conducive to genius. From an early age, however, he was exceptionally curious, interested in natural history, with a talent for languages. An outstanding student, he early on manifested a strong personality. Classmates used to call him their "king."

Virchow's medical education was exemplary, combining the new German science with the advances in clinical pathology associated with the Paris hospital system. After graduating from gymnasium, Virchow in 1839 entered the Friedrich Wilhelm University in Berlin. This state school offered a free medical education to a small number of students, with the proviso that they serve as army physicians after graduation. Virchow was lucky enough to study under the charismatic Johannes Müller (p. 67), who became his formative teacher in the laboratory; in the clinic he was influenced by another famous investigator, Johann Schönlein. Virchow received his medical degree in 1843 and was appointed to the distinguished Charité Hospital in Berlin as a "company surgeon." He not only worked as a clinician, but undertook research as well.

The decline of the romantic *Naturphilosophie* in Germany at midcentury, after a generation of domination in the universities, created unusual opportunities for new influences. Within only two years of gaining his medical degree, Virchow had become a well-known, articulate, and outspoken physician. In 1845 he gave two speeches before large audiences at the Friedrich Wilhelm University, in which he set out an ambitious agenda for medicine in terms of experiment and research. Arguing the views of Theodor Schwann and others, Virchow was already proclaiming the central importance of the cell as the basic unit of life. He challenged and derided vitalism and humoral pathology, and spoke in favor of the new, reductionist, scientific medicine. In 1847 Virchow became editor of the *Archiv für pathologische Anatomie und Physiologie und für klinische Medizin (Archive for Pathological Anatomy, Physiology and Clinical Medicine)*, soon to be known popularly as "Virchow's Archive," the most prominent medical journal of the time. Virchow would serve as its editor until his death.

Contributing to Virchow's growing authority was his own experimental research. A popular theory held that phlebitis, or inflammation in a vein, played a causal role in diseases of all sorts. The idea was plausible because at autopsy pathologists would frequently find clots of blood, or thrombi, in the bloodstream. Fibrin—the fibrous substance of the clots—was thought to be a "vital" substance. Charged with verifying these notions, Virchow came to quite different conclusions. He debunked the idea that fibrin was "the stuff of life" and suggested it was a chemical artifact, a mechanical result due to other circumstances. In the course of this work Virchow coined the term *thrombosis*—formation of the thrombus, or intravascular blood clot. He described a new phenomenon, *embolism,* in which a foreign body moves through and lodges somewhere in the bloodstream, with various pathological results. Virchow's "inflammatory" theory of the formation of arterial plaques, though not finally correct, was influential, detailed, and spawned much useful research.

All this early work, undertaken with the help of the recently improved microscope, indicates Virchow's ability to develop significant generalizations from experimental data. The same was true for the disease known as "white blood." At autopsy Virchow recognized that the proportion of white blood cells to red blood cells was inverted. Familiar with the normal proportions

through his work with phlebitis, Virchow had discovered and went on to describe leukemia. Virchow would make numerous other contributions toward describing various cancers, and he also undertook chemical studies which, though now forgotten and obsolete, were valuable at the time.

Virchow's research career was interrupted by the social unrest that coursed through much of Europe in the late 1840s. First, he was sent to direct a medical survey in Upper Silesia, where a typhus epidemic had broken out among the impoverished Polish minority. Reporting to the government, Virchow wrote a politically radical prescription for reform. He suggested that the causes of the epidemic were essentially social. Self-government, separation of church and state, taxing the rich, and improved agricultural techniques were among his recommendations. Virchow subsequently developed the constructive idea of the "artificial epidemic," which posited outbreaks of disease as due to social conditions, and he cited typhus and tuberculosis as examples. In this context, Virchow viewed doctors as "natural attorneys for the poor" and argued they should take an active role in solving social problems.

Virchow was truly awakened to political change with the onset of the 1848 revolution, as Austria lost control of the German states. He served ineffectively on the barricades, but remained committed to socialism and revolutionary ideals after it was over. He became editor of a radical weekly, *Die Medizinische Reform (Medical Reform)*, and participated in meetings and demonstrations that soon brought him a partial suspension from Charité.

The decade of the 1850s was Virchow's most fruitful in terms of medicine and pathology. In 1849, with the onset of a reactionary political climate, Virchow moved to the University of Würzburg. He embarked on a program of research and publication, and consolidated his reputation as a teacher. He undertook publication of a massive six-volume handbook of pathology and therapeutics—one of the first of many such *Handbücher* to issue from German science. Virchow also began his long service as one of the editors of an annual, *Canstatt's Jahresbericht,* a yearbook of medicine that was a great storehouse of medical knowledge, read by an international audience of anatomists, pathologists, surgeons, and physicians.

In 1856 Virchow returned to Berlin, where a chair of pathological anatomy was established for him at the Friedrich Wilhelm University. His teacher Johannes Müller was largely responsible for this call, and a special building for the Pathologisches Institut was constructed for his work. From this institute, near the Charité, Virchow would train two generations of physicians, and his reputation and influence would become worldwide.

The appearance of Virchow's *Die Cellularpathologie (Cellular Pathology)* in 1858 is a genuine landmark in scientific medicine. It is a series of twenty lectures that revamps a half century of the science of pathology. Historically, first the individual organ, then various types of tissue had been considered the fundamental sites that undergo change in disease. Now came the cell. In the body, comprised of a vast assemblage of individual cells, all disease processes affect cells' normal functioning. With Virchow, pathological anatomy becomes cellular pathology.

In addition, the cell was no longer simply a structural entity, but now evoked an entire biological system. Virchow as early as 1852 had rejected the idea, closely associated with Theodor Schwann, that cells emerge from an undifferentiated blastema. Rather, he adopted — with scarce acknowledgment — views first put forward by Robert Remak, a Polish researcher. Remak had criticized Schwann's views and, with frogs' eggs, had concluded "that the independent production of nuclei or cells is really only division of preexisting nuclei or cells." When Virchow took up this concept in his lectures on cellular pathology, he expressed it as a powerful formula: *Omnis cellula e cellula* (Every cell arises from another cell).

The doctrine of cell self-replication opened a path to unify biology and medicine. "Throughout the range of living beings, plants, animals, or the constituent parts of one or the other," Virchow proclaimed, "there rules the eternal law of continuous development.... We must reduce all tissues to a single simple element, the cell." *Cellular Pathology,* wrote Ralph Major some years ago, "caused a revolution in medical thinking.... In a brief time, the medical world *in toto* became disciples of Virchow." A direct application of cell theory to medicine came with Virchow's work on tumors, *Die krankhaften Geschwülste (The Pathology of Tumors)*, published between 1863 and 1867.

Virchow had the privilege of a life as healthy as it was long, and had a second career as a politician, and a third as a physical anthropologist. In 1862 he was elected for the first time to the Prussian House of Representatives. He opposed forced reunification of an armed German state, and soon became an enemy of Otto von Bismarck, who once challenged him to a duel. (Virchow is supposed to have replied by saying that he would accept the challenge only when Bismarck became his peer in the realm of morality.) From 1880 to 1893 he served in the Reichstag and also was a member of Berlin's city council. Among other things, his political work helped achieve reform in hygiene and improved the municipal hospital system. Berlin could also thank Virchow for better sewage disposal and a potable water supply.

As an anthropologist, Virchow was also influential, with over a thousand published contributions. In 1869 Virchow founded the Berlin Society of Anthropology, Ethnology, and Prehistory, which he directed for more than thirty years. Anthropology was a relatively new science, and Virchow became a powerful figure for its development in Germany. He also influenced Franz Boas, who went on to found American anthropology. Virchow's archaeological activities were many. He excavated widely in Prussia's eastern provinces, where he had been born and raised. He enjoyed taking issue with German chauvinists. With excavations in Pomerania, he undermined the idea of a unified and culturally advanced German race. He showed that primitive tribesmen there inhabited caves while elsewhere in the world high civilizations flourished. Virchow also became friend and sponsor to Heinrich Schliemann, the rediscoverer of Troy, and accompanied him to Egypt in 1888.

In his personality, Rudolf Virchow possessed a certain coldness that corresponded poorly with his professed love of humanity. Pugnacious in debate, in personal relations he was unaware of how his words could sting. Modest and even ascetic in personal habits, he had no interest in becoming wealthy. As a teacher he was known as "Pope" or "Pascha" but was open to students' ideas and was adept at collaboration. He was said to be capable of gaiety, especially with his family. His marriage to Rose Mayer, when he was a firebrand in 1848, endured and produced six children. Virchow's death, from cardiac disease, came several weeks after he suffered a broken femur in a streetcar accident. When he died on September 5, 1902, Berlin gave him a public funeral.

Throughout his career, Virchow made errors, large and small. He opposed hand washing as advocated by Ignaz Semmelweis (p. 165) in 1849, and his admission that he was wrong, years later, was less than generous. He was not much kinder to the far more successful bacteriological theories later proposed by Louis Pasteur (p. 18), Robert Koch (p. 24), and others. Virchow extensively studied and wrote about tubercular illnesses, but he did not view tuberculosis—which has numerous sites and manifestations—as a single disease entity. Indeed, he seriously muddied the waters after a firm foundation had been laid by René Laennec (p. 62) and other investigators. Finally, Virchow's suspicion of Darwin's theory of evolution, despite his interest in anthropology, is evidence of the rigid cast of mind that characterized some of his views in later years.

But none of this should detract from Virchow's central influence on the course of medicine and medical research. He was, writes Erwin Ackerknecht, "more than a medical scientist; he was also a great helper and saver of lives—a great doctor in the full sense of the word."

# Claude Bernard [1813–1878]

## Medicine and Modern Experimental Physiology

Claude Bernard's host of discoveries and wealth of insights into the way the human body functions, in health and in sickness, make him a central figure in the development of modern medicine. Building on fruitful investigations in anatomy and pathology about the turn of the nineteenth century, Bernard forged a physiology based on function. His emphasis was on experiment and vivisection, and his work foreshadows modern biological and biochemical explanation. This renders him notably modern to contemporary eyes, as does his conceptual sophistication and ability to provide a unifying vision of the body at work. "His philosophy," writes Rosalyn S. Yalow (p. 287), "provides the basis of interdisciplinary research which has become increasingly important in modern science as the boundaries between the various disciplines appear to merge."

Indeed, any listing of Bernard's accomplishments must include a catalog of both his specific discoveries and his theoretical principles. Early in his career, Bernard showed how the pancreas works to digest fats and how the liver stores, processes, and secretes sugar. He made numerous discoveries concerning the operations of various nerves, and by demonstrating the action of the poison curare became a key figure in the history of pharmacology. But in addition, as he grew older, Bernard was responsible for broad and solid generalizations about human physiology and the nature of disease. His most famous concept, that of the *milieu intérieur,* became the basis for what Walter B. Cannon would later call *homeostasis* — since become a fundamental tenet across biology. Overall, write Hugh LaFollette and Niall Shanks: "Bernard shaped the mechanistic physiological paradigm that has reigned for most of the twentieth century."

Relatively little in Claude Bernard's upbringing indicates a capacity for dedication to science and medicine. He was born on July 12, 1813, in Saint-Julien, a village in the Beaujolais region of France, to Pierre François Bernard, a winegrower; his mother, with whom he enjoyed greater affection, was Jeanne Saulnier. Claude was educated in religious schools, and although intrigued by nature from a young age, he received no training in science. While apprenticed to a pharmacist, Bernard developed an interest in the theater. After enjoying provincial success with one of his comedies, he wrote a play, *Arthur de Bretagne,* and moved to Paris with the hope of becoming a successful playwright. But after being rebuffed by a well-known critic, Bernard turned his back on a literary career. He obtained the baccalaureate degree and entered medical school. An average student, he graduated toward the bottom of his class and became an intern in 1839.

While still a student, Bernard was greatly impressed by the lectures of François Magendie (p. 71). He appreciated the great pathologist's skepticism and mistrust of contemporary physiology, which relied heavily on accumulated observation and inductive reasoning, but little on experiment. At the Hôtel-Dieu, Bernard became a member of Magendie's staff. As his internship ended, he maintained his relationship with Magendie by becoming his assistant from 1841 until 1844. Although he received his medical degree in 1843, Bernard would never practice clinical medicine.

For a number of years Bernard worked in a private laboratory, and on a shoestring. He was helped out by the large dowry he obtained when he married Marie Françoise Martin in 1845. This marriage of convenience would come to haunt him. Many of Bernard's experiments were carried out with animals—indeed, they showed the way for much of twentieth-century research. But his wife and the couple's two daughters were repelled by this work and became antivivisectionists.

Bernard pursued several different lines of research at a time. Two of his principal foci were digestion and metabolism. His doctoral thesis, from 1843, concerned the chemistry of digestion, and in 1849 Bernard published a landmark paper on the role of the pancreas, showing its crucial contribution to the metabolism of fats. This kind of description and demonstration of a particular activity linked to a broader theory of function was characteristic of Bernard's great work. Previously, the science of physiology had been largely limited to classification, with explanation of function often based on speculation. Bernard's approach was revolutionary.

Equally important were Bernard's studies of liver function. He demonstrated, about 1848, that the blood of healthy people, not just diabetics, contains sugar. He then used this work to develop a broader theory of hepatic function. He showed that the liver adds sugar to the blood as it passes through the hepatic veins and also secretes bile in the course of digestion. The liver's double function became a linchpin in the new, broader understanding of nutrition and intermediate metabolism. In 1850 Bernard's paper, "On a New Function of the Liver," won him the prize in experimental physiology from the Academy of Sciences—for the third time—and became the basis of a thesis with which he obtained a doctorate in natural sciences in 1853. In 1857, Bernard chemically isolated glycogen, the liver's stored form of sugar.

Another focus of Bernard's research was the nervous system. In 1843, investigating the facial nerve known as the chorda tympani, he was not at first notably successful. But beginning in 1851 he undertook experiments which eventually showed that certain nerves—the vasomotor nerves, as we would say today—control the vascular system. By 1858 he discovered the vasodilator nerves that regulate the diameter of the blood vessels. These research efforts were interwoven, to some extent, with work on circulation in organs at rest or at work. Bernard published *Leçons sur les propriétés physiologiques et les altérations pathologiques des liquides de l'organisme (Lectures on the Physiological Properties and Pathological Changes of the Liquids of the Organism)* in 1859.

Although not trained in chemistry himself, Bernard benefited greatly from work with at least two excellent chemists, his friends Jules Pelouze and Charles-Louis Barreswil. Chemical reactions were an especially important part of Bernard's experiments with poisons and drugs. Specific poisons, he found, can reveal the chemistry of physiological action. For example, Bernard discovered that carbon monoxide asphyxiates because it replaces oxygen in red blood cells, to lethal effect. He also experimented with curare, opium, strychnine, and various anesthetics.

From about 1855, after long gestation in his notebooks, Bernard's writings took a turn toward conceptual development and the philosophy of medical investigation. This may have been due in part to the obligations of stature. In 1854 he had been elected to the Academy of Sciences. He took up a professorship of general physiology at the Faculty of Sciences in Paris, and in 1855, upon Magendie's death, Bernard became professor of medicine at the Collège de France. Yet it was remarkable all the same, for Bernard, after years as an assiduous experimenter, emerged as one of the most significant figures in the philosophy of medicine and medical research.

Bernard's *Introduction à l'étude de la médecine expérimentale (Introduction to the Study of Experimental Medicine)*, conceived in 1858 and published seven years later, remains one of the most influential books in modern medicine. Bernard had taken the time to read various philosophers, including Immanuel Kant and Auguste Comte, and he developed an astute and sophisticated argument for "experimental reasoning." Medical research, writes Bernard, ought to proceed stepwise in three stages:

*Observation,* which stimulates the imagination to develop a *hypothesis,* which leads to *experiment.* His overarching goal was to "conquer living nature, act upon vital phenomena and regulate and modify them." Bernard was a strong determinist, and he set himself against vitalism.

Another central concept in Bernard's thought, extensively discussed in his introduction to *Experimental Medicine,* is the *milieu intérieur,* a concept that took shape gradually in the course of his work during the 1850s. Bernard viewed the "internal environment" of the body as necessarily stable, the better to provide "constant conditions of temperature, moisture, availability of oxygen, without which the organs cannot be nourished." Several decades later, with a more fully developed cell theory, the discovery of hormones, and an improved grasp of the sympathetic nervous system, Walter B. Cannon (p. 210) would develop the more modern concept of homeostasis. As a generalization in physiology, the *milieu intérieur* was a powerful organizer.

Bernard became a figure of great renown as he grew older, which must have been consolation for several bouts of illness. From 1869 his lectures were attended not only by medical students and physiologists, but by the rich and famous. Bernard became known to many of the French literary giants, and Émile Zola's *The Experimental Novel* was an unsuccessful effort to parody *Introduction to the Study of Experimental Medicine.*

Bernard's domestic life was not happy, and after 1869 he lived apart from his wife and daughters. He took as his intimate Madame Raffalovich, young and attractive, intellectual, and the wife of a banker. Bernard's letters to her were eventually published in 1950 as *Lettres beaujolaises.* Admired by Louis Napoleon, Bernard was named a senator in 1869 and became a rubber stamp for the authoritarian government. Upon his death on February 10, 1878, Bernard received a state funeral—the first French scientist to be so honored. The procession ended at Père Lachaise cemetery, and Gustave Flaubert described it later with a touch of irony as "religious and very beautiful." Bernard was an agnostic.

A caveat should be added to any evaluation of Bernard's achievements. Although nearly unparalleled, his scientific heritage may be described as mixed. His powerful paradigm for experimental research also involved skepticism of clinical medicine, unnecessary distrust of statistics and epidemiology, and an unfortunate rejection of evolutionary thinking. "The costs of researchers' continued acceptance of the Bernardian paradigm are substantial," write Hugh LaFollette and Niall Shanks in a recent assessment. "Physiology's continued insensitivity to evolution has led it further and further away from the other biological sciences." Modern medicine's enshrinement of Claude Bernard may be ascribed as much to cultural values as to the scientist himself—who discovered, in the view of his student Paul Bert, "as others breathe."

# Louis Pasteur [1822-1895]

## The Germ Theory of Disease: Microbiology

Louis Pasteur is commonly portrayed as one of the great heroes of medicine. He is popularly credited with the establishment of the germ theory of disease—gradually outlined by experiment and theory over several decades before being fully enunciated and demonstrated about 1880. Microorganisms would henceforth be identified as the infective agents for a host of specific diseases. Pasteur developed one of the first preventive vaccines, against anthrax, in 1882. Extended to hygiene and sepsis, the germ theory had a cascade effect on medical research, practice, and eventually, therapeutics. Indeed, with Louis Pasteur the vast potential for a scientifically based amelioration of the physical ills of human life through medicine was, for the first time in history, obvious, if not at hand.

Pasteur's career has a definite trajectory and his personality, a distinct character. He was trained as a chemist, and he moved early in his career to investigate significant issues in biology. His work in pathology was closely linked to expanding French industry and was in significant measure patriotic. Undrinkable beer, spoiled wine, and diseases of silkworms were the subjects of Pasteur's initial studies. He turned to anthrax, a disease of cattle, in 1878. Development of a human rabies vaccine represented the climax of his career. Pasteur put his work powerfully, sometimes dramatically, before colleagues and an enthralled public. "He made happiness around him whilst he gave glory to France," wrote René Vallery-Radot of his father-in-law, in a eulogistic biography. The reality of Pasteur is more complex than the legend, and more interesting.

The only son and second of four children, Louis Pasteur was born in Dole on December 27, 1822. His mother was Jeanne-Etiennette Roqui. Jean-Joseph Pasteur, his father, was a tanner by profession and a highly decorated veteran of Napoleon's army. Pasteur always recalled him with expressions of devotion and credited him for his own perseverance and patriotism. Indeed, during his early years in school, when he performed only moderately well, his father tutored him. Louis grew diligent, industrious, and perfectionist. In 1838 he entered a preparatory school in Paris. In his youth Pasteur enjoyed painting and, as surviving portraits attest, was a promising artist. But at age nineteen he abandoned art for science.

He was initially most attracted to physics and trained in chemistry at the prestigious École Normale Supérieure. He received his *agrégation*, with theses in both subjects, in 1846.

Pasteur's move from physical chemistry to biology came through research into what may be called the "tartaric acid problem." Tartaric acids had been first identified as the deposits in wine casks about 1770. As various tartrates were discovered, they were recognized to have the same chemical composition (they were early examples of isomerism) yet quite different properties. However, in 1844 two tartrates were discovered to have every property identical save one: the capacity to polarize light. How could they be the same? Here Pasteur began his work. With painstaking examination of crystals of the tartrate known as racemic acid, using a hand lens, he discovered two asymmetric forms, one the mirror image of the other. Indeed, he could separate the crystals into two groups and show that light would rotate to the left through one group and to the right through the other. This was brilliant work, and also a lucky discovery. To Pasteur is owed the famous, often heard "Chance favors only the prepared mind."

Pasteur's work on the tartrates of wine casks evolved into an investigation of fermentation after he became professor and dean of the Department of Science at Lille in 1854. This industrializing area in central France was known for its manufacture of alcohol from beetroot sugar. At the urging of a local industrialist, Pasteur carried out a long series of experiments aimed at understanding fermentation and the associated problem of spoilage. He continued this work when he returned to Paris to direct the École Normale, his alma mater, in 1857.

Fermentation, when Pasteur began to study it, was widely considered a purely chemical process, according to a famous theory of the great German chemist Justus von Liebig. But Pasteur now stepped forward to claim that "lactic yeast," comprised of living organisms, was responsible for the transformation of sugar into lactic acid—of which sour milk and yogurt are common products. He published an audacious paper, "Mémoire sur la fermentation appelée lactique" ("Note on So-called Lactic Fermentation"), in 1857. Pasteur went on, in 1860, to treat of alcoholic fermentation, showing that all the various types and processes involved the presence of "organic beings." Control of the fermentation process, an enormous advance for industry, was the practical result of this work. In theoretical terms, Liebig and Pasteur were each half right: Yeast is a living organism but fermentation is a chemical, enzymatic process.

Pasteur's study of fermentation in turn led him to investigate "spontaneous generation." The idea that certain forms of life arise from nonliving matter—as flies seem to emerge full-grown from the soil—was much discussed just about the time Pasteur was formulating his ideas concerning yeasts and fermentation. Pasteur carried out a long series of ingenious experiments showing that atmospheric air is never free from living organisms. Water that was boiled to destroy germs could remain sterile indefinitely—unless opened to the air. In 1864 Pasteur re-created his experiments before an illustrious audience at the Sorbonne, describing how one could wait forever for life to arise from a sterile solution. "And I wait, I watch, I question it, begging it to recommence for me the beautiful spectacle of the first creation." But nothing happens, because, as Pasteur puts it, "Life is a germ and a germ is Life. Never will the doctrine of spontaneous generation recover from the mortal blow of this simple experiment."

Industry remained the driving force of Pasteur's research projects during these years. In 1862 he had suggested a new practical means for manufacturing vinegar and controlling its ferments. In 1863, at the request of Napoleon III, he began work on various problems associated with wine, increasingly a French export. Certain wines reacted poorly to heat, storage, and transport. Pasteur investigated the underlying microbiology that can turn wine sour, cloudy, bitter, or too acidic. He made a variety of recommendations, most significantly that of heat treatment to preserve and even improve quality. Several years later, in 1871, Pasteur investigated beer, again showing that microorganisms would affect fermentation and suggesting how their presence could be controlled. In sum, the yield of Pasteur's research into wine and beer was the development of *pasteurization,* a process eventually also applied to milk products. About the same time, Pasteur also studied two contagious diseases that were destroying silkworms and ruining the silk industry in France. He showed how fairly simple measures could remediate or prevent recurrence of the problem.

From at least the time of his election to the Academy of Medicine in 1873, Pasteur was interested in applying his developing germ theory to diseases of humans and animals. He was gratified to learn how his experiments had proved crucial to the work of Joseph Lister (p. 94) in developing antiseptic measures in surgery in England, and of similar improvements in French hospitals. He suspected that microorganisms were responsible for gas gangrene and, perhaps, childbed fever. In 1878 and 1880 Pasteur offered both observations and therapeutic suggestions concerning the "germ theory" before the French Academy of Sciences. Together with Robert Koch's work on anthrax, these papers constitute the first essential articulation of the germ theory of disease.

Pasteur's studies of anthrax, begun in 1877, were dramatic because the disease was killing sheep in Europe in epidemic numbers. He benefited from the description by Robert Koch (p. 24) of the life cycle of the anthrax microbe, while his own contribution was the development of a preventive inoculation. This came about through studies of chicken cholera, which was not a common disease but proved a useful model. Pasteur discovered that virulence could be slowed and finally would subside. Attenuated blood product from chickens with mild illness could serve, Pasteur realized, as a protective inoculation. The vaccine "merely communicates to animals a benignant malady," he wrote, "which preserves them from the deadly form."

Skepticism met Pasteur's claim for an anthrax vaccine, and so opened a path to great success. An agricultural society offered sixty sheep for experiment, and Pasteur readily took up the challenge. The public avidly followed the story, widely reported in the press, as it unfolded. On May 5, 1881, at Pouilly-le-Fort, Pasteur caused twenty-five unvaccinated animals to be infected with anthrax. Another twenty-five were first vaccinated, then infected. (Ten sheep served as a control group.) Within a month the results were clear and stunning. The vaccinated sheep all remained alive; twenty-one of the unvaccinated animals were dead, the others dying. Pasteur's triumph was complete. He christened his method "vaccination" to honor Edward Jenner (p. 152), who had coined the term (from the Latin *vacca* for "cow") for his cowpox-derived smallpox inoculation. The germ theory of disease could explain not only smallpox and anthrax, but in principle, any number of other infective diseases.

Pasteur's culminating achievement came with rabies. An ancient disease known to be transmitted from animal to human, rabies (or hydrophobia) attacks the nervous system. With its dramatic symptoms, rabies was a well-known danger in a world that was still largely rural. Over several years, beginning in 1880, Pasteur discovered that he could reduce the virulence of rabies, as he had done with cholera and anthrax, by passing the disease from animal to animal. (He could not isolate the agent, a virus.) He announced these results but was not initially tempted to experiment on humans. However, on July 6, 1885, he was confronted with Joseph Meister, a young man who, two days before, had been badly bitten by a dog that seemed certain to be rabid. He was still without symptoms when Pasteur decided to employ his vaccine. Under his direction, doctors gave young

Joseph thirteen inoculations. After three months, when the boy had not fallen ill, Pasteur proclaimed success. In October he treated another case, and soon announced to the Academy of Sciences, "I have perfected a practical and rapid means of prevention [of rabies]," and he believed it could be applied safely to human beings as well as to animals.

Pasteur, already famous, was covered in glory when his vaccine against rabies proved successful. Three years later, in 1888, the Institut Pasteur opened in Paris and became a major research institution that is still in business today. Pasteur himself never really had a chance to work there, for he increasingly fell prey to illness. He had suffered a stroke which left him hemiplegic in 1867, and almost thirty years later he was suffering from cardiovascular problems as well. Offered a cup of milk on September 27, 1895, he murmured, "I cannot," and according to Vallery-Radot, "looked around him with an unspeakable expression of resignation, love and farewell." A devout Catholic, he lay with a crucifix in one hand, beside his wife, Marie Laurent, whom he had married half a century before. He died the next day.

A good deal of confusion exists concerning Pasteur's personality. Thanks to numerous adulatory biographies, he is still sometimes described as "warm, effusive, personal, emotional." Pasteur could be affectionate with family and colleagues, but in fact he was driven and devoted to work, dour in temperament, and lacked any sense of humor. "Worship great men," Pasteur once told students, and he himself cultivated the myth which grew up around and eventually enveloped him.

A historian, the late Gerald Geison, has recently brought the master down to earth as a scientist, in his exceptional *The Private Science of Louis Pasteur*. This study, based on Pasteur's laboratory notebooks, does not accord with received wisdom in various respects. For example, Pasteur concealed the fact that, in his famous anthrax trials at Pouilly-le-Fort, he employed a chemically attenuated vaccine originally developed by a rival, Jean-Joseph Henri Toussaint, instead of the atmosphere-attenuated vaccine he had originally advocated. In developing his rabies vaccine, he seems to have appropriated methods developed by a colleague, Émile Roux. Pasteur's own theory of "biological exhaustion" to explain pathogenicity was flawed, and it would seem that he eventually adopted practical and theoretical ideas of others that he had previously criticized—but without acknowledgment. Geison also details ethical lapses connected to Pasteur's decision to employ the rabies vaccine on an asymptomatic patient.

Although historians have in recent years questioned the ethical purity of other scientific heroes, none was so entrenched and widely known as Pasteur. Accordingly, Geison's work met with both relief and resistance after it was published in 1995. No less a light than Nobel laureate Max Perutz attacked the effort to deflate what has become known as the Pasteurian legend. While Geison's tone is sometimes denunciatory, his study points out Pasteur's flaws, properly assesses the rhetorical aspects of his great successes, and deflates his mythic status. Although Pasteur was a captivating speaker, bold in his writing—his addresses and papers still make compelling reading—there is no reason to worship him. Pasteur's influence on science and on medicine will abide without genuflection.

# Robert Koch [1843–1910]

## Foundations of Bacteriology

If Louis Pasteur (p. 18) was a scientific genius possessed of vision, Robert Koch was the tireless and methodical virtuoso who tracked down the bacteria responsible for a host of diseases. Anthrax, typhoid fever, gonorrhea and syphilis, leprosy, and pneumonia all were in some measure unraveled in Koch's laboratory. Among his greatest triumphs were identification, in 1882, of the microorganism that causes tuberculosis and isolation of *Vibrio cholerae* in 1884. Tuberculosis was the nineteenth century's great scourge, and cholera was a fearsome disease and often epidemic.

From the beginning of his career, Koch developed new techniques in microscopy and novel procedures for culturing microbes. The fact that "Koch's postulates"—rules for accepting any particular microorganism as causing a specific disease—are still frequently cited today is alone testament to his influence on medicine over the century past. Insight, perseverance, and methodical technique characterized his cultivated persona. "Bacteriology's consolidation into a scientific discipline," writes Roy Porter, "was due mainly to Robert Koch."

Robert Koch, one of eleven boys and thirteen children, was born on December 11, 1843. His father, Hermann Koch, was a mining engineer whose work had brought him to Clausthal-Zellerfeld, a city in the Harz Mountains. His mother, Mathilde Julie Henriette Biwend, was the grandniece of his father. Growing up in a harmonious family environment, Robert was a favored son, intellectually precocious, with a strong interest in nature. Wandering the mountains equipped with a field guide, he collected rocks, lichen, moss, and insects. He graduated at the head of his class in the gymnasium, and an upturn in family fortunes enabled him to begin at the University of Göttingen in 1862. He was already interested in medical research. Using himself as an experimental subject, he began eating 500 grams of butter per day, intending to measure the levels of succinic acid in his urine. He became ill, but his report on the experiment earned him his dissertation, and he graduated in 1866.

Koch's decision to enter private practice derived from his wish to marry Emmy Fraatz, as he did in 1867. He had trouble generating income, and for a time worked at an asylum for retarded children. With the outbreak of the

Franco-Prussian War in 1871, Koch served in the military as a field hospital physician. At war's end he settled down as a young district medical officer in the provincial town of Wollstein (today Wolsztyn, Poland). Essentially a country doctor, Koch set up a home laboratory and, armed with a microscope, a birthday gift from his wife, he began his career in research.

By the 1870s considerable interest had developed around pathogenic bacteria, spurred by the improved microscope and much suggestive experimentation. That Koch, however, working in rural isolation, could address the problem of anthrax is a measure of the comparatively elementary state of the science. Anthrax, a disease that kills cattle and can be transmitted to humans, was in those years epidemic in both France and Germany. The anthrax bacillus had been viewed under the microscope as early as 1849, but its role in the disease remained unclear. Mysteriously, anthrax could arise even where the bacteria seemed not to be present.

The key to the disease lay in the bacterium's life cycle. This Koch discovered and described. In 1876 he wrote to Ferdinand Cohn, the most prestigious researcher in Germany, and won an immediate invitation to present his findings at the Botanical Institute in Breslau. Koch outlined his work during three days in the spring of 1876, illuminating for his distinguished audience the metamorphoses of the anthrax bacterium from cradle to grave. He showed how it multiplies quickly under favorable conditions but assumes a dormant, sporelike shape at other times. News of his discovery, published within weeks, spread rapidly. Soon thereafter, with much fanfare, Louis Pasteur in France would develop a vaccine.

While Koch returned to his homemade laboratory in Wollstein, his reputation was further consolidated by two other exceptional papers. His discoveries concerning anthrax were largely due to his innovations in microscopy, which he now described to the world. An enthusiastic photographer, Koch had adapted and developed new methods for fixing, staining, and photographing bacterial slides. In addition, he also published, in 1878, "The Etiology of Traumatic Infective Diseases." It is from this paper that scholars frequently date the founding of the germ theory of disease. In 1880, with the backing of Cohn and others, Koch was appointed to the Imperial Health Office in Berlin, where he was provided a laboratory and funds for research.

Koch's demonstration that specific diseases, arising from various wounds, may be traced to species of bacteria, to be named and classified, is a landmark in the history of bacteriology. Yet there is an important caveat. Koch's insistence that each disease was caused by an invariant form of a microbe was unfortunate. It led to a debate between Koch's "monomorphism" and the "pleomorphists." Carl von Nägeli, notably, presented a more complex picture of an evolving microworld tailored by natural selection. Koch, who was suspicious of Darwinism, was not inclined to agree. His greater authority was difficult to overcome, and recognition that microbes of a species are genetically varied was, arguably, long delayed.

Koch's innovations in the laboratory were both simple and deeply influential. At the International Medical Congress in England in 1881 — Virchow and Pasteur also were present — Koch demonstrated his new method for growing bacteria. Pasteur preferred flasks for his cultures, but Koch worked out a method that was simple, eminently replicable, and inexpensive. A shallow glass plate, covered by gelatin infused with a meat broth for nourishment, became a transparent medium in which pure cultures of bacteria could be easily and selectively grown. (A slight innovation with an enduring legacy, the petri dish, was named after Koch's laboratory assistant, Julius Richard Petri, who fitted the shallow glass dish with a cover to keep out contaminants.) Koch also played a significant role in the practical evolution of asepsis in clinical medicine. He suggested replacing carbolic acid, as Joseph Lister recommended, with mercuric chloride, and he recommended steam for sterilization.

Koch's new culturing methods were central to his most spectacular discovery: isolation of the bacterium that causes tuberculosis. One of the most baffling and confusing diseases to plague the nineteenth century, its symptoms had been much studied, and Jean Antoine Villemin and others had provided suggestive but inconclusive evidence that the disease could be transmitted to animals, but no bacterial culprit had been detected. Koch made the bacteria visible by staining tissue samples with (thanks to the German dye industry) methylene blue. He discovered rod-shaped bacteria in large numbers in "all locations where the tuberculosis process has recently developed and is progressing most rapidly." In his 1882 paper, Koch wrote decisively, "I consider it as proven that in all tuberculosis conditions of man and animals there exists a characteristic bacterium which I have designated as the tubercle bacillus, which has specific properties which allow it to be distinguished from all other microorganisms." It was the keystone for future research into a complex disease—a "red letter day in bacteriological history," wrote Claude Dolman—and for it Koch would be awarded the Nobel Prize for physiology or medicine in 1905.

In 1890, Koch set forth a group of requirements for determining whether a microbe is to be considered the cause of a disease. Koch's postulates, as they are known today, are four in number: (1) the organism can be demonstrated to be present in every case of the disease; (2) a pure culture of the organism must be obtainable; (3) the culture must produce the disease when inoculated into healthy, susceptible animals; and (4) the organism must be found in sick animals. It should be added that these postulates adapt ideas put forward by Koch's teacher, Jacob Henle (p. 84). Koch's postulates, although useful to medical science over more than a century, have certain limitations. They work better with bacterial than with viral infections, and there are always exceptions—if only because microbes don't read textbooks on disease.

Koch's career and the birth of the germ theory of disease coincided with the European imperialist expansion into Africa, Asia, and the Indian subcontinent. Colonials and soldiers were beset by old sicknesses as well as diseases never before encountered. In 1883 Koch led a commission to Egypt to investigate cholera. He later studied the disease in India and isolated the *Vibrio cholera*, confirming stagnant water as its principal route for transmission. In South Africa in 1896, Koch studied rinderpest, a disease of cattle, and although he could not isolate the organism responsible, he developed a means of immunization. The next year he studied bubonic plague in Bombay. In East Africa in 1902, at the request of the German government, Koch investigated the parasitic diseases carried by the tsetse fly, and four years later he headed a commission to study sleeping sickness.

Indeed, once he achieved eminence, Koch's services were in constant demand, frequently requested by the government, sometimes sponsored by industry, and widely reported in the press. His work on the various pathogenic bacteria, although not in every case fully successful, virtually beggars summation. Koch held several appointments in later years. In 1885 he was named to a specially created post as professor of hygiene at the University of Berlin where he also directed the Institute of Hygiene. From 1891 to 1904, Koch directed the Institute for Infectious Diseases in Berlin, although frequently from afar, for he traveled constantly.

Koch made an egregious error in 1890 when he suddenly announced that he had discovered a remedy for tuberculosis. He called the agent "tuberculin," and a great deal of publicity ensued. Victims of the disease flooded Koch with letters begging for the medicine, and many made their way to Berlin. Thousands were given the medicine. But it soon became clear that tuberculin was positively dangerous for patients with pulmonary tuberculosis. Secretive about its actual composition, Koch was eventually compelled to reveal his formula, which turned out to be only a glycerol-containing extract of tubercle bacilli. The whole episode was extremely embarrassing, and Koch soon took an extended voyage to Egypt.

In Koch, as with Pasteur, one finds admixed with scientific talent, and even genius, considerable measures of ambition, egoism, and jingoism. If personal and cultural competition is common in medical research, each instance might well be measured against the rivalry of Robert Koch and Louis Pasteur. In terminology Pasteur preferred "microbiology" while Koch liked "bacteriology"—and that is only the beginning. While the germ theory of disease was inaugurating a revolution in medicine, its two most prominent founders engaged in backbiting and polemics. This running dispute during the 1880s had as its immediate background the Franco-Prussian War, which France had lost in 1871, much to Pasteur's chagrin. In 1882 Koch credited Jean-Joseph Toussaint, Pasteur's rival, with discovery of the anthrax vaccine. Koch's less attractive qualities were on display in his relations with Pasteur.

In everyday life, Koch was friendly and enthusiastic; his characteristic pugnacity acquired a certain arrogance in later life. He loved nature, the "wonders of Africa," and archaeology. It is not surprising to find that he was an avid chess player, nor that he was uninterested in religion or politics. Although Koch's wife, Emmy, had set Koch upon his career with her gift of a microscope, the couple was not really compatible. They had one child, a daughter, while remaining together a quarter century; they eventually divorced. In a much publicized affair, about 1891 Koch became enamored of Hedwig Freiberg, an attractive art student thirty years his junior, whom he married in 1893. Upright Germans were scandalized, but Hedwig became Koch's constant companion and long outlived him, dying in 1945. Koch's health declined during 1909, and at the famous spa in Baden-Baden, on May 27, 1910, at age sixty-seven, he died of a heart condition

The adulation customarily accorded Robert Koch had its downside. Koch's "utterances were carefully recorded and repeated," writes his biographer Thomas D. Brock. "A Koch myth developed: the great Koch could do no wrong....Unfortunately, even Koch had trouble distinguishing the myth from the reality." To his contemporaries, however, his greatness was transparent. Upon his death, his ashes were deposited in an urn at the institute he founded. Elie Metchnikoff (p. 186) carried a plaque from Paris to Berlin, while in Japan his celebrated colleague Shibasaburo Kitasato erected a shrine that included a tuft of Koch's hair.

# Hippocrates [c. 460–370 B.C.]

## Rational Medicine

In Greece, about the sixth century B.C., there emerged the basic lines of a rational attempt, based on recognizably Western ideas, to understand the human body and its afflictions. In the midst of folk healing and traditions of gods and heroes associated with sickness and health—the most famous was Asclepius—arose schools in which evolved theories of illness and treatments to cure it. Ancient Greek physicians were craftsmen who did not have a high social status and who frequently traveled in search of work. Under the influence of early philosophers such as Pythagoras and Empedocles, some among these physicians eventually began to write, preparing catalogs of observations, elaborating on concepts of health, and setting out terms of moral obligation. The most famous of such writings is a group of about sixty works, known collectively as the *Corpus Hippocraticum*. It is associated with the name of Hippocrates.

Hippocrates of Cos is traditionally considered the founder of Western medicine, and in this regard he has no rivals. But little or nothing is known about his life; ancient Greek literature provides scant information. Although one cannot say with complete assurance that Hippocrates ever lived at all, it is only fair to recognize him as a historical, not a mythic, figure. He lived about the same time as a clutch of other commanding figures in Western culture, including Aristophanes and Sophocles, and the statesman Pericles. The only more or less contemporary references to Hippocrates come in the works of Plato. In the *Phaedrus* it is implied that he wrote medical books; in the *Protagoras,* he is mentioned as a physician and teacher. A generation later, Aristotle brings up Hippocrates in connection with his stature—he would appear to be more renowned than his small size would suggest.

On the other hand, long after his death, in the flourishing intellectual center of Alexandria, several authors developed fairly extensive biographies of Hippocrates—about which nothing can be verified or accepted at face value. Hippocrates is said to have been born about 460 B.C. on Cos (or Kos), one of the Dodecanese islands in the Aegean Sea, which today form a department of modern Greece. His mother was Phenarete; his father was Heraclides, a physician with whom he studied. Hippocrates traveled

throughout Greece, according to the old biographies. In 430 B.C. he lighted bonfires in Athens to drive away the plague. Among his best-known cases was a Macedonian tyrant, whom he cured of lovesickness. When Hippocrates died no one knows; he reached an age variously given from 85 to 109 and was said to be buried in Thessaly.

The Hippocratic corpus was not "published" in any ordinary sense. It is a collection of texts, perhaps the remains of a library, written in the Ionian dialect and probably assembled by scholars at Alexandria about 280 B.C. Its sixty books are the works of various authors, and the corpus covers a wide variety of issues, from illness and injury to problems concerning law and conduct. The author of *On the Sacred Disease*—that is, epilepsy—aims at a lay audience and makes an effort to demystify a frightening disease, which in the ancient world was easy to ascribe to demonic or divine intervention. *Air, Waters and Places* is more or less a handbook, meant to help the physician who arrives in a new city or town and needs to cope with local conditions and diseases. The subject of *Decorum* is bedside manner. Traditionally the most popular Hippocratic text is the *Aphorisms*, which were reprinted time and again over the centuries and inspired endless commentaries.

Observation, with a view to developing a prognosis, emerges as the basic stance of the Hippocratic physician. Diagnosis and treatment were not easy or painless, and so emphasis on describing for the patient what might be expected was a prudent course. A definite advantage accrued to the ancient physician who did not promise to fix or cure what could not be treated. An adequate prognosis protected the physician from accusations of wrongdoing and also brought the competent practitioner recognition for perspicacity.

The entire Hippocratic corpus shares an essentially rationalist outlook. Disease is viewed as a process in nature, during the course of which crucial signs and symptoms may be discerned. "Examining the body requires sight, hearing, smell, touch, taste and reason," claimed the author of the Hippocratic *Epidemics*. This perspective of observation and scrutiny, and use of the five senses, is essentially the first such instance of a naturalistic, reflective approach in Western medicine. It is not found, in any direct form, in shamanistic or magical medicine; it does not characterize medicine as practiced in Egypt or Mesopotamia.

Underlying the basic attitude of the Hippocratic physician was the doctrine of humors. Of immeasurable historical importance to Western medicine, humoral doctrine was initially based on a philosophical, cosmological idea. Empedocles, who lived from about 490 – 430 B.C., was the first to suggest that the entire universe is comprised of four elements: earth, air, fire, and water. These were associated in various ways with the winds and seasons, and eventually with the humors, as an adaptation to the human subject. Predictably, there were four humors, consisting of four bodily fluids and discharges. (The term "humor" was originally descriptive of any fluid found in an animal or a plant.) *Blood,* associated with childhood, invokes heat and the season of spring; it is the primary humor. *Bile* (meaning yellow bile) is dry, associated with youth and the summer. *Phlegm* is connected to old age and winter. *Black bile* is associated with adults, the cold of autumn, and melancholy. With the Hippocratic treatise *On the Nature of Man,* humoral theory enters medicine as a general theory of bodily function and of disease.

The humoral system was also, in great part, the way by which ancient Greek medicine understood the interior of the human body. The humors provided the basis for beautiful, analogical descriptions of how the body worked, which would later appeal to Medieval churchmen. The eye is compared to a lantern; the stomach, to an oven. The kidneys are like cupping glasses, drawing fluid into themselves. "Spongy, porous parts, like the spleen, lungs and breasts," according to the author of *On Ancient Medicine,* "will drink up readily what is in contact with them, and these parts especially harden and enlarge on the addition of fluid." The humoral schema is at once rational and dogmatic, based on observation but in no wise on experiment. Hippocratic interest in the body did not include extensive classification or investigation of its interior; few surgical procedures were allowed.

When applied to disease, humoral concepts of the Hippocratic physician were holistic. From humoral theory arises the familiar and still popular idea that health implies equilibrium. Disease is the result of an imbalance of humors, and treatment is designed to restore balance. Too much phlegm, for example, caused epilepsy. Excessive drinking or debauchery disturbed the humors, as did hot or cold weather, or not sleeping enough. It was the nature of the body to reestablish equilibrium through its warmth, by which humors were matured and expelled. This provided an explanation for fevers, and if the body failed in its restorative work, the patient died.

With its powerful, rationalistic explanations, humoral theory retained a firm place in medical practice for well over two thousand years. Its definitive decline did not really come until well into the nineteenth century, with the rise of a dependable chemistry and, somewhat later, the coming of biochemistry. The concept of "humoral" (as opposed to "cellular") immunity persisted into the twentieth century, and such concepts as "stress" could for a long time be described as belonging to humoral theory. It ought to be added that the humors also possessed a psychological aspect: their mixture was supposed to determine an individual's personal temperament. It is interesting to note that today genetics research based on molecular biology has led, via sociobiology, to a new emphasis on basic temperament and a corresponding de-emphasis on the intricacies of personality. Humoral theory has, in effect, been replaced by molecular explanations—with the same functional value but with a limited depth of vision.

Finally, there is the oath. It remains the most significant remnant of Hippocratic medicine, and parts of it are still recited by graduating medical students. Extensively studied by philologists, the oath essentially has two parts, the first of which constitutes a contract of indenture between master and student. The second part delivers the duties of physicians to society—principally in terms of what is forbidden. The oath prohibits poisoning, abortifacients, abetting suicide, performing surgery using the knife, and sexual relations with patients and other breaches of confidence. "If I fulfill this oath and do not violate it, may it be granted me to enjoy life and art, being honored with fame among all men for all time to come; if I transgress it and swear falsely, may the opposite be my lot." The Hippocratic oath, which may have been composed as early as the sixth century B.C., or perhaps considerably later, has parallels with beliefs found in the cult of Pythagoras and is consonant with principles of the early Christian church.

Hippocrates's durability in medicine is both logical and adventitious. In presenting medicine as a rational endeavor, essentially unmixed with supernatural or mystical elements, Hippocrates set the agenda for Western medicine. He has been perpetually rediscovered. His fame was championed by the Greek physician Galen (p. 34), who served as the arbiter of Medieval medicine. In the seventeenth century, Thomas Sydenham (p. 132) became known as the "English Hippocrates." After the French Revolution, when modern medicine dawned in Paris, a Hippocratic professorship was established. By midcentury a new and important edition of the whole corpus, published by Émile Littré, established the basis of a modern picture of Hippocrates. He has continued to interest scholars throughout the twentieth century, down to a recent work, *Hippocrates*, by Jacques Jouanna, that affirms the continuing relevance of the corpus as a monument to the Western intellectual tradition and the significance of Hippocrates as a historical figure. Although his system and practices have been mostly scrapped or transformed, Hippocrates continues to exemplify, writes Oswei Temkin, "the autonomy of medicine as a sphere of life."

# Galen [c. A.D. 129–204]

## Western Medical Tradition

The most significant prescientific figure in Western medicine, who indeed fashioned the crucible from which it emerged, is Galen of Pergamum. Living at the time of the Roman Empire, he represents the culmination of the long and essentially fruitful history of Greek medicine. Possessed of a controversial, often antagonistic personality, Galen was much celebrated in his own lifetime and, for the breadth of his work, he is often compared to Aristotle. He was an exceptional anatomist and attempted to synthesize all that was known of the human body and disease. Although no stylist, he was an immensely prolific writer. As the "climax and flower of the experimental spirit in antiquity," wrote Charles Singer some years ago, Galen "presents a unique phenomenon in the history of science and one perhaps unique in cultural history as a whole."

Historically, Galen's legacy is complex. His status was magnified in the Middle Ages, when his works became the principal authority in medicine, adopted by the scholastics and taught as dogma. Galen's influence diminished, but by no means ended, with the advent of such figures as Paracelsus (p. 50) and Vesalius (p. 41), and subsequently, the scientific revolution. The reason for Galen's enduring influence is that, unlike other medical thinkers of antiquity, his focus was the structure and function of the human body. The anatomical concept of disease belongs first of all to Galen. Excepting Hippocrates (p. 29), Galen is, by fair consensus, the most influential source of Western medicine.

Born to a wealthy family about A.D. 129, Galen was the son of Nicon of Pergamum (today Bergama, in the Izmir province of Turkey), a prosperous city and cultural center of the Roman Empire. His mother is described as irascible and unpleasant, a cantankerous woman who "sometimes bites her maids." But Galen wrote, "It was my good fortune to have a father who was perfectly calm, just, gallant, and devoted." Under his tutelage, Galen studied philosophy, mathematics, and literature. A dream of his father's in which he was visited by Asclepius—in Homer's *Iliad*, the father of good doctors—may have impelled Galen to devote himself to medicine. His education was long, peripatetic, and comprehensive. After several years at the medical school in Pergamum, Galen studied anatomy at Smyrna. Here he wrote his first treatise, *On Medical Experience,* about the year 149. After further travels, Galen studied for some five years at Alexandria, long the center for medical studies but—as Galen seems to have found it two centuries after its peak of influence—bereft of new ideas. He subsequently traveled through Egypt, and assimilated much useful medical lore.

Galen started practicing medicine when he returned to Pergamum, about 157, at age twenty-eight. As physician to gladiators at the city's stadium, Galen had the opportunity to gain considerable knowledge about both anatomy and treating wounds. He developed a considerable reputation for his skills, and characteristically he claims to have been immensely successful. About 162 Galen moved to Rome, for reasons not clear, and discovered that his fame preceded him. He gave public lectures, served as physician to the learned and renowned, and made a famous cure of his former instructor in philosophy, Eudemus. In 166 he suddenly left Rome, whether to avoid an epidemic (perhaps of smallpox) or to escape professional animosities is not clear. In 168 he was asked by Marcus Aurelius to accompany him on a military expedition; this was a request from a friend and protector that Galen could hardly refuse. He returned to Rome with the army in 169. There he remained, often in imperial service, for much of the rest of his life.

Galen was heir to a long and productive series of traditions in Greek medicine, developed over the course of 600 years. Various sects and schools had evolved, and in the early Alexandrian period dissection was allowed, so anatomy flourished. The early theorists, from dogmatists to methodists, made creative attempts to understand and treat disease. Although none of their ideas developed into a complex, comprehensive system, they helped shape Roman medicine during the empire.*

Galen entirely refashioned this lore, benefiting from the powerful philosophical traditions established by Plato and Aristotle. His work, both in theory and therapeutics, represents a creative synthesis of the medical knowledge of his time. He recognized the prominence of Hippocrates while writing that the father of medicine "has not gone as far as we could wish." Galen adds of Hippocrates: "His writings are defective in order, in the necessary distinctions; . . . he opened the road, but I have rendered it passable."

---

*As with Aristarchus, who believed the earth and planets traveled around the sun, basically correct ideas were sometimes sketched only to be eclipsed. One of the founders of Alexandrian medicine, Erasistratus (c. 300–225 B.C.) believed that the elements comprising the body were composed of atoms and nourished by air; he also held a mechanistic conception of digestion.

The most prolific medical writer until modern times, Galen is credited as the author of over 300 works, running to some 8,000 pages. (A standard edition, in twenty-two volumes, was published in the early nineteenth century.) He was not a stylist and is not easy to read, often moving from one subject to another without warning. "We have, then, it seems, arrived at the subject of Nutrition," writes Galen in *On the Natural Faculties,* switching gears after an acute but rambling discussion of growth. He wrote in Attic Greek, the main literary dialect and standard form of the language. Although he specialized in medicine, Galen also wrote on linguistics and philosophical issues. Some five of his treatises concern the ancient comic poets. Most of his nonmedical writings, however, are lost.

Among Galen's most important and influential books is *De usu partium corporis humani (On the Actions of the Parts of the Human Body).* A textbook of physiology and anatomy, replete with experimental demonstrations, it became the fundamental teaching tool of the scholastics. Galen's *De anatomicis administrationibus (On Anatomical Procedures)* was the starting point for Vesalius's anatomical studies. Other important works include *De ossibus ad tirones (On Bones for Students),* based on human skeletons, and *De locis affectis (On Disordered Parts),* a book on disease which was highly influential, after being printed in 1500, from the sixteenth to the eighteenth century. As with those of many of the ancient authors, Galen's works were first translated into Arabic, then into Latin, at first with much distortion. Only in 1453, when Constantinople reverted to Christian rule, were the original writings in Greek returned to the West.

As an investigator, Galen's most intriguing quality is his willingness to scrutinize, experiment, and demonstrate. Although human dissection was by his lifetime forbidden, Galen dissected many kinds of animals, especially the macaque monkey, found in Asia and North Africa. A brief perusal of any Galenic text indicates his observational stance. Galen showed, for example, that the voice originates from the larynx, not the lungs as earlier ancients had assumed. While he confused tendons and nerves—he had no magnifying glass—Galen showed that the nervous system would not work if the nerves were cut. He made many errors in description, but by viewing the three principal organs of the body as the heart, liver, and brain, he adumbrated a paradigm useful to Western medicine from then until now.

Galen supported and to some extent helped shape the theory of the humors as it would evolve in Western medicine after Hippocrates, principally by making it compatible with Aristotelian physics. Fire, air, earth, and water were the basic elements, according to Aristotle, and all matter was comprised of them in admixed quantities of hot, cold, dry and moist. Galen thought of the humors as combinations of these elements and qualities in living bodies. He derived from them a scheme of nine related temperaments that referred both to psychological type—a person was by degrees sanguine, phlegmatic, choleric, or melancholic—and also to the various organs themselves. A heart that was warm and dry could be detected: "The pulse is hard, big, rapid and frequent, and breathing is deep, rapid, and frequent." This kind of heart would be found in tyrannical, quick-tempered people "ready for action, courageous, quick, wild, savage, rash, and impudent."

An aspect of Galen's basic outlook that made him highly attractive to the medieval scholastics involved the concept that living creatures belonged to a world spirit, and that the structure and function of the human body reflected the perfection of Nature. A good example is Galen's view of the liver: It is the place where the natural spirit is manufactured and sent out into the body through the veins, transmuted into vital spirit and distributed through the arteries to nourish the body as well as the brain. In the brain, vital spirit is transformed into animal spirit and is in turn distributed to the nerves. This broad concept of irrigation corresponded to natural processes and was meaningful both in Galen's world and through the end of the Middle Ages.

Galen's ability as a clinician must have been impressive to ancient eyes. He could treat fractures and dislocations and perform simple operations to excise polyps, but he also undertook more complex and painful procedures, such as the removal of bladder stones. He describes arrhythmia of the heart, was a strong proponent of bleeding, and, being Galen, he developed rationales for how much blood would best be drawn from which part of the body to cure a specific illness. Nutrition, in Galen's humoral scheme, played an important role in health, and he recommended prophylactic and therapeutic regimens. His cast of remedies included opium, castor oil, tannic acid, and many others. The "Galenical" remedies, as they eventually evolved, could be complex, with dozens of ingredients. But Galen himself had a complicated classification in which there were twelve degrees of drug action—and it too fit into his metaphysical scheme. Altogether, Galen's broad knowledge, together with his unrivaled reputation, made him a formidable authority.

Galen's personality, which comes through forcefully in his writings, tempers his brilliance by extravagant ambition; he could be obnoxious, self-aggrandizing, and deceitful. Galen was, however, an egoist on a mission, and in this respect he was not unlike many of the important physicians and researchers today. The year of Galen's death is uncertain. Most often he is said to have died about A.D. 200, but sources suggest it may have been as late as 216, and by the evidence of the manuscripts, this is not unlikely.

"He is the upholder of an impressive creed," writes Vivian Nutton in a recent appraisal, "the unity of the eye and hand, of reason and experience, of past learning and future performance. To say that Galen endeavored to fulfill his own ideal, and in large part succeeded, is to pay him the compliment of genius."

# Part II   The Principal Transformations

# Andreas Vesalius [1514–1564]

## The *Fabrica* and the New Anatomy

In 1543, from Basel, issued a work of art and science that would influence the annals of Western medicine forever after. *De humani corporis fabrica* was one of the first anatomy texts to systematically provide descriptions derived from actual dissection of the human body. Its brilliantly detailed drawings represented a break with the scholastic model of the body based on the work of Galen (p. 34), then over a thousand years old and, not surprisingly, rife with errors. Above all, the *Fabrica* embodied the Renaissance and its new vision of humankind, less encumbered by religion, unbound by dogma. Its author, Andreas Vesalius, is as a consequence traditionally classed with such historic figures in medicine as William Harvey (p. 45) and Ambroise Paré (p. 119).

Andreas Vesalius was born to Isabella Crabbe and her husband, Andreas, on December 31, 1514, in Brussels. The paternal side of his family was steeped in medicine, from his father, apothecary to the Hapsburg emperor Charles V, to his great-great-grandfather, a renowned physician. The Vesaliuses were prosperous and possessed a library, and young Andreas became absorbed by books. Other details of his early education are lacking — it is said that he dissected animals — but he entered the University of Louvain in 1528. He received an extensive education there before going on to study medicine at the University of Paris in 1533. At that conservative institution he did not learn a great deal, he said, but he became committed to anatomical studies. Dissection of human corpses had been common in medical schools since the fourteenth century. One of Vesalius's teachers was Johann Guinther of Andernach, a translator of Galen's anatomical work, but not much of an anatomist himself. Another professor was Jacobus Sylvius, remembered for helping to develop a rational terminology for anatomy.

Vesalius did not graduate before being compelled to leave Paris after Charles V invaded France in 1536. Returning to the Low Countries, Vesalius soon became known for his anatomical knowledge, and it is during this period, as he later recounted, that he went to great trouble to obtain his first skeleton, from an executed prisoner. Bodies were customarily left at the gallows after hangings, and the flesh would soon rot and be eaten off the bone by animals. "After I had brought the legs and arms home in secret...I allowed myself to be shut out of the city in the evening in order to obtain the thorax which was firmly held by a chain. I was burning with so great a desire...that I was not afraid to snatch in the middle of the night what I so longed for...." Vesalius subsequently conducted dissections before fellow students. But he soon moved on to Padua, a hub of culture and learning during the Renaissance. The faculty at the University of Padua awarded Vesalius his medical degree with high distinction in 1537.

Young Vesalius's anatomy demonstrations were popular among students. They were distinctive in two ways. First, Vesalius dissected the cadavers himself. This contravened the usual procedure, in which the professor read from a Galenic text while the body was opened by a menial, or prosector. In addition, and as a consequence, Vesalius began to employ drawings to clarify the various structures of the body. Success with this method led him to publish his charts. The *Tabulae anatomicae sex (Six Anatomical Charts)*, with drawings by Jan Stefan van Calar, appeared in 1538. They depict the reproductive organs in both the male and female, the liver, and the vascular system. The influence of Galen remained strong in this early work, with the liver drawn as a five-lobed organ, and the heart is that of an ape. Nevertheless, the charts were an immediate success and were widely plagiarized.

Over the next six years Vesalius worked, as he had hinted he would, on a larger and more comprehensive work. He had the advantage of a good supply of cadavers, which emboldened him to put realism before Galenic dogma. In 1543—within weeks of the publication of Copernicus's *De revolutionibus*—appeared Vesalius's masterpiece, *De humani corporis fabrica libri septem (Seven Books on the Structure of the Human Body)*. Beautifully printed by Johannes Oporinus of Basel, the books represent a marriage of objective description to the new realism in art characteristic of the Late Renaissance. There has been much discussion over the identity of the artist or artists responsible for the plates. It is thought today that several were at work, among them Vesalius himself, but also the artists of the celebrated school of Titian, considered the greatest of the Venetian painters.

Although a revolutionary work, the *Fabrica* could not escape the influence of Galen, which still permeated thinking about the body. Thus, elements of Galenic anatomy strongly persist, while the book as a whole moves medical thought in another direction entirely. The *Fabrica* aimed to elucidate the real human body for the benefit of students. It is at once a descriptive catalog of the human body and a didactic guide to dissection. Bones and muscles are detailed in Books I and II, and Book III attempts to

describe the vascular system. Book IV, on the nervous system, shows how Vesalius could be led astray by the Galenic classification of nerves. Book V describes the abdominal and reproductive organs—the liver is now the real, human liver. In Book VI, Vesalius expresses clear suspicion concerning the septum of the heart. Galen had assumed it must be permeable in order to allow the flow of venous blood, which he believed was produced in the liver, to enter the arterial system. Book VII describes the brain.

Publication of a volume that was, in effect, an assault on established authority was bound to raise some hackles. *De fabrica* quickly won attention, some of it negative. It was denounced by Vesalius's former teacher Sylvius of Paris, among others. Sylvius went to extraordinarily vituperative lengths to denounce Vesalius—calling him a madman—though with no great results. The *Fabrica* became an authoritative work within a short time.

It seems odd that the publication of the *Fabrica* concluded Vesalius's career as an anatomist, but essentially that is what happened. Vesalius would continue to follow developments in anatomy, and he saw to press a second, lavish edition of the *Fabrica* in 1555. But, perhaps with the help of his father, in 1544 he sought and obtained appointment as imperial physician to Emperor Charles V. It used to be thought that Vesalius had hoped that by entering royal service he would evade the enmity aroused by the *Fabrica*. More likely, though, the move represented fulfillment of ambition. Vesalius did find time to defend himself against Sylvius in a brilliant 1546 epistle to a friend, known to history as the "China Root" letter—so-called because it contained advice on a sarsaparilla-like remedy touted at the court of Charles V.

For two decades as royal physician, Vesalius was associated with high-profile cases and surgical interventions of great skill. In 1548 he dramatically foretold the imminent demise of Maximilian of Egmont, a prognostication which became the talk of Europe. Vesalius acquired a lifetime pension when the emperor abdicated in 1556. He continued at the royal court, however, now in the service of the new monarch, Charles's only son, the King of Spain, Philip II. Neither Vesalius nor Ambroise Paré could do anything for the jousting wounds sustained by King Henry II of France in 1559. Vesalius's last great case, in 1562, involved the unbalanced son of Philip, Don Carlos. The young prince fell down a flight of stairs—reportedly while making sexual advances to a maid—and received a head wound that soon became infected. Vesalius's ministrations brought the patient back from death's door, and Philip was grateful.

However, restoring the prince to health had a fateful consequence. For some, it appeared to be rather like dangerous witchcraft. Vesalius was compelled to give up royal service and, to expiate his sins, make a pilgrimage to Cyprus and Jerusalem. A number of memoirs, all in some degree dubious, provide accounts of his demise. What seems certain is that his return voyage was a mariner's disaster. Vesalius became ill or was shipwrecked on the island of Zante, near the Peloponnesus. There he died.

Vesalius's personality has been the subject of debate over four centuries. He has been described in first-hand accounts as "choleric," and also characterized as disputatious and querulous, wrathful, schizoid, depressed, a butcher at heart, and avaricious. But he has also been endlessly admired. As evidenced by his writings, Vesalius was aggressive, well aware of his own historic significance, and possessed of a broad grasp of the whole range of medicine in his time. "I could have done nothing more worthwhile," he wrote, "than to give a new description of the whole human body, of which nobody understood the anatomy."

# William Harvey [1578–1657]
## Circulation of the Blood

W illiam Harvey was a physician to the King of England and a contemporary of William Shakespeare and Thomas Hobbes, and of Galileo and Johannes Kepler. In 1628 he demonstrated that the heart is a pump which causes the blood to circulate through the body, passing from the arteries to the veins. Harvey's discovery, which controverted the ancient theory of Galen (p. 34), is one of the vital, incontestable breakthroughs in the history of science and medicine. Like the rediscovery by Vesalius (p. 41) of the fabric of the human body through dissection, Harvey's discovery lacked any immediate clinical application. But it was a first step toward a new understanding of how the body works. Its more general significance lies in Harvey's use of scientific method and quantitative reasoning to yield dependable knowledge. "I do not profess to learn and teach Anatomy, from the axioms of the Philosophers," wrote Harvey in the introduction to his historic treatise, commonly referred to as *De motu cordis*, "but from Dissections and the Fabrick of Nature."

Born in Folkestone, Kent, on April 1, 1578, William Harvey was the eldest of nine children born to Thomas Harvey, a yeoman farmer who prospered enough to join the gentry, and his wife, a "Godly, harmless woman," Joan Halke. His early education included five years at the King's School in the Cathedral of Canterbury, where he learned Latin and Greek. In 1593 William, having obtained a scholarship, entered Gonville and Caius College, at Cambridge. Four years later, after receiving his bachelor's degree, he journeyed to Italy to study at the celebrated University of Padua. He received medical degrees from both Padua and Cambridge in 1602.

Harvey's education at Padua was of decisive importance for his discovery of the circulation of the blood. He surely absorbed the secular, cosmopolitan atmosphere at this Late Renaissance seat of learning, where Copernicus had been schooled and Vesalius dramatically transformed the teaching of human anatomy. But specifically, Harvey studied with Fabricius of Aquapendente. An Aristotelian anatomist concerned with structure and function, Fabricius had noted "little doors"—the valves—in the veins. He misinterpreted their function along Galenic lines, believing that they served to slow the flow of blood to the extremities. In fact, Harvey would later realize, the valves served as sluice gates helping to pump blood back to the heart. Later in life, Harvey would tell chemist Robert Boyle that learning of the existence of the valves had been decisive to his later grasp of circulation.

Scholastic authority in matters anatomical had been eroding since the second half of the sixteenth century. The churchmen's use of Galen, like their philosophical dependence on Aristotle, was dogmatic. But it should be remembered that the Galenic concept of the blood and humors was not only ingrained, but satisfying, if not beautiful. In brief, blood was thought to be manufactured constantly in the liver with nourishment taken up from the intestines. The blood moved up to the heart, presumably passed through "pores" in the septum (the partition which separates the heart's atria), and mixed with "pneuma" to produce arterial blood. The resultant image of the ebb and flow of blood and "vital spirit" through the body, as water irrigates a field, made for a powerful construct.

Though this rational scheme could not withstand the claims of Renaissance science, it did not go down without a struggle. In 1553 Michael Servetus, a Spanish physician, put forth the notion of pulmonary circulation, but the religious context of his work led to his being burned at the stake for heresy, and copies of his book, *The Restoration of Christianity*, disappeared with him. Servetus had studied with Vesalius, who in 1543 doubted, and twelve years later stated definitively, that the "pores" in the septum did not exist. Harvey knew of the pulmonary transit of the blood (from right to left heart via the lungs), which had been confirmed by Realdo Colombo in 1559. A prevailing basic conservatism in anatomy had accepted this discovery while preserving spiritual loyalty to Galen. Harvey, by contrast, living several decades later in England, far from the authority of the Catholic Church, was well placed to dispute Galenic ideas.

From early in his career Harvey practiced medicine in high circles. He married the daughter of Dr. Lancelot Browne, Queen Elizabeth's physician, and became associated with St. Bartholomew's Hospital in 1609. Here he would remain some thirty-four years. In addition to practicing medicine, he undertook extensive anatomical observations, dissecting many different species of animals, as well as humans. In 1615 he was honored by the Royal College of Physicians as Lumleian lecturer in surgery. Harvey became one of the royal physicians in 1618, serving first King James I and later King Charles I. Some of his lecture notes, rediscovered in 1876, show that he was teaching the circulation of the blood as early as 1616. "It is certain from the structure of the heart," read his notes for that year, "that the blood is perpetually carried across through the lungs into the aorta as by two clacks of a water bellows to raise water."

*Exercitatio anatomica de motu cordis et sanguinis in animalibus (On the Motion of the Heart and Blood in Animals)* is the definitive text, written in Latin, published in Frankfurt in 1628. A brief volume of seventy-two pages and seventeen chapters, *De motu cordis* begins with a critical analysis of the Galenic conception of the pulse. Indeed, the heartbeat—systole and diastole had long been known—becomes a kind of observational probe for Harvey throughout the book. The heart, Harvey realizes, is an expulsive pump; its work as a muscle is evinced by the pulse. From the beginning, he points out the "incongruous and mutually subversive" opinions which held that the arteries contain "fuliginous vapours," spirits, or air—while Galen himself had admitted that in any artery you open, "you will find nothing but blood."

Harvey went on to lay the groundwork for his own theory, in part through quantitative analysis. He showed that the liver could not be expected to produce as much blood as Galenic theory required. Based on examination of a human heart, Harvey estimated the amount of blood it might expel with each beat. If all that blood were created in the liver on demand, Harvey noted, an estimate of 500 ounces per half hour, or any similar estimate, would always be a larger amount of blood than is found in the entire body. His calculations were in fact quite faulty (the heart pumps far more blood and counts twice as many beats as he supposed), but they proved his point.

Circulation of the blood, Harvey showed, with the heart as a pump, was the more reasonable alternative to the Galenic analysis. "For it is the heart by whose virtue and pulse the blood is moved, perfected, and made nutrient, and is preserved from corruption and coagulation," wrote Harvey, adding extravagantly, "[I]t is the household divinity which, discharging its function, nourishes, cherishes, quickens the whole body, and is indeed the foundation of life, the source of all action."

To support the concept of circulation, Harvey employed famous experiments that could be repeated by any reader. If a vein is located, say, in the arm, and pressure is exerted between valves, the venous blood can be seen and felt to flow not back and forth but ineluctably toward the heart. Similarly, if a bandage is wrapped around the arm so as to block the flow of blood through the veins while leaving open arterial flow, the veins (but not the arteries) will swell. If the arteries are also blocked, however, the veins will not swell. This was presumptive evidence for Harvey's theory that blood passed to bodily extremities via the arteries and returned to the heart through the veins.

It is important to note that in this explanation Harvey provides one of the great inductive insights in the history of science. Harvey knew that the tubelike venous system is distinct from the more muscular arteries, and he could show that perfusion in the lungs could account for communication between the arterial and venous systems. But how was the circle completed? How did Harvey think that arterial blood could enter the venous system in the extremities? In fact, he speculated, writing, "It is absolutely necessary to conclude that the blood in the animal body is impelled in a circle, and is in a state of ceaseless motion." It would remain for Marcello Malpighi, founder of microscopic anatomy, decades later, in 1660, to discover the capillaries.

*De motu cordis* excited considerable attention on its publication. Harvey's critics, whom he characterized as "crack-brained," published a number of attacks, but overall, they had a hard time. One highly vocal attack came from Jean Riolan the Younger, in Paris, who would write a detailed description of the coronary vessels in 1648. Riolan recognized some of the implications of Harvey's theory for Galenic medicine: the function of the liver was put into question, as were rules for bloodletting and the rationale for various medicines. Harvey responded to Riolan with a treatise published the next year, ridiculing his views.

Harvey's subsequent influence on science and medicine has long been considered of the first order, and was both direct and diffuse. The publication of an English-language version of *De motu cordis* in 1653 is indicative of the work's popularity. More generally, as a famous physician, Harvey served as a model to those who would pursue science and research. He became an important figure for anatomists, chemists, and physiologists through the last half of the seventeenth century, who saw themselves as part of a Harveian revolution. Over the course of several generations, writes Robert G. Frank, Jr., these researchers "completely refashioned our knowledge of the function of the human body." Though their conclusions would be limited in terms of achieving medical advances and a satisfactory physiology, the "totality of [their] work was an accomplishment of a magnitude unsurpassed again in the medical sciences for over a century."

Harvey's later career was partly shaped by his royal duties and by the English civil war. He was a Royalist who remained in the company of the king from 1642 until his surrender in 1646. He did not suffer physically either during the conflict or afterward, but he was much aggrieved when Puritans ransacked his home and confiscated his papers. Much of his output was thus lost to posterity.

*Exercitationes de generatione animalium (On the Generation of Animals)*, a work of some importance to the history of embryology, was published six years before his death. Harvey's interest in embryology was notable for reflecting his teleological, Aristotelian worldview, which valued sensory experience while assuming ultimate perfection to exist in Nature. Harvey observed and recorded the day-by-day development of chicks, but he was limited once more by lack of a microscope. The microscope had been invented as early as 1590, but it still remained, for scientific purposes, a curiosity.

The picture of William Harvey left to history is owed largely to John Aubrey, a contemporary and author of *Brief Lives*. It is a lively, not altogether reliable portrait. Well-liked in spite of being temperamental and eccentric, Harvey had been hot-blooded as a youth and had sported a dagger. He and his wife, Elizabeth, were childless, although they kept an "impudent and sensual" parrot that nested nights in Mrs. Harvey's bosom. She left him a widower in 1645. Harvey subsequently lived with one or another of his brothers, who had all become successful merchants.

In 1655 Harvey retired from the Lumleian lectureship. During his last years he suffered from gout and kidney stones, but Aubrey remarks that his blood was kept warm by a "pretty young wench" whom he remembered in his will. On June 3, 1657, the faltering septuagenarian suffered a stroke and sent for his young relatives. They began a death vigil. He could not speak clearly, and asked that his tongue be bled. He lost consciousness and died before the day was out. He was first buried in a family plot, but, thanks to the Royal College of Physicians, the remains of William Harvey lie today in Hempstead Church, Essex.

# Paracelsus [1493–1541]

## A New Tradition in Medicine

With the disputatious and controversial physician and natural philosopher Paracelsus, the authority of medieval medicine suffers a rupture. Although his work is rife with mysticism and he often takes recourse in magic—like other great figures of the Renaissance—Paracelsus represents a defiant turning away from scholasticism to scrutinize the real world. He harvested knowledge from "tramps, butchers and barbers" as he traveled amongst common folk, burned the books of Galen, and won the enmity of the medical establishment. From ancient mystical beliefs he fashioned a complex, protoscientific universe. The result was a new tradition in medicine. His beliefs were taken up and modified by later followers and had great influence over the short term and a lasting impact on medical thought—shades of which linger today.

Paracelsus is notable in modern eyes for groping toward a chemical interpretation of the world, and also for introducing the concept that diseases have external causes. His writings are frequently esoteric, but also witty, outrageous, and passionate. He is noted for his commitment to patients. "No one requires greater love of the heart than the physician," writes Paracelsus. "For him the ultimate instance is man's distress." Brilliant, frustrating, and contradictory, Paracelsus has been admired for centuries by historians and philosophers. "It is difficult," writes one of his biographers, Walter Pagel, "to overrate the effect of Paracelsus's achievement on the development of medicine and chemistry."

Philippus Aureolus Theophrastus Bombastus von Hohenheim was born in Einsiedeln, which is a Swiss Alpine commune today but was part of the Holy Roman Empire in 1493. Sickly while an infant, as a boy he enjoyed a close relationship with his father, the physician and alchemist Wilhelm von Hohenheim, "who never forsook me." His mother, Els Ochsner, probably the bondswoman of the famous Benedictine abbey of Einsiedeln, died when Theophrastus was young. After her death, father and son moved, about 1502, to Villach, a mining district in Austria. Wilhelm taught his son some version of natural philosophy as well as botany and mineralogy. Theophrastus had other early teachers, including Johann Trithemius, a well-known adept of the esoteric and occult.

Paracelsus studied at various Italian universities, but evidence that he received a degree is circumstantial. His travels provided his real education. The itinerant physician was not a rare phenomenon in Renaissance Europe, but Paracelsus took the opportunity to amass a trove of medical folk wisdom and knowledge as practiced in different lands. He writes that he studied in Egypt and the Holy Land. He visited Russia and served as a surgeon for mercenary armies in Italy. During the Neapolitan Wars he came to possess a long sword, which he always wore thereafter. Everywhere he went, Paracelsus learned, not only from physicians but from barbers, healers of all kinds, alchemists, and magicians.

Indeed, Paracelsus's connection to ordinary people and his hostility to academia are defining features of his career. Early in his wanderings, or perhaps as late as 1529, Theophrastus had taken the name Paracelsus, perhaps to indicate his superiority to the Roman medical author Celsus (p. 375), whose works had been published half a century earlier to widespread admiration. In Salzburg for the Peasants' War in 1525, Paracelsus apparently was arrested for taking the peasants' side. In Sweden he investigated the diseases that afflict miners—one of the first studies of occupation-related disease—and identified both tuberculosis and silicosis.

In 1526 Paracelsus's career took a new turn. That year he had settled in Strasbourg, where he wrote a number of treatises and developed a successful practice. But his sojourn there was brief. He was soon called to Basel, where with conservative treatment he successfully brought the famous printer Johannes Froben through a serious illness. Not only was Froben grateful, so was his houseguest, the great humanist, Erasmus. In consequence, church reformers appointed Paracelsus municipal physician and invited him to lecture at the university. His reputation was already considerable when he arrived, and controversial. Paracelsus did not disappoint. He gave his lectures in German rather than Latin, and is supposed to have told students, "The patients are your textbook, the sickbed is your study." He dramatized this rejection of book learning by solemnly burning in public the works of Galen (p. 34) and Ibn Sina (Avicenna) (p. 379) during a student festival. None of this endeared him to the local church-men, who attacked him as "Cacophrastus"—a scatological insult—and scathingly compared him to Luther. Paracelsus replied with his own insults. When his friend and protector Froben died suddenly in 1528, Paracelsus was compelled to leave Basel. He resumed his wanderings.

During his remaining thirteen years, Paracelsus was both a traveling physician, treating rich and poor alike, and a prolific writer. His work ranged across alchemy, astronomy, religion, and philosophy as well as medicine. He expounded on all these topics in his most celebrated book, *Buch paragranum (Against the Grain)*, published in 1530. He augmented this work the next year with *Opus paramirum,* in which he subsumes humoral theory under his no-tion of five *entia,* or powers, as governing the mind and body.

Impoverishment did not quell Paracelsus's pen, although many of his works would not appear until after he was dead. He published a book on surgery in 1536, entitled *Grosse Wundarzenei.* His *Astronomia magna,* from 1538, is a chaotic effort to create a system of natural philosophy. It includes much reliance on magic, but it should be added that this was not unusual for a rebellious intellectual at the time. Johannes Kepler, from the same era, cast astrological charts, and much mysticism pervades his great works on astronomy. But such extravagance in a practical craft is more problematic. It is difficult to distinguish Paracelsus's useful contributions, not least because even when true they are couched in self-adulation. "Come then, and listen," Paracelsus urged his adversaries,

> imposters who prevail only by the authority of your high positions! After my death, my disciples will burst forth and drag you to the light, and shall expose your dirty drugs, wherewith up to this time you have com-passed the death of princes....Woe for your necks on the day of judge-ment!...Not that I praise myself: Nature praises me.

"Is this rhetoric," asks historian of chemistry William H. Brock, "or the ravings of a lunatic?"

The major ideas of Paracelsus clearly set him apart from the Galenic tradition long dominant in Europe. His influences include notions drawn from gnostic and Neo-Platonic traditions. He viewed man, for example, as a microcosm of the universe: "For the sun and the moon and all planets, as well as all the stars and the whole chaos, are in man. . . . For man was cre-ated from heaven and earth, and is therefore like them!" The world itself is comprised of spiritual forces, including those that direct digestion; and the poisons that create illnesses might come from the stars. Paracelsus also be-lieved in the doctrine of signatures, by which a plant or root constitutes medi-cine for the body part that it resembles—the orchid for testicles, for example.

Much of this may today appear bizarre and mystical. That perception is deceptive. Paracelsus was laying the basis for a medicine in which chemistry plays a central role and diseases are not seen as resulting from humoral imbalances in the body, but as entities in the world, discrete and invasive. In place of the basic elements and humors to which mainstream medicine then subscribed, Paracelsus held to three primary substances found in matter: salt, sulfur, and mercury. These are basic principles from which the world is made. Mercury was spirit; sulfur, the soul; salt, the body. Is this strange? Consider salt in its various forms relative to the body—kidney stones as one visible, painful example.

Paracelsus employed laboratory techniques to isolate or purify the "quinta essentia" of various substances. The grand alchemical theme, the transmutation of base metals, didn't much interest Paracelsus, but his work includes one of the first efforts ever made to create a chemical system. It is not surprising that he employed analogical thinking. He related salt, sulfur, and mercury to the trinity of body, spirit, and soul. The Paracelsian *tria prima,* writes Allen G. Debus, "has a special significance in the rise of modern science." Viewed as a new system of elements, it could "[call] into question the whole framework of ancient medicine and natural philosophy."

Indeed, historians have long understood Paracelsus's revolutionary significance. The new tradition that begins with him was broadly expanded in the late sixteenth century as works of Paracelsus began to be widely distributed and some of his basic ideas gained adherents, especially among Protestants. (Paracelsus himself had heard Luther at the Diet of Worms, but in religion he was neither Catholic nor Lutheran.) Paracelsians found support among the crowned heads of Europe, particularly in the German empire. The science that emerged from Paracelsus's work came to be known as *iatrochemistry,* or medical chemistry. Just like Paracelsus, iatrochemistry was influential, anti-elitist, and part and parcel of Reformation thinking. Its considerable influence would last until it was absorbed by advances in natural philosophy and new ways of thinking about medicine and the human body.*

---

*Iatrochemistry flourished after Paracelsus's death and attracted a number of brilliant and idiosyncratic physicians. The Flemish physician Joan Baptista van Helmont (1579–1644) moved chemistry further toward its eventual emergence as a discipline and to some extent systematized Paracelsus's concept of disease. Franz de la Boë, or Sylvius (1614–72), was clinically oriented and concerned in great part with physiology and specific diseases; he was more skeptical than mystical. Daniel Sennert (1572–1637) was highly influential in Germany and attempted to adapt Paracelsian ideas to traditional humoralism.

Although their theories could not be sustained, Paracelsus and his later followers brought (or returned) to medicine numerous remedies, including the use of opium, lead, arsenic, copper sulfate, potassium sulfate, and iron—as well as mercury and sulfur. All these were largely unknown to Galenic medicine, and many of the new remedies, in various forms, found their way into the seventeenth-century pharmacopoeias.

Paracelsus's complete works take up fourteen volumes. Often obscure and always in need of exegesis, he has generated endless commentary over the centuries. His life has been a source of fascination for many and, not surprisingly, there is also a literature of denigration. (One is reminded of the late twentieth-century reaction to Sigmund Freud [p. 173].) Enemies took advantage of Paracelsus's eccentricity to tar him posthumously. According to one detractor, he "lived liked a pig, looked like a drover, found his greatest enjoyment in the company of the most dissolute and lowest rabble, and throughout his glorious life he was generally drunk." These insults always have some basis in fact. Paracelsus did like to drink, was an expert on wine and vintage, and if one believes an eyewitness account by his amanuensis, Johannes Oporinus, he was an angry, irascible drunk.

Not much is known of the last few years of Paracelsus's life, but by the summer of 1540 he was in Salzburg, where Archbishop Ernest of Wittelsbach invited him to enjoy his protection. Paracelsus did not marry and left no heirs when he died, shortly after suffering a stroke, on September 24, 1541. His grave soon became a pilgrim's shrine for those ill and infirm who believed in his powerful ideas and remedies. In a celebrated poem by Robert Browning, he forecast his enduring reputation. "But after, they will know me," says Paracelsus—

> If I stoop
> Into a dark tremendous sea of cloud,
> It is but for a time; I press God's lamp
> Close to my breast; its splendour, soon or late,
> Will pierce the gloom: I shall emerge one day.
> You understand me? I have said enough.

# Giovanni Morgagni [1682–1771]

## "His Anatomical Majesty"

The idea that symptoms of diseases, from colds to cancer, arise from changes in organs and tissues of the body seems commonplace if not banal. But the systematic correlation of the clinical history of disease with structural changes seen at autopsy was once a novel concept. For centuries in Western medicine, with time out for figures such as Paracelsus (p. 50), diseases were thought to result from an imbalance of the body's four humors. This idea persisted into the Enlightenment. In 1761, however, consolidating more than a century of anatomical investigation, the Italian physician and anatomist Giovanni Morgagni published *On the Sites and Causes of Disease*. "It was Morgagni," writes Roy Porter simply, "who thus finally clinched the direct relevance of anatomy to clinical medicine." By this achievement, Morgagni is a pivotal figure, a bridge to modern medicine. His words, as an old man, to James Boswell, who visited him in 1765: "I have passed my life amidst books and cadavers."

Giovanni Battista Morgagni was born in the small town of Forli, Italy, on February 25, 1682, the son of Fabrizio and Maria Tornieli Morgagni. Precocious as a child, he wrote poems and essays. In 1698 he began attending the University of Bologna, not far from his home, where he received his degree in philosophy and medicine at the young age of nineteen, in 1701. His most important teacher was Antonio Maria Valsalva, a pupil of Marcello Malpighi, the famous founder of microscopic anatomy who discovered the capillaries. Morgagni remained at the university to work as Valsalva's assistant and became a demonstrator himself.

Morgagni's early years in medicine cast the successful shape of his entire career. While still a student he was admitted to the Accademia degli Inquieti, serving as its head beginning in 1704. The next year Morgagni discussed the material for his *Adversaria anatomica prima (Notes on Anatomy)*, to be published in Bologna in 1706. In this work of descriptive anatomy, Morgagni corrects errors of his predecessors and describes a number of original discoveries. He also included new and better detailed descriptions of the larynx, the male urethra, and the female genitals.

In 1709, after about two years in Venice, where he collected fine books and looked into the anatomy of fishes, Morgagni returned to Forli, his native town, to work as a general practitioner. In this as in everything else, Morgagni was successful. He married Paola Verzeri, and together they would raise a large family of three sons and twelve daughters.

In 1711 Morgagni accepted a professorship of theoretical medicine at the University of Padua. Four years later he took over the chair of anatomy once held by Vesalius and a whole succession of eminent teachers. Morgagni became a popular professor, and his presence drew students from Venice and abroad. Because he enjoyed the cooperation of both secular and religious authorities, Morgagni received as many cadavers as he could use. Individuals of all classes wished themselves to be autopsied by Morgagni. He published additional volumes of *Adversaria anatomica* in 1717 and 1719.

About 1740, Morgagni became interested in a gargantuan but flawed effort by Théophile Bonet, a Swiss-born pathologist, to relate findings at autopsy to discrete diseases. Bonet's encyclopedic work, *Sepulchretum sive anatomia practica,* had been first published in 1679 and was a standard reference. Morgagni found it too disorderly and inaccurate to be of much use. As a consequence, he began to gather material himself. Versed in all aspects of medicine, Morgagni was well-organized, excellent at deductive reasoning, and an elegant writer in Latin. He would gather material over the next two decades.

Morgagni was not only an acclaimed anatomist but also a physiologist and physician who continued to practice throughout his career. In conducting physical examinations, Morgagni did not recoil from the human body. Unlike most of his colleagues at the time, he used his eyes to scrutinize the surface of the body and even its orifices, his hands to palpate, his ears to auscultate. He is even said to have employed percussion.* Morgagni engaged in many medical consultations, often by letter. Although he did not have the concept of underlying disease, he evaluated symptoms and looked for proximate visible signs of illness. Following Enlightenment thinking, Morgagni viewed the body as basically mechanical. When parts break down, the harmony of the whole machine is disturbed and illness or death results.

Not until 1761, when he was seventy-eight years old, did Morgagni publish *De sedibus et causis morborum per anatomen indagatis (On the Seats and Causes of Disease).* It represents a fundamental departure in

---

*Percussion, or tapping the chest and abdomen for diagnostic signs, was systematized near the end of Morgagni's career, with a famous book by the Viennese physician Leopold von Auenbrugger.

medical history. There are records of 640 dissections, and the book is arranged in five parts. Morgagni records case histories supplied by his teacher, Valsalva, and includes more from his own experience and still others from citations found in the medical literature. He discusses diseases of the head, respiratory and heart disorders, sickness in the belly, and surgical conditions; a supplemental section is epistolary. The records include information about symptoms of each disease and a clear history of the case in question, including treatment, course, and findings at autopsy. Four indexes render the book eminently useful for clinicians.

Overall, *De sedibus* is a fascinating series of excursions into the human body. It includes a host of discoveries and descriptions with sufficient clarity for the modern clinician to understand and unravel. Morgagni describes the cancerous stomach and distinguishes the gastric ulcer. He records the changes found in the heart after death from myocardial infarction. He delineates heart-block syndrome (now called Adams-Stokes syndrome), which involves fainting or seizures, and so calls it "epilepsy with a slow pulse." Such essentially correct and congenial descriptions abound. After two centuries, "his work remains alive and complete," writes Roberto Margotta, "so that one can today give exact diagnosis to the cases he describes." Indeed, long after Morgagni's death, twelve volumes of his letters were discovered and published in 1935 as *Consulti medici*.

It is easy to see why Morgagni's work has received extravagant praise, especially from physicians themselves, across two centuries. Rudolf Virchow (p. 8) said that, with Morgagni, "the new medicine begins." He might also be said to represent a continuation of the Renaissance tradition in medicine that begins with Vesalius (p. 41) and includes William Harvey (p. 45) and Marcello Malpighi. At the same time, Morgagni represents a movement toward clinical pathology that would finally become signally important in the nineteenth century. His *De sedibus* would later be extended by the work of Xavier Bichat (p. 58), René Laennec (p. 62), and Virchow himself, among many others.

Renowned as "his anatomical majesty," Morgagni counted among his friends Hermann Boerhaave (p. 136) and his former student Albrecht von Haller. Given the patience with which he compiled *De sedibus*, it is not surprising that he was said to possess a serene disposition. At eighty-two he "yet reads without spectacles and is as alert as a Man of 50," wrote an American visitor in 1764. Indeed, Morgagni lived seven years more. Upon his death on December 5, 1771, an autopsy was performed. It showed a ruptured myocardium, suggesting a heart attack.

# Xavier Bichat [1771–1802]
## Doctrine of Tissues

French surgeon and anatomist Xavier Bichat founded the discipline of histology, the study of tissue, and he is sometimes called the "father of descriptive anatomy." In the course of a fleet career that ended with his death at age thirty-one, Bichat published four major works that created a springboard for the transformation of medicine through physiological investigation. Classification of tissue provided a new elementary unit for understanding disease, and in a sense sounded the death knell for humoral pathology—the idea that disease is due to an imbalance of essential humors. Over the short term Bichat became immensely significant. "His works have become a species of holy scripture," wrote John Cross in 1820, "from which one cannot depart without sacrilege."

Although his direct authority would soon fade as advances in chemistry and the development of cell theory rendered his classification obsolete, Bichat's historical influence abides. The program outlined in *Recherches physiologiques sur la vie et la mort (Physiological Researches on Life and Death)* represented Bichat's belief, writes John Lesch, that "he had fulfilled the long-standing eighteenth-century ambition to do for physiology and medicine what Newton had done for physics." Indeed, together with Philippe Pinel (p. 148) and several others working in the Parisian hospitals, Bichat was a primary figure among those responsible for a series of radical advances toward a scientific medicine at the turn of the nineteenth century.

Marie-François-Xavier Bichat was born on November 14, 1771, at Thoirette-en-Bas, a village in Bresse (later the department of Jura) in eastern France. He was the son of Jean-Baptiste Bichat, a physician who had trained at Montpellier, and his wife and cousin, Jeanne-Rose Bichat. In his early schooling Marie-François studied the humanities and took courses in rhetoric, but he became interested in medicine and began studies in anatomy at Lyons in 1791. During the Revolution, Bichat gained practical experience as a surgeon with the Army of the Alps. In July 1794, the same month the Reign of Terror collapsed, Bichat moved to Paris to complete his training.

At the Grand Hospice de l'Humanité (as the Hôtel-Dieu was known during the Revolution), Bichat came under the formidable influence of

Pierre Desault, a renowned surgeon and professor. Desault's teaching methods brought his students close to patients both dead and alive. Bichat's talent was noted, and he soon became not only Desault's most valued pupil but a lodger in his home. After Desault's sudden death in 1795, Bichat apparently suffered a nervous breakdown. But when he returned to the Hôtel-Dieu, it was with the ambitious aim of organizing his teacher's wealth of observations and insights and providing them with a new theoretical foundation. Desault had been a surgeon, but Bichat would adapt his methods and his approach to physiology.

Indeed, where Desault's major focus had been on patients and clinical medicine, Bichat's main interest lay in the theoretical yield of anatomical observation. In 1796, he and several other colleagues formally founded the Société d'Émulation de Paris, which provided an intellectual forum for debating problems in medicine. At the same time, Bichat performed a great number of autopsies, opening as many as 600 corpses in a year. In spite of his extensive work and growing reputation, Bichat initially had no official title within the French hospital system. He held the unofficial post of *chirurgien-externe*, and gave private courses in anatomy. But in spite of his association with Desault, not until 1801 was Bichat appointed physician to the Hôtel-Dieu.

In 1798 Bichat began to publish articles concerning the potential classification of various tissues apart from the organs they formed. A book, *Traité des membranes (Treatise on Membranes)*, was published in 1799, and two years later he produced *Anatomie générale appliquée à la physiologie et à la médecine (General Anatomy Applied to Physiology and Medicine)*.

Taken together, these works express a major simplification. Although subsequent research would revise most of the essentials, it is easy to see why Bichat had such an impact at the turn of the nineteenth century. The organs, wrote Bichat, "are themselves composed of several tissues of very different nature, which truly form the elements of these organs. Chemistry possesses its simple bodies, which, by various combinations, form compound bodies . . . likewise anatomy has its simple tissues, which by combining . . . compose the organs." Bichat's allusion to chemistry—he is writing within a decade of the death of Antoine Lavoisier—is a stamp of his modernity. It is not a surprise to learn that his admirers included Auguste Comte, or that the German philosopher Schopenhauer called himself a disciple of Bichat.

To see the power of Bichat's histological approach, one need only consider the heart. Bichat correctly distinguished the heart's muscle tissue (the myocardium) from the membranous tissue enclosing it (the pericardium), and from the tissue lining the chambers (the endocardium). Each of these three tissues can be attacked by disease, leading to three different conditions. Instead of "inflammation of the heart," Bichat made it possible to distinguish pericarditis, myocarditis, and endocarditis.

Bichat's predominant role in the development of histology needs to be qualified in several ways. In classifying twenty-one kinds of tissue, Bichat relied on external appearance as well as on determining how each type reacted with chemicals and other means of "de-composing." He soaked tissue, baked it, boiled it, dried it out, and observed how it rotted. He examined how it reacted to acids and alkalis. Bichat did not make significant use of the microscope, however, which would not be improved until the 1830s. Both that technical innovation and the cell theory that arose soon after would be crucial developments. When medical students study histology today, it is in effect the study of tissue via microscopic anatomy—further refined through the use of the electron microscope and all the methods of chemistry and molecular biology. As a consequence, credit for founding histology must include not only Bichat but Marcello Malpighi, Rudolf Virchow (p. 8), and Jacob Henle (p. 84), among others.

Publication of *Recherches physiologiques sur la vie et la mort* in 1800 represented Bichat's even larger aim of refashioning physiology. Bichat proceeded in two ways. He took over and extended the classificatory enterprise that had developed in medicine during the eighteenth century. Also, using his experience in surgery and at autopsy, he applied experimental procedures to understand function. Moving from taxonomy to grasp of function in science is fairly common, but rarely does one individual achieve both. This was the case with Bichat, as reflected in his *Recherches physiologiques*. According to John Lesch, in his lucid *Science and Medicine in France,* one consequence is that, although Bichat's system of tissue classification is today useless, it remains "a starting point and exemplar for the scientific physiology" that would transform medical thinking in the nineteenth century.

Bichat was, much like Albrecht von Haller in the eighteenth century, a vitalist who believed that animals must obey a separate set of laws from both plants and inorganic matter. Although vitalism often had religious undertones, for Bichat it was a powerful classificatory device, shaped more by his experimental agenda than by any concern for maintaining a distinctive place for humans in the cosmic hierarchy. Although vitalism would prove unsustainable, Bichat's arguments in its favor remained bastions for its proponents for decades to come.

Modest in demeanor and rather shy, Xavier Bichat lived an immensely active life, but it was not destined to last long. He is said to have sometimes slept by night in the morgue where, by day, he dissected cadavers. On July 22, 1801, write his recent biographers in an excess of adulation, death avenged itself upon "this audacious young man, who had undertaken to rob it of its terrible secrets and put them at the service of life." Bichat's autopsy, as it would be interpreted today, shows that he died of acute meningitis brought about by tuberculosis. A revered figure in France, he was not dead ten days before Napoleon ordered a bust sculpted in his memory.

# René Laennec [1781–1826]

## The Physician's New Gaze

The stethoscope is closely linked to the revolution in medicine dating to the first quarter of the nineteenth century in France. The instrument's inventor, René Laennec, employed it to develop a taxonomy of sounds correlated with findings at autopsy, the better to diagnose diseases of the heart and lungs. Though its usefulness is reduced today relative to new technologies, there is little question as to its historic significance. With the stethoscope, medicine became ever more occupied with finding aural or visual signs of pathology that linked symptoms to specific types of lesions. Many later instruments, from the various endoscopes to X rays to magnetic resonance imaging (MRI), are effectively the progeny of Laennec's invention.

René Théophile Hyacinthe Laennec was born in the old walled port town of Quimper, in Brittany, France, on February 17, 1781. He was the first-born son of Michelle-Gabrielle Félicité Guedson, a frail woman who died when René was five years old. René's father was Théophile-Marie Laennec, a lieutenant in the admiralty and a civil servant. He was of a capricious nature and had no talent for raising children. After his mother's death, René and his brother were therefore sent to live in Nantes with his paternal uncle Guillaume, a successful doctor and university scholar. He became a second father to René, and clearly was the one who inclined him to become a physician. Guillaume once told René that a calling for medicine "is like a set of chains that one must carry at all hours of the night."

Laennec's childhood coincided with the French Revolution and subsequent civil wars. But during the Reign of Terror, even while the guillotine worked in Nantes, René attended classes in rhetoric and achieved excellent marks. He considered pursuing a career in engineering and had numerous interests, including botany and music, but he decided on medicine. During the revolutionary wars, Laennec received a commission as a surgeon as early as 1795, with his uncle's help, and gained experience treating wounds. In 1799 he renewed this commission and participated in an early Napoleonic campaign after the Eighteenth Brumaire. He returned to medical studies in 1800, to which end he moved to Paris in 1801. Laennec was brilliant and ambitious, and set himself the highest goals.

Laennec took full advantage of the unprecedented atmosphere of progress in the Parisian hospital system at the turn of the nineteenth century. He studied at Charité and the Collège de France, and he collaborated with Gaspard Laurent Bayle, a charismatic and influential anatomist. But Laennec's most significant teacher was Jean Nicolas Corvisart. To become Bonaparte's personal physician, Corvisart, a key figure in Parisian medicine, had rescued from oblivion the work of Leopold von Auenbrugger, the Viennese physician. In 1760 Auenbrugger had systematized the practice of diagnosis by percussion, or tapping patients' chests. Laennec learned about percussion directly from Corvisart, who studied the practice and improved it, so it may be seen as a direct precursor to the stethoscope. It is interesting to note that, on a personal basis, Laennec did not particularly like Corvisart. "His character pleases me so little," he wrote, "that I have scarcely sought to know him better."

While still a student, Laennec joined the cohort of Parisian doctors who were attempting to link clinical history and symptoms with findings at autopsy. He wrote articles on a variety of topics, becoming an expert on parasitology, and he is credited with a number of discoveries in pathological anatomy. By the time he received his diploma in 1804, Laennec already had a reputation as an important—and, to some extent, arrogant—young researcher. At the same time, he always respected the important historical figures in ancient medicine, and his doctoral thesis concerned the usefulness of Hippocratic thinking about contemporary problems. He edited the *Journal de médecine* until 1808 and was exceptionally active in the Société de l'École from about 1804 to 1811.

By about 1810, writes his recent biographer, Jacalyn Duffin, "Laennec had established himself as an expert in the new science of pathological anatomy, conscious of both its potential and its limitations." He was the first to describe the symptoms of the deadly abdominal inflammation that he named peritonitis. A fine example of his work is found in his research on the liver, the favored organ of French medicine. He coined the term cirrhosis, derived from the Greek *kirrhos*. The postmodernist author Michel Foucault, in his famous *The Birth of the Clinic,* was impressed by the "extraordinary beauty" of Laennec's description of the "first cirrhotic liver in the history of medical perception." Indeed, from Laennec's careful gaze and examination came nuanced prose to describe the distressed organ, "reduced to a third of its volume . . . hidden in the region that it occupies, its external surface, slightly mammilated and emptied . . . yellowish-gray in color." Much of Laennec's work, it should be evident, was primarily descriptive; neither a functional physiology nor an improved therapeutics was within his reach.

Although it was not his ambition, Laennec became a successful Parisian physician. His private practice became the main source of his income after 1808. He bought a carriage, hired a cook, and attended daily to a full waiting room of patients. In the aftermath of the Revolution, his hospital career was slower to start. He did not receive an important appointment until 1816, when he was made chief of the medical service at Hôpital Necker. By then he was especially interested in problems associated with tuberculosis, which he recognized as a complex and multifaceted disease. Among those patients he saw in consultation was Madame de Châteaubriand, wife of the famous writer and statesman. Whereas another physician had pronounced her close to death from tuberculosis, Laennec saw a case of bronchitis. He was right, and she lived until 1847.

Laennec's invention of the stethoscope in 1816 is one of medicine's famous discoveries made through happenstance. Laennec had been consulted by a young woman with heart disease. Percussing the chest yielded no information because of the patient's "great degree of fatness." Laennec's sense of delicacy made it impossible for him to put an ear directly to the chest, as he might have done with an older patient. One can imagine his frustration. Then, recalling how boys at play might listen to the scratching of a pin transmitted along a stick of wood, a basic principle of acoustics occurred to him. Laennec wrote, "I rolled a quire of paper into a sort of cylinder and applied one end of it to the region of the heart and the other to my ear." With the improved sound, Laennec immediately recognized that he had found a new way of listening to the sounds emanating from within the chest. The technical term would be *mediate auscultation*.

Experimenting with shapes and materials, Laennec graduated from paper and tried various kinds of wood. He found that chest sounds were best detected by "a cylinder which is perforated throughout, and excavated into somewhat of a funnel shape, at one of its extremities, to the depth of an inch and a half." He himself turned his first stethoscopes, as he eventually called them, on a lathe. He presented his work to the Academy of Sciences in 1818, and *De l'auscultation médiate (On Mediate Auscultation)* was published the next year. When one bought the book, a Laennec stethoscope was provided for a few extra francs.

Physicians using the stethoscope could follow Laennec's descriptions and learn to distinguish, among other sounds: rales, bruits, fremitus, egophony, pectoriloquy, and bronchophony. These indicated various diseases, most connected with breathing: pleurisy, emphysema, pulmonary infarction. In general, Laennec had a better grasp of lung sounds than heart sounds. The heartbeat and sounds associated with cardiac disease were more difficult to classify, largely because the complex physiology of the heart remained poorly understood. But Laennec's contribution to the diagnosis of pulmonary tuberculosis using the stethoscope was significant. Although the cause of tuberculosis would not be discerned for the best part of a century to come, nor would it be curable for fifty years after that, Laennec's stethoscope represented a considerable advance for diagnostics.

The "great and wonderful discovery" that "will mark an era in the history of medical art" won acclaim from the moment it was introduced. Stethoscopes of various kinds became widely available in the medical shops of Paris within a few years. Laennec's book was translated into English by 1821, and his ideas were spread far and wide by his students. Originally a cylinder, the stethoscope underwent a number of improvements and innovations. By midcentury George P. Camman introduced a "self-adjustable double stethoscope" with the same shape as stethoscopes used today.

Although it would become popular and ultimately indispensable, the stethoscope played an important role in shifting the "medical gaze" from the stories patients told about themselves to the objective physical signs of illness. This was no small affair, and the stethoscope, to judge from contemporary prose and parody, caused some psychological discomfort. Rudyard Kipling portrayed Laennec as a witch. The skeptical physician Oliver Wendell Holmes wrote "Stethoscope Song," in which a "young man of Boston town" purchases one of the fashionable instruments, and so—

> It happened a spider within did crawl,
> And spins him a web of ample size,
> Wherein there chanced one day to fall
> A couple of very imprudent flies.

For others, however, the stethoscope clearly embodied progress. George Eliot found it emblematic of science in medicine. "I believe that you are suffering from what is called fatty degeneration of the heart," Mr. Lydgate informs Mr. Casaubon in *Middlemarch*. A disease, he adds, "first divined and explored by Laennec, the man who gave us the stethoscope...." As an example of resistance to technology, some physicians rejected the stethoscope altogether into the twentieth century, preferring to apply an ear directly to the chest.

Like the Austrian Auenbrugger, who had tapped beer barrels as a child and chests as a physician, Laennec was a musician who excelled on the flute. He also was athletic, enjoyed hunting, and was enamored of the Breton language. But his health was not excellent, and by 1819 Laennec had developed tuberculosis. Fatigued, for two years he retired to his country manor at Kerlouarnec and took up the life of a gentleman farmer. Feeling better, he returned to Paris in 1821 as professor at the Collège de France, a doctor at the Charité, and personal physician to the Duchess of Berry. A conservative Royalist in post-Napoleonic France, Laennec accumulated honors and fame. He was elected to the Academy of Medicine in 1823 and the next year was joined to the Légion d'honneur.

In his personal life, Laennec was pious and taken with a melancholic idea of his own fate. After a brief romance as a young man, he lived as a bachelor for many years. But in 1824 he married Jacquemine Guichard Argou, a distant cousin and a Bretonne, who had become his housekeeper. It was a marriage of affection, not convenience, as it is sometimes portrayed, but their time together was short. Laennec fell ill again. He left Paris and busied himself with an extensive revision of *De l'auscultation médiate*. "In returning [to Kerlouarnec] last year in order to finish my book, I knew that I was risking my life," he wrote. "But the book that I am going to publish will be useful enough, sooner or later, I hope, to be worth more than one man's life, and, as a consequence, my duty was to finish it, whatever might happen to me." René Laennec died on August 15, 1826.

After his death Laennec was long subject to — in some ways the victim of — overstatement and adulation. He was compared to Isaac Newton and Galileo, and his fame, narrowly connected in popular accounts to his simple invention, distorted and obscured his real accomplishments. Hagiographic biographies, inadequate and old-fashioned, were long the only ones available. This was remedied recently by Jacalyn Duffin's exceptional work in English, *To See with a Better Eye*. From this book Laennec may be viewed as less a holy relic than "a vigorous if challenging specimen" whose work promoted a transformational shift in the way doctors view patients and understand illness.

# Johannes Müller [1801–1858]

## The Rise of German Medicine

When scientific materialism and laboratory medicine took hold in German universities in the mid-nineteenth century, one of the chief instigators and most influential teachers was Johannes Müller. From his laboratory for over two decades beginning about 1820, there issued a cornucopia of new knowledge about how the human body works. Müller worked in comparative anatomy, neurophysiology, and pathology, and those who studied under him included Carl Ludwig (p. 80), Jacob Henle (p. 84), the great physicist and physiologist Hermann von Helmholtz, and Rudolf Virchow (p. 8). His reputation brought medical students on pilgrimages to Germany, according to one extravagant account, "with full hearts, in a glowing fervor, like pilgrims to a shrine."

Müller's *Handbook of Human Physiology* was a modern textbook, perhaps the premier such comprehensive fund of durable knowledge, and his published works are estimated to run some 15,000 pages. When he died in 1858, Müller won praise from former students that would have borne him to paradise in a first-class coach. "So magnetic was his personality, a glance from his splendid eyes made such a lasting impression," wrote medical historian Victor Robinson, "that in an earlier century Müller could easily have become the founder of a religion.... Emerson wrote an essay on Character, but Johannes Müller lived it." Virchow asked: "How can a single tongue adequately praise a man who presided over the whole domain of the science of natural life?..." Such untamed eulogies seem overblown and even amusing today, but they represent Müller's due stature as his students perceived it.

Eldest of five children, Johannes Müller was born on July 14, 1801, in Koblenz, a city near Cologne. His father, Matthias Müller, from a family of winemakers, was a shoemaker who achieved a level of prosperity that enabled him to hope for his son's education. Johannes was intelligent and competitive, but also a sensitive child, close to his mother. He collected butterflies and disliked spiders. For a time he considered entering the priesthood, but he decided, in 1819, to study medicine. At Bonn University, where he excelled, Müller's education was strongly influenced by the reign of *Naturphilosophie*—the romantic philosophy of Friedrich

Schelling, embraced by Goethe and Schiller. At the Faculty of Medicine, some of Müller's professors believed in supernatural remedies; and, for a time, so did he.

After receiving his medical degree in 1822, Müller committed himself to studies in anatomy and physiology. He spent a year and a half at the University of Berlin, studying with Carl Rudolphi, one of the greatest German anatomists. Rudolphi was an enemy of mysticism, and Müller, who also read the Swedish chemist Jöns Jacob Berzelius during this period, now embraced the growing scientific mainstream. His *Über die phantastischen Gesichtserscheinungen,* from 1826, is an intriguing transitional work in which Müller investigates the way the eye reacts to internal stimuli, such as the imagination. In 1824 Müller had qualified to teach, and he made rapid progress at the University of Bonn. By 1830 he was a full professor.

Müller's research in microscopic and embryonic anatomy cannot be briefly summarized, but was both detailed and broadly significant. For example, he demonstrated that enfolded membranes represent the basic common structure of the various glands, and his discovery of the embryonic duct that bears his name clarified the embryogenesis of sex determination. (In females, Müller's duct develops into the fallopian tubes, uterus, and vagina; in males it atrophies.) Müller also unraveled the fine structure of Bowman's capsule—important for understanding how the kidneys work—and he made many other similar investigations. His studies in glandular physiology were published as a book in 1830. *De glandularum secernentium structura penitiori earumque prima formatione in homine atque animalibus,* translated as *The Intimate Structure of Secreting Glands,* advanced embryology and histology, and laid some of the physiological groundwork for endocrinology.

In neurophysiology, Müller laid a basis for understanding the nerves as part of a unitary system. He proposed the "law of specific nervous energies," which states that nerves have discrete qualities—that visual nerves, for example, do not transmit pain. To Müller is also owed an early modern formulation of the concept of reflex action: the basic idea that coughs, sneezes, and hiccups belong to the same class of phenomena.

Müller also proved the Bell-Magendie Law, which represents an axiomatic idea in neurology: The ventral (or anterior) nerve roots issuing from the spinal column control motor function, while the dorsal (or posterior) nerve roots transmit sensation. In a famous experiment that untold numbers of medical students have performed since, Müller cut the anterior roots of the nerves that lead to the hind leg of a frog. The limb was paralyzed but still reacted to irritation. By contrast, when he cut the posterior root, the frog could still move its leg, but the leg was insensitive

to stimulation. This experiment, simple and impressive, was a clear experimental demonstration of the sensory/motor division of the spinal roots, which for Charles Bell and François Magendie had been the source of a rancorous priority dispute.

In 1833, when his mentor Rudolphi died, Müller wrote the ministry of education that "With the exception of [Friedrich Theodor] Meckel, no one in Germany can fill this post as well as I." He received the coveted professorship of anatomy, physiology, and pathology at the University of Berlin, and from there would issue his most important discoveries. Müller became the central figure in an educational system that made German medical research the most advanced in the world. In 1834 he began publishing the *Archiv für Anatomie, Physiologie und Wissenschaftliche Medizin*, which became known throughout Europe as *"Müller's Archiv."*

Müller's most influential work, *Handbuch der Physiologie des Menschen (Handbook of Human Physiology)*, was published between 1834 and 1840. It is a summary text of all the advances made in understanding human physiology over the previous half century. "It contains such an unbelievable amount of new and even revolutionary information," wrote one commentator, that even a century later it could be read with profit.

One aspect of the *Handbuch* indicates a retention of Müller's early philosophical views: a long, eighty-page discourse on the soul. Like many nineteenth-century scientists, Müller was a vitalist. He believed that some life-giving principle must inhabit living things. No religious agenda attended Müller's vitalism. He did not know, but wondered, whether the soul was a thing united with the physical body, or if it was a force inherent in all matter. In support of the view that the soul is not simply located somewhere in the brain but is "more widespread in the organism," Müller pointed to such creatures as earthworms, which remain alive when cut in two.

The nature of tumors became another focus of Müller's activity, and his studies were useful, descriptive, and gave him a claim as founder of pathological histology. His research became the basis for a number of diagnostic procedures that physicians would use for decades to come. Virchow, as one of Müller's most celebrated students, would later amplify this research.

After 1840 Müller turned from human physiology to comparative anatomy and zoology. One important reason was that he became uneasy with the practice of vivisection. He tolerated, but came to dislike using higher animals in physiological research, believing too much suffering was involved. Müller's zoological work was concerned mainly with invertebrates and ocean fauna, and classification was his major aim. He made numerous field trips to collect a great variety of creatures—first amphibians and reptiles, and later primitive invertebrates, such as lampreys.

Müller married Nanny Zeiller as a young man, and they had two children. There is some speculation that Müller suffered from bipolar disorder. He endured bouts of depression as a young man in 1827, and again in 1840. The revolution in Germany in 1848 put him for a time at anxious odds with his students, and he was depressed that year as well. In 1857 he grew ill once more and was found wandering the streets of Berlin, filled with anxiety. On April 28, 1858, he was found dead in his bed. The cause of death was never known, because Müller himself had forbidden an autopsy. Some said apoplexy, others arteriosclerosis. But one of his students, the eminent Ernst Haeckel, strongly suspected an overdose of morphine.

# François Magendie [1783–1855]
## "A Science in the Making"

The physiology on which modern medicine is founded dawned in France, in the wake of the Enlightenment and Revolution, at the beginning of the nineteenth century. Its most durably influential figures were not preoccupied with building complex theoretical systems, but based their work on observation, classification, and experiment. We have discussed René Laennec (p. 62), who developed the stethoscope, and Xavier Bichat (p. 58), who simplified the classification of tissue. Another central figure was François Magendie. He made a legion of discoveries, is considered a principal artificer of modern pharmacology, and was a major influence on Claude Bernard (p. 14). "I compare myself to a ragpicker," Magendie once told Bernard, "with my spiked stick in my hand and my basket on my back, I traverse the field of science and I gather what I find." His motto was *La médecine est une science à faire*, "Medicine is a science in the making."

Magendie's fame in his own time was such that Honoré de Balzac cast him as Dr. Maugredie in his novel *La peau de chagrin (The Wild Ass's Skin)*, and the portrait is so concise that it deserves repeating. "He found some value in all theories," wrote Balzac, "adopted none of them, claimed that the best way to proceed in medical matters was to do without theory and stick to the facts." He was "this great explorer, this great scoffer, this champion of desperate expedients." As the fictional Dr. Maugredie examines the magical hide, he remarks (as indeed Magendie might have) that "the shriveling of cutaneous tissue is an inexplicable and yet natural phenomenon which from the beginning of time has caused despair among doctors and pretty women."

François Magendie was born on October 15, 1783, in Bordeaux. His mother was a Parisian, Marie Nicole de Perey Delaunay. His father, Antoine, was a surgeon and an ardent follower of Jean Jacques Rousseau. A firm supporter of the French Revolution, in 1791 Antoine moved his family to Paris, where his wife soon died. At age ten François had not yet attended school or learned how to read and write. This was in keeping with his father's Rousseauian precepts, which were nicely vindicated when François made rapid progress over the next few years. At age fourteen he won a national contest for his essay on the rights of man, a burning issue of the time.

Most of Magendie's training coincided with Napoleon's institutionalization of the Revolution's major reforms, which strongly affected medical education. New emphasis on clinical experience in a hospital setting worked much to Magendie's advantage. As early as 1799, still a teenager, he was apprenticed to an eminent surgeon, Alexis Boyer—who later became Napoleon's personal surgeon—who taught François much about dissection. Two years later he entered the École de Médecine, and in 1803 became an intern at the Hôpital St. Louis.

When he received his medical degree in 1808, Magendie was already giving courses in anatomy and physiology, and he also taught surgery. Within two years he was well placed to become a central figure in French medicine. His skeptical attitude toward theories of physiology inclined him to emphasize experiment. Magendie was clear, in his earliest papers, about his distaste for ideas that had even a whiff of the metaphysical, such as the "vital force." "It would be more advantageous for physiology," he wrote, "to begin only at the moment the phenomena of living bodies become detectable to our senses."

Magendie's experiments with poisons make him a founder of modern pharmacology. Beginning in 1809, he performed experiments designed to elucidate the action of strychnine, from the plant *Strychnos,* used by hunters in Borneo and Java. Experimenting on dogs, Magendie showed how death was caused through asphyxiation. But how was the poison absorbed? A theory popularized by William Hunter and John Hunter (p. 140) held that absorption of nutrients occurred exclusively through the lymphatic system. This was a logical idea, but wrong. Magendie, without suggesting an alternative theory, nonetheless demonstrated the existence of other pathways. He went to great lengths to inject the poison at various sites and then compared its actions. This enabled him to conclude that the blood transported the poison to the spinal column, and that its lethal effect was on the nervous system.

Magendie foresaw that strychnine might have medical uses, as could other alkaloids such as codeine, quinine, brucine, and morphine. While only a small dose of strychnine, for example, was lethal, in even smaller doses it had various nonlethal effects. Magendie's researches in pharmacology were immensely aided by advances in chemistry. In 1821 he published *Formulaire pour la préparation et l'emploi de plusieurs nouveaux médicaments (Formulary for the Preparation and Use of Several New Drugs).* This guide, by emphasizing the value of plant-based drugs, met resistance from some physicians. But it was so useful, and progress was so

rapid, that it was revised no less than eight times over the next fifteen years. Magendie's little volume represents an important entry point of science into medical practice in the nineteenth century.

Magendie's early work gained him respect, but he did not advance through the university system. In 1813 he opened a private practice and organized a course in physiology. Three years later he published the first volume of his *Précis élémentaire de physiologie (An Elementary Compendium of Physiology)*; the second volume appeared in 1817. This work was soon translated into a number of languages, including English and German, and, writes M. D. Grmek, "exerted a very profound influence on physicians and biologists during the first half of the nineteenth century." Magendie was elected to the Royal Academy of Medicine and the Academy of Science in 1821. The same year he founded the *Journal de physiologie expérimentale (Journal of Experimental Physiology)*, the first specialized review of physiology ever to appear, which provided a stage for Magendie's work and, more generally, his overall blueprint for physiology. Finally, in 1831, Magendie was appointed to the Collège de France as professor of anatomy.

Work on the nervous system led Magendie to, among other things, a new appreciation of the significance of the cerebrospinal fluid. At the time, when dissectors hammered open the skull at autopsy, thus breaking the protective membrane, the fluid spilled out. Magendie recognized the importance of more careful procedures and nuanced investigation. In 1842 he published a work, *Recherches physiologiques et cliniques sur le liquide céphalo-rachidien ou cérébrospinal,* that reported his results. Magendie also saw the need for a new nomenclature for neurological diseases, based on careful pathological investigation, and his work helps explain why terms such as "apoplexy," encountered in both medical and literary texts, seem today so perplexing. With the advent of a tissue-based pathology, they became vague and metaphorical.

Clinically, Magendie made several interesting errors. He believed that putrefaction was responsible for transmitting disease, and as a consequence he doubted cholera was contagious, even in the context of the 1832 and 1849 epidemics. For the same reason he also opposed imposing quarantine for yellow fever. This was especially unfortunate in that during the outbreak of 1848 he held a top appointment on the Advisory Committee on Public Hygiene. Most surprising, though, was Magendie's lonely but fierce opposition to ether anesthesia after its efficacy had been demonstrated in 1847.

Other clinical evaluations of Magendie's were acute. He was scornful of bloodletting, for example, which during the 1820s was in vogue in French medicine. In spite of his concern to align medicine with the exact sciences, Magendie's awareness of individual variation served him well, for example, with respect to sexual orgasm in women. He sketched various physical and emotional reactions, and added, "In reference to all these phenomena, there are perhaps no two women who are precisely similar." Magendie published his *Leçons sur les phénomènes physiques de la vie (Lessons on the Physical Phenomena of Life)* in four volumes from 1839 to 1841.

There is room to mention only a few of Magendie's many other studies of structure and function. Discovery in 1827 of the aperture in the brain's ventricular system known as the "foramen of Magendie" came about through his description of nerves of the skull. His investigations of the phenomena of vomiting showed how the stomach's role is essentially passive. His experiments on the absorption of nutrients are sometimes viewed as having pointed the way for others' discoveries, especially those of Frederick Gowland Hopkins, that led to the concept of vitamins.

Magendie's colleagues considered him difficult—too frank and too quick to take offense. Said to be sensitive but idiosyncratic, Magendie was known as a gentle and understanding physician. He was nonetheless pilloried by antivivisectionists for alleged cruelty to animals. In 1830 he married a young widow, Henriette Bastienne de Puisaye, and in this way he became owner of an estate in Sannois, in the old commune of Seine-et-Oise, not far from Versailles. He moved there after leaving the Hôtel-Dieu in 1845, and he eventually allowed Claude Bernard (p. 14) to take over his teaching duties at the Collège de France. In his final years he undertook experiments in horticulture. The year after Balzac published his characterization of the famed doctor in *La peau de chagrin*, Magendie died, on October 7, 1855.

# Pierre Louis [1787–1872]
## The Numerical Method

After French physicians had revolutionized medical diagnosis at the beginning of the nineteenth century, an equally important step was taken about 1825 when Pierre Louis introduced what he called the "numerical method." Insisting that it is "indispensable to count," Louis brought quantification forcefully to bear on medicine. With Louis it became possible "to appreciate the value of symptoms," he wrote, "to know the progress and duration of diseases, to assign their degree of gravity, their relative frequency." Causes of disease would be clarified; so, too, the value of various therapies. Louis's work represented the debut of biostatistics and clinical epidemiology.

Pierre Charles Alexandre Louis was born on April 14, 1787, in Ai on the Marne River, in the province of Champagne. He was the son of a prosperous wine merchant. Growing up during the French Revolution, Louis was initially inspired to study law, but after several years he switched to medicine. He began his studies at Reims but completed them in Paris, receiving his medical degree in 1813.

Louis's early career was unusual and disposed him to "therapeutic skepticism," then common among influential physicians, especially in France. Soon after graduating, having no fixed future, Louis decided to accompany a family friend, the Comte de Saint-Priest, to Russia. At St. Petersburg, Louis secured permission to practice medicine, and then for several years traveled with the count, who was a prominent provincial governor. In 1816 Louis settled in Odessa and developed a successful private practice, earning the honorary title of physician to the Czar. In 1820, however, his inability to effectively treat patients during a diphtheria epidemic strongly affected him. Louis returned to France, intent on further study.

Louis's original statistical work took place in the Paris hospital system. At La Charité, in the wards of a former classmate, Louis initially served without pay. He was a doctor with a mission, intent to learn from experience. For over six years he worked incessantly, night and day. He lived at the hospital in a room in the entresol. It was said that he left the wards only to visit the autopsy room. He took copious notes on cases he saw and on postmortems he examined, and he accumulated great quantities of data.

"He consecrated the whole of his time and talents," wrote a student, "to rigorous, impartial observation." His motto was *Ars medica tota in observationibus*, "The art of medicine is all in observation."

Mathematical analysis was critical to this project. During the 1820s, Pierre Simon de Laplace (1749–1827) was at the height of his influence. Laplace had introduced into science generally the concept of statistical correlation, and Louis effectively appropriated it for medical research. He conceived the idea of breaking observations down into units of data and counting them as a path to new insights.

Beginning in 1823 Louis began publishing studies employing this method on a variety of topics, from perforation of the small intestine to the phenomenon of sudden death. Most significant was his work on tuberculosis. The incidence of this disease was surely rising by the early nineteenth century. When Louis started his tabulations, a great deal of effort had already gone into gaining a better understanding of its symptoms and course. Much credit was due to René Laennec (p. 62), who had developed a unitary idea of tuberculosis and its manifestations in 1804. But symptoms of the disease vary widely in their severity and according to which organs are affected, so that the overall picture remained unclear, as did actual morbidity rates. In this context now appeared, in 1825, Louis's *Recherches anatomico-pathologiques sur la phtisie (Pathological Researches on Phthsis).*[*] His data had been gathered from 123 cases which he had himself seen, and he described lesions and symptoms with meticulous attention to detail. In this volume, too, he enunciated what became known as "Louis's law"—the observation that tuberculosis originates most often in the left lung and may subsequently be found elsewhere in the body. The *Recherches* became a significant contribution to an extensive literature on tuberculosis.

In 1829 Louis published two volumes on what was then called typhoid fever—a most confusing disease, as indicated by his title, which would translate as *Anatomical, Pathological and Therapeutic Researches upon the Disease Known by the Name of Gastroenteritis, Putrid, Adynamic, Ataxic, Typhoid Fever, &c., Compared with the Most Common Acute Diseases.* In brief, Louis scrutinized lesions in some fifty patients who had been diagnosed with typhoid fever and compared them with lesions in other similar illnesses. This represented a considerable achievement in classification, although the "continued fevers" would not be well categorized or better understood for some years to come.

---

[*]"Phthisis" was the older term for the disease. In 1839 a Swiss professor of medicine, Johann L. Schönlein, renamed it "tuberculosis" based on the lesion that seemed to characterize it: "tubercle" means small protuberance or node.

Perhaps Louis's most famous and influential work was his examination of the efficacy of bloodletting. This ancient remedy enjoyed a resurgence in the early nineteenth century, in part because of the limitations of various other therapies. Its new champion was François Broussais, a prominent physician strongly critical of the major currents in Paris medicine. Broussais believed that an underlying, nonspecific inflammation accounted for almost all diseases. As a consequence, he ordered the use of leeches to treat virtually every illness. With the popularity of Broussais's teaching, France came to import, for the year 1827, some 33 million leeches.

Louis focused on the usefulness of bloodletting in pneumonia. He published a paper in 1828 and a book seven years later, *Recherches sur les effets de la saignée dans quelques maladies inflammatoires (Research on the Effects of Bloodletting in Some Inflammatory Diseases)*. These landmark publications in clinical epidemiology were recognized, even at the time, to introduce "a new era in our science," as an American reviewer wrote in 1836. Louis had considered some seventy-seven cases matched by diagnosis, age, and general health. He took careful histories, noting when in the course of the illness (early or late) patients were bled. He compared this data to the outcome—whether the patient got well or died. The results, although not a blanket condemnation, represented an unambiguous withdrawal of enthusiasm for bloodletting. Patients who were bled early in the disease, Louis found, tended to recover, while patients bled later tended to die. No extravagant claims on behalf of bloodletting for pneumonia or its various manifestations could be supported. Louis concluded that various factors "all establish narrow limits to the utility of this mode of treatment." Bloodletting would not disappear as a therapy for some years, but its reputation as a therapeutic staple entered a decline from which it never emerged.*

---

*It is interesting to note that, in France at least, literary lights, including Molière, questioned the usefulness of bloodletting even while physicians prescribed it. René Le Sage satirized the practice in his famous novel *Gil Blas* as early as about 1715. At the end of the eighteenth century, the Marquis de Sade made it a subject of hilarious satire in his great novel *Justine*.

By the time his work on bloodletting appeared, Louis was renowned. In 1832 some of his students created the Society of Medical Observation, with Louis designated as president in perpetuity. This organization met once a week around a horseshoe-shaped table with participants ready to analyze and criticize cases brought before them. The numerical method was the source of a complex debate at the Academy of Sciences in 1837, and opponents would continue to argue its merits for years to come. Louis, meanwhile, became a physician at La Pitié Hospital, and an eminent teacher. From the United States, especially, he drew the cream of university-trained doctors. His American students included Oliver Wendell Holmes, who wrote that Louis was "the object of our reverence, I might say almost idolatry." Another American strongly influenced by Louis was Henry L. Bowditch, who initiated the Clinical Medical Conference at Harvard Medical School in 1857.

Louis is sometimes credited with creating the form for the standard medical history: careful interrogation about the patient's background and general health, followed by an effort to establish a narrative concerning symptoms. Louis viewed symptoms as pointing toward signs of particular abnormalities—as lesions, for example, that bespeak a specific disease. "With Louis," writes Stanley Reiser, "the patient's narrative assumed renewed importance in diagnosis." Because he had rules for examining the patient, "it became a wholly different clinical instrument."

Louis's methodical procedure emerged from and was a necessary adjunct to the numerical method, which required orderly collection of data. His use of such a narrative long remained popular and is still fundamentally valid. It is interesting to note that, in combining narrative and statistical analysis, Louis was integrating contrasting approaches of the physical and social sciences. In 1894, Wilhelm Windelband named these approaches *nomothetic,* meaning an effort to find general laws, and *idiographic,* or the study of particular cases.

Descriptions of Pierre Louis emphasize his sincerity and unostentatious personality. As a lecturer, he was dull. He married late and fathered one son, Armand, who, still a boy, developed tuberculosis in 1853 and died the next year. Louis was heartbroken. His commitment to daily practice as a physician soon ended. He continued, however, to participate in medical meetings and to work as a consultant for two decades more.

One drawback to worshiping great men while they are alive is that the magic fails with a new generation. This was the case with Louis. He was greatly admired in his active career by "academic progeny" who "knew no distinction of race or even colour, but coalesced into a noble band of enthusiasts in the cause of medicine, of science, and of humanity." But Louis's death, on August 22, 1872, passed unremarked by some American medical journals. Even in France he was forgotten, perhaps due to Claude Bernard's dim view of statistical medicine. In 1905 an aging William Osler (p. 181), in Paris for a conference on tuberculosis, led a score of colleagues to Louis's tomb in the cemetery at Montparnasse. There he talked a little about Louis and his accomplishments and placed a wreath of autumn leaves on the mausoleum steps.

# Carl Ludwig [1816–1895]
## An "Integrated Approach" to Physiology

In the historic city of Leipzig, resonant with the warmer aspects of German culture, the Physiological Institute opened its doors in 1869. Conceived on a grand scale, the building itself was shaped like the letter E. Each of its three wings was devoted to a single branch of investigation: physiological chemistry, histology, and the study of physiological problems. The place was congenial both to basic research and learning. Each afternoon at four o'clock the institute's founder and director took to the podium to lecture advanced students from all over Europe and the United States. This was Carl Ludwig—"the great inaugurator and discoverer," wrote Karl E. Rothschuh, "to whom we owe a great number of new physiological facts."

Carl Ludwig is still recalled as one of the intellectual potentates in the development of modern physiology. He lived and worked during the second half of the nineteenth century when, at several flourishing German universities, the systems and functions of the human body were described, measured, and analyzed. Ludwig's "integrated" approach launched microscopic anatomy and animal experiments as interpreted by physical and mechanical laws. A reductionist view of the body emerged. Within the limits of an imperfect but improved science of chemistry, a wealth of new research data helped lay the foundation for twentieth-century medicine. Of Carl Ludwig, William Osler predicted, "When the history of experimental physiology is written his name will stand pre-eminent with those of Magendie and Claude Bernard. . . ."

Carl Friedrich Wilhelm Ludwig was born on December 29, 1816, in Witzenhausen, near the city of Kassel, capital of Westphalia, in what today is part of Germany. His father, Friedrich, had been wounded as a cavalry office during the Napoleonic wars that devastated the region, and he was rewarded with a post as a civil servant in the city of Hanau. There Carl was raised and attended the gymnasium. In 1834, he entered the University of Marburg, where he received a considerable scar on his upper lip in a duel. Having been expelled, probably for political activities, Carl was allowed to return after studying at Erlangen and Bamberg, and he received his degree in medicine from Marburg in 1839. He remained at the university and became prosector under his mentor and friend, Ludwig Fick. In 1842 he received the privilege of teaching medical students, and four years later he was named associate professor of comparative anatomy.

Ludwig was from the beginning of his career in favor of physical and chemical explanations and opposed to vitalism. The romantic school of German *Naturphilosophie,* which espoused this view—that living things obey a different set of laws from inorganic matter—was in decline by the 1840s. Nothing better illustrated opposition to it than Ludwig's doctoral thesis, "Beiträge zur Lehre vom Mechanismus der Harnsecretion"—an investigation of how the kidneys work.

For vitalists, the kidneys served as a prime example. How could these organs draw waste into themselves from the blood and secrete urine? The laws of kidney function could not—so it seemed—be reduced to chemical and physical terms. Ludwig attempted to show otherwise. In the kidneys, blood filters through the tiny structures known as glomeruli. This, he maintained, is the first stage in the precipitation of urine. No vital principle is needed, because a simple hydrostatic model will suffice. Although Ludwig could not entirely account for the composition of urine in this way, the filtration model was a convincing first step. These researches represented the first physiological explanation of liquid diffusion through membranes. A definitive explanation of the entire process of kidney function, as Ludwig himself realized, awaited a better understanding of chemistry and improvements in microscopic anatomy.

By 1847, Ludwig's basic commitment to experimental science was fully articulated. That year he met with three protégés of Johannes Müller (p. 67): German physicist and physician Hermann Helmholtz, Viennese physiologist Ernst Brücke, and Emil du Bois-Reymond, the discoverer of neuroelectricity. Together they issued a manifesto proclaiming that all vital (that is, living) phenomena could be explained through physical and chemical laws. The social context for this militant and influential assertion, it should be noted, was formed by the broader social changes associated with the political uprisings that swept Europe in 1848.

In 1849, after three years as associate professor at Marburg, Ludwig was appointed professor of anatomy and physiology at the University of Zurich. The first volume of his *Lehrbuch der Physiologie des Menschen (Textbook of Human Physiology)* was published in 1852; the second volume appeared four years later. It has been called a "veritable turning point" as well as the "first modern text book of physiology," by virtue of its organization, subjects covered, and overall aim. "The task of a scientific physiology," asserted Ludwig in the book's famous first sentence, "is to determine the functions of the animal body and deduce them as a necessity from its elementary conditions." Ludwig's reductionist view is an early expression of the physiochemical form of explanation that would soon become the hall-mark of medical research.

Ludwig's intent to deduce function from objective data led him (like his friend Helmholtz) to make several inventions. His adaptation of the kymograph, or "Wave-writer," allowed various physiological events such as blood pressure and muscle contractions to be measured. It was clock-driven and consisted of a stylus that recorded the change in a mercury manometer on a rotating, paper-covered drum. Ludwig's description in 1847 of sinus arrhythmia, an irregular heartbeat of no great significance, represents the beginning of cardiac monitoring. The instrument required insertion of a catheter, which made it impractical for clinical medicine, and it remained a laboratory tool.

Cardiovascular dynamics was a major focus of Ludwig's research. The isolated frog heart came into use as a basic model after Ludwig discovered, in 1856, that it could be revived and kept beating by perfusion of the coronary arteries with defibrinated blood. Ludwig's research was extended and refined in many ways, and was used to discover various laws of cardiac function. Among them: the all-or-none law, which states that the heart muscle contracts when stimulated independently of the strength of the stimulus; and the "Treppe" or staircase phenomenon, which describes how the heart beats more forcefully when stimulated.

Ludwig also did research in the related area of respiratory exchange. In 1859, together with Ivan Sechenov, his Russian student, Ludwig developed the mercury blood pump, by which the gases in blood could be separated and measured. This instrument made possible considerable progress in understanding the physiology of respiration and oxygen exchange. Otto Warburg (p. 218), among others, would continue this line of research.

As a teacher, Ludwig accepted his responsibilities with great seriousness. "Destiny has conferred on us professors the favor of helping the responsive heart of youth to find the right path," he wrote to a student. "In the seemingly insignificant vocation of the school master there is enclosed a high, blessed calling. I know no higher."

In 1865, after a decade as professor of anatomy and physiology at the Josephinum Academy in Vienna, Ludwig was called to the University of Leipzig. He planned the construction of and headed the Leipzig Physiological Institute, built with funds provided by King Johann of Saxony as part of a general renovation of the medical facilities. The institute, opened in 1869, soon became the most famous training ground in Europe, a magnet for students of medicine and physiology, who went on to spread Ludwig's methods throughout the industrializing world.

Ludwig's institute embodied a historic shift of emphasis in medical research that favored physiology over anatomy (even microscopic anatomy) and morphology. Physiology, Ludwig wrote, "is nothing other than applied physics." But Ludwig's work also encompassed an awareness of the growing significance of chemistry. "I hope that you are in agreement with me," Ludwig wrote his friend Jacob Henle (p. 84), "that in our field chemistry in the true sense of the word provides the prospects for the most significant advances." In terms of the discoveries that would empower medicine in the twentieth century, this was an excellent prediction.

Although Ludwig was not thought to possess the creative brilliance of Claude Bernard (p. 14), he left behind a more powerful school. A legion of discoveries is owed to work carried out at his institute or by his students. He was a "great inaugurator and discoverer" whose influence may be counted as greater than that of his teacher, Johannes Müller. Ludwig's name is not found so often in modern textbooks, however, in part because he did not systematically add his name to students' papers.

As in the case of Müller—and because of Ludwig's eminence—one can read numerous articles about Ludwig without gaining the least insight into his personality. Nearly a century passed before a full-length biography appeared. George Rosen's description of the man, notes Louis Acierno, is made "in such superlative terms that it is hard to imagine that Ludwig was indeed a human being." Enthusiasm for work, generosity, a sense of humor, and modesty are all supposed to have been his traits. He was not religious. William Henry Welch, one of his most famous pupils, described him as "formal but very kindly." Ludwig's marriage to Christiane Endemann in 1849 produced two children. Weakened by a bout with bronchitis, Ludwig died at age seventy-nine on April 27, 1895.

# Jacob Henle [1809–1885]

## Anatomy, Histology, Physiology, and Pathology

The work of Jacob Henle, like that of Carl Ludwig (p. 80), represents a switch to the express track of modern medical research. Another student of Johannes Müller (p. 67), Henle is responsible for a multitude of discoveries in the mid-nineteenth century. With the benefit of both an improved microscope and the renascence of German science, Jacob Henle helped reinvent the medical image of the body in sickness and in health. He revised and reorganized histology, or the study of tissue, as first set forth by Xavier Bichat (p. 58), described a host of hitherto unknown anatomical structures, and brought new optimism to the study of pathology. His influential textbooks fused science and medicine in the minds of students all over Europe and North America.

Famously, Henle was also author of the first essentially valid hypothesis of contagion. Although too early by a generation when it was proposed, Henle's theory subsequently had an indirect impact on microbiology via Robert Koch (p. 24), one of his students. The significance of Koch's postulates governing the isolation of disease-causing agents is still much discussed today.

Jacob Henle was an eldest child, born on July 19, 1809, in Fürth, near Nuremberg in the German state of Bavaria. His mother, Helena Sophia Diespeck, was the daughter of a rabbi. Wilhelm Henle was an indulgent father, but his business frequently took him away from home. The Henles prospered during Jacob's childhood and, as was not uncommon at the time, they eventually converted from Judaism to Evangelism. For a time Jacob considered studying theology. His early education emphasized the classics and language; he was an excellent artist and had musical ability. The desire to study medicine did not come to him until one day at a musicale when he met Johannes Müller. In 1827 he entered the University of Bonn, where Müller taught, and he received his medical degree in 1832. His dissertation on the embryological development of the eye was the first of a number of works he produced on ocular anatomy.

Coming of age during a politically volatile period had nearly dire consequences for Henle. As a student in 1829, he joined one of the student associations, or *Burschenschaften,* that aimed at the unification of Germany—a

liberal goal considered to be subversive. Henle's brief period of activism came back to haunt him after he received an academic appointment at the University of Berlin in 1833. He was not allowed to lecture—indeed, in 1835 he was arrested. Henle passed a month in jail before intervention by Alexander von Humboldt, the famous naturalist, gained his release. He still had to face trial, and in 1837 was condemned to six years in prison. Illustrious connections won him a pardon, however. When he finally assumed his academic duties at Berlin, Henle's research career commenced in earnest.

Henle's early work in anatomy quickly brought him notice, and he made numerous contributions to Müller's *Archiv.* In general, improvements made in the microscope around 1830 permitted a revision of the histology established by Xavier Bichat a generation earlier. After Bichat had shown it was possible to classify and describe the various tissues, progress was hesitant, as Brian Bracegirdle has written, "with isolated steps forward but much confusion." Cell theory, though still in its infancy, was gradually taking shape, first via botany, notably with the work of Matthias Schleiden and Theodor Schwann. Using the microscope to develop anatomical description, Henle became one of the earliest medical authors to regularly use the term "cell."

In 1837 Henle set the stage for a major departure in histology by describing and defining the epithelial layer of tissue. Epithelium was previously thought to be a lifeless exudate from living tissue. Henle distinguished several types and showed that, "All free surfaces of the body, and all the inner surfaces of its tubes and canals, and all the walls of its cavities, are lined with epithelium." The body was paved, in effect, with stuff alive. Henle provided, writes Henry Harris, "the most systematic and wide-ranging study of epithelia that had so far been made and [it] remained for years the standard work on the subject."

In addition to his anatomical studies, Henle also had a serious interest in pathology. Unlike some of his colleagues, he was optimistic about the prospects of discovering the causes of disease. In 1840 he published *Pathologische Untersuchungen (Pathological Investigations),* which historian George Rosen called "a landmark in the history of bacteriology and clinical diseases." The book's stature derives from its first section, "Of Miasmata and Contagia and of the Miasmatic-Contagious Diseases."

Henle suggests that living, microscopic agents enter the body, multiply, and cause disease. He distinguishes *miasma* as the infective substances that enter the body from the surrounding environment. *Contagia* are transmitted by person-to-person contact. Many diseases are "miasmatic-contagious" and can be transmitted either way. The kind of extreme transformations seen with disease, Henle recognized, would have to be produced by something living. "The material of contagions is not only an organic but a *living* one," wrote Henle, "and is indeed endowed with a life of its own, which is, in relation to the diseased body, a *parasitic organism.*"

Included among the diseases Henle discussed are rabies, smallpox, and tuberculosis. He studied their exudates and made interesting observations but could not offer solid experimental evidence that showed cause and effect. The immediate influence of this work was therefore limited. As Henry Sigerist has pointed out, at a time when German science was emerging from the more speculative *Naturphilosophie,* hard evidence was especially valued and speculation denigrated. However, Henle's views on contagion would help shape the thinking of Robert Koch. In considering how his theory might be confirmed, Henle suggested that this would require that disease-causing "parasites" be isolated, be found in every victim, and be shown to cause the disease in other animals when transmitted. These ideas became the basis of Koch's postulates.

In 1841 Henle published his seminal *Allgemeine Anatomie (General Anatomy).* It represents a considerable advance over Bichat's earlier classification of tissue. Henle, unlike his predecessor, made extensive use of the microscope. He constantly attempted to relate structure to function. His goal, he wrote, was to "understand the processes and symptoms of disease as the law-like reactions of an organic substance endowed with peculiar and inalienable powers against abnormal external influences." According to the great German biologist Walther Flemming, Henle's *Allgemeine Anatomie* "contained the first real, rational tissue theory of the animal body, so comprehensive and many-sided, that it earned the admiration of the entire biological world."

Henle's early work brought him fame and attention, and he held three major academic appointments. In 1840 he moved to Switzerland, taking a professorship of anatomy at the University of Zurich. In 1844, he moved to the University of Heidelberg, and in 1852, to Göttingen, where he would remain for the next thirty-three years.

At Göttingen Henle produced the *Handbuch der Rationellen Pathologie (Handbook of Rational Pathology),* published between 1846 and 1853. The audience for this book was the medical student who fully embraced scientific medicine. Written in an elegant style, the *Handbuch* is filled with instructive epigrams: "A hypothesis which becomes dispossessed by new facts," writes Henle, "dies an honorable death; and if it has already called up for examination those truths by which it was annihilated, it deserves a moment of gratitude." "The physiology of the sick and of the healthy are not different," Henle proclaimed, as principle: "physiology and pathology are one."

Over the years, Henle became a force in German medicine. Between 1866 and 1871 he published the three-volume *Handbuch der systematischen Anatomie des Menschen (Handbook of Systematic Anatomy)*. Frequently translated and republished, this work was of central importance to medicine for decades. Henle was also involved in the publication of an important journal, the *Zeitschrift für rationelle Medizin (Journal of Rational Medicine)*, founded in 1842 and published until 1869. Henle himself contributed a great number of reports and also provided annual reviews of continuing progress in physiology, pathology, histology, and anatomy.

Henle's extensive work on the frontiers of tissue classification ensured that his name would be associated with a host of small structures that medical students still learn in courses on anatomy, histology, and physiology. Most famous perhaps is *Henle's loop,* the hairpin turn in the kidney's filtering units known as nephrons. But there is also *Henle's layer,* found in hair follicles. *Henle's fissure* is a patch of connective tissue in the heart. *Henle's sphincter* is the band of muscle fibers that surrounds the prostatic urethra. *Henle's glands* are tubular in shape and found in the conjunctiva of the eyelids. Not to mention: *Henle's warts* and *Henle's spine.*

Jacob Henle was remembered as a sparkling, sociable intellectual. He was an excellent violinist who hosted musicales and concerts. Politically he remained a liberal all his life, sharing the general outlook of Rudolf Virchow (p. 8). As a young man, he was romantically involved with the daughter of composer Felix Mendelssohn. He eventually fell in love with the beautiful Elise Egloff, the illegitimate daughter of a Swiss bourgeois and a governess, when they met in Zurich. They married in 1846. Elise's lack of social graces, for which her beauty was compensation, was put to rights by Henle's sister. This fix came to naught within two years, however, as Elise died from tuberculosis. (Her fate was widely bruited and inspired a novel and a play.) Henle's more durable second marriage to Marie Richter, daughter of a Prussian army officer, produced four daughters and two sons.

Another of Henle's charms was that his good nature apparently did not succumb to illness. He suffered from neuralgia and from a chronic case of periostitis, a frequently painful inflammation of the vascular membrane covering the bones. At the end of his life he developed cancer of the kidneys and spinal sarcoma. He died on May 13, 1885.

# Florence Nightingale [1820–1910]
## Modern Nursing

Nursing is an ancient occupation, if by it one means taking care of the sick and wounded. Records from ancient India describe attendants who prepared and administered medication, and in ancient Roman households such tasks were frequently assigned to slaves. For centuries in Christian Europe, the sick were cared for in a limited way by members of religious orders. But in the nineteenth century, new and unprecedented needs arose. With growing urban populations, ever more sanguinary warfare, and a more complex medical establishment, nursing begged to be professionalized. The modern era in nursing is usually dated to the work of the British heroine Florence Nightingale.

An intriguing figure in the history of medicine, Florence Nightingale's fame and eccentricities should not overshadow the breadth of her vision and accomplishments. In addition to helping create the image of the professionally trained nurse, Nightingale made important contributions to sanitary reform and military medicine. She is also credited with pioneering the use of statistics. "Much of what now seems basic in modern health care," suggests historian of science I. Bernard Cohen, "can be traced to pitched battles fought by Nightingale in the nineteenth century." Immensely famous in her own day, she was the subject of a celebrated—some say scandalous—sketch by Lytton Strachey in his *Eminent Victorians*. Today she remains a literary figure in her own right, through her extraordinary correspondence.

Florence Nightingale was born on May 12, 1820, the daughter of William Edward and Frances Nightingale. She was named for the city in which she was born, as was her sister, Parthenope. The Nightingales were wealthy, upper class, and progressive. William Nightingale himself supervised the education of his daughters, ensuring that they learned history, philosophy, and ancient Greek and Latin, as well as German and the Romance languages. Florence's education was unusual for a woman of her day and probably exceeded college standards; it surely lent depth to her distinctive personality. Although a young woman of her station was expected to marry, near her seventeenth birthday Florence had a religious experience that influenced the course of her life. She believed God had called her to serve, without yet specifying an assignment. An attractive young woman when

presented at court in 1839, over the next several years she was pursued by several young men, including linguist and political reformer Richard Monckton Milnes. But she determined not to marry. Indeed, Florence said that she considered an ordinary domestic arrangement akin to suicide.

By 1844 Nightingale was aware that she was destined to aid the sick in hospitals. "If I should determine to enter nursing," she asked American reformer Julia Ward Howe, "and to devote my life to that profession, do you think it would be a dreadful thing?" In fact, Nightingale's wishes met violent and lengthy opposition from her family, particularly from her mother and sister. One general objection held it inappropriate for a woman of her social class to become a nurse. Hospitals were dreadful and deadly places; nurses were reputed (often unjustifiably) to be dissolute drunks and former prostitutes, drawn from the most impoverished ranks of society. Charles Dickens caricatured nurses—"Mrs. Sairey Gamp" and "Mrs. Betsy Prig"—in his novel *Martin Chuzzlewit*, published the same year Nightingale decided on her career.

Nightingale's determination would not be curbed, however, and a crucial component of her interest in nursing was reform. She grasped that nursing could be a structured, autonomous profession for women involving a fund of special skills and dedicated to service to the patient. For a long time Nightingale studied the profession through reports on sanitary conditions and public health. She became an expert on contemporary nursing practices, which in some places were already moving beyond the Catholic "sisterhood conception" of nursing. She trained in Paris with the Daughters of Charity for a short time and spent several months at the Deaconess Institute in Germany. Started in 1836 by Theodor Fliedner and his wife, Friedriche, the Deaconess originally helped female prison convicts before it evolved to treat the poor and the sick. Nightingale later called it her "spiritual home."

In 1853, with her family's approval hard won, Nightingale accepted the offer to superintend the Harley Street Nursing Home, an establishment for "Gentlewomen during illness." Here Nightingale proved an effective administrator, and she put into practice ideas she had developed during her apprenticeship. Patients were provided bells to call for help; food was delivered to them in the wards. Religious requirements were abolished and sanitary conditions were improved.

Florence Nightingale's sudden catapult to fame came with the Crimean War in 1854. This significant nineteenth-century conflict arose when Russia's imperialist designs on Turkey were contested by Britain and France. In general, the British side of the war was ineptly managed and was fought during a period when the influence of the press was growing. Reports on the dire lot of the ordinary soldier, published in the *Times* of London, sparked public outrage. Hospital conditions were particularly appalling, and the ensuing scandal threatened the government itself. "Why have we no Sisters of Charity?" demanded a letter to the *Times* after correspondent W. H. Russell described conditions for the soldiers and unfavorably compared the British to the French. At this point, Sidney Herbert, the secretary of war, contacted Nightingale, who was already preparing to offer her services.

Herbert appointed Nightingale superintendent of the female nursing establishment. She sailed with thirty-eight nurses, whom she herself had recruited from various hospitals, on October 21, 1854. Nightingale's friendship with Herbert and his wife thus provided an upper-class conduit for the emergence of modern nursing. Herbert himself was aware of the significance of the enterprise. If it succeeded, he wrote, "a prejudice will have been broken through and a precedent established, which will multiply the good to all time."

Within a fortnight of her arrival in Constantinople, Nightingale confirmed the worst reports of chaos and disarray in the hospitals. The war had generated a huge number of casualties. Hygienic conditions were ghastly, with no regard for clean bedding—and there were, at one point, some four miles of beds. The water supply was polluted. There were only twenty chamber pots to serve all the patients, while one thousand among them suffered from diarrhea.

Initially Nightingale and her nurses met resistance to their presence from physicians and surgeons. Strategically, Nightingale did not at first allow her authority to intrude in the wards. Rather, she took control of the kitchen and directed the food service. This led to her taking charge of cleaning the bathrooms. She subsequently created a laundry service. Finally, with the consent of the doctors, her nurses began entering the wards to bathe, clothe, and comfort the patients.

Nightingale's work was reported by the press in heroic terms. The care that she and her staff took with patients, and her concern for soldiers suffering and dying—in contrast to doctors' apparent complacency—

won the hearts and minds of the British public. Eventually the idea would arise that she was responsible for a remarkable drop in mortality at the hospital. (Nightingale herself was much more circumspect.) When she returned to England in 1856, she was treated as a heroine, toasted, and brought before the queen. Victoria presented Nightingale a brooch with the words "Blessed are the merciful." She was "Santa Filomena" in one of Henry Wadsworth Longfellow's popular and overly sentimental poems:

> *A lady with a lamp I see*
> *Pass through the glimmering gloom,*
> *and flit from room to room.*

Over the next several decades, Nightingale put her authority and eminence to practical use in a variety of ways. Nursing remained the axis of her fame, although not always the focus of her attention. By public subscription she was able to raise enough funds to open a school of nursing at St. Thomas's Hospital in 1860. She designed buildings for the hospital that still stand today, and her book *Notes on Hospitals,* published in 1858, established her as innovative expert in hospital architecture. There emerged from these endeavors what was sometimes called the "Nightingale system" for educating nurses.

Nightingale's most popular book, her *Notes on Nursing,* appeared in 1859, and became a classic that remains in print today. "I use the word nursing for want of a better," wrote Nightingale. In her holistic conception, the nurse did not merely administer medicines and the like, but served as a positive force in treating the patient. Nursing, she wrote, "ought to signify the proper use of fresh air, light, warmth, cleanliness, quiet, and the proper selection and administration of diet—all at the least expense of vital power to the patient."

But Nightingale's influence extended well beyond nursing. She succeeded where earlier reformers had failed in addressing issues of public health policy. Her work also had significant impact on military medicine. In 1858 she published and distributed at her own expense an 800-page report, "Notes on Matters Affecting the Health, Efficiency, and Hospital Administration of the British Army." In this work Nightingale made extensive use of statistical comparison, employing graphical representations which she believed would help gain legislative reform. A member of the International Statistical Congress, Nightingale was particularly indebted to Adolphe Jacques Quételet (1796–1874), whose *Sur l'homme* (*A Treatise on Man*), published in 1835, showed how probability might be applied to social issues.

Nightingale's work in military medicine had further repercussions. She became an important part of the sanitary reform movement then under way in England. She also devoted considerable attention to problems of cleanliness and hospital medicine in India, then part of Britain's colonial empire. Nightingale authored two books, *Notes on the Sanitary State of the Army in India,* published in 1871, and *Life and Death in India,* from 1874. She called attention to poor sanitary conditions and intemperance among soldiers, with adverse consequences for discipline and morale. She had never been to India, however, and the results, writes Colleen Hobbs, represent "an ambiguous combination of her upper-class bias, farsighted belief in the importance of public health, and her complicated, often contradictory attempts to maneuver her highly political projects past resistant government administrators."

Nightingale's own health is a striking and much debated aspect of her later life. After returning from the Crimean War, Nightingale became, for want of a better description, a bedridden invalid. Her vaguely defined symptoms may have been psychosomatic, but a more recent retrospective diagnosis has her suffering from brucellosis, an infectious disease that can result in chronic ill health. Recently, Hugh Small has suggested that the British government's unwillingness to acknowledge its role in unnecessary deaths among soldiers caused Nightingale's breakdown. In any event, she subsequently exercised her influence by writing notes and letters—from her bedroom. She distanced herself from friends and family, and visited the Nightingale School only in 1862, long after it opened.

From the 1870s, Nightingale felt herself grown old. She gradually withdrew from the political arena and did not keep up with the progress of nursing. Although she eventually advocated sterilization techniques and asepsis, she believed too much emphasis was placed on the causes of disease; more important was its management. In other respects Nightingale eventually became an old-fashioned figure. There had always been a spiritual element to her thought, and when in 1873 *Fraser's Magazine* published extracts from her quasi-religious tract *Suggestions for Thought,* Thomas Carlyle compared her to "a lost lamb bleating in the mountain."

Complex, intelligent, and temperamental, Nightingale was a passionate woman capable of self-torment and of tormenting others. Her correspondence resonates with a gift for language, and the collection of her manuscripts is one of the largest in the British Library. Reading her letters, one can easily see why Nightingale became so influential. By turns solicitous and manipulative, she used the epistolary form to its fullest. Her letters—a recent collection is entitled *Ever Yours, Florence Nightingale*— are filled with subtleties, with sometimes scathing wit, and with beautiful phrasings. "I am an egg full of meat," she wrote Sir Douglas Galton in 1889, "and you might have come and cracked me if you had made an appointment."

In her last decade, retired entirely from public view, Nightingale became blind and senile. She died on August 13, 1910, copiously mourned the world over. In a tribute, the Indian nationalist Mohandas Gandhi wrote that upon her passing, "Thousands of soldiers wept bitterly like little children, as though they had lost their own mother." She did not want to be buried in Westminster Abbey; instead she lies with her family in East Wellow, Hampshire.

# Joseph Lister [1827–1912]

## Antisepsis and Modern Surgery

Joseph Lister's development of antiseptic procedures in surgery is a landmark accomplishment in the history of medicine. He was not the first to recommend such techniques, but he was arguably the first to understand why they might work. For, in 1865, after reading about research by Louis Pasteur (p. 18) that indicated the presence of invisible living organisms in the air, Lister recognized how wound infection might be avoided by the use of a germicidal dressing. Initially doubted and hotly debated, Lister's methods were accepted by the surgical establishment only with difficulty and over the course of two decades. But asepsis—the absence of germs—proved to be the linchpin of safe surgery, and so led to a cascade of new procedures around the turn of the twentieth century. Today, Lister's contributions remain a prime example of the power and authority of a practical discovery in medicine derived from basic research.

Joseph Lister was born to a prosperous family on April 5, 1827, at Upton, Essex, England. He was one of seven children, all of whom lived to adulthood. His father, Joseph Jackson Lister, was a wine merchant, a Quaker leader, and an amateur scientist who discovered the principle by which opticians could grind an achromatic lens—one that would transmit light without breaking it up into its component colors. Iridescent blurring of microscopic objects, or chromatic aberration, had been a troublesome problem with the compound microscope for two centuries, and the elder Lister's achromatic lens opened the way to the modern microscope.

As a child strongly influenced by his father, Joseph interested himself in the world of the microscopic, and (like Louis Pasteur) he was an excellent draftsman who might have made a fine artist. At London University, which he began to attend in 1843 at age sixteen, Lister initially entered the arts faculty, graduating with a bachelor of arts degree in 1847. But he had already decided to study medicine, and while still an undergraduate he witnessed the first demonstration in England of anesthesia. Lister heard surgeon Robert Liston tell his audience on December 21, 1846, after amputating the leg of an etherized patient, "This Yankee dodge, gentlemen, beats mesmerism hollow." Lister received his degrees in medicine and surgery in 1852.

Lister's talents in research were recognized from the beginning of his career. He initially practiced at Edinburgh University with James Syme, a highly respected professor of surgery whose resident house surgeon Lister became in 1854. In 1856 he married Syme's daughter, Agnes, which led him to convert from Quakerism to Anglicism. During the course of the couple's extended wedding journey, Lister visited the major medical centers in Europe. Returning to Edinburgh, he took up duties as assistant surgeon at the Royal Infirmary, where he also began teaching.

With a background in microscopy as well as in surgery, Lister was well prepared to study the interrelated problems of inflammation, gangrene, and wound healing. In 1858 he published several important papers, including "On the Early Stages of Inflammation," in which he recounted his observations of the tissue of a frog's web when it was irritated with various substances. How the capillaries became engorged with blood during inflammation was not well understood, and Lister's experiments presented some intriguing data—for example, that arteries in a frog without a brain or spinal cord do not dilate. His ultimate theory, however, that inflammation was of two kinds, nervous and local, was not correct, although he believed this to the end of his life. In general, Lister's work on inflammation was impeded by medicine's limited grasp of disease processes and biochemistry. But it was well done, and Lister became highly regarded. He was appointed professor of surgery at the University of Glasgow in 1859, and a year later, at the young age of thirty-three, he was named a fellow in the Royal College of Surgeons.

Lister's interest in wound healing and infection only became more acute when, in 1861, he began directing the surgical ward of Glasgow's Royal Infirmary. Even with the introduction of anesthetics in the 1840s, surgery remained a procedure of last resort. Death rates of up to 50 percent for some operations were not uncommon, and a trip to the hospital for the simplest procedure could well be a death knell. Why wound infections killed people was unclear, but, following from the views of the great and influential German chemist Justus von Liebig, putrefaction in surgical infections was thought to be due to some sort of combustion. This was a logical idea—digestion, after all, is chemical combustion—and one consequence was that surgeons of Lister's generation attempted to protect wounds from oxygen. Various dressings, wet and dry, were applied to wounds, or plasters were used to cover them up. But the concept was mistaken, and none of these measures prevented the dreaded, often deadly infection known as "hospitalism."

At Glasgow's Infirmary, Lister employed techniques conducive to cleanliness, such as those advocated by Florence Nightingale (p. 88). He belonged to what was known as the "cleanliness and cold water school," in which doctors and nurses were to keep things clean and wash their hands. Initially this brought him no significant success. However, in 1865 Lister read the groundbreaking papers recently published by Louis Pasteur concerning fermentation and putrefaction. Pasteur contested Liebig's theory and suggested that the agents of fermentation in wine and milk, for example, were submicroscopic organisms. Lactic fermentation was a kind of putrefaction caused by germs from the surrounding air; alcoholic fermentation was the same process caused by germs that are anaerobic—that is, they live without oxygen. Lister connected Pasteur's concepts with surgical wounds: "[I]t occurred to me that decomposition in the injured part," he later wrote, "might be avoided without excluding the air, by applying in a dressing some material capable of destroying the life of the floating particles." This was the concept of antisepsis.

Lister was not the first to suggest that germs caused hospital disease or that antiseptic measures were the solution. In 1861 Ignaz Philipp Semmelweis (p. 165), a Hungarian obstetrician, had published *The Etiology, Concept and Prophylaxis of Childbed Fever,* but he was ignored and his contribution would earn only retrospective credit. In addition, others had read Pasteur's papers, and Thomas Spencer Wells had given an address in 1864 in which he suggested—but made no experiment—that infection might be due to microorganisms. Lister's great contribution was, therefore, a marriage of theory with practice, and of both with rhetoric. He recognized that from Pasteur's work might be extrapolated an explanation of infection, and he saw how antiseptic measures could be implemented. He was a respected figure, and his views commanded attention.

In 1865, Lister began a program of antisepsis using carbolic acid—which had been used with impressive results in treating sewage—to dress compound fractures, which involve rupture of the skin. Significantly, he persisted after two initial failures, and waited for months before another similar case was brought to the hospital. This time, with an eleven-year-old boy named James Greenlees, Lister had an excellent result when his young patient was discharged with two working legs. Using the same methods, in which carbolic-acid-soaked lint was applied to the wound, he eventually succeeded with nine of eleven cases. In August 1867 Lister could describe his surgical division of the Glasgow Royal Infirmary—hitherto a notoriously fatal place—as having had no deaths whatever from blood poisoning over the previous nine months. *Lancet* published Lister's "On a New Method of Treating Compound Fracture, Abscess, etc., with Observations on the Conditions of Suppuration" beginning on March 16, 1866.

Although Lister's papers excited much publicity in British newspapers and magazines, acceptance of his dramatic results was not immediate. Surgeons were not always susceptible to scientific arguments, and were often hostile to the notion that they would need to adjust their procedures to defeat invisible organisms. In addition, Lister's techniques, still undergoing refinement, allowed considerable room for argument. In one particularly uncharitable attack, Sir James Young Simpson, the famous obstetrician who discovered chloroform, claimed that Lister had merely brought European procedures to bear on problems of healing wounds. Indeed, he bitterly accused Lister of having in effect plagiarized the work of Jules Lemaire, a French chemist who had described the medical worth of carbolic acid in a book published in 1863. Even after Lister repeated the experiments of Pasteur for his medical colleagues, many remained skeptical, attributing lower mortality statistics to other causes, such as improved diet and better nursing.

In 1869 Lister was made professor of clinical surgery at the University of Edinburgh. There over the next eight years he continued to test and improve antiseptic methods. For the ideal bandage, Lister eventually settled on muslin gauze, which remained popular for decades. He also developed such innovations as rubber drainage tubes for wounds and sterile catgut ligatures. Not all his ideas proved successful. About 1870 he introduced what became known as the Lister Spray, in which the surgeon infused the surrounding air with carbolic acid mist. Unpopular and ineffective, the method was abandoned in 1887. Lister was distinctly able to give up methods when he recognized their failure, and he once said that "next to the promulgation of new truth, the best thing, I conceive, that a man can do, is the recantation of a published error."

Antiseptic ideas continued to be controversial in England through the 1870s. When Lister resettled in London, at age fifty, resistance and doubts among British anti-antiseptic surgeons were still not ready to fade. However, a growing body of evidence supported antisepsis. Neither could Lister's growing acceptance in Europe be easily ignored. The eminent German surgeon Theodor Billroth (p. 169) capitulated in 1878, as did a host of other highly regarded foreign surgeons. The next year Lister was treated to a tumultuous ovation at the Sixth International Medical Congress. "History will infallibly say, even if the details of Mr. Lister's methods are superseded," wrote the editors of the *British Medical Journal* in 1879, "that the man who has done the most to take the 'disgrace' out of surgery is Mr. Lister." This was one among many tributes that foreshadowed Lister's victory over his critics.

In general, the principles of antisepsis were expanded in the last two decades of the nineteenth century, both with Lister's help and, more integrally, with widespread acceptance of the germ theory of disease. "Aseptic" methods, in which the absence of germs became the goal, replaced Lister's antiseptic methods, and heat eventually replaced chemicals. Lister himself had paid no attention to the surgeon's dress—he simply spread a clean towel across his abdomen—but bacteriology suggested the use of sterile gowns, masks, and instruments. Both Pasteur and Robert Koch (p. 24) suggested as much, and during the 1880s laboratories in Germany, especially, investigated aseptic procedures and set empirically based standards for sterilization that eventually were adopted throughout surgery and medicine. These practices, it might be added, are still evolving and changing today.

Lister's later years were filled with honors of all sorts. Lady Lister's death in 1893 caused Lister such grief that he abandoned both private practice and experimental research. But he remained a dignitary in British science and in 1895 was elected president of the Royal Society. In 1897 he was the first surgeon to be made a peer. In 1909 his *Collected Papers* were published with his editorial help, but thereafter he entered a decline. He suffered from rheumatic ailments, and his hearing and eyesight began to fail. His death on the morning of February 10, 1912, put a merciful end, wrote a friend, "to that later life of sorrow and misgivings." Although it was widely hoped that Lister might be buried in Westminster Abbey beside such notables as Sir Isaac Newton and Charles Darwin, his own desire to lie beside his wife in West Hampstead prevailed.

Joseph Lister remains one of the icons of medicine. W. E. Henley wrote a poem about him entitled "The Chief," and typically one used to allude to "the rare nobility of his character." Lister's personality resists the burnishings of reverence, however, and his psychological travails bespeak Victorian repression. Although he treated patients with great consideration, Lister was cool and aloof in professional relationships. His marriage was said to be excellent, and Agnes helped him considerably in the laboratory. But the couple was childless. After his brother's death in 1848, Lister suffered a nervous breakdown, and in later years, according to his biographer Richard B. Fischer, he "was positively afraid of emotional display." He entirely lacked a sense of humor, and his only response to "Let us-s-pray"—a student's pun apropos of carbolic acid—was a condescending, pitying glance. He was notoriously unpunctual in appointments and so shy about money as to refuse to name a fee.

From a technical point of view, Lister was not an exceptional surgeon, and it was no accident that he limited himself to setting bones and performing relatively simple operations. Nevertheless, it is on account of Lister's work that after centuries of relative impotence, surgery was able to become enormously sophisticated, as the frock coat and bloody scalpel were replaced with gowns, gloves, and every appurtenance of sterility. "Only those who lived in pre-Listerian days can appreciate the revolution which has taken place in surgery," wrote William Osler (p. 181), who lived through the transition. "As with everything else that is worth preserving in this life there has been evolution; but from the great underlying principle on which Lister acted there has been no departure."

# Wilhelm Conrad Röntgen [1845–1923]

## The Discovery of X Rays

Powerful astonishment greeted the announcement of the discovery of X rays in January 1896. "Her noseless, eyeless face looks into mine," to cite just one of the poems published soon after,

> And I but whisper, "Sweetheart, je t'adore."
> Her white and gleaming teeth at me do laugh.
> Ah! Lovely, cruel, sweet cathodagraph!

Apart from wonder and bewilderment, when the dust settled, the discovery of X rays was a watershed for medicine. Radiology technology would provide an entirely novel way of probing the interior of the human body. From the beginning X rays were employed to locate bullets and view broken bones, and they were soon used to diagnose tuberculosis and a wide variety of pathological conditions. X rays also represented a fundamental advance in physics, a crucial event in the development of modern atomic theory. Their discovery is the principal achievement of the German experimental physicist Wilhelm Conrad Röntgen.

Born March 27, 1845, in Lennep im Bergischen, a small town in the Rhine province, Wilhelm Röntgen was the only child of a prosperous cloth merchant, Friedrich Conrad Röntgen, and Charlotte Constanze Frowein. As a child, Wilhelm was keen on the outdoors and liked to use his hands to make mechanical gadgets. In 1862 he entered the Utrecht Technical School, a private school, preparatory to a technical college. Röntgen was only an average student, although he excelled in mathematics. He could be rowdy and insubordinate, and he was soon expelled for refusing to denounce a fellow student's caricature of a teacher. This incident seemed to undermine his chance of receiving a higher education of any kind, and his father was heartbroken. But a solution came when Wilhelm was allowed to enter the Polytechnikum in Zurich, Switzerland, beginning in 1865. Here he took a diploma in engineering in 1868. By the time he received his doctorate in 1869 from the University of Zurich, Röntgen's focus had become experimental physics.

Early in his career, while teaching at the universities of Strasbourg and Giessen, Röntgen developed a solid reputation as a physicist known for his meticulously designed experiments. He studied properties of gases and crystals, working alone in his laboratory with apparatuses which he constructed himself. In 1888 he confirmed an important prediction of Maxwell's theory of electricity: that a magnetic effect will be observed in a dielectric—a material such as plastic—whenever the field changes. This effect was named the "Röntgen current" by Hendrik Antoon Lorentz, who used it to help reformulate and reinterpret the theory of electricity, essentially to include the concept of electrons. In this sense Röntgen was right to say that he considered his work on the dielectric effect of equal importance to his discovery of X rays.

Like many physicists in the late nineteenth century, Röntgen was intrigued by the cathode ray tube. When a glass tube, evacuated of air but containing some rarefied gas, is subjected to a sufficiently powerful electrical charge, it begins to glow. The properties of the luminescent rays—which do not behave like light waves—intrigued physicists for years before the flowering of the atomic theory of matter. In 1894, soon after he was appointed rector at the University of Würzburg, Röntgen began to use the cathode ray tube for examining the effect of the discharge of electricity through various gases.

On Friday, November 8, 1895, Röntgen was at work in his laboratory. His broad aim was to gather data that might be plugged into some recent theoretical work. He intended to test how the cathode rays, produced from one of his Crookes tubes, fluoresced on a paper screen coated with crystals of barium platinocyanide. This involved, as a preliminary, entirely covering the tube in a black cardboard sheath to protect it from outside light. In the darkened room, as Röntgen turned on the tube to test the opacity of the sheath, he noticed that the paper screen, lying on a table, began to glow. This was entirely unexpected. Although others who had worked with cathode ray tubes had noticed unusual effects, no one until Röntgen possessed any notion of their remarkable implications. Röntgen, well-versed in contemporary physics and the broad ramifications of the new electrodynamics, was prepared to grasp the fundamental nature of what he saw.

Over the next six weeks, Röntgen intensively studied the properties of what he came to understand was a new kind of ray. He called them "X rays" because they behaved like no known ray—not like the waves of visible, ultraviolet, or infrared light. Unlike light waves, they could not be reflected or refracted. But they were also quite unlike cathode rays, in that they were unaffected by magnetic fields or electrostatic charge. Most significantly, Röntgen discovered that X rays traveled in a straight line and created shadows of various objects interposed between the tube and the fluorescent

screen. Indeed, their prime quality was that they passed through all sorts of opaque material, from cardboard and clothing to thin sheets of metal. Something thick, such as a disk of lead, however, stopped the rays cold. And so, when Röntgen held his hand up before the fluorescing screen, he was astonished to see the bones within his thumb and forefinger.

This was the first, fortuitous X ray, and it is fitting that Röntgen was emotionally shaken by the experience. After viewing the interior of his own body, Röntgen seems to have stopped his experiments for a time, concerned for his reputation. Taking advantage of Christmas vacation in 1895, he resumed work intensively, in complete privacy, not even informing his laboratory assistants. He used photographic plates to record the effects, coming away with pictures of such items as a lead weight within a wooden box and the interior of a shotgun barrel. The hand of his wife was particularly dramatic. The whole technology of photography was indispensable for Röntgen's work—and later, for acceptance of his discovery.

Röntgen's famous announcement came in January 1896, in an article entitled "Eine neue Art von Strahlen" ("A New Kind of Ray") in the journal of the Würzburg Physical and Medical Society. It is a clear, simply written account of his experiments and his conclusions; two other reports would follow. As Röntgen understood it, X rays "are not identical with cathode rays, but . . . are produced by the cathode rays in the glass wall of the discharge apparatus." This is not wrong, but it would not be until 1912 that the nature of X rays would be clarified, by Max Laue, as a form of electromagnetic radiation with waves much shorter than those of visible light.

X rays excited almost instantaneous public interest. On January 7, 1896, the *Frankfurter Zeitung* told of a "Sensational Discovery" which, if confirmed, "constitutes an epoch-making result of research in exact science." There soon followed an untold number of articles in the popular press. Images of feet within shoes and coins inside purses soon appeared in newspapers and magazines. Articles explained how an X-ray apparatus could be constructed. There were studios for "bone portraits" and "skiagrams." The inventor Thomas Edison set about developing processes and devices. Concern was voiced for morality in an age where machines could reveal what was underneath clothing. In fact, pioneer X-ray photographs, including sepia-toned prints and careful reliefs that resemble engravings, are aesthetically pleasing in ways that could scarcely be reproduced today. Röntgen's discovery may be viewed, in a sense, as a defining moment for a culture which, over the course of the twentieth century, would be consumed by every kind of electronically generated image.

The prospects for medicine were apparent from the beginning—to Röntgen himself and to everybody else. Physicians and surgeons, according to the article in the *Frankfurter Zeitung*, "will be very much interested in the practical use of these rays, because they offer prospects of constituting a new and very valuable aid in diagnosis." Within weeks, physicians were examining the inside of the body using X rays. Before 1896 was out, medical journals on radiology were published in Germany, America, and Britain. When the Spanish American War took place in 1898, a photographer radiographed casualties. X rays were made for fractures and bullets and such things as kidney stones. Veins were too soft, but it was soon realized that they could be injected with contrast material, which would make them visible.

X rays "not only changed medical practice," writes Ronald G. Evens in a recent historical evaluation, "but dramatically transformed the philosophy and culture of medical science in several fundamental ways." More than the stethoscope or any of the nineteenth-century aids to physical diagnosis, X rays became part of the popular image of medicine. At first they caused some to question the usefulness of physicians—as the computer does today—and Thomas Edison wondered if there might not one day be an X-ray machine in every home. But soon radiology departments sprang up in hospitals, as the complexities of diagnosis dictated that radiology become a medical specialty.

Wilhelm Röntgen accepted the directorship of the physical institute of the Ludwig-Maximilians University in Munich in 1900, where he remained for the last two decades of his career. He was honored endlessly for his discovery. He received the first Nobel Prize in physics in 1901, and later his statue was erected in Berlin on the Potsdam Bridge. The biographical memoirs are elegiac. As a human being, Röntgen possessed only virtues. He was, wrote William Woglom a half century ago, "robust, erect, vigorous, and devoted to his science; full of humor, never arrogant or biased, but open to everything new that did not seem to him extravagant or just superficially clever." But he had a fiery temper. In 1872 Röntgen married Anna Bertha Ludwig, whom he had met in Switzerland. They apparently could not have children, and in 1887 they brought into their home, and eventually adopted, Bertha's niece, Josephine Bertha. Röntgen was said to be a stern *pater familias*.

But Röntgen's last years were not easy. His wife became ill, suffering from an inoperable kidney stone for which only morphine brought relief. He had to attend to her constantly. Röntgen had refused patents on anything connected with X rays, and had donated his Nobel Prize money. After World War I, hyperinflation in Germany stripped him of what fortune he possessed. By 1922 he was in constant distress, probably from cancer of the intestine. Röntgen died on February 10, 1923. His body was committed to the family grave at Giessen. In 1932, a museum in his memory was opened in Lennep.

# Theodor Boveri [1862–1915]
## The Chromosomes

A foundation for understanding genetic inheritance was laid down in the last three decades of the nineteenth century, and a number of signal developments mark the way amidst considerable confusion. In 1882, when biologist Walther Flemming summarized the whole of cytology, the study of cells, he noted the behavior of the threadlike *chromosomes* that arise within the nucleus during cell division. The next year embryologist Wilhelm Roux speculated that these structures constitute the material of heredity. The experimental demonstration of this, however, owes much to the work of the German scientist Theodor Boveri.

"There is no doubt," writes Ernst Mayr, "that Boveri, more than anyone else, supplied the decisive proof for the theory of chromosome individuality." Without his work, Mendel's laws, rediscovered in 1900, would not have had a solid physical interpretation. Boveri, who had great range as a theorist, was one of the first to recognize that "the characters dealt with in Mendelian experiments are truly connected to specific chromosomes." The chromosomal theory of inheritance developed continuously thereafter, acquiring further specificity from biochemistry and culminating at midcentury with the discovery by Francis Crick and James Watson of the structure of DNA.

Theodor Boveri was born on October 12, 1862, in the Bavarian city of Bamberg. He was the second of four sons and the namesake of his father, a physician of Frankish descent. His mother was Antonie Elssner Boveri. At age thirteen Theodor was sent to the Realgymnasium at Nuremberg. He graduated in 1881. Artistic and musical, he would have liked to have become a painter. At the University of Munich Theodor had planned to study history and philosophy, but after a single semester he switched to the natural sciences. Boveri initially studied anatomy, not embryology. He eventually served as an assistant to Carl von Kupffer at the university's anatomical institute. He received his doctorate in 1885 summa cum laude; his thesis concerned the structure of nerve fibers.

Boveri's major achievements are largely connected to the experimental work he undertook between 1885 and 1890. He remained at Munich, but moved from the anatomy division to the Zoological Institute. Boveri had the excellent luck to receive the Lamont-Stipendium, a five-year fellowship later extended to seven years, that left him free to do research. Under the influence of the eminent zoologist Richard Hertwig, whose assistant he became in 1891, Boveri developed skills in cell biology—most especially in the study of cell development. He augmented his work at Munich with field trips to the famous Zoological Station at Naples. In 1893 Boveri became director of the Zoological-Zootomical Institute in Würzburg, as well as professor of zoology and comparative anatomy.

In general, cytology made great strides from about 1870, when it was recognized as probable that the major chemical reactions in the cell, including reproduction, take place in the nucleus. Demonstration in 1875 that fertilization depends on fusion of nuclei from spermatozoa and eggs gave support to this hypothesis. Four years later, Walther Flemming gave the name "chromatin" to a distinctive substance—it would stain red—found within the nucleus. Observing the course of cell division, Flemming saw that chromatin organized into units, assumed rodlike shapes, and split longitudinally, with half of the material passing into each daughter cell. These squiggly shapes, as seen under the microscope, would soon be called chromosomes.

This was how the cellular stage was set when Boveri began his major investigations, and he moved toward proving the chromosomal theory of inheritance in what seems like stepwise fashion. Working initially with a species of roundworm (*Ascaris megalocephala*) in 1887, he established several key events in the process of cell mitosis, or division. He showed how, as the process begins, a "spindle" appears, to which chromosomes attach themselves, emerging from a minute body in the cytoplasm that he termed the "centrosome." Boveri's detailed account provided a basis for viewing mitosis as a highly organized process. The character and plausible significance of the chromosomes emerged from this work.

In his next long study, published in 1888, Boveri showed that, as the chromosomes sort out during cell division, each possesses an organized and regular structure. Chromosomes, he could now suggest, "are independent individuals that preserve their individuality even in the inactive nucleus." This idea ran counter to the belief that chromosomes simply dissolve in the course of cell division and are re-formed with the beginning of mitosis in the daughter cells—a view that some cytologists would maintain for many years, in spite of Boveri's evidence.

Boveri went on to develop a view by which the chromosomes are not just individual but dynamic entities. The chromatic material that assumes equivalent positions in nuclei during cell division, Boveri came to believe, is not passive but active. Considering the technical limitations of the light microscope, this was an extraordinary theoretical leap—and in fact

Boveri had at first only a few good examples. Moving beyond description, he wrote, "I regard the chromosomes as the most elementary organisms, which carry on an independent existence within the cell."

Boveri found better evidence of what he began to call the "continuity of the chromosomes" by moving from roundworms to the eggs of sea urchins, which possess only two chromosomes. One sea urchin egg fertilized by two sperm can generate tripolar mitosis: three cells from one egg. These cells contain an unequal distribution of chromosomes, but can continue to develop with various defects in most, but not all, of the larvae; a predictable percentage would receive a normal complement of chromosomes. Boveri followed the process of cell division in some 719 triaster eggs, of which 79—or 10.98 percent—developed the usual, distinctive "painter's easel" shape. This again strongly suggested the individuality of chromosomes and their continuity over generations, which is what would be expected if chromosomes contained the hereditary material of the cells. By 1891 Boveri was able to write, "We may identify every chromatic element [chromosome] arising from a resting nucleus with a definite element that entered into the formation of that nucleus." And he was able to conclude that "in all cells derived in the regular course of division from the fertilized egg, one half of the chromosomes are of strictly paternal origin, the other half of maternal."

Although by 1890 Boveri's work, as Jane Oppenheimer writes, "completed the shift of emphasis from the nucleus as a whole to the chromosomes as the agents of inheritance," it did not everywhere meet with acceptance. Chromosomal inheritance was rejected for a time by some eminent scientists, and disagreement over the function of the chromosomes mirrored a period of extensive discovery and confusion in biology at the turn of the twentieth century.

Indeed, chromosomal inheritance was only fully resolved with the establishment of classical genetics. Briefly, in 1902 Boveri welcomed the rediscovery of Mendel's work, which laid hereditary traits at the door of discrete parental "factors" that could clearly reside in the chromosomes. A "specific assortment of chromosomes is responsible for normal development," wrote Boveri in 1902, "and this can mean only that the individual chromosomes possess different qualities." That same year Edmund Beecher Wilson, the influential American zoologist, wholeheartedly embraced Boveri's theory as laying "the basis for the cytological explanation of Mendel's law of heredity." And in 1903 another American, Walter Sutton, published "The Chromosomes in Heredity," and similarly brought Mendel's genetics to bear on cytology. What became known as the Boveri-Sutton hypothesis continued to rouse hope and doubt until 1910. In that year one of the skeptics, Thomas Hunt Morgan, in experiments with fruit flies, essentially confirmed both Mendel's rules for inheritance and the chromosomal hypothesis at one stroke.

Boveri was the author of many other contributions, too numerous or esoteric to mention here, but his hypothesis concerning cancer should not be entirely neglected. At the end of his life, in 1914, he published a theory suggesting that malignant tumors might arise from an abnormal number of chromosomes. This notion had no influence, but it was a prescient idea, foreshadowing today's still evolving theory of carcinogenesis.

In 1898 Boveri married Marcella O'Grady, an American biologist who had come to Würzburg to work with him. She often aided him in his experiments. They had one child, a daughter Margret, who became a well-known writer and journalist. Although considered witty and, in later life, cool and self-possessed, Boveri sometimes suffered from depression and self-doubt, and seems to have had several nervous breakdowns. The first occurred as early as 1890, when his father was in financial trouble and his mother was sick. In 1913 Boveri refused a call to move to the Kaiser Wilhelm Institute, mainly because of ill health. He wrote to his friend and colleague Hans Spemann (p. 232), "I have gradually grown to be like that chandelier of [the famous aphorist] Lichtenberg which, while no longer lighting the place, serves at least as decoration." But not for long. Boveri's well-being did not improve over the next year, and he died, as World War I raged, on October 15, 1915.

# Santiago Ramón y Cajal [1852–1934]

## Discovering the Neurons

The famous philosopher Julian Offray de La Mettrie, in the eighteenth century, considered the brain an "enlightened machine." Yet for more than a century afterward, and for a generation after the body was understood to be a community of cells, the composition and organization of the brain and nervous system remained a dark continent. How the brain worked could not be described, much less explained. One popular theory held that the nervous system was a "protoplasmic network"—a diffuse gray mush. It is not hard to understand why. Nerve cells cannot be easily viewed under a light microscope, and in the brain they are densely packed, like brambles stuffed to bursting in a small gray suitcase.

But at the end of the nineteenth century, as a powerful example of bonds forged between science and medicine, comes the work of Ramón y Cajal. To him is owed, more than to any other single investigator, the description of nerve cells and the concept of the neuron as the basic unit of the nervous system.

Ramón y Cajal is often regarded as the "father of modern neuroanatomy," and his work emerges logically from the refined taxonomy of tissue that arises in the mid-nineteenth century. It is conceptually based on the insights of Rudolph Virchow (p. 8) and strongly indebted to staining techniques for microscopy developed by the German chemist Paul Ehrlich, as well as by Camillo Golgi. An artist and scientist of high caliber, Ramón y Cajal is one of the most attractive and colorful figures in the history of medicine.

He had an exceptionally fascinating childhood. Ramón y Cajal was the first-born son of Antonia Cajal and Justo Ramón y Casasús, born on May 1, 1852, in Petilla de Aragón, Spain, a small village in the Pyrenees. His father had been trained as a barber-surgeon and rose to become a full-fledged physician and eventually a professor of anatomy. He was a disciplinarian who used to beat his son within an inch of his life, and sometimes liked to lock him in a dark room. But Santiago loved his father with ardor, while at the same time developing an aggressive personality with a strong need to be punished. As a youngster he enjoyed stealing fruit from orchards and bringing down birds with a slingshot—but he was also a keen bird-lover. He is one of the few great scientists to have belonged to an adolescent gang.

A reluctant student, Ramón y Cajal detested the school of the Aesculapian fathers (a Catholic order dedicated to education), where he was sent at age ten. Although he did better at the Institute of Huesca, his father, believing there was no hope for his son to achieve a learned education, apprenticed Santiago to a cobbler. It was a year before Don Justo permitted him to return to school, at age sixteen. But now he improved dramatically, and soon was studying at the University of Zaragoza, where his father taught applied anatomy. His interest in art and drawing—which his father had deplored—now became useful to science and medicine. After receiving his medical degree in 1873, Ramón y Cajal spent time in the army, where he nearly died of malaria and dysentery. But he returned to Spain to continue his studies and received a doctorate in medicine in 1879.

Ramón y Cajal's talents were recognized early in his career, and he won an appointment as director of the University of Zaragoza's anatomical museum. In Spain his medical education had been sorely deficient; as a student he did not even look through a microscope. Soon after graduating, however, he set about teaching himself microscopic anatomy.

In 1884 Ramón y Cajal became professor of descriptive anatomy at Valencia. He soon had a growing reputation as a prodigious investigator, and he published studies on a wide variety of anatomical structures, from the muscle fibers of various insects to the crystalline lens of the eye. Over several years he published *Manual de histología normal y técnica micrográfica (Manual of Histology and Micrographic Technics)*, a breathtaking 700-page work. In 1887 Ramón y Cajal moved to the University of Barcelona, where he became professor of histology. In 1892 he moved to the University of Madrid, where he would remain based for the rest of his academic career.

Ramón y Cajal's research into the nervous system began early and evolved into a cascade of basic discoveries. In 1888—"my greatest year, my year of fortune"—Ramón y Cajal began experimenting with the "silver stain" method developed by the Italian histologist Camillo Golgi. He improved this method and used it to examine the nervous tissue of small mammals and birds. Importantly, he recognized, as others had not, that unambiguous results could be obtained by studying embryonic tissue instead of tissue from fully developed animals. His results were dramatic. The nervous system was not a vast network of interconnected *fibers,* as Golgi and many others had imagined. It was comprised of *cells* of various shapes. Ramón y Cajal recognized that these cells, to be called *neurons,* constitute the basic functional units of the entire nervous system.

Ramón y Cajal's challenge to the "continuity doctrine" was controversial, but eminent colleagues soon overcame their initial skepticism and embraced his findings. A turning point came in 1889, when Ramón y Cajal read a landmark paper to the German Anatomical Society and put his skills as a draftsman to use. Ramón y Cajal's powers of persuasion, together with beautiful slides demonstrating his microscopic descriptions of nerve cells in the spinal cord, gained his ideas considerable attention.

"I began to explain to the curious in bad French what my preparations contained . . . ," recalled Ramón y Cajal, and soon, "the prejudice against the humble Spanish anatomist vanished and warm and sincere congratulations burst forth." Previous researchers had described neurons, but none before him had shown convincingly that these were cells, discrete like every other kind of cell, communicating but not continuous with their neighbors. The "neuron doctrine" represented the culmination of years of suggestive experiment. Ramón y Cajal had built a scientific bandwagon in Spain, and now his European colleagues climbed aboard.

Although the vast complexity of Ramón y Cajal's contributions is far beyond the explorative scope of this work, it should be emphasized that he made major contributions to both the detailed picture of the brain and nervous system and to the general underlying theory of how the nervous system functions. Thus, from his detailed microscopic investigations of the nerves of the eye and nose, there emerged what Ramón y Cajal called the "doctrine of dynamic polarization." Ramón y Cajal distinguished a neuron's *dendrites*, the filaments emanating from the nerve cell body, from its long and slender *axon*. Axons, Ramón y Cajal noted, all point in the general direction of the brain, while the network of dendrites runs in the opposite direction. Axons, Ramón y Cajal concluded, function to transmit electrical messages, while the dendrites receive them. "Dynamic polarity" became one of the fundamental pillars of neuroanatomy.

Ramón y Cajal's equally fruitful "neurotropic" theory, or "chemotactic hypothesis," dating to 1892, suggested how nerve cells find their way during embryonic growth to their predestined terminals. He believed, correctly as it turned out, that chemical pathways were key. In its fundamental outlines, the neurotropic theory forms the root of a vast elaboration of neuroscience still in progress today.

From 1894 to 1904 Ramón y Cajal published three volumes of his *Textura del sistema nervioso del hombre y de los vertebrados (The Nervous System in Man and Vertebrates)*. This was a huge work of synthesis. Douglas W. Taylor wrote that this "classic of medical science," as he called it, ". . . contains the cytological and histological foundations of modern neurology." It is by no means simply a work of classification and description, but an effort to understand patterns of function, all in the context of evolution of structure.

In 1906, Ramón y Cajal was awarded the Nobel Prize for physiology or medicine. He shared the award with Camillo Golgi, the Italian researcher who had developed the silver nitrate stain that made possible much of Ramón y Cajal's early work. At the awards ceremony, Ramón y Cajal provided a straightforward account of his basic discoveries. Golgi, in contrast, gave a speech that denigrated Ramón y Cajal's theories and attempted to revive his own, now obsolete, theory of neuronal networks.

Ramón y Cajal was as prolific as he was original, publishing some 20 books and over 250 papers. In addition to his scientific works, he also wrote literary works, including *Cuando yo era niño (When I Was a Child)* and *Reglas y consejos (Rules and Counsels)*. In old age he wrote an intriguing autobiography—florid, propulsive, digressive, and colorful—*Recuerdos de mi vida,* published in abridged form in English as *Recollections of My Life.* He also published an aphoristic *Charlas de café,* translated as *Conversations at the Café,* which Fielding Garrison described as observations of a Latin cast of mind, pessimistic as well as "direct, mordant and uncompromising."

Ramón y Cajal invested his private life with the same sense of self-importance and missionary zeal as was found in his science. In 1880 he wed Silvería Fañanás García, to whom he was initially attracted not only physically but "by a certain air of child-like innocence and melancholy resignation emanating from her whole person." She "devoted herself to caring for me and establishing my health upon a firm basis." They had eight children. One of the most famous Spaniards when he died on October 18, 1934, Ramón y Cajal's likeness graced postage stamps and Spanish pesetas. His complete literary works were published, with the help of the Spanish government, in 1947.

# Oswald Avery [1877–1955]

## The "Transforming Principle": DNA

The discovery that DNA (deoxyribonucleic acid) controls protein synthesis and the transmission of hereditary characteristics is a keystone
in twentieth century medical research. Francis Crick and James Watson
are credited with the discovery of the structure of DNA in 1953, but a host
of scientists made a variety of discoveries, piecemeal, during the jigsaw
dawn of molecular biology. In retrospect, the most profound was the revelation, which dates to 1944, that DNA could cause genetic transformations
among strains of certain bacteria. This discovery "marked the opening of
the contemporary era of genetics," writes Joshua Lederberg, "its molecular
phase." It was principally due to the work of an eminent microbiologist at
the Rockefeller Institute — Oswald Avery.

The middle of three sons, Oswald Theodor Avery was born on October 21, 1877, to English parents who had emigrated to Halifax, Nova Sco-
tia. His father, Joseph Francis Avery, was a Baptist pastor; his mother, also
actively religious, was Elizabeth Crowdy. At age five, young Oswald witnessed what he believed was his mother's death from a fever. Her recovery,
some have speculated, had a psychological impact that turned Oswald in
the direction of medicine. In 1887 the Averys relocated to New York City,
where Joseph took charge of the Mariner's Temple, which still stands on
the famous Lower East Side of Manhattan. An excellent student throughout his childhood, Oswald attended Colgate University, where he received
a liberal education and earned his bachelor of arts degree in 1900. He
went on to study medicine at the Columbia University College of Physicians and Surgeons and received his medical degree in 1904.

Although Avery practiced medicine in New York for several years, he was
discouraged by his inability to treat many of the common and lethal diseases.
His interest turned to research, and he soon took a position at the Hoagland
Laboratory in Brooklyn. At this private laboratory, connected with the Long
Island Medical College, Avery had the opportunity both to teach and to do
research. One of his early papers, on tuberculosis, so impressed Rufus Cole,
director of the hospital of the Rockefeller Institute, that he visited Avery at
his laboratory bench. In 1913, at Cole's invitation, Avery moved to the Rockefeller, and there he would remain for the rest of his career.

Avery's major research effort was directed at gaining a better understanding of the bacteria that cause pneumonia, then a leading cause of death. An acute infection of the alveolar spaces in the lung causing severe pulmonary congestion, pneumonia in the days before antibiotics was frequently fatal. Louis Pasteur (p. 18) had isolated the first strain of pneumococcal bacteria as early as 1881, and over the next half century numerous other pneumonia-causing bacteria were identified. Avery and his laboratory at the Rockefeller Institute played an important role in typing the various strains of pneumococci, which, as Avery and his colleagues understood matters, were distinguished by shape and other significant characteristics. Some strains were lethal, and others were relatively harmless.

Avery's work during the years after World War I profited from the increasingly potent tools of biochemistry. Together with Raymond Dochez, whose lifelong friend he became, Avery discovered that if pneumococci were removed from the culture in which they had been grown, certain types left behind traces of "soluble specific substance," or SSS. Avery and Dochez eventually recognized that this substance constituted the capsule in which the organism was encased. White blood cells could engulf and digest unencapsulated pneumococci, but encapsulated bacteria were indigestible and could proliferate rapidly. These types were lethal. From this taxonomy emerged, in principle, therapeutic potential.

In 1928, Frederick Griffith, a British scientist, made a startling discovery. By chance and against all expectation, he found that when he injected killed but lethal *encapsulated* bacteria into mice together with living but harmless *unencapsulated* bacteria, the mice developed pneumonia. How could dead bacteria, harmless if injected alone, have lethal effects when injected with living but harmless bacteria? Griffith's experiments stunned the world of microbiology. An assumption that immunological types of bacteria were stable and fixed was strongly embedded in medical research—no less so for Avery, who had worked with the various strains for years. Indeed, Avery doubted Griffith's results when they first appeared. His laboratory repeated and confirmed the experiments in 1929.

How the transformation of pneumococci occurred remained unknown for several years. Griffith's own explanation was that the dead bacteria might furnish some nutrient to the living bacteria by which they developed a capsule and became lethal. This was a good idea, but it proved wrong. In addition, as Avery discovered in 1931, the mice could be ignored in the equation. For the transformation to take place, it was enough to put the two types of bacteria together in a petri dish. Avery's question then became, and for some years remained, "What is the substance responsible?"

The problem of isolating and purifying the agent that transformed the bacteria occupied Avery and his colleagues for about five years, from 1932 until 1937. His laboratory became highly proficient at effecting transformation. Beginning with some 20 gallons of bacteria, Avery and his colleagues employed centrifuges, filters, and chemical reagents in attempts to isolate the substance by which harmless pneumococcal bacteria turned deadly. As early as 1936 Avery suggested—but only wistfully—that the "transforming principle" seemed to be neither a protein nor a carbohydrate, but a nucleic acid.

Knowledge about the nucleic acids dated to the latter part of the nineteenth century. "Nuclein" was identified as the principal substance of the nuclei of cells in 1871; DNA and RNA (ribonucleic acid) were distinguished in the 1920s. Although suspected of playing a role in metabolism, the nucleic acids seemed simple in composition, and their specific biological role remained unclear. The presumption, meanwhile, was that the hereditary material—the stuff of genes—was probably a protein. But when Avery and his colleagues attempted to disable the transforming mechanism in pneumococci by removing protein, they failed. When enzymes that attacked protein were applied, the transforming principle remained active. However, when enzymes that attacked DNA were used, the principle became inactive. Separated by centrifuge, the "transforming principle" proved to be a homogeneous substance that could be matched to DNA from calf thymus. Using electrophoresis, another technique for analysis, the substance behaved—like DNA.

By the early 1940s, Avery recognized the broader implications of his experimental work with the "transforming substance." At the time, most scientists doubted that the genetics of bacteria and those of higher organisms would involve the same essential biochemistry. However, in a famous letter to his brother Roy—a "rambling epistle," he called it—Avery wrote that his results might indeed mean that nucleic acid was the substance by which "it is possible to induce *predictable* and *hereditary* changes in cells. . . . Sounds like a virus—may be a gene." He added, a measure of his characteristic caution, "It's lots of fun to blow bubbles—but it's wise to prick them yourself before someone else tries to."

Avery's research at the Rockefeller Institute attracted considerable attention among a handful of eminent scientists. In 1943 both Theodosius Dobzhansky, the evolutionary geneticist, and Macfarlane Burnet (p. 280) visited Avery's laboratory. The latter wrote immediately that Avery had showed "nothing less than the isolation of a pure gene in the form of deoxyribonucleic acid." But for publication, Avery's caution prevailed. In 1944, together with colleagues Colin MacLeod and Maclyn McCarty, Avery published a landmark paper in the *Journal of Experimental Medicine*. Its unprepossessing title was "Studies on the Chemical Nature of the Substance Inducing Transformation of Pneumococcal Types." The nucleic acids, Avery suggested, might possess a hitherto unguessed significance, but he did not go so far as to suggest that DNA would constitute the chemical basis of heredity.

And in fact Avery's discovery alone did not lead to recognition that DNA is indeed the molecule of heredity. In 1950 Erwin Chargaff showed that DNA from various organisms had regular but distinctive proportions of the four chemical bases that comprise it. Making use of the work on bacteriophages initiated by Max Delbrück, experiments in 1952 by Alfred Hershey and Martha Chase showed still more conclusively that DNA was responsible for genetic transformation in bacteria. About the same time, Linus Pauling brought forth an inspired—but mistaken—structural model of DNA as a triple helix. With the help of X-ray diffraction techniques, recognition that the structure of DNA was instead "double-helical" and ladderlike—suggesting "a possible copying mechanism for the genetic material"—was finally delivered by Francis Crick and James Watson, in a letter published in *Nature* in 1953.

Oswald Avery was quiet and reserved. He rolled his own cigarettes and evinced bafflement by passing a hand across his bald pate. A Republican in politics, a painter who worked in watercolor, a musician who played the cornet, he was friendly and sensitive, optimistic and persistent. His discovery of the "transformational principle" came toward the end of his career, and his death a few years later denied him the opportunity for a Nobel Prize. After formally retiring from the Rockefeller Institute in 1947, Avery continued working there for a time. But in the end he moved to Nashville, Tennessee, where he spent his last years with his brother's family. He died from liver cancer on February 20, 1955.

# Part III  Figures of Constant Reference

# Ambroise Paré  [1510–1590]

## The Rise of Surgery

Ambroise Paré developed and popularized a profusion of new surgical techniques for coping with insults to the human body. With the increasing use of firepower on the battlefield — gunpowder enters the Western armamentarium in the fourteenth century — it is no accident that Paré's reputation was first gained as a military surgeon. Famously, he used gentle dressings to treat gunshot wounds instead of cauterizing them with boiling oil. But more generally, Paré displayed such flexibility and freedom from dogma that he has been widely praised over the course of more than four hundred years. He is, in short, the great surgeon of the Renaissance. "Chyrurgery is an Art," he wrote, "which teacheth the way by reason, how by the operation of the hand we may care, prevent, and mitigate diseases, which accidentally happen unto us." From a humble background, Paré went on to become surgeon to five kings.

Paré was a contemporary and probably a friend of the great anatomist Vesalius (p. 41). His voluminous writings had considerable practical influence and covered a broad range of medical and surgical topics. They are written not in Latin but in lively French, and display a personality at once genial and combative. Paré's books were translated into other languages of Europe and even into Japanese, and were used by surgeons for over two centuries. In addition, his famous *Apologie et voyages* has substantial literary value and bears reading today. Paré, writes Harold Ellis in a recent assessment, is "one of those great landmarks that punctuate surgical history; a surgeon who, through his example and writings, greatly influenced progress in the management of wounds."

Ambroise Paré was born about 1510 near Laval, the old city near Rennes, in Brittany, France. His father, a valet and barber, made a meager living. Paré became apprenticed to a barber-surgeon and at age nineteen moved to Paris, where he learned his craft. In French medicine there existed then a tripartite hierarchy: physicians, guild surgeons, and barber-surgeons. Paré was destined by background to join the last, who performed such tasks as bleeding and cupping, as well as wound management. His training at the Hôtel-Dieu he counted as exemplary, later writing that "I had the meanes to see and learne divers workes of Chirurgery, upon divers diseases together

with the Anatomy, upon a great number of dead bodies. . . ." After three years at the hospital, Paré entered the army to put these skills to work as a regimental surgeon.

The years of Paré's youth were marked by the ascendancy of Francis I, who, four years after becoming king in 1515, lost his bid to become emperor of the Holy Roman Empire. This led him into a series of wars with Charles of Hapsburg that were fought largely on the Italian peninsula. There, at the siege of Turin in 1537, Paré made his first and most famous innovation.

As was customary, Paré and his fellow surgeons treated gunshot wounds by cauterizing them with boiling oil of elder, which was thought to prevent death from "gunpowder poisoning." This method caused terrible agony and more damage to the flesh than the projectile had. At Turin, the oil ran out. As a stopgap, Paré covered the wounds with a salve composed of egg yolk, turpentine, and oil of roses. One night he wrote, "I could not sleep . . . for I was troubled in minde, and the dressing of the precedent day, (which I judged unfit) troubled my thoughts; and I feared that the next day I should finde them dead, or at the point of death by the poyson of the wound, whom I had not dressed with the scalding oyle." In fact, these patients were still alive and in better condition than the men who had been treated with cauterization. Paré continued to treat casualties in this way, he added, and "When I had many times tryed this in divers others I thought this much, that neither I nor any other should ever cauterize any wounded with Gun-shot."

Returning to Paris in 1541, Paré formally qualified as a master barber-surgeon, and within a short time he became an authority for his peers. He was not necessarily inclined to write about his innovative work until this was suggested one day by Jacobus Sylvius, one of his teachers. In 1545 Paré published his *Method of Treating Wounds,* a brief guide that became the vade mecum for military surgeons throughout Europe. He also recognized the significance of anatomy—Vesalius had published his highly influential *Fabrica* two years earlier—and Paré spent several years in anatomical studies. His *Briefve collection de l'administration Anatomique,* first published in 1549, served as a practical guide. It included advice on obstetrics, with an explanation of the "podalic version," the shifting of the fetus for feet-first delivery.

Paré became famous through his writings. His works reached an audience hungry for pragmatic knowledge about surgery. In 1552 Henry II appointed him surgeon-in-ordinary. Two years later Paré was accepted into the elite and staid Confraternité de St. Côme—highly unconventional for a barber-surgeon, but, given his standing with the king, understandable. When Henry II's luck ran out during a tournament joust in 1559, Paré could not save his life—nor could Vesalius, called in on consultation. But Paré remained in royal favor, serving as surgeon to Henry's three sons, each of whom became king in turn: Francis II, Charles IX, and Henry III. One is not surprised to learn that Paré was an exceptional presence at bedside. In his classic account of the duc d'Auret's recovery after infection due to a gunshot wound, he explained that he ordered musicians and comics to the sickroom.

Paré published voluminously and expansively on a variety of topics. In his *Dix livres de la chyrurgery,* published in 1564, for example, he provides a careful investigation of how thigh amputations might be made to work. He proposes the use of fifty-three ligatures—a reminder that the tourniquet would only be invented in the eighteenth century. In 1572 his work on fractures and dislocations appeared: *Cinq livres de la chyrurgery.* Two more books, on obstetrics, appeared the same year. Paré even published *Traité des rapports,* a book for surgeons called to testify in court about the nature of lethal wounds, causes of death, or, in matrimonial cases, the state of the hymen (a spouse whose marriage had not been consummated had ecclesiastical grounds for divorce).

Paré was also a pioneer in prosthetics and obstetrics. He invented artificial limbs and eyes, nasal prostheses, lightweight trusses for hernia, and many other contrivances "to repair or supply the natural or accidental defects or wants in Man's bodie." In addition to devising innovations in obstetrics, he also founded a school for midwives and was a major influence on, for example, Louise Bourgeois (p. 383).

Many of Paré's beliefs reflect the age in which he lived. Probably a Huguenot, he was protected from harm in 1572 by Charles IX, even as the king, encouraged by his mother, ordered the killing of thousands of French Protestants. Paré believed in witches and was convinced that the stars influence disease. He had a fascination with the still largely unexplored world—the earth, but also the oceans and heavens—that seemed filled with exotic creatures and monsters, from Sarmatian snails to African elephants, sea devils, and scale-covered mermaids. *On Monsters and Marvels,* first translated into English only in 1986, is a little compendium that features various birth defects, and in Paré's commentaries, as Janis Pallister notes, "We can see many of the modern sciences in their embryonic form."

Ambroise Paré was shrewd, modest, and pious. Nothing indicates this better than his famous saying, *Je le pansay, Dieu le guarit*—"I dressed him, God cured him." Ambroise Paré lived into old age, dying renowned on December 20, 1590.

# Bernardino Ramazzini [1633–1714]

## Occupational Diseases and Environmental Hazards

The Western medical tradition, with its emphasis on humoral imbalance as the cause of illness, for centuries did not really favor the idea that certain diseases might be due to one's occupation or environment. Egyptians knew that the blacksmith was "grilled" by the furnace, and in Roman times Lucretius mentioned the "malignant breath" of gold miners, and noted "how speedily men die and how their vital forces fail when they are driven by dire necessity to endure such work." But only with the development of new means of exploiting the earth, as well as of new ways of looking at its products, was illness linked to occupation. In the sixteenth century the ever insolent Paracelsus (p. 50) wrote a monograph on diseases of metal workers, and the metallurgist and physician Georgius Agricola connected the injured lungs of Silesian miners to the dust they breathed. But the founder of investigation into occupational and environmental diseases is generally conceded to be the great Italian physician Bernardino Ramazzini.

Bernardino Ramazzini was born in Carpi, in the duchy of Modena on the Italian peninsula, on November 5, 1633. As a boy he was educated by the Jesuits. For three years, from 1652 to 1655, he attended the University of Parma, which had been reorganized in 1601. He received his medical degree, the Master of Arts and Doctor in Medicine, in 1659.

Initially Ramazzini practiced near Rome, in the small towns of Canino and Marta. Malaria was prevalent at the time, and Ramazzini acquired a case of it. That his own illness, as he undoubtedly realized, was linked to location may have sensitized him to consider environmental causes of disease in general.* He returned to his native Modena. In his home town of Carpi he soon developed a successful practice and came into favor at the ducal court of Francis II. In 1682, after the duke constructed the University of Modena, Ramazzini was appointed professor. Here he met, and was perhaps influenced by, the philosopher Gottfried Wilhelm von Leibniz. During

---

*Malaria was epidemic in Rome during the later empire because of its surrounding swamps. For centuries afterward the area was depopulated.

the 1690s Ramazzini kept a meteorological journal and also recorded more general environmental conditions. In 1700 he moved to the University of Padua, and there he would remain until his death.

While still in Modena, Ramazzini had become interested in the diseases associated with various occupations, initially by accident. The privy in his home—his "house of offices"—was cleaned out every two or three years. This was a grisly task that invariably fell to the poorest workers in the city. Ramazzini happened across them one day, in the midst of their emptying his "dismal Vault." Noticing one man who was particularly agitated, Ramazzini writes, "I asked the poor Fellow, Why did he not work more calmly and avoid over-tiring himself with too much Straining?" He learned that the worker was concerned about losing his sight, and he saw that his eyes were "very red and dim." A few hours of such work, and he had to spend a day in a dark room, washing out his eyes with warm water. "After this," writes Ramazzini, "I took notice of several Beggars in the City, who, having been imployed in that Work, were either very weak-sighted, or absolutely blind."

By the time Ramazzini began compiling information, there already existed a small literature on occupation-related diseases. In addition to Paracelsus and Agricola, the German physician Ulrich Ellenbog had published a small pamphlet on the fumes and smoke that affected goldsmiths. It was written in German and probably circulated among workers. Several other such papers appeared in Latin for physicians; these also discussed diseases of miners. Ramazzini made excellent use of these sources, but in addition he visited workers and noted their illnesses and infirmities. He descended into the mines—sometimes a risky thing to do—and visited the workshops. "[O]ut of these Places I have endeavored to pick whatever might best please the taste of the Curious; and chiefly indeed to suggest such Cautions as may serve to prevent and cure the Disease to which Tradesmen are usually subject."

*De morbis artificum diatriba* was published in 1700 and immediately found an audience. The English translation appeared just five years later: *A Treatise of the Diseases of Tradesmen, Shewing the Various Influence of*

*Particular Trades upon the State of Health; and with the Best Methods to Avoid or Correct It, and Useful Hints Proper to Be Minded in Regulating the Cure of All Diseases Incident to Tradesmen.*

Ramazzini makes a broad distinction between occupations such as soldiering, which are dangerous in and of themselves, and those involving work-related hazardous materials. In his first edition, Ramazzini addresses some forty-two groups. Miners are discussed in the first chapter, for their suffering is most pronounced and the cause is obvious. But artisans of all kinds are represented. There are chapters on diseases of apothecaries, bakers, millers, painters, and soap makers. Ramazzini details metal poisoning in metal workers, and silicosis in stone masons. The seventeenth chapter is devoted to tobacco workers, and as Cesare C. Tedeschi notes, it "could have been written in our days." Ramazzini did not describe lung cancer, but he noted that tobacco workers had lungs that were "flaccid and dry," all to nourish a vice which "will always be condemned and always clung to." The most amusing story comes in the tenth chapter, on sulfur workers. When her husband comes home unexpectedly, a woman hides her lover under the bed. But she covers him with a blanket just cleaned with sulfur. The residue makes him cough and sneeze, betraying the tryst.

In addition to illuminating occupational imperilments, Ramazzini outlines the concept of environmental hazards. He recounts the story of a lawsuit brought by a citizen of the town of Finale against a certain manufacturer of sublimate. When vitriol (in this case, probably sulfuric acid) was roasted in the factory ovens, it gave off powerful fumes, which, as it appeared to the citizens of the town, made people sick. In spite of evidence and testimony for the plaintiffs by the town physician, this hotly contested issue ended with a victory for the manufacturer. In retrospect, all one can say is that sulfuric acid is indeed powerfully corrosive to body cells, causes skin irritation on contact, and damages the intestinal tract; injection of a small amount can be fatal.

Ramazzini was a follower of the "Divine Hippocrates," and he made a suggestion that was incorporated into the clinical interview. "On visiting a poor home a doctor should be satisfied to sit on a three-legged stool in the absences of a gilt chair, and he should take time for his examination; and to the questions recommended by Hippocrates he should add one more — 'What is your occupation?'" On this point Ramazzini's influence was fairly direct and widespread. Giovanni Morgagni (p. 55), a good friend of Ramazzini, seldom fails to mention the occupations of his patients in *De sedibus et causis morborum.*

*A Treatise of the Diseases of Tradesmen* became a perennial classic. Its influence dominated works published on occupational disease through the eighteenth century. But at the same time, it played no part in the concerns of manufacturers during the Industrial Revolution. Ramazzini's essential humanity and his empathic view of individual workers in 1700 stand in contrast to the insensitivity that marked the rise of manufacturing over a century later.

As one might expect, Ramazzini possessed an attractive personality. He was married to Francesca Righi, who descended from a noble family. Their two daughters grew up to marry physicians; their one son died at eight months. Ramazzini was loved, according to Dr. James, his English translator, for "his singular Learning, the Sweetness of his Temper, the Candour of his Judgment, the Uprightness of his Intentions, the Honesty of his morals, the Industry with which he discharged his various offices, and the Success of his practice."

In spite of blindness in old age, Ramazzini continued to teach. On his eighty-first birthday he was preparing a lecture when he suffered a stroke. He died on November 5, 1714.

# Girolamo Fracastoro [c. 1478–1553]

## A Poem About Syphilis, a Theory of Contagion

Physician and scholar Girolamo Fracastoro, who as an author used the name Fracastorius, wrote two books of signal interest to the history of medicine. One is a poem concerning a horrifying and apparently new disease in Europe, to be known eventually, through his works, as syphilis. The other book, still more important, is *De contagionibus,* which provides a nascent theory of contagious disease traditionally considered the first in the history of medicine.

Renowned as a physician, Fracastoro fully belongs to the Italian Renaissance and classical Humanism. He followed contemporaneous discoveries closely and was an astronomer who in a limited way anticipated Copernicus. As a botanist he contributed to the era's materia medica. He was also a mathematician and a philosopher.

Girolamo Fracastoro was born in the Venetian city of Verona; the year 1478 is an intelligent approximation. (Hieronymus Fracastorius, the name he used in his writings, is the Latinized version.) He studied law at Bologna before enrolling at the University of Padua. Established in the early thirteenth century, Padua was the second oldest seat of learning on the Italian peninsula. By the time Fracastoro arrived there in 1501, it was also the liveliest. Less than fifty years had elapsed since Constantinople had been conquered by the Turks, an event that caused a number of Greek scholars to flee to Italy. For the next century Padua would remain emblematic of the Renaissance, home to Aristotelian thought and emergent Humanism.

Fracastoro studied mathematics and philosophy as well as medicine at Padua, and he received his bachelor's degree in 1502. He remained at the university to teach for a year or perhaps a little longer, but soon enough he returned to Verona to practice medicine. He became successful and renowned. Famously, he preferred the country and lived in an elaborate estate near the city that was equipped with a fine library and boasted a fireplace in each room. He would read Plutarch as he was driven in his coach to see patients.

Among the baffling diseases that Fracastoro attempted to treat was one that seemed new. Horrible in many of its symptoms, it was talked about all over Europe and became known by many different names.

Italians and Germans associated it with the French, but it was also called the "Spanish disease" and the "Neapolitan itch"—all wanted to export the blame. By the sixteenth century the most popular term, both among doctors and patients, was the "French pox." In the seventeenth century the term venereal disease (lues venera) came into wide use. "Syphilis," Fracastoro's name for the disease, would not become common until the early nineteenth century.

The origin of the disease in Europe was from the beginning, and remains to this day, controversial. Perhaps the oldest and most celebrated theory holds that it was brought back to Spain from the New World by sailors under Christopher Columbus. Another possibility is that *Treponema pallidum,* the spiral-shaped bacterium that causes syphilis, arose in Europe as a genetic mutation in the context of urban congestion and social change. Today, after nearly five hundred years, there are several competing theories, each with merit, that draw increasingly on evidence from microbiology and paleoanthropology. The debate will no doubt continue in the twenty-first century with help from the new discipline of genomics.

When Fracastoro wrote about it, syphilis was recognized as being transmitted sexually at least part of the time. In this way the mercenaries of King Charles VIII of France, dispersed after the unsuccessful siege of Naples in 1494, carried the disease all over Europe. By 1497 the Scots of Aberdeen called for town prostitutes to "decist fra thar vicis and syne of venerie" or risk being branded. But the vagaries of infection undermined a clear appreciation of the actual route of transmission. Syphilis was originally more aggressive and more often fatal than it would be today.

"I sing of that terrible disease," begins Fracastoro, "unknown to past centuries, which attacked all Europe in one day, and spread itself over a part of Africa and Asia." Published in 1530, *Syphilis sive morbus Gallicus (Syphilis, or the French Disease)* was dedicated to Cardinal Pietro Bembo, a well-known scholar, papal secretary, and one of Lucrezia Borgia's numerous lovers. Writing in blank verse in Latin, Fracastoro laid claim to classical Greek and Roman sources.

The poem has three books. In the first, Fracastoro describes the emergence of the disease and the puzzlement it has caused. The second book discusses the various treatments and the adventures of a husbandman, Ilceus, who finds his cure in mercury baths. The third book is the allegorical tale of a shepherd named Syphilus, whose worship of a worldly king incited the anger of the sun god. In consequence he suffered from "the foul sores in his own body; first he knew sleepless nights, his bones ached mercilessly." The poem was frequently translated and eventually was published in over one hundred editions. The book's widespread distribution attests to the prevalence and severity of the disease.

Fracastoro's other great book is *De contagionibus,* published in 1546. It is a shrewd combination of observation and reasoning. His theory offers three interrelated possibilities to explain the nature of contagious disease in general. First, a disease can be transmitted by direct contact. Fracastoro gives the potent example of grapes or apples rotting side by side. He had no good explanation for the mechanism of putrefaction, but the result was undeniable. A second possibility would be infection by what he called *fomes* (fomites). These are vectors of infection—cloth or linen, for example—"which foster the *essential seeds* of the contagion and thus cause infection." (This would be the case with syphilis.) The third category is the type by which diseases and various fevers can be transmitted "at a distance." Throughout, Fracastoro is sensitive to the selectivity by which plants, animals, humans, and even individual organs, are subject to specific diseases. "The affinities of infection are numerous and interesting," writes Fracastoro. "Thus there are plagues of trees which do not affect beasts and others of beasts which leave trees exempt."

Most fascinating, in modern terms, is Fracastoro's concept that "germs of contagion" multiply. He has the idea that they adhere to specific humors of the body and "generate and propagate other germs precisely like themselves, and these in turn propagate others, until the whole mass and bulk of humors is infected by them." Fracastorius's concept is striking, but it is not a direct forerunner of the germ theory of disease. Rather, it should serve as a reminder that the idea that disease is caused by infinitesimal things has roots in ancient folklore. Historically, speculations on contagion were made by Galen (p. 34), as well as by the Roman scholars Marcus Terentius Varro (116–27 B.C.) and Pliny the Elder. Just as in *De rerum natura* the Roman poet Lucretius beautifully reprises Democritus's atomic theory, in *De contagionibus* Fracastoro offers a philosophical structure for thinking about infinitesimal, invisible causes of disease. Fracastoro, writes C.-E. A. Winslow, "worked out a clear and essentially accurate analysis of the way in which living 'germs' operate, without ever suspecting that they were living." Although his efforts were widely admired, Fracastoro's work could not have produced a scientific theory without something like modern biology, the microscope, and at least a partly reliable chemistry.

Finally, Fracastoro also discusses various diseases in detail. Drawing careful distinctions between the various "fevers" and their symptoms, he may be considered one of the discoverers of typhus and a predecessor of

Thomas Sydenham (p. 132). Fracastorius's treatment of syphilis in *De Contagionibus* includes a canny appraisal—in prose this time—of its origin and development in Europe. Early twentieth-century scholars admonished Fracastoro for blaming the onset of the epidemic on an astrological configuration, but nothing would be less surprising for a Renaissance thinker. More importantly, Fracastoro's explanation of syphilis by contagion departed obviously if not heretically from scholastic medical views, by which diseases were due to humoral imbalances that arose from within an individual. The appearance of syphilis in the wider world of Renaissance trade, commerce, and warfare probably demanded some kind of explanation such as Fracastoro provided.

It is instructive to compare the fate of Fracastoro's theory of contagion with the theory of a sun-centered planetary system developed by his classmate at Padua, Nicolaus Copernicus. Within one hundred years of the publication of *De revolutionibus orbium coelestium (On the Revolution of the Heavenly Bodies)*, Copernicus's work had been taken up and developed by Johannes Kepler, Galileo, and others. The Copernican revolution culminated in the immensely successful theories of Isaac Newton. Intellectually, it contributed mightily to European thought, and indirectly to discovery and conquest, and the creation of the modern state.

By contrast, Fracastoro's theory of contagion was not further developed. Evidence that might have supported his theories—much of it deep in the microscopic world—was not at hand or sought after, and his views did not achieve any dominance. Three centuries would elapse before the advent of the germ theory of disease around 1880. When it came to syphilis, still another generation would pass before the bacterium was isolated in 1905. For treatment Fracastoro recommended an ointment made with quicksilver; a truly effective medicine would come only with penicillin in the 1940s.

Fracastoro had a hand in, but did not much influence, a variety of other pursuits. As an astronomer, he wrote *Homocentricorum sive de stellis liber (Homocentricity, or The Book of Stars),* published in 1538, in which he suggested that the earth and planets might rotate along spherical orbits around a fixed point. This was an Aristotelian concept, not the revolutionary advance that would be proposed by Copernicus. Fracastoro's contribution to geography was greater. He suggested the use of rectilinear maps, and to him is owed the derivation of the word "poles" for the ends of the earth's axis. The flooding of the Nile and the underlying character of wine—is it hot and wet?—were other inquiries of his. His *L'Alcone* is a poem about hunting dogs.

Famed and celebrated for all his scholarly pursuits, Fracastoro was honored by princes and solicited by churchmen. For a time Pope Paul II made him a *medicus ordinarius,* in which capacity he recommended moving the Council of Trent to Bologna, the better to avoid a plague. (Political maneuvers moved it back.) But Fracastoro soon returned to his country estate. There, while seated at his dinner table on August 8, 1553, he suffered a stroke, at age seventy-five. He died later that evening, leaving unfinished a discussion of the soul. Within two years the Veronese honored him with a monument in stone on the Piazza dei Signori.

# Thomas Sydenham [1624–1689]

## The "English Hippocrates"

A sked to recommend the best textbook in medicine, Thomas Sydenham famously suggested Cervantes' *Don Quixote*. "It is a very good Book," he said. "I read it still." Sydenham's sardonic disdain for academic medicine, and for what he viewed as the lamentable state of the art, was coupled with acute observational skills and a bedside approach to treating illness. For this Sydenham has come down through history as the "English Hippocrates." He worked within a humoral framework, and he did not contribute much to the understanding of disease causation. But as an iconoclast who largely disliked theories and books, he developed new ways of viewing illnesses as classifiable entities, and he simplified many treatments. This skeptical and practical stance won him great influence and established him as a harbinger of clinical medicine.

*The Whole Works of that Excellent Practical Physician, Dr. Sydenham*, his collected writings, was reprinted throughout the eighteenth century. "His plain dogmatic style, his emphasis on personal observation," writes Geoffrey Meynell, "the vivid clinical descriptions and the temperate nature of his treatments, come like a blast of fresh air into a frosty over-crowded room." Celebrated in his own time, he was friends with early scientists Robert Hooke and Robert Boyle as well as philosopher John Locke, who wrote a poem praising his methods and did much to magnify his reputation. Sydenham's fame eventually extended from England to the European continent, where it is said that Herman Boerhaave (p. 136) never mentioned his name without tipping his hat, and called him "that shining light of England, that Apollo of the art."

The early life of Thomas Sydenham — indeed, his first thirty years — strongly reflects the social upheavals which culminated in the English civil war. The fifth of seven sons and ten children, he was born in early September 1624 in the hamlet of Wynford Eagle, Dorset. His father was William Sydenham, a country squire and well-known politician. In 1643, at age seventeen, Thomas entered Magdalen Hall, Oxford University. But he studied for only two months because the war broke out. Thomas joined the Parliamentarians and returned to Dorset, where, with his father and brothers, he made ready to fight.

The Sydenhams were committed Puritans, and local skirmishes were brutal. Thomas's mother, Mary, was killed in a raid; one of his brothers subsequently avenged her death. Thomas himself escaped the first round of the war unscathed. He even returned to Oxford in 1647, and soon transferred to Wadham College. He received his bachelor's degree in medicine in 1648 and was elected a fellow of All Souls' College. His degree was by "actual creation" of the university's Puritan chancellor, however, and was essentially a formality. The disorganization of academic life wrought by the war ensured that Sydenham had little in the way of a real medical education, and consequently he had little respect for its teachings. In 1651, now in his mid-twenties, Sydenham returned to the military as a captain in one of Cromwell's regiments. According to some sources, he was seriously wounded at a battle — documents do not clarify which — and left for dead on the field.

Returning to London, Sydenham began practicing medicine part-time in Westminster as early as 1655. But, having fought on the victorious side in the war, he now found much of his time given over to supporting his brother William, who played a powerful role in the Cromwell government. For a time in 1655, he held a government sinecure as Comptroller of the Pipe. Sydenham was defeated, however, when he stood for Parliament in 1659, the year in which Cromwell's death led to the Restoration. Both his brother and father, crushed by this political reversal, died within a couple of years. Sydenham thereafter devoted himself to medicine. He practiced at first without a medical license, which he only received in 1663 after passing requisite exams. He would not receive a doctorate in medicine until 1676, from Cambridge, at age fifty-two. This degree, like his earlier one, was also conferred by mandate.

On the advice of the great philosopher and chemist Robert Boyle, Sydenham began to study epidemic diseases in the early 1660s. Inasmuch as the Great Plague of London in 1665, against which medicine was helpless, was followed by a series of minor epidemics, this research was not surprising. In 1666 he published the first edition of his study of fevers, *Methodus curandi febres.* Ten years later, much expanded and recast, this work appeared as *Observationes medicae*. Sydenham turned careful clinical observations into a significant new system of classification of various febrile and epidemic diseases. These diseases included pleurisy, pneumonia, and the skin disease known as erysipelas, as well as rheumatism and quinsy, a painful throat infection. One of Sydenham's most significant therapeutic advances was to employ Peruvian bark to treat the "agues"— the acute chills and fever which, as would eventually be understood, characterize malaria, a disease that was epidemic in Europe beginning in the sixteenth century. Quinine was the active ingredient in the bark, and it saved many thousands of lives. It is thought that this was the first specific remedy for a febrile disease.

During the 1660s Sydenham became one of the most successful practitioners of his time, with a wealthy clientele. From his writings it is easy to see why. He took the part of the layman against the learned, but frequently impotent, physician. He once wrote that "the usual pomp of medicine exhibited over dying patients is like the garlands of the beast at the sacrifice." More often than did his colleagues, he opted for noninvasive therapies such as rest, fresh air, and travel. He avoided overmedication and surgery, which patients particularly dreaded. Sensitive to the sufferings of his patients, he prescribed opium for pain, and by adding wine he developed the highly drinkable "Sydenham's laudanum." Another treatment he pioneered was that of giving iron for chlorosis, an anemic condition (seldom seen today) that lends the flesh a greenish hue. In general, Sydenham's search for specific remedies ran counter to the period's dependency on "blunderbuss" formulas, derived from Galenic medicine, in which many ingredients were mixed together. It exemplifies his emphasis on using experience and observation, as opposed to induction based on rational (but often unhelpful) principles.

Perhaps Sydenham's most intriguing regimen was his advocacy of the cure known as accubitis: prescribing a dog or child to lie with a sick person. Treating a woman for dysentery, Sydenham had her son, "a plump hot lad of thirteen years of age, and her nurse's son of six or seven years, to go to bed to her naked and to lie the one close to her belly, the other close to her back…." In this case the patient recovered. Accubitis, if not always successful, was at least warm and familiar.

Chronologically and conceptually, Sydenham's work stands midway between the older humoralist ideas, which he did not attack—Nature tries to effect a cure, he believed—and scientific medicine, then possessed of only a weak base of knowledge. So, while creating a new bedside approach that relied on observation and led to valuable concepts of classification, Sydenham also de-emphasized anatomy and thought little of the microscope. However, although he disdained theories, he could not entirely avoid formulating them. Few were successful. His understanding of epidemic disease, for example, "in its vagueness," observes Erwin Ackerknecht, "did little either to explain the data or further the development of epidemiology." In particular, Sydenham believed smallpox to be a natural process to which everyone was subject. He made the claim, for which he was stridently criticized by some and defended by others, that many deaths from smallpox were due to physicians' interference with this natural process.

Sydenham did not limit himself to studying only bodily afflictions. His *Epistolary Dissertation on the Hysterical Affections,* from 1682, is a penetrating treatise that describes the various symptoms of hysteria, from insomnia and hypochondria to morbid jealousy. As treatment he sometimes prescribed bleeding; he also recommended horseback riding. But Sydenham often enlisted only "the prince and pattern of physicians—Time." He knew that hysteria could affect both men and women, and might involve such symptoms as headache and nausea. Indeed, his concept was modern in that he accorded hysteria a psychological dimension. From a medical point of view, his discussion was far more canny than the rather eccentric reflections found in Robert Burton's 1621 book, *The Anatomy of Melancholy.* It was not so influential as the rest of his work, however, and the view of hysteria as a disease specific to women would persist to the end of the nineteenth century.

Sydenham's personal life, after the civil war, was fairly tranquil. Like a number of powerful doctors (today as well as through history), he had a bit of a persecution complex, and saw himself as somewhat further outside the establishment than he really was. He married Mary Gee in 1655, and the couple had three sons. While still young, as early as 1649, Sydenham was afflicted by gout. His book *Tractatus de podagra et hydrope,* a book on gout and dropsy published in 1683, includes a classic description of the disease. Sydenham suffered from other problems as well, including anemia, for which he prescribed his own laudanum. Any rough walk or ride brought blood into his urine. For that he drank beer for supper and again at bedtime "in order to dilute and cool the hot and acrid humours lodged in the kidneys, which breed the stone." In 1677 he wrote his friend John Locke, "I am in dispaire of being ever well agayne." Yet Thomas Sydenham lived twelve years more, dying in London on December 29, 1689.

# Hermann Boerhaave [1668–1738]
## Medicine in the Eighteenth Century

H ermann Boerhaave is the magisterial figure credited with setting the agenda for medicine in the eighteenth century. He revived and to some extent systematized the emphasis on bedside observation that was original with and characteristic of Hippocratic medicine. Upon this clinical foundation he brought to bear an eclectic group of the most advanced scientific theories of his day. In 1724 Boerhaave provided the first modern case history, detailing a physical examination, diagnosis, course of disease, outcome, and results of autopsy. He became the most renowned professor of medicine in Europe—historian Henry Sigerist calls him the "undisputed master"—and his works were widely translated. During his lifetime and for some years after his death he was highly influential and the epitome of all that medicine knew or thought it knew. To understand him, writes historian Lester King, "is to understand all the currents of medicine in the early eighteenth century."

Boerhaave's limitations are as interesting as his range of accomplishment. Although recognizably a scientist and physician, he was not a highly original thinker and made no signal discovery. He tried. But the scientific revolution, in his time realizing mainly mechanical advances, offered few remedies and little genuine insight into the way the body works. In sum, Boerhaave's life and work amount to a historical prescription for what Western medicine needed—namely, a new biology and a valid chemistry. Neither would actually become available for therapeutic purposes for more than one hundred fifty years after his death.

The eldest child and only son of a minister, Hermann Boerhaave was born on December 31, 1668, in Voorhout, Netherlands. After the death of his mother, Hagar Daelder, when he was about five, his father, Jacobus, married Eva Dubois, who became an affectionate stepmother. Highly educated, Jacobus lavished his son with care and educated him in ancient Greek, Latin, and Hebrew, with a view to making him a minister. Boerhaave wrote later that his father "molded my character from childhood with Socratic devotion."

In 1683 Hermann entered the University of Leiden to study theology, at which he excelled. He qualified in philosophy in 1687 and received his doctorate in 1690. But he was also interested in, first, mathematics and science, and then, by 1691, medicine. He obtained his medical degree in 1693 from the University of Harderwijk. Initially, Boerhaave both practiced medicine and worked as a minister—a dual occupation that was not unusual but, in his case, lasted only a short time. According to friends, during a voyage on a canal boat, Boerhaave made the mistake of intervening in an argument and speaking in favor of being fair to the philosopher Baruch Spinoza, whose pantheistic philosophy was considered atheistic and subversive. Boerhaave's name was noted on the spot, and he was subsequently suspected of supporting Spinoza's heretical views. Boerhaave, believing that now he would never obtain a pastorate, devoted himself solely to medicine and to studying physics and chemistry. He became lecturer in medicine at the University of Leiden in 1701 and professor of medicine and botany in 1709.

Boerhaave's inaugural lecture at the university in 1701 is a masterful summation of his program for medicine and reflects his impressive background in classical literature and philosophy. He extols the virtues of Hippocrates but also touches on other major figures of medicine, from Andreas Vesalius (p. 41) in the Renaissance to his own near contemporary, Thomas Sydenham (p. 132). In a sense Boerhaave systematized Sydenham's emphasis on observation and his Hippocratic style by integrating teaching with clinical demonstrations. In 1714, after being made vice chancellor of the university and teaching the course on clinical medicine, he began taking students to Caecilia Hospital to observe patients at first hand and discuss their afflictions. Thus Boerhaave emphasized, with greater force than was common in an academic setting, that the aim of medicine was to give ease to suffering.

During his lifetime, and for a generation or more afterward, Boerhaave's work was widely taught. Two books in particular were translated and published throughout Europe. His *Institutiones medicae*, a classification of disease, was first published in 1708. The next year there appeared the *Book of Aphorisms*, a practical and Hippocratic guide to help physicians treat patients. Aware of the importance of botany to medicine, Boerhaave had established a garden, and in 1710 he published *Index Plantarum*, which eventually listed 5,846 species. Botany, in the eighteenth century, was taught as a medical subject; the botanist, often a physician, studied and taught the medicinal properties and uses of plants. Boerhaave's lectures on botany were later collected by students and published as *Historia Plantarum*.

Boerhaave was a forerunner of scientific medicine in a number of respects. In addition to emphasizing the importance of observation, he understood from the beginning of his career the relevance of chemistry to medical knowledge. This probably spared him from adopting an overly mechanistic outlook. Boerhaave's biographer G. A. Lindeboom has suggested, "Perhaps it is not too much to say that he is the father of physical chemistry"—and, indeed, Antoine Lavoisier praises him highly. With its clear explanations, *Elementa chemiae (Elements of Chemistry)*, published in 1732, became one of the most famous works of its time. Boerhaave had considerable perseverance at the laboratory bench. It is said that he heated mercury day and night for fifteen years and six months in the hope of discovering some therapeutic benefit.

In retrospect, it is easy to see Boerhaave's limitations. The physician, he wrote, "builds for himself a clear idea of the human frame." But by this he meant the human organism was a mechanical instrument, complete with fluid flowing through tubes under pressure, balance maintained through movement, and illness resulting from some imbalance or obstruction. Besides prescribing exercise and a good diet—he was fond of milk as an elixir—Boerhaave was woefully limited in terms of therapeutics and was desperately eclectic. Purging with powerful laxatives, bleeding and cupping, and bathing in warm water were the main methods with which he treated most of his patients. He also employed remedies of iatrochemistry and iatrophysics—the chemical and mechanistic theories applied to medicine—without committing himself to either. These remedies did not work for many illnesses, and the best that can be said today is that Boerhaave was not blind to their limitations.

Boerhaave's personality, even among those who knew him, was enigmatic. This is not surprising in view of the blanket of veneration bestowed upon him by students. He is said to have projected great serenity and apparent tranquillity of mind. He was honest, humble, and religious. But even his letters express little in the way of emotion.

In 1710 Boerhaave married Maria Drolenvaux, who was the daughter of a wealthy merchant and had once been his patient. Of the couple's four children, just one daughter lived to adulthood. After 1729, Boerhaave cut down his workload, and later in life he suffered a great deal from gout. He died, probably of heart failure, on September 23, 1738. His wife wrote letters to inform the scientific and medical societies at home and abroad. All Europe mourned.

The nature and extent of Boerhaave's fame and influence is a fair lesson in the history of medicine. In his time he was immensely renowned, and once received a letter from a Chinese mandarin which had been addressed only to "Boerhaave, celebrated physician, Europe." Upon his death, he could not be praised highly enough. His direct importance and exceptionally wide influence continued until new systems of medicine, such as those advocated by William Cullen, were designed later in the eighteenth century.

However, once the scientific approach to medicine that Boerhaave had attempted to promote started to yield results, his reputation began to decline. By the late nineteenth century Charles Daremberg could find little of interest in Boerhaave. Historian Charles G. Cumston said that he was a "passing light, and after his death soon forgotten." With the rise of the history of medicine as a separate discipline in the twentieth century, however, the wheel turned once more. In 1968, Lindeboom's excellent biography was one of a number of documents that rectified this imbalance. Taking into account the number of Boerhaave's students who themselves became eminent teachers, E. Ashworth Underwood pronounced Boerhaave "probably the most successful medical teacher who ever lived." Today Boerhaave's reputation for stimulating research in physiology and spreading the practice of observation in clinical medicine in the early eighteenth century is assured.

# John Hunter [1728–1793]

## Beginnings of Scientific Medicine and Surgery

One day in 1783 a human giant purchased a coffin made of lead. In anticipation of his own end—he was tubercular and ravaged by alcoholism–Charles Byrne also contracted with several sturdy Irishmen: when he died, they were to sink his body into the Thames River. Byrne hoped by these uncommon arrangements to avoid becoming a medical specimen. Byrne's remarkable body—he was eight feet two inches tall—was much desired by London anatomists.

However, when Byrne did die, his Irish guardians betrayed him. Bribed with the huge sum of £500, they stripped his corpse naked and under cover of night sent it off in a carriage across London. Before dawn the body had been dismembered and the flesh boiled off the bones. Not until three years later, for the sake of prudence, was the skeleton of a "tall man" first shown. Encased in glass, it was exhibited beneath the much smaller Sicilian Fairy in the famous museum of the great surgeon and anatomist John Hunter.

Surgeon, anatomist, physician, and naturalist, John Hunter exemplifies the unprecedented curiosity about nature that belongs to the second half of the eighteenth century.

For many years Hunter was a hero of British medicine, and he remains today a figure of constant reference. His accomplishments include various practical surgical innovations. One of these was an operation to treat an aneurysm by damming the bloodstream instead of amputating a limb, an approach that "excited the greatest wonder and awakened the attention of all the surgeons in Europe." He also wrote one of the pioneering treatises in dentistry and an influential tract on gunshot wounds. He was a tireless teacher and enjoyed an international reputation. Importantly, Hunter's experimental and practical work was also undergirded by a broader interest in the natural world. A great collector, Hunter amassed a huge trove of plant and animal specimens—as well as humans such as the gigantic Byrne. He was a taxonomist who reveled in the diversity of nature, and he is sometimes cited as a precursor of Charles Darwin (p. 3). Because he made no dramatic discovery, Hunter is not as well known as, say, Louis Pasteur (p. 18). But his major works, taken together, "mark the rise of surgery," writes Roy Porter,

"from manual craft to scientific discipline." From a contemporary perspective, John Hunter is one of the early founders of modern medicine.

John Hunter was born near East Kilbride, Scotland, on February 13, 1728. His mother, Agnes Paul, was the daughter of a Glasgow maltster. His father, for whom he was named, was a grain merchant become gentleman farmer who died in 1741. John's education was basic. He did not like the rigid, hewn-to-theology Scottish school, and stopped attending at age thirteen. As the youngest of ten children, of whom only several lived to adulthood, he may have been spoiled and allowed to indulge what was, at any rate, an unquenchable curiosity. "When I was a boy," he later wrote, "I wanted to know all about the clouds and the grasses and why the leaves changed colour in the autumn. I watched ants, bees, birds, tadpoles, and caddisworms. I pestered people with question about what nobody knew or cared anything about." John's brother William, ten years his senior, moved to London and became a celebrated surgeon, specializing in obstetrics, and a teacher. After a period spent with an uncle as a cabinetmaker's apprentice, John was sent to join William in 1748.

John Hunter's skill with his hands and his intellectual gifts both became apparent over the next several years and compensated for his lack of social polish. Initially he helped prepare cadavers for William; soon he was so adept that he started doing dissections himself and supervising his brother's students. He attended classes in surgery and also became a pupil of William Cheselden.* At St. Bartholomew's Hospital he worked under Percival Pott, another famous surgeon, and learned from him to trust, insofar as possible, the restorative powers of the body. By 1753, Hunter was appointed master of anatomy. He entered St. George's Hospital in 1754, as a surgical pupil, and two years later was named house surgeon.

---

*Cheselden, who lived from 1699 until 1752, was celebrated as a surgeon who, before the advent of anesthesia, could remove a bladder stone in an operation lasting, objectively, just two minutes. He was also the author of *Anatomy of the Human Body*, published in 1713.

Hunter would be associated with St. George's for the rest of his life.

An army surgeon from 1759, during the Seven Years' War Hunter sailed with the British navy in 1761 when it set out to capture the small but strategically important Belle Île-en-Mer off the French coast. Caring for casualties, Hunter was shocked by the primitive treatment of wounds, writing that "It was hardly necessary for a man to be a surgeon to practice in the army." Hunter recognized, as surgeons of his day generally did not, that the body would adjust to many wounds, and intervention was often unnecessary and harmful. (In clinical medicine, Thomas Sydenham (p. 132) had understood something similar a century before.) With the Treaty of Paris in 1763, Hunter returned to London and the wards of St. George's. His *Treatise on the Blood, Inflammation, and Gunshot Wounds* was eventually published in 1794, a year after his death, and became exceptionally influential.

Hunter's rise to fame represents, in part, the advantages of practical experience that surgeons enjoyed over better-educated physicians, who were still content to consult, listen, advise, and prescribe. This led both John and William to original research in specialized areas of anatomy. The lymphatic system, for example, had been first discovered in the early seventeenth century and its anatomy was gradually elucidated; but it was not well understood in terms of function. The Hunters demonstrated how lymphatic flow is toward the heart, rather than away from it, and John eventually recognized how the lymphatic system was implicated in certain cancers. John and William also showed how the circulatory system in the fetus is independent of that of the mother, and thus they became founders of placental anatomy. No less significant were their investigations of the structure and function of the bones, in which endeavor the brothers were immeasurably aided by people known as "resurrectionists," or grave robbers.

John Hunter, by the 1760s, had won renown and acceptance by the surgical and scientific establishment. He was elected to the Royal Society in 1767 and the next year was officially awarded a diploma of the Company of Surgeons. He developed a prosperous private practice and was named physician extraordinary to King George III in 1776. He was awarded the Copley Medal in 1787. Three years later he became deputy surgeon to the army and was named inspector general of hospitals.

To both his work in anatomy and his research in clinical medicine, Hunter brought a positive attitude toward experiment and classification. His two-part *Treatise on the Natural History of the Human Teeth*, published in 1771 and 1778, was a landmark—anatomical rather than clinical in intent, but full of useful information. One of Hunter's experiments was to transplant a human tooth into the comb of a rooster. The classification of teeth as molars, bicuspids, cuspids, and incisors is owed to Hunter's work, as is the practice of using braces to correct overbite.

In 1767 Hunter made an unfortunate mistake. Many of his patients suffered from venereal disease, which was still little understood, and he hypothesized that gonorrhea and syphilis were two types of the same disease. But how to find out? He took the extreme measure of infecting himself with what he thought was simple gonorrhea. When he identified the characteristic chancre on his penis—it became known as the Hunterian chancre—Hunter thought his hypothesis confirmed. He was wrong. In all probability the patient from whom he contracted gonorrhea also suffered from syphilis, which is, of course, far more serious and persistent. For the purpose of study, Hunter endured its external lesions—and put off his marriage—for several years before dosing himself with mercury. His *Treatise on Venereal Disease* was published in 1786. It is wrong in many respects but, it should be added, contains much sound observation on contagion.*

Hunter's most visible and celebrated legacy is his museum. At his death it contained some 13,500 specimens. It represented his love of collecting wedded to his passion as an anatomist. Hunter dissected many animals, from bulls to whales, and solicited specimens from friends and colleagues. Eventually the collection was sold to the British government, and the Hunterian Museum for many years was housed in the Royal College of Surgeons. It was heavily damaged by German bombs during World War II, but was subsequently restored and reopened.

John Hunter possessed a canny, scientific personality, whose insight shows clearly through the rough-hewn texture of his writings. He married Anne Home in 1771, and of their four children, two survived to adulthood. Although John and his brother William collaborated early in their careers, their personal relationship deteriorated over the years, and bitterness burst forth publicly in 1780. The cause of the rupture was John's claim that he deserved full credit for discovery of the structure of the placenta in 1755, when he was still much the younger brother.

It is fitting that Hunter studied his own decline in old age. During his last years he developed angina pectoris. He described his symptoms in great detail—all the while refusing to admit the diagnosis. His former

---

*Along similar lines, Hunter's remarks on the psychology of sexuality are inordinately modern. Hunter dissented from the common view that masturbation led to impotence. He recognized the psychological component of male impotence, writing that "the mind is subject to a thousand caprices, which affect the action of those parts."

student and friend Edward Jenner (p. 152) understood. "I am fearful (if Mr. H. should admit this to be the cause of the disease)," he wrote, "that it may deprive him of the hopes of recovery." Hunter was aware that the disabling pains that shot through his chest frequently came when he was angered. He said, in an oft-quoted remark, "My life is in the hands of any rogue who chooses to provoke me."

Indeed, it was under just such circumstances, at a meeting of the Board of Governors of St. George's Hospital, that John Hunter collapsed and died on October 16, 1793. Members of the Board could have cared less and offered no condolences, while his wife could not afford the fees to have him buried in Westminster Abbey. But that is where his remains were moved in 1859 by the Royal College of Surgeons, in "admiration of his genius" and the better to record "their grateful veneration for his services to mankind as the Founder of Scientific Surgery."

# Pierre Fauchard [1678 – 1761]

## Founder of Modern Dentistry

The functions of the various teeth were described in the Hippocratic corpus, and the Roman encyclopedist Celsus (p. 375) had suggested filling cavities with lint. The Middle Ages saw the use of resins and waxes, and the Renaissance brought gold. Yet, though teeth long preoccupied people and caused them pain and suffering, dentistry was slow to develop as an integral profession with a fund of written knowledge. Only in the sixteenth century did *Libellus de dentibus* (*Pamphlet on Teeth*) arrive, composed by an Italian anatomist, Bartolomeo Eustachio. And not until the mid-eighteenth century, by traditional consensus, did modern dentistry take shape—with Pierre Fauchard.

Trained as a surgeon, in 1728 Fauchard published a comprehensive treatise on teeth that effectively established dentistry as a field of medicine, separate from surgery and at professional remove from the tooth pullers. Practitioners had formerly jealously guarded technical knowledge and in this way cultivated incompetence. But *Le chirurgien dentiste, ou traité des dents* (*The Surgeon-Dentist, or Treatise on the Teeth*), Fauchard's seminal work, inspired the development and free exchange of knowledge about the teeth. It formed a solid foundation for schools and other professional institutions established in the nineteenth century. Chapin A. Harris, the American dentist who wrote *Dental Art* in 1839, was clear about Fauchard's significance: "He found the dental art a crude branch of mechanics," wrote Harris; "he left it a digested and systematic branch of the curative art."

Pierre Fauchard was born in 1678 in Brittany. Little is known about his early life, but in 1693 at age fifteen he entered the French navy as a student in surgery. "From my youth I was destined to the surgical profession," he wrote; "the other arts I have practiced have never made me lose sight of it." In general, surgery in the eighteenth century was more advanced in France than elsewhere. Fauchard's teacher was Alexandre Poteleret, a surgeon-major in the navy who, because of the then common scurvy disorders, was familiar with diseases of the mouth.

Fauchard remained in the navy for three years; when he left, a reversal of family fortunes compelled him to look to dentistry as a livelihood. In

1696 Fauchard began practicing in Angers, the old city near Nantes. Over the next two decades he developed a lucrative practice. In 1719 he made the logical move to cosmopolitan Paris and opened an office on the Rue de la Comédie-Française. His reputation soon became established. His clientele was drawn from both the nobility and the growing numbers of wealthy bourgeoisie. He called himself *dentiste*, and as Roger King observes, "Fauchard used the title deliberately to mark as new territory what he and his colleagues were doing, as something quite different from what had gone before."

*Le Chirurgien dentiste, ou traité des dents,* was first published in 1728. It defines the entire field of dentistry, setting out the various paths to be developed over the next two centuries. Fauchard describes the anatomy of the teeth and their morphology, and discusses their anomalies. He delineates what today are the subdisciplines of oral surgery, prosthodontics, orthodontics, periodontics, and endodontics. Partly because he was so clever and inventive, but also owing to exceptional clarity of expression, *Le chirurgien dentiste* remains in print after nearly three hundred years— a rare distinction in the history of medicine. "Even today it is a treasure trove of still useful information for the inquiring dentist," wrote Bernhard W. Weinberger in 1941. "When first published it started a revolution which made a profession of what had been a craft."

One need not be a dentist to appreciate *Le Chirurgien dentiste.* Fauchard dismisses the theory that cavities are caused by worms—an idea that dates to the ancient Sumerians—and laments the overconsumption of sugar. As an Enlightenment figure, he condemns mountebanks who would work by means of prayer and who promise miracles. Quacks irritate Fauchard no end. He is more than aware of the dangers patients face with an inexperienced or clumsy tooth puller. He describes one whom he identifies as the "Roche Operator," who, in trying to extract a tooth, drove it into the nasal cavity known as the maxillary sinus. The Operator thought that, because the tooth was no longer visible, the patient had swallowed it. It subsequently reappeared as a "little hard tumor" on the patient's cheek, and had to be removed by "cutting through the gums, seizing the roots with straight pincers, and yanking out the whole tooth."

Fauchard writes extensively on the subject of tooth decay and dental caries. He understood the importance of carefully cleaning cavities before filling them. For this he used cautery and oil of cinnamon, and employed fillings made from iron or, as he preferred, tin. Although he did not use casts in making bridges and dentures, he used human teeth, ivory, walrus tusk, or ox bones. He eventually invented a means of retaining the upper denture through the use of steel springs. Custom dictated that the patient sit on the floor, with the surgeon standing over him. Fauchard introduced the chair.

Fauchard also discusses prophylaxis, and gives attention to the gums and gum disease, and to straightening teeth. He describes about one hundred diseases of the mouth, teeth, and gums; and in the second edition of his treatise, published in 1746, he provides what became a celebrated description of pyorrhea alveolaris, or purulent periodontal disease. Again, Fauchard was exceptionally modern in believing that scaling and debriding the root surfaces of teeth could prevent or contain gum disease. In a sense, Fauchard brought forth the concept of oral hygiene more than a century before it was applied in hospitals and surgical techniques. He suggested that patients have their teeth cleaned once or twice a year.

Obviously, Fauchard's knowledge was limited. In line with the still prevalent humoral theory, he believed that decay represented imbalance. Unusual to modern thinking was a treatment that he claimed "brought a great deal of relief to a number of persons" suffering from multiple caries. This was, in a word, urine. An ancient remedy employed in cultures the world over, urine has many interesting uses. Fauchard recommended that patients rinse their mouths carefully with several teaspoonfuls, just passed and still warm. Although he acknowledged it was not really an agreeable remedy, its success with patients who followed this regimen made him ask the rhetorical question: "But what will one not do for relief and for health?"

Fauchard was married three times. Of his first wife there is no record. His second marriage, in 1729, was to Elisabeth Guillemette Chemin, who was from an eminent family and whose brother was also a well-known dentist. This marriage produced two children but ended with Elisabeth's death in 1739. At age sixty-nine, Fauchard married Louise Rousselot, who would outlive him. Fauchard's son from his second marriage, Jean Baptiste, became "Grandmesnil," a famous actor whose name is as well known in France today as is his father's. Fauchard's death came on March 21, 1761. He was buried in a church which was subsequently destroyed. Today the resting place of Pierre Fauchard is unknown.

# Philippe Pinel [1745–1826]

## Treating the Insane

A tall tale, convincing if fanciful, from the French Revolution during the Terror of 1793: Philippe Pinel, gentle and soft-spoken physician, pays a visit to Georges Couthon, the fiery, merciless leader of the Committee of Public Safety. Pinel describes the shocking conditions of inmates at the Hospice de Bicêtre. Unmoved but curious, Couthon, a cripple, is taken to view the hospital's 300 filthy, disorderly, shackled lunatics. Questioning them, he receives shouts and insults in reply. He turns to Pinel and says, "Ah, ça! citoyen, es-tu fou toi-même de vouloir déchainer de pareils animaux?" ("Well, Citizen, are you yourself mad to want to unchain such animals?") But when he does not forbid Pinel to do as he pleases, there begins one of the most fortunate experiments in the history of psychiatry. The spirit of the Enlightenment and revolutionary ideals transform the treatment of mental illness.

Psychiatry actually has far more beginnings. Madness is discussed in the Hippocratic corpus; Aretaeus described mental illnesses in the second century A.D. Paracelsus (p. 50) and early humanists such as Erasmus viewed insanity with something like compassion. Johann Weyer challenged the link between madness and witchcraft during the Renaissance. Later, in the eighteenth century, British medicine gave rise to theories about mental illness. And ever since, though its history has been one of uneven development and tortuous steps forward and back, modern psychiatry has its own identity and history. Its founder, it is often said—mythmaking aside—is indeed the French reformer and humanitarian, the physician and scientific theoretician Philippe Pinel.

Philippe Pinel was born on April 20, 1745, near the old city of Castres in southern France. His father was a country doctor, and his mother, Elisabeth Dupuy, was from a family of physicians, apothecaries, and surgeons. Pinel was educated at a local seminary, where he was taught geography, history, and literature. He eventually became familiar with the writings of John Locke and Etienne Bonnot de Condillac. From these thinkers Pinel developed a humanist outlook, a disrespect for metaphysical theorizing, and a theory of knowledge based on sensation. At the University of Toulouse Pinel studied theology from 1767 until 1770, when he switched to the faculty of medicine. He received his medical degree from Toulouse at age twenty-eight in 1773.

Pinel spent the first several years of his career at Montpellier, the old university city in southern France. He worked as a physician and supplemented his income by giving mathematics lessons, anatomy courses, and ghostwriting theses for prosperous students. In 1777, two papers on mathematical aspects of human anatomy demonstrated his grasp of scientific thinking and won him respect. The next year Pinel moved to Paris, where he became acquainted with Pierre Cabanis, an eminent physician and Enlightenment figure who introduced him to the lively salon of Madame Helvétius. In 1784 Pinel was named editor of the *Gazette de santé*, and began to publish articles concerning problems of lunacy. In 1785 he also translated, and was influenced by, *First Lines of the Practice of Physick*, by the Scottish physician William Cullen.

Interest in understanding and treating the insane developed around the time of the French Revolution. Several physicians, in Italy and in the German states, had suggested reforms. As just one example, in Florence in 1788 Vincenzo Chiarugi demanded improved conditions for the mentally ill. In England, in 1792 Quakers under the aegis of William Tuke, a layman, planned what became the York Retreat, which emphasized fresh air, decent food, and wholesome occupations instead of shackles and beatings.

But the Revolution gave direction to Pinel's work and spread its influence. In 1793 he was appointed director of Bicêtre, the general hospital for men in Paris. Here he discovered that pandemonium reigned, and he later wrote that "everything presented to me the appearance of chaos and confusion." Removing chains from the insane, on the initiative of his administrator, Jean Baptiste Pussin, had good results. Pinel eventually developed a therapeutic approach that he called "moral treatment," which, according to some, "represented the first attempt at individual psychotherapy." Pinel's accounts of his mental patients are early versions of today's case histories in psychotherapy. He became the first to urge physicians, for therapeutic purposes, to learn compassionately about the lives of their mentally ill patients.

Pinel's concept of "moral treatment" is a psychological theory, an alternative to treating the insane by manipulating the body. Instead of constraint or such remedies as bleeding and cupping, "gentleness" is a basic strategy that presupposes the basic humanity of the patient. The authority of the physician is another of Pinel's principles—recognition that the patient has some capacity to react to another. The therapeutic aim in any event is to extirpate the pathological ideas that have laid siege to the patient's mind. Management of "passions" was for Pinel a major goal.

Although he would use the straitjacket when he deemed it necessary, he avoided most violent treatments.

A scientific and practical typology of the mental disorders was a further outcome of Pinel's work when, in 1801, he published *Traité médicophilosophique sur l'aliénation mentale (A Treatise on Insanity)*. Recognizing the limitations of classification based on imperfect knowledge, he retained the categories of mania, melancholy, dementia, and idiocy. He considered that heredity, predisposition, and what he called "individual sensitivity" could be factors in the development of mental illness.

In 1795 Pinel was appointed to Salpêtrière, Paris's general hospital for women, where he would stay for the rest of his career. At this huge institution, with as many as five thousand patients, there was a large ward for the mentally ill. From this station, Pinel's influence on the problems of treating mental illness was directly felt in Europe. Pinel himself examined, treated, and reported on hundreds of individual patients. The Parisian medical establishment, with increasing authority, "adopted the moral treatment on its own initiative beginning in the 1790s," writes Jan Goldstein, "and used it to ground claims for the establishment of a new psychiatric specialty." A generation of physicians, taught by Pinel, disseminated his thought.

Pinel's ideas, it should be noted, did not create a consensus. From the outset they were challenged to some extent by the Catholic Church. In the latter part of the nineteenth century the work of Emil Kraepelin would establish a more pessimistic attitude toward treatment, built on the belief that insanity represents a diseased brain. Although there are consensual aspects to diagnosis, intellectual disagreements on most aspects of treatment continue to characterize psychiatry today.

Although he is most remembered for his work with the insane, in his own time Pinel was considered an internist, and his influence on medicine was more general. He recognized the importance of taxonomy, and in 1798 he published his *Nosographie philosophique, ou la méthode de l'analyse appliquée à la médecine*. This textbook, which would undergo six revisions over the next twenty years, made Pinel one of the most famous and influential European physicians of his time. He was himself strongly influenced by the taxonomies of Carolus Linnaeus, and broadly speaking, his conception of disease as an entity that follows a natural course is not wrong. "He wanted, as practical-minded doctors had again and again wanted before his day," writes Henry Sigerist, "to extricate medical science from uncertainty, so that it should no longer grope in the dark." Although his classificatory scheme did not long survive, it was an important influence on the physiological scheme of Xavier Bichat (p. 58).

Pinel's work makes a strong impression, even today, with respect to its scientific character. In therapeutics he was conservative, partly because he conducted rigorous experiments with drugs. Some of his pet dislikes were unfortunate: he used neither quinine for malaria nor opium for pain. But he strongly approved of the stethoscope when it was introduced in 1816 by René Laennec (p. 62). One is not surprised to find that Pinel, soon after the publication of the convincing book on smallpox vaccination by Edward Jenner (p. 152), opened the first clinic for inoculations in 1799 at Salpêtrière.

In 1792 Pinel married Jeanne Vincent, with whom he had three sons. One of them, Scipion, became a well-known psychiatrist who, envious of his father's fame, spread the oft-repeated tale of Pinel's unchaining the inmates at Bicêtre, the better to depict him as an "irrelevant philanthropist." After he was widowed in 1811, Pinel married Marie-Madeleine Jacquelin-Lavallée. He possessed a serene personality, and his friendliness was an asset in surviving the French Revolution. "Almost imperturbable yet sensitive," wrote Gregory Zilboorg years ago, "he was polite, composed, matter of fact yet quick witted." When a young friend suffered from depression, Pinel asked him a favor. "Please come to see me every day," he wrote him, "and let us read together a few pages of Montaigne, Plutarch, and Hippocrates."

# Edward Jenner [1749–1823]

## Vaccination Against Smallpox

S mallpox was "the most terrible of all the ministers of death," as historian Thomas Macaulay described it. It is estimated to have claimed some 40 million lives worldwide during the eighteenth century, and in some years it was responsible for up to ten percent of all deaths. Smallpox killed up to fifty percent of the time, while victims who survived might be left sterile, blind, or disfigured. Indeed, it was sometimes called the "speckled monster." In organized medicine, practical helplessness against the scourge ended with the introduction of the first vaccine in 1796 by Edward Jenner.

Often portrayed by popular writers as a humble country doctor who came upon vaccination through sharp observation, Edward Jenner in fact emerged from a highly influential segment of British medicine. He was a pupil and close friend of the great physician John Hunter (p. 140) and a member of the Royal Society. He was also a naturalist and ornithologist, a musician, and, while not an exceptional medical writer, a poet. Although the smallpox vaccination is not, by most standards, a great scientific break-through—without the germ theory of disease, Jenner could not explain the result—it became an important symbol of medical advance. Today, smallpox has become the only contagious disease ever to be effectively eliminated worldwide from the human population.

Edward Jenner was born on May 17, 1749, the third son and youngest of six children of Sarah and Stephen Jenner, a clergyman and landowner. His birthplace was Berkeley, a vicarage in Gloucester still renowned for its sour, tasty cheese. After the deaths of his parents when he was just five years old, Edward was raised by his uncle, also a clergyman. After a classi-cal elementary education he was apprenticed, at about age thirteen, to Daniel Ludlow, a local surgeon, with whom he studied for about seven years. In 1770 Edward moved to London to continue his education. He became one of the favorite pupils of John Hunter, under whom he worked at St. George's Hospital, serving as his assistant in anatomy. Jenner did not take a formal medical degree until years later, in 1792, at age forty-three, from St. Andrew's University.

To practice medicine, meanwhile, Jenner returned to Berkeley in 1773. Although he was to remain a country doctor until the end of his life, he

retained his ties with John Hunter, now his friend and colleague. The two corresponded extensively. Jenner was himself a naturalist, and from the Gloucester countryside and along the Severn River he collected specimens for Hunter's famous museum in London, sending along such finds as a cuckoo's stomach, eels, porpoise bones, and salmon spawn. His observations of the cuckoo's breeding habits led to his being elected, in 1789, to the Royal Society.

Smallpox was an ancient disease, and the story of vaccination begins with various practices of inoculation, originally outside the Western medical tradition. The Chinese used to blow flakes from the disease's scabs into the nostrils of healthy patients, and similar means of preempting the illness were used in Persia and, perhaps, in India. The famous physician and philosopher Muhammad ibn Zakariya' al-Razi (in the West known as Rhazes) wrote the first comprehensive treatise on smallpox, *Liber de pestilentia,* in the ninth century A.D.

The direct ancestor of Jenner's smallpox vaccine was promoted in the early eighteenth century by Lady Mary Wortley Montagu. Living in Constantinople as the wife of the British ambassador, she had learned of "engrafting." This was a practice of certain Turkish women, who would scratch the skin with a pin that had been dipped into a smallpox sore. A case of the disease would follow, but in most instances it was not fatal. Lady Montagu, who had suffered from smallpox herself and lost her brother to it, was especially sensitive to its ravages. She successfully protected her son in this way in 1721 and lobbied for more general use of what came to be known as "inoculation." Princess Caroline of Anspach, wife of King George II, had the royal children inoculated during an epidemic, and they did not contract smallpox.

Inoculation, however, did not represent a plausible solution on a large scale. "Inoculation hospitals" for variolation were available in the eighteenth century, especially for well-to-do families. Jenner himself had been inoculated as a child, in an unpleasant experience that involved a course of bleeding, purging, and quarantine. George Washington had the Continental Army inoculated during the American Revolution, and there were other instances of mass variolation. This person-to-person procedure carried a risk — estimated at three to five percent — that the full-blown illness would develop and prove fatal. This high mortality rate prevented variolation from becoming more widely employed, and made it largely a province of specialists.

Jenner's development of the smallpox vaccine from cowpox pustules was in essence the result of insight into the pertinence of folk wisdom. Even as an apprentice, Jenner was aware of the belief around Gloucestershire that, once milkmaids and dairymen caught cowpox, a disease which mainly afflicted cattle, they were immune from smallpox. One local farmer, Benjamin Jesty, was known to have vaccinated his family with cowpox using a darning needle. Jenner investigated the issue as early as 1775. He came to distinguish two types of cowpox. One type he viewed as the true form of the disease, which he believed appeared in humans as smallpox. Indeed, after about seven years' practice in Berkeley, Jenner had formulated a theory about the transmission and possible prevention of the disease.

On May 14, 1796, Jenner took some pus from a sore on the hand of Sarah Nelmes, a dairy maid whom he knew to be suffering from cowpox. With this he vaccinated, via superficial incisions, an eight-year-old boy, James Phipps. Shortly thereafter, James came down with a fever and a pustule sore that scabbed and scarred. But that was all. Six weeks later, Jenner challenged the reaction by injecting James with matter from smallpox sores, taken from a recent case. In ethical terms, it should be said that Jenner's procedure, although not fully defensible in tody's terms, was essentially variolation; he was not necessarily courting any greater risk. In any event, to Jenner's relief, James remained well, as he did when the challenge was repeated several months later. (James would live to be an old man.) Encouraged, Jenner tried several more cases over the next year, with the same success.

Reaction to Jenner's work on smallpox was initially skeptical. His paper about his procedure for inoculation was rejected by the Royal Society. In consequence Jenner prepared *An Inquiry into the Causes and Effects of the Variolae Vaccinae*, which he published privately in 1798. A brief book of seventy-five pages, Jenner included records of twenty-three cases of immunity induced by inoculation. *An Inquiry* received a loud and controversial reception. But most importantly, as Alfred W. Crosby writes, "a member of the elite had introduced an account of the technique [of inoculation] into print for the whole world to read, and that made all the difference." Indeed, within several years Jenner's book had been translated into the major European languages.

Promoting the smallpox vaccine became Jenner's principal activity by the turn of the nineteenth century. For a time it was widely adopted in England, by everyone from doctors to school teachers. Some attacked it, including the influential Thomas Malthus, who viewed anything that might increase the numbers of the poor as misguided. Eventually, however, the vaccine was distributed throughout the British empire. In the United States, Benjamin Waterhouse promoted the vaccine, which led President Thomas Jefferson to have his family and neighbors inoculated. In Vienna, Jean de Caro championed its use throughout Europe. Napoleon promoted the vaccine and personally admired Jenner.*

Smallpox prevention, however, was not simple in the early nineteenth century. To be potent, the vaccine had to drawn from pustules. To transport it to America, for example, unimmunized boys were used as reservoirs. Like all prophylactic measures, Jenner's vaccine was only as good as the public health system, which in England was not far advanced in 1800. By 1808 the British government had set up a National Vaccine Establishment, a publicly-funded program that provided free vaccine to practitioners, but this did not ensure mass vaccination. And so, through the first half of the nineteenth century, local epidemics continued to occur. Further government action in 1841, in the wake of several years of severe epidemic, lowered the death rate, but smallpox still claimed some five thousand lives in 1850. Infant vaccination was made compulsory in Britain in 1853. An excellent indication of the vaccine's worth would come during the Franco-Prussian War in 1871. Some twenty thousand unvaccinated French conscripts died of smallpox, compared to only a small number of German soldiers: the Germans had been vaccinated. By World War I, among some four million soldiers, only 853 smallpox cases were recorded, of which only 14 were fatal.

As his work became appreciated, Jenner was showered with honors — but at the expense of his practice. He was soon broke. Parliament rewarded him with £10,000 in 1802, and twice that sum five years later. In 1804, even though France and England were at war, Napoleon struck a medal in Jenner's honor. The chieftains of the Five Indian Nations sent Jenner a belt and a string of wampum and, in addition, petitioned "the Great Spirit to take care of you in this world and in the land of the spirits." This gesture was poignant: Smallpox had been exported to North America by Europeans and had decimated the Native Americans.

---

*That the terms *vaccine* and *vaccination* became generic is owed to Louis Pasteur (p. 18), who proposed them in honor of "the merit and immense services rendered by one of the greatest men of England, your Jenner."

Jenner, who called fame a "gilded butt, for ever pierced with the arrows of malignancy," was well liked for his charm and personality. After once being jilted as a young doctor, Edward Jenner married Catharine Kingscote in 1788. They raised four children in their country house in Berkeley. After Catharine died, in 1815, Jenner seldom left his natal vicarage. He lived through a mild stroke in 1820 but did not survive another one three years later, and died on January 26, 1823.

Smallpox is the only contagious disease ever to have been eliminated from the human population. The last case in the United States was recorded in 1949; with new techniques of vaccine manufacture, the smallpox virus became a candidate for worldwide eradication by the 1950s. The World Health Organization (WHO) adopted a resolution to this end as early as 1958, and eventually carried out an extensive program of vaccination in the developing world that reached the remotest corners of the earth—where as late as 1966 an estimated two million people died from smallpox. This program was a success, however, and the last cases of the disease were reported in Somalia in 1977 and in England in 1978. Eradication was certified in 1980.

However, another part of the WHO strategy was a plan to destroy the last stocks of smallpox virus. This proved to be an interesting utopian dream, originating during the Cold War era, that eventually ran into a series of real-world obstacles. First, advent of the deadly AIDS epidemic eroded the fantasy of being able to abolish infectious diseases. In addition, advances in molecular biology suggested that the smallpox genome might contain potentially useful biological information, of particular concern in an era in which germ warfare could pose a significant threat. This was especially the case after the end of compulsory smallpox vaccination left large populations vulnerable to an epidemic. Until its collapse, the Soviet Union seems to have pursued the use of smallpox as a potential weapon, and today it may be on the secret agenda of several governments and terrorist organizations. In brief, two hundred years after Edward Jenner vaccinated young James Phipps, smallpox was vanquished but had not vanished, while the larger prospect of conquering infectious diseases had essentially come and gone.

# William Thomas Green Morton [1819-1868]

## The Demonstration of Anesthesia

Anesthesia was the first great medical breakthrough to be made in the United States, and so it is fitting that the tale of its discovery combines avarice and invention, not to mention insanity. Its significance is beyond doubt. A substance and method to deaden the senses was past due by the 1840s. Neither alcohol nor the more effective drug, opium, could relieve pain during invasive surgery. Anesthesia, together with the subsequent introduction of antiseptics, would enable a revolution. The demonstration of ether in 1846, writes Ulrich Tröhler, "can be seen as a heroic landmark in the history of modern surgery."

Anesthesia was not the invention of a single individual or even a team working together. Indeed, the lack of a systematic effort to discover it reminds us that modern medical research was based first of all in the autopsy room, where cessation of pain has already occurred. Several individuals in the backwater of medicine actually hit upon a chemical solution to pain at about the same time. The dramatic demonstration in 1846 at Boston's Massachusetts General Hospital was the key event, for the setting conferred the power of prestige. It is through a confluence of circumstances, not genius, that the major credit for this demonstration goes to a dentist, William Thomas G. Morton.

Born in Charlton City, Massachusetts, on August 8, 1819, William Thomas Green Morton was the son of a shopkeeper and landholder. His father was ambitious for him, and William, as he later avowed, wanted from an early age to be a doctor, and made pills for friends from bread and leaves. He was too poor, however, to enter medical school. For a time he may have attended the Baltimore College of Dentistry. In 1843 he moved to Boston. Acutely aware of his limited education, Morton sought to improve himself. He began attending Harvard Medical School the next year and joined Boston's scientific and intellectual community. He boarded with and engaged as a private tutor the chemist Charles T. Jackson, who was gifted but also moody and sometimes grandiose. Morton's success in bettering himself is indicated by his marriage, in 1844, to Elisabeth Whitman. Her highly regarded family overcame its objections to Morton's origins.

But most significantly, Morton became partners in a dental business with Horace Wells in Boston in 1843. The older Wells, a well-known dentist and author of a book on dental care, must have been impressed by Morton's ingenuity. In any event, together they took up the vexing problem of creating improved dentures. In a city such as Boston, with both wealthy Brahmins and an expanding middle class, there existed a strong demand for good teeth. Hoping to become rich, Morton and Wells worked on a spring-free denture plate. Their enterprise was impeded, however, by the requirement that, to insert the plate for the false teeth, all roots and stumps of the patient's original teeth had first to be removed. This was a bloody, excruciatingly painful procedure. Wells soon gave up the partnership and returned to his home in Hartford, Connecticut. Morton, for his part, prospered with his private dental practice. But he was acutely aware of the pain suffered by his patients and of the need for a reliable anesthetic.

The chemicals that would be used in anesthetics had long been available. Sulfuric ether dated from 1540, and in 1819 its properties were discussed by the chemist John Dalton. Nitrous oxide had been first described by Joseph Priestley in 1772, and Sir Humphry Davy had recognized its potential for surgery in 1799. Although these substances were not employed in medicine, "laughing gas" and ether became the stock-in-trade of traveling showmen, especially in the rural, entertainment-starved regions of the United States. Inhaling the gas would induce a harmless, limited euphoria. Audience participation hilarity provided a crucial avenue for the discovery of anesthesia.

In 1842, Crawford Long, a doctor in Georgia, administered ether to a friend before excising two tumors from his neck. Although he performed several more operations, and obtained affidavits of the efficacy of ether, he did not trumpet his discovery or spell out its broader implications. And in 1844, Horace Wells, Morton's erstwhile partner, also recognized the value of "laughing gas." Using it, he had one of his own teeth pulled without pain. "A new era in tooth-pulling," he is said to have remarked. The next year, with Morton's help, Wells attempted to demonstrate the benefits of nitrous oxide at the Massachusetts General Hospital. He failed: he did not administer enough of the gas to dull sensation, and the patient screamed in agony.

However, beginning in the summer of 1846, Morton himself began experiments on ether. By his own later admission, he learned more about sulfuric ether from Charles Jackson without telling him about his aims; he was, he wrote, not "possessed by the most disinterested spirit of philosophic enthusiasm, clear of all regard from personal rights and benefits." He worked in secret, fearing that whatever process he devised would be stolen. His early experiments involved worms, insects, goldfish, and even a dog. Morton could not be sure of his results, partly because animals cannot talk. But he tried sulfuric ether on himself with considerable success. On September 30, 1846, Morton received at his offices a cracker maker who bore the beautiful name Eben Frost. Frightened at the prospect of suffering, yet already in pain from a decayed bicuspid, Frost needed an immediate extraction. Morton had little trouble convincing Eben to inhale ether. Throughout the operation, Frost slept. Upon awakening he attested to the fact that he had felt no pain.

Morton's historic demonstration of anesthesia took place two weeks later. It was arranged with the help of John Collins Warren, a founder of Massachusetts General Hospital and an eminent professor of surgery at Harvard University. He was pleased to help Morton try to show the effectiveness of ether, just as he had been open to Horace Wells. Morton worked feverishly over several days to create an inhalation apparatus. He came up with a sponge, soaked in ether, within a glass vessel fitted with valves to ensure proper dosage.

On October 16, 1846, Morton arrived late and breathless as Dr. Warren prepared to excise a tumor on the neck of a young man, Gilbert Abbott. He administered the gas and told Dr. Warren, "Your patient is ready, sir." Dramatically, Abbott did not respond when Warren made the initial cut. After the operation the young man said, "No. It didn't hurt at all, although my neck did feel for a minute as if someone were scraping it with a hoe." Now Dr. Warren turned to the assembled surgeons and students and said, "Gentlemen, this is no humbug."

Word of this demonstration created an international sensation. Another operation was performed the next day, with the same pain-free result. On November 18 a professional paper by Henry Bigelow announced the procedure, and in December anesthesia was used successfully in England for an amputation by surgeon Robert Liston. Although it would be some years before anesthesia was used systematically in surgery and in dentistry, its value was no longer in doubt. "Unrestrained and free as God's own sunshine," Morton wrote later, "[ether] has gone forth to cheer and gladden the earth; it will awaken the gratitude of the present, and all coming generations."

In fact, one of Morton's principal motivations was to obtain a patent and make money. He was not avaricious, he maintained, but "I am not able to be a philanthropist. I must make a living out of this discovery." It did not prove easy. Ether unimproved could not be patented, and so Morton called his substance "Letheon" and planned to license its use for a hefty fee to individual doctors. He came in for considerable criticism by seeking such financial gain. The fact that his apparatus was no better than a doused handkerchief did not help. When military doctors simply began using ether anyway, particularly during the Mexican War, Morton's intellectual cache was lost. And, having sacrificed his dental practice, Morton now acquired a large debt.

When Morton's patent effort came to nought, he sought out the eminent physicians and surgeons at Massachusetts General Hospital. They agreed to help him gain formal recognition and compensation from the U.S. Congress. This was a good idea. Governments can always gain a public relations advantage by granting a citizen a small monetary reward for a great discovery. However, there now loomed the issue of who, in fact, had discovered ether anesthesia. As has happened many times since in the history of medicine, a priority dispute erupted. No fewer than four principals were involved: Morton, his former teacher Charles Jackson, his former partner Horace Wells, and the Georgian doctor Crawford Long. All except Jackson have had their defenders, in terms of their rights of priority, up through the twentieth century.

The complex tale of Morton and his adversaries—a lesson in the problems created by claiming the air as one's own invention—will be simplified here. Briefly, in 1849 Crawford Long emerged from obscurity to stake his claim, for which he possessed attestations on paper, but little else. He did not succeed. In later decades the subject of ether became painful for him to discuss, but he would spend hours with his affidavits, kept in a trunk in his attic. Toward the end of his life, in the wake of Southern pride following the Civil War, his claim was revived. Historian James Thomas Flexner supported Long as codiscoverer with Morton in a famous article entitled "The Death of Pain."

Charles Jackson, Morton's chemistry tutor, made numerous efforts to claim priority, both in the United States and in France, where his reputation as a chemist gave him entrée into all sorts of official precincts. But Jackson was clearly unbalanced. He had earlier sued Samuel Morse over invention of the telegraph and would eventually claim to have invented guncotton, an explosive. Jackson spent the last years of his life, from 1873 till his death in 1880, in a mental asylum.

Morton's former partner, Horace Wells, did not fare better. Soon after Morton presented his petition claiming priority, Wells also went to Washington, and later to France. But Wells's life also unraveled. In 1848 Wells was arrested for throwing acid in the face of a woman whom he accosted one evening on Broadway in New York. In prison, he opened a femoral artery and committed suicide. This end did not help Morton. Wells's wife then claimed that her husband had been driven insane and had killed himself because Morton had stolen his discovery.

Morton himself, on account of the priority battle, believed he was being persecuted, and he became a physical wreck. Each refusal of Congress to grant him compensation—there were several petitions—caused him more grief. He was in financial straits for the rest of his life. Flexner's 1868 article reviving Long's assertion to have discovered ether brought Morton to the edge of a nervous breakdown. He went to New York and soon asked his wife to join him, for he was sick. On July 15, 1868, they went riding in a coach in Washington Heights in Upper Manhattan. It was in the midst of a heat wave, and Morton apparently suffered a stroke. He died that day.

It is sometimes said that the discovery of anesthesia was "overdue" or "postmature," and in a sense this is certainly true. But if one considers how doctors perceived and thought about their patients' experience of pain, the delay is not so surprising. Reading Morton's essay on anesthesia, one sees why a generation separates the invention of, say, the stethoscope and the use of ether. Once given the anesthetic, writes Morton, "the patient should be told, in a loud, distinct tone, to open his eyes; and, if he does *not* do so, the operation should be immediately commenced." To ignore a patient's objective reactions to pain is one thing; for a doctor to have to infer insensitivity to pain is something different. This is the context by which Morton's significance, born of perseverance and a willingness to entertain such ideas, may be judged. In her recent history, *Ether Day,* Julie M. Fenster judges Morton a "thinking opportunist" and "not a great man at all, but a man who had given the world a great discovery." On a monument in Mount Auburn Cemetery in Cambridge, Massachusetts, are lines by the surgeon, Dr. Jacob Bigelow. William Thomas Green Morton—

> *Inventor. Revealer of Anaesthetic Inhalation.*
> *By whom pain in surgery was averted and annulled.*
> *Before whom in all time surgery was agony.*
> *Since whom science has control of pain.*

# John Snow [1813–1858]

## Field Epidemiology Begins at the Broad Street Pump

For nearly two centuries after the plague of 1665, England was free of serious epidemics. But in 1831, thanks to travel, trade, and colonialist expansion, cholera reached England, probably from Asia. Eventually it would touch virtually every country the world over. Cholera can begin with diarrhea and spasmodic vomiting, and end in death within hours. It became the century's classic scourge, creating immense consternation and, before the advent of the germ theory of disease, much confusion. But in 1854, the British physician John Snow recognized that cholera was caused not by general conditions of filth, but by some specific agent in the London water supply.

The story of Snow and the Broad Street pump is one of the first great successes in the field of public health, and it constitutes the beginning of modern field epidemiology. Snow's work, coming a generation before the foundation of the germ theory of disease, complements the work of Pierre Louis (p. 75) and the birth of clinical epidemiology. It also underscores the pragmatic aim of the study of disease distribution: to discover and break the chain of transmission, even if the causative organism remains unknown. Snow, an eminent physician, was also famous in his day for advocating and developing the use of anesthesia in England.

Much of what is known about the early life and personality of John Snow, who was from a working-class background, comes from a memoir written by a friend. He was the eldest of nine children, born on March 15, 1813, in York. His father was an unskilled laborer who apparently had higher aspirations for his children at a moment in history when they might be realized. John attended a private school, or day school, which in England at the time meant a school for poor children. John apparently did well, especially in mathematics. At age fourteen, probably with the help of a relatively affluent uncle, he left York for Newcastle. There he worked at the local infirmary and entered the service of surgeon and apothecary William Hardcastle. His apprenticeship began in 1827 and lasted six years.

In 1836, after three years' practice, Snow moved to London and studied at the Windmill Street School. He qualified as a surgeon two years later, at age twenty-five. Continuing his studies, he received a bachelor of medicine

degree at the University of London in 1843 and a doctorate in medicine the year after. Snow's extensive education was not required for him to practice as a family physician, but it enabled him to advance socially. It also inclined him to scientific investigation.

From his home and office on Frith Street, Snow closely followed new developments in medicine. His practice was not heavy at first, perhaps because he was studious and shy. He wrote papers, such as "On Asphyxia, and on the resuscitation of still-born children," from 1841. Most important was his work with anesthesia, introduced in Britain in 1846 within weeks of William Morton's (p. 157) demonstration of it in the United States. Snow immediately perceived that procedures needed to be standardized to avoid a high percentage of failures. Working first with ether and later with chloroform, Snow developed an improved inhaler and performed experiments upon a variety of animals and upon himself to better determine dosage and administration. With the publication in 1847 of a small book entitled *On the Inhalation of the Vapour of Ether in Surgical Operations,* Snow became the celebrated expert in England. He was twice called to anesthetize Queen Victoria, and had great success in doing so.

Snow's work on cholera begins with the epidemic of 1848, which caused a devastating 53,000 deaths in England alone. Snow had first encountered cholera while an apprentice at Newcastle, when it struck the area's coal miners. In 1849, a year after the first round of the new epidemic, Snow published a brief pamphlet in which he doubted the current theory that the disease was airborne and contagious by inhaling putrid gases known as "miasma." He argued instead the case for transmission via the water supply. This hypothesis guided him toward a serious epidemiological study. Snow came to believe that cholera was due to fecal contamination of water and that the disease-causing particles were too small to be seen.

The next serious round of the epidemic enabled Snow to test his views. He focused on "the most terrible outbreak . . . which ever occurred in this kingdom"—which was in a small area around Broad Street, Golden Square, in August 1854. When more than five hundred people died of cholera over the course of ten days, Snow suspected the water that residents drew from a common street pump. With help from the city bureaucracy, he compiled a record of some eighty-three deaths that had occurred over a three-day period; almost all these victims had drunk from the Broad Street pump. Snow convinced the Board of Guardians in St. James Parish to disable the pump by removing its handle. Although new cases were already declining, the death rate for the area's inhabitants now sharply declined. In 1854 Snow discussed his involvement with the nascent epidemic in a second version of his 1849 pamphlet, "On the Mode of Communication of Cholera."

Importantly, Snow developed corroborating evidence, making use of effective control groups. He noted that workers in a brewery on Broad Street did not fall ill, and that the plant had its own water well. Inmates in a nearby workhouse with a pump-well on premises also escaped the disease. By contrast, a number of workers in a percussion-cap factory that was supplied with water from the Broad Street pump became sick.

Still more convincing was Snow's South London water supply study, in which he traced the source of water from several companies. The Vauxhall and Southwark companies took their water from the Thames, downstream of considerable discharge of raw sewage. Households from these two companies had a death rate from cholera of some 71 cases per 10,000 households. The Lambeth company's water pumps, by contrast, were located upstream of the outfall. Lambeth households had only 5 deaths per 10,000. Cleaner water meant less cholera.

Snow's work had its effect—he spoke to a select committee of the House of Commons in 1855—but was not considered definitive. His views were contested, ironically, by sanitarians, who believed cholera was essentially a disease of environmental filth. Snow's inability to locate the agent responsible weighed against him. Only in 1883 would Robert Koch (p. 24), working with cholera patients in Egypt and in Calcutta, identify and isolate the *Vibrio cholerae*. London in the meantime had undertaken a vast civil engineering project to clean its water supply—provoked not by Snow's work, however, but by the famous "Great Stink" of 1858 that had forced a halt to the proceedings of Parliament.

By the mid-1850s Snow had become an eminent figure in British medicine. In 1855 he was elected president of the Medical Society of London. In his personal habits he was irreproachable, if one can believe the memoir composed by his friend and younger colleague Benjamin Ward Richardson. Retiring, generous, mildly eccentric, Snow was a vegetarian all his adult life. He never touched alcohol. Indeed, he was a temperance crusader. But these virtues did not result in a long life. John Snow died on June 16, 1858, at age forty-five.

# Ignaz Semmelweis [1818–1865]
## Tragic Insight into Childbed Fever

Behind doctors' self-admonition to "Wash your hands" lies an intriguing tale, complete with tragedy. In 1850 Ignaz Semmelweis, a Hungarian physician practicing in Vienna, proposed that puerperal fever, a fatal and too common disease, was transmitted to women during childbirth by physicians themselves. Invisible particles clinging to the fingers, Semmelweis maintained, were deposited in the uterus, causing disease and death. Although his arguments were buttressed by dramatic clinical evidence, Semmelweis's hypothesis was attacked by conservative forces. He continued to fight for his views for over a decade, even as sanity deserted him. "[Y]ou are a murderer . . . ," he wrote one of his opponents not long before his death, and it "would not be unjust to you if [history] memorialized you as a medical Nero, in payment for having been the first to set himself against my life-saving doctrine."

Ignaz Philipp Semmelweis was born on July 1, 1818, in Buda, Hungary; his family was of German extraction. His father, Joseph, was a prosperous shopkeeper; his mother was Terézia Müller. From 1835 until 1837, Ignaz studied law at the University of Pest. He initially planned to join the Austrian bureaucracy and moved to Vienna to continue his legal education. But medicine attracted him, and he entered the Second Vienna Medical School, well known for its amalgam of clinical and laboratory medicine, receiving his degree in 1844. Semmelweis subsequently took a brief course in midwifery and qualified as a surgeon. He decided to specialize in obstetrics at a time when it was still essentially a branch of surgery limited to delivering babies. But importantly, Semmelweis also had considerable training in anatomy and dissection.

Childbed, or puerperal, fever had become epidemic in various countries in Europe during the seventeenth century. At the Vienna General Hospital, where in 1846 Semmelweis was appointed assistant professor in the maternity department, it was a serious problem. Indeed, the mortality rate in the obstetrical ward over the two decades preceding his arrival had risen tenfold. The disease essentially referred to serious infections in the reproductive organs appearing soon after delivery. In an era before antibiotics—most cases were probably due to streptococcal infections—the frequent outcome was death.

Semmelweis's insight into this persistent, recurrent tragedy and vexing problem came through careful reasoning and an unusual concatenation of circumstances. At the Vienna General Hospital there were two maternity clinics. The First Maternity Clinic, in which Semmelweis worked, was staffed by physicians. In 1839 a second clinic had been set up with a view to instructing midwives. While the two clinics had a similar clientele, they produced vastly divergent statistics for mortality from childbed fever. In the physician-staffed first clinic in 1846, maternal deaths were 13.10 percent; in the midwives' clinic, mortality was only 2.03 percent. These numbers caused much puzzlement among doctors and terrible anxiety for expectant mothers. "One has to watch the heart-rending scenes with individuals kneeling and wringing their hands," wrote Semmelweis in his diary, "begging to be released, having wished to go to the second clinic and . . . being sent to the other."

Viennese physicians considered several explanations. Most were related to "miasma" and other atmosphere-related theories, but with the two clinics adjacent to each other, how could any such interpretation succeed? Indeed, some physicians resorted to extravagant speculations. They wondered, for example, whether the frequent appearance of priests on the ward might account for the disease. Johann Klein, director of the First Maternity Clinic and Semmelweis's direct superior, himself suggested that male doctors (as opposed to female midwives) brought on the disease by offending women's modesty. Semmelweis explicitly did not share these hypotheses. "I could not understand how fear, a psychological condition," he wrote, "could bring about such physical changes as occur in childbed fever."

From his conviction that the various explanations were untenable, Semmelweis set out to discover the real cause of the high rate of mortality in the physicians' maternity clinic. An important clue came when a friend and colleague at the hospital, Jacob Kolletschka, died after receiving a puncture wound while performing a dissection. At Kolletschka's autopsy, Semmelweis observed pathological changes similar to those seen in the victims of childbed fever. In place of an atmospheric explanation, Semmelweis began to consider the possibility that some "decaying animal-organic matter" caused the disease. The chain of infection became clear when he realized that students in the maternity clinic often arrived at the lying-in ward directly from the dissecting room. (Dissection and pathological anatomy were emphasized in the curriculum at Vienna.) Students' hands, Semmelweis realized, might bear the substance that caused the fatal infection.

Beginning in May 1847, Semmelweis demanded that his students cleanse their hands with a solution of chlorinated lime and scrub their fingernails using a brush. Before the end of the year, the mortality rate for childbed fever had dropped to 3.04 percent, and during the next year, to 1.27 percent. This was a startling decline. Semmelweis continued to improve his preventive measures and began cleaning instruments as well as hands.

Semmelweis himself did not publish his results immediately. Rather, they were presented in the leading Viennese medical journal with the support of one of his former teachers, the eminent clinician Joseph Skoda. Semmelweis also had the support of Carl Rokitansky, a champion of pathological anatomy. But other powerful figures in the Viennese medical establishment did not accept Semmelweis's views—although some admitted that hand washing might be a good idea on sanitary grounds. Semmelweis's evidence was circumstantial and statistical—compelling but not decisive. His major adversary was Klein, head of the clinic, who in March 1849 refused to renew Semmelweis's appointment. In addition, the ministry of education refused to create a commission to investigate his claims. Semmelweis was clearly disappointed, but for a long while he seemed unable to react with appropriate rhetorical force.

Finally, in May 1849 Semmelweis spoke out in a lecture before the Vienna Medical Society. Every case of childbed fever, he suggested, was due to decayed matter that passed into the genital tract during parturition. This strong view would be at odds with a multifactorial theory of the disease that would remain dominant through the 1850s. In a book published in 1855, Carl Braun, an eminent obstetrician, listed no fewer than thirty possible causes of childbed fever. Braun disliked Semmelweis intensely, and neglected his viewpoint.

Without a hospital post or a means to perform research, Semmelweis left Vienna suddenly in late 1850—much to the detriment of his theory. He returned to Hungary. In 1851 he became head of the maternity ward at St. Rochus Hospital, and in 1855 he was appointed to a chair of midwifery at the University of Pest. Again, Semmelweis enjoyed considerable success in combating childbed fever at his clinic, instituting strict hand-washing procedures as well as more general measures, such as adequate ventilation and clean linen and bandages.

In 1860 Semmelweis published his major work, *Die Aetiologie, der Begriff und die Prophylaxis des Kindbettfiebers (The Etiology, the Concept and Prophylaxis of Childbed Fever)*. Written in German, it was discussed through the rest of the decade. The book was replete with statistics and was argued with force. But it also contained much brooding and bitter polemic. Several unfavorable reviews led Semmelweis to respond with a series of open letters in which he gave vent to considerable hostility. In one he wrote, "I myself will say to the helpless public, 'You, father of a family, do you know what it is to summon an obstetrician or a midwife to your wife? . . . It is as much to expose your wife and your yet unborn child to the danger of death.'" In another, to the influential obstetrician Joseph Spaeth, Semmelweis wrote, "This murder must cease, and in order that the murder cease, I will keep watch, and anyone who dares to propagate dangerous errors about childbed fever will find in me an eager adversary."

The paranoid flavor of Semmelweis's outbursts in this final period may have been due to organic brain disease. Opinions differ on the diagnosis. Sherwin Nuland has suggested he suffered from early-onset Alzheimer's disease; tertiary syphilis is another possibility. In 1863 Semmelweis apparently suffered a physical breakdown, and by 1865 his wife, Maria, could no longer care for him. In August of that year, she took him to Vienna, and he was committed to an asylum for the insane. He died just two weeks later.

Ignaz Semmelweis's influence remains a complex issue. Thirty years after his death, Joseph Lister (p. 94) recognized Semmelweis's contribution as having predated his own work. Thereafter, he was held up in popular histories as an example of the visionary innovator unable to uproot entrenched dogma. "It is always difficult to overcome human stupidity," wrote Hermann Glasscheib, "and even more difficult to jolt human beings out of their indolence." By this view, Semmelweis's work, done a generation before the establishment of the germ theory of disease, survives as a splendid case of heroic insight married to statistical analysis—but it was not very influential.

At a distance of a century and more, however, it is plausible that Semmelweis's work was more instrumental than once supposed. His theory was widely discussed during the 1860s, and quite possibly was adopted without attribution by Carl Mayrhofer, who also worked in the Vienna maternity ward. Far from being forgotten, Semmelweis was cited rather often after about 1872 in the growing literature on the germ theory of disease. His work, according to the controversial view of K. Codell Carter, "contributed importantly to the theoretical development of germ theory." In any event, less than a tragic hero, Semmelweis was victimized, writes Sherwin Nuland, by "his own faulty nature, and not, as popular historians have told us for generations, by the overwhelming gods of a backward medical establishment."

An infection not unlike puerperal fever led to Semmelweis's death, on August 13, 1865—adding irony to abject misfortune. More recently, moreover, others have noted that institutional brutality may have played a role. Sherwin Nuland, examining autopsy reports and X rays of Semmelweis's remains, concluded that he was quite possibly beaten and abused by asylum attendants. The infection that killed him may have been due to the wounds he sustained.

# Theodor Billroth [1829–1894]

## Surgery Comes of Age

Surgery reinvented itself in the late nineteenth century. While advances in physiology and pathology made it possible to understand the architecture and some of the dynamics of the human body, anesthesia and asepsis made it plausible to open it up and repair it. Theodor Billroth was well suited to be the leading innovator. He was a surgeon of great technical skill, but he was also at home in the laboratory, eager to experiment, and a celebrated teacher who drew students from all over the world. He developed operations which everyone thought possible, but only he could orchestrate. He was particularly famous for novel interventions in the gastrointestinal tract, resecting (removing all or part of) the esophagus, larynx, stomach, and pancreas. He also attempted to treat ovarian and breast cancer. If Billroth's efforts were often unsuccessful, his careful reporting of outcomes helped shape rapid progress in a complex field.

Albert Christian Theodor Billroth was born on April 26, 1829, to a family of Swedish origin on the Baltic island of Rügen, then part of Prussia. His father, Carl Theodor, was a Lutheran pastor who died in 1834 and left his wife, Christine Johanna Nagel, a widow and mother to five. Although he excelled in music, Theodor was not a superb student. He had difficulty with languages and mathematics, and was tutored remedially at home. Sensitive by temperament, he was attracted to the ministry. At his mother's urging, though, he chose medicine. He studied at the University of Greifswald for a time before moving to the University of Göttingen and then to the University of Berlin. Here Billroth received his medical degree in 1852.

For about three years Billroth looked into such specialties as dermatology and internal medicine. He had a brief and deceptively disappointing start in private practice—he went two months without a single patient—before becoming assistant to Bernhard von Langenbeck, a renowned anatomist and surgeon at the famous Charité in Berlin. Here Billroth had great success, both in the operating room and at the laboratory bench. His early research (he was an exceptional microscopist) was spent in classifying tumors of the breast and lymphoid tissue. In 1856 he was appointed a lecturer in surgery and pathological histology, beginning a teaching career that would eventually make him the most famous professor of surgery in the world.

In 1860 Billroth was offered a double appointment at the University of Zurich: professor of surgery and director of the clinic. He received over eight thousand patients during the next seven years. In 1863 Billroth's reputation was assured with the publication of a series of fifty lectures entitled *Die allgemeine chirurgische Pathologie und Chirurgie in fünfzig Vorlesungen (General Surgical Pathology and Therapeutics)*. A testament to the growing influence of science on surgery, the book became a classic and was constantly re-edited and widely translated. Billroth soon consolidated his fame with the *Handbuch der allgemeinen und speziellen Chirurgie (Handbook of General and Specialty Surgery)*, which he prepared in collaboration with Franciscus J. Pitha.

In 1867 Billroth was appointed professor of surgery at the University of Vienna, and was provided with his own clinic. Over the next twenty-seven years he would perform the surgical interventions and innovations for which he is best remembered. In 1872, he made the first resection of the esophagus, and the next year he performed a complete laryngectomy, the removal of the voice box, to treat cancer. Billroth was noted for the scrutiny to which he subjected his own work. He carefully published the results of his cases, successful or not. "Criticism is the principal need of our day," he wrote, "and for this, knowledge, experience, and calm are requisite." Billroth would make good on this throughout his *Chirurgische Klinik,* a four-volume collection of cases published from 1869 to 1876.

Initially, Billroth was not receptive to the idea of antisepsis, the key development that would empower many of his innovations. Nor was he convinced by early work on the germ theory of disease by Louis Pasteur (p. 18).* He changed his mind only in the wake of work by Robert Koch

---

*Billroth published a widely read work on the nature of wound infections. He took the view that in all probability there existed a single microbe, infinitely variable, that produced a toxin that caused infection. One intriguing result of his research was a report that the *Penicillium* fungus halted the growth of microbes in urine. The significance escaped him. Over half a century later, Howard Florey (p. 245) would develop Alexander Fleming's discovery of penicillin, the first effective antibiotic.

(p. 24) in 1878. That year, Billroth finally lent his prestige—indeed, his enthusiasm—to the concept of antiseptic (later aseptic) surgery originally promoted by Joseph Lister (p. 94). This necessary capitulation reverberated throughout the world of surgery.

Billroth's contributions to gastric surgery were most notably the eponymous operations he designed to treat stomach cancer and peptic ulcer. These were gastrectomies, removal of part or all of the stomach. He first performed the procedure that became known as Billroth I on January 29, 1881, by excising a tumor that afflicted the pyloric sphincter, which governs the passage between stomach and intestine. He then stitched what remained of the stomach to the duodenum (the first part of the small intestine). Initially the patient recovered, and within a week Billroth reported the procedure in the Vienna medical press. Like other surgeons through history, he was well aware of the significance of being the first to perform a specific operation.

Billroth II was a similar operation, developed in the hope of better long-term success. The earlier operation appeared to allow leakage, and subsequent infection, because the stomach's larger opening was a poor fit to the duodenum. Therefore, in 1885, after several years' preparation, Billroth employed an innovation that one of his students first tested in animals. Instead of reconnecting the stomach directly to the intestine after removing the cancerous tissue, he created a detour from stomach to jejunum (the midportion of the small intestine); the openings are the same size. Then he simply stitched shut the cut end of the stomach and the top of the duodenum. When Billroth's patient lived for eighteen months after the surgery, the intervention was judged a success. This operation is still employed; the first laparoscopic Billroth II was done in 1992.

Although Billroth's heroic operations opened the whole field of abdominal surgery, as might be expected in the nineteenth century, patients often did not survive very long. Thérèse Heller, for example, the first patient to undergo Billroth I, died four months after the operation. Billroth, scrupulous about reporting bad results as well as good, experimented with the limited forms of chemotherapy then available—mostly medications made from arsenic and antimony, or copper. But with cancer, long-term survival was rare.

Reliance on statistics, attention to advances in physiology, and careful preparation and training using animals all became aspects of what eventually became known as the "Billroth school." Its founding was, Billroth himself maintained, his most important accomplishment and "the greatest joy in my rich life." To study at the Billroth Clinic in Vienna became the aim of many young surgeons, not only in Germany but elsewhere in Europe and in the United States. Many returned home with a mission and went on to become leaders in various surgical specialties. They exerted influence throughout the fields of abdominal, gastroenterological, and gynecological surgery. Although Billroth himself was not prepared to operate on the heart, he is often cited as having laid the clinical and conceptual groundwork for cardiac surgery.

Theodor Billroth was "one of the most congenial characters in the history of surgery," wrote Henry Sigerist. His personal charisma augmented his skill and science and made him a hero to surgeons everywhere. This view abides among them today. A recent assessment calls him "intuitive, sensitive, humane, and inventive." If praise be long, it is no surprise to learn that he is the subject of a 1,300-page biography. He married Christine Michaelis in 1858, and of their four children, three daughters lived to adulthood. His home in Vienna, write Leo Zimmerman and Ilza Veith, "was a center of social activity which drew the intellectual and artistic leaders of the great Austrian capital." In the Billroths' drawing room one frequently heard the newest pieces of his friend, Johannes Brahms, whose uncongenial disposition must have made for fine counterpoint; to Billroth, he dedicated two of his string quartets. When Billroth died, on February 6, 1894, he was working on a book, published posthumously, entitled *Wer ist musikalisch?—Who Is Musical?*

# Sigmund Freud [1856–1939]

## The Rise, Decline, and Persistence of Psychoanalysis

Psychiatry did not benefit substantially from the development of scientific medicine around the turn of the twentieth century. Its diagnoses were not based on physical evidence and the drugs it employed were not effective. A system of classification of mental illness, first proposed by Emil Kraepelin in 1883, represented a major step forward, but the outlook for treating the various disorders—most of them severe—remained persistently grim. About 1900, however, psychiatry's agenda, and its boundaries and constraints, were radically changed with the advent of Sigmund Freud and psychoanalysis.

Psychoanalysis was devised in the decades before World War I, and became a powerful current of thought during the interwar years. Its period of greatest influence came after World War II, when it flourished in the United States and elsewhere for about twenty years. Psychiatry was never fully beholden to psychoanalysis; many psychiatrists were thoroughly eclectic in practice while others remained skeptical or rejected Freudian thought outright. For a variety of reasons, the prominence of psychoanalysis began to diminish by the 1970s. But many concepts in psychiatry today are owed to Freud, and his overall impact on European and American thought has been as fruitful and exceptional as it has been controversial.

Sigmund Freud was born on May 6, 1856 in Freiberg, East Moravia, today part of the Czech Republic. He was the eldest son of Jacob Freud, a fairly unsuccessful businessman, and Amalia Nathanson, an attentive and caring yet at times distant mother. Genteel poverty, anti-Semitism and some traumatic childhood experiences also may have helped shape Freud's later view of the psyche, the world, and his own place in it. The Freuds moved to Vienna in 1860, and Sigmund, after receiving excellent marks at the gymnasium, entered the University of Vienna in 1873.

Freud's medical education was extensive and included several years of laboratory research. After early work in zoology, he moved to the university's Physiological Institute, where Jacob Brücke, a dedicated positivist and opponent of vitalism, was Freud's most significant teacher, from 1876 until 1882. But Freud also pursued medical studies, and he received his medical degree in 1881. The next year he became engaged to Martha Bernays, and his need for financial security led him instead to practice medicine. At the Vienna General Hospital, Freud gained experience in the fields of neurology and psychiatry; he also undertook research in brain anatomy, and in 1885 he became a lecturer in neuropathology. His first book, a study of aphasia, the puzzling brain disorder in which the ability to comprehend or produce speech is absent or impaired, was published in 1891.

Freud's early career demonstrates his interest in therapeutic innovations and ambitious theoretical aims. In 1885, after a decisive six months in France with the eminent neurologist Jean-Martin Charcot, Freud returned to Vienna and attempted to treat hysteria. This perplexing illness, in which various somatic complaints do not have a physical cause, is today considered one of the somatoform disorders. Charcot's belief that hysteria had a psychological rather than physiological cause, and his perception that it often seemed to have a sexual component, strongly influenced Freud. His positive report on Charcot's work, which included the idea that men as well as women could suffer from hysteria, met with some hostility in Vienna medical circles — or so Freud would maintain for the rest of his life.

After opening his practice in 1886, Freud found ineffective massage and electrotherapy, the current treatments for treating hysteria and disorders such as neurasthenia, then a popular term for various symptoms attributed to "nervous exhaustion." For a time he employed hypnosis, as Charcot had done, impressed by the "possibility that there could be powerful mental processes which nevertheless remained hidden from the consciousness of men." But therapeutically, hypnosis also disappointed.

Early steps toward psychoanalysis began during the 1890s, owing to Freud's relationship with Josef Breuer, a distinguished physician. Breuer was intensively treating a patient, to become known as "Anna O.," and he enlisted Freud's help in understanding a whole gamut of perplexing symptoms, which included hysterical manifestations, a dual personality, and hallucinations. Breuer in practice, and Freud in theory, began to explore the possibility that Anna O.'s bewildering somatic symptoms were disguised expressions of psychological conflicts that could be treated by what the patient herself described as the "talking cure." Anna O. was the most elaborate of several case histories presented in *Studies in Hysteria,* by Breuer and Freud, in 1895.

In addition, during the 1890s Freud began a passionate epistolary friendship with a Berlin doctor, Wilhelm Fliess, which allowed him to develop the broad outlines of several theories about mental functioning. He investigated his own emotional life as well as that of patients, and started considering the role of childhood experience, including the concept of infantile sexuality, in the genesis of adult psychological conflicts and in personality development. Freud's own "self-analysis" was probably not a success except in intellectual terms, but it was nonetheless significant in creating the kind of self-scrutiny that later characterized psychoanalytic thinking. Freud first used the term "psychoanalysis" in 1896.

As author of a radical new form of therapy and a theory of mental development and functioning, Freud began to acquire disciples around the turn of the century. His imaginative hypotheses and innovative form of treatment had considerable appeal. *The Interpretation of Dreams,* which appeared in 1900, was a brilliant effort to explain dreams in terms of emotional life and the press of unconscious wishes. Similarly, his brief but momentous *Three Essays on the Theory of Sexuality,* from 1905, provided a biopsychological-stage theory of how the mental life of infants and children was shaped around body and sensation; and he discussed the various transformations of puberty. A drawback to Freudian theory, now and later, would be a tendency to make overreaching claims: the interpretability of *all* dreams, or the *universality* of the Oedipal conflict—originally, a boy's rivalry with his father for his mother's love.

Freud also articulated highly original therapeutic ideas, such as the technique of "free association" (the patient says whatever comes to mind) and the notion of "transference" (feelings displaced from parents or others onto the analyst). In retrospect, Freud was not notably successful as a therapist in terms of outcome—his own views to the contrary. But the concept of a talking therapy in which the analyst does not employ coercion, offer advice, or sit in judgment, was a powerful innovation that could be extended in many ways and adapted to many kinds of patients. Without changing the basic therapeutic stance, for example, Freud's own early emphasis on exposing unconscious aggressive and sexual wishes would be superseded by efforts to examine intricacies of the self and psychological defense mechanisms.

Freud became celebrated in the years before the First World War and remained active for two decades afterward. In *The Ego and the Id,* published in 1923, he established a fruitful "structural" model of psychological development and intrapsychic conflict. In Freud's view, from an undifferentiated "id," responsive to instinct and physical need, there emerges an "ego" as the basis of self, and later a "superego" that incorporates the demands and strictures of parents and civilization. These psychic agencies, functionally defined, in their English translation miss Freud's attempt to employ terms from ordinary language. This tripartite view of the mind survived the intellectual elaboration of later psychoanalysts under the rubric of "ego psychology" and it remains useful today.

Freud's later work was of mixed quality. His concept of the "death instinct," developed in 1920 in *Beyond the Pleasure Principle*, was widely discussed but found little acceptance even among Freudians. In 1931, Freud reexamined the problems of trauma and anxiety in *Inhibitions, Symptoms and Anxiety*—an important work for later analysts. *The Future of an Illusion*, which appeared in 1927, represented Freud as a militant atheist; his famous *Civilization and Its Discontents*, published in 1930, is beloved by some, viewed by others as overly pessimistic.

In general, Freud's ability to situate psychiatric diseases within a broader context of normal human experience, as sculpted in his writings through a sensitive use of language, helps account for his impact. He influenced several generations of intellectuals, and Freudian concepts eventually passed into common parlance and created new avenues of discourse in art, literature, and everyday life. Freud's work advanced in the real world the new emphasis on subjectivity found in such philosophers as Arthur Schopenhauer and Friedrich Nietzsche. "The greatest legacy of psychoanalysis," suggests Robert T. Fancher, "is its highly developed art of listening for what is not being said, for self-deception that is being perpetrated, and for the wishes and terrors that patients cannot own honestly. When psychoanalysis functions at its best, it makes possible a level of honesty . . . [that] is about unrivaled by any other institution in our society."

Freud continued to live and work in Vienna, the charismatic leader of the psychoanalytic movement until June 1938, when, old and suffering from cancer, he was extracted from Austria on the eve of World War II. He resettled with his immediate family in London, where he died on September 23, 1939. Of Freud's five children, his youngest daughter, Anna, had been the most devoted to him; she became a founder of child psychoanalysis and was influential in her own right.

Psychoanalysis became particularly important in Britain and America after World War II, and served as the basis for a proliferation of therapies with various aims and methods employed by psychiatrists and other mental-health professionals. A diverse community of émigré European analysts protected the tenets of pure "classical" psychoanalysis, which both enhanced its reputation and sowed the seeds of its eventual decline. Psychoanalysis was costly and its effectiveness could not be easily demonstrated statistically. Drug treatments for anxiety and depression gradually became available; during the 1980s the arrival of the selective serotonin reuptake inhibitors (SSRIs), which could be used to treat mild depression and other disorders, was particularly significant. By then, the popularity of psychoanalysis had been severely compromised and marginalized by rising health-care costs. Freud's psychodynamic principles remain at the root of much though by no means all psychotherapy—but the future of such therapy in psychiatric practice, and the prospects for psychiatry as a whole, remain unclear.

How finally to understand Freud himself? There have been any number of biographies—worshipful, critical, impartial, mean-spirited—since psychoanalyst Ernest Jones published a massive three-volume life of Freud in the 1950s. In the 1970s, historian of science Frank Sulloway critically examined the development of his thought in *Freud: Biologist of the Mind*, while Paul Roazen's *Freud and His Followers* examined Freud's life in minute detail, down to the toothbrush his wife prepared with toothpaste before bedtime. Ronald Clark's dependable *Freud: The Man and His Cause* set a standard of objectivity; Peter Gay's *Freud: A Life for Our Time* showed that an accurate but adulatory biography was still possible at the end of the twentieth century. Louis Breger's recent *Freud: Darkness in the Midst of Vision* is both balanced and excellent at providing historical context; its major demerit is that it is not comprehensive.

There was always a negative middlebrow reaction to Freud, and an extensive literature of denigration has grown up in recent years. Although some psychoanalysts had wrestled with the changing landscape of scientific  discourse, they created no consensus, and the charismatic Freud eventually reaped a whirlwind of Whiggish abuse. Philosopher Adolf Grünbaum challenged the scientific pretensions of psychoanalysis, and this work became a foundation for later critiques. More recently, Frederick Crews accused Freud of "medieval (spirit-possession) and romantic (little elves make deeper selves) conceptions" and blasted him for his "egocentric and prurient encouragement to look for low motives in everyone but oneself." On a more mundane plane, Jeffrey A. Masson imputed to Freud cowardly motives in abandoning his early "seduction theory" that suggested infant and child sexual abuse (as it would be called today) lies at the root of neurosis. Peter J. Swales suggested that Freud had an affair with his sister-in-law and might have tried to murder his friend Fliess.

When the dust settles, the historical Freud might best be viewed as a latter-day Paracelsus (p. 50). Like that central and influential figure, Freud viewed himself in somewhat aggrandized terms and developed overarching theories that challenged received ideas about the nature of human beings and their afflictions. There was much truth in Paracelsus's views, although, as in Freud's case, they were cast in terms that were sometimes arcane. Freud did not burn the classics like Paracelsus did— rather, the Nazis consigned his books to flames. But he called for a new view of the human psyche much as Paracelsus insisted on exogenous causes of disease. Paracelsus's followers were an "odd bunch" and so were Freud's disciples. The ideas and language of Paracelsians were eventually transformed by and incorporated into chemistry—and, with advances in brain science, Freudian ideas might someday find the same fate. With such a legacy, Freud himself might be content.

# Part IV  Creating Modern Medicine

# William Osler [1849–1919]

## Modern Clinical Medicine

William Osler is one of the most eminent figures in modern clinical medicine. Perhaps the best-known physician in the English-speaking world in 1900, he was also a teacher and humanitarian. Osler made his reputation in the United States, but he was born in Canada and was of British ancestry. Optimistic, urbane, and an excellent writer, Osler was one of the "Baltimore four"—the group that made the Johns Hopkins Medical School and Hospital a widely emulated model for educating and training physicians.

Although Osler made important contributions to research, his greatest impact was as a teacher of clinical medicine. Osler was charismatic. From his own day to the present he has inspired almost unbelievable adulation and reverence. The surgeon John Miller Turpin Finney wrote of the "'magic spell' of Osler's influence," and added, with quaint sententiousness, that this was "an influence so subtle, and yet so compelling, that one could not remain in his immediate environment for any length of time without experiencing in some form or other its lasting effect." So emblematic of modern medicine was Osler that for decades throughout North America his portrait was frequently found in doctor's offices.

William Osler was born on July 12, 1849, in Bond Head, a parsonage in Tecumseh Township, Ontario. His father was Featherstone Lake Osler, an Anglican priest, and his mother was Ellen Free Pickton; both were English-born missionaries to the Canadian wilderness. Osler, the youngest son of eight children, attended the Anglican School at Weston. There he became familiar with *Religio Medici*, whose author, Sir Thomas Browne, he would consider his "lifelong mentor."* William originally considered studying theology but became interested in medicine while at Trinity College, Toronto. In general, Osler's devout parents and religious inclination help explain his influential personality. Osler brought a spiritual and high moral tone into what had become a largely secular profession.

---

*Thomas Browne (1605–1682) was trained as a physician, and his *Religio Medici* (*A Doctor's Faith*) is a stylistic masterpiece that mingles faith, skepticism, and wit.

After receiving his medical degree from McGill University in Montreal in 1872, Osler undertook what became a long and determinative postgraduate education in pathology and clinical medicine. In England for about fifteen months, he studied with eminent physiologists and physicians, including John Burdon-Sanderson at University College, London. Perhaps even more influential were Osler's studies in Germany and Austria. In Berlin he viewed some of the stunning demonstrations of postmortem pathology by Rudolf Virchow (p. 8). Osler was strongly impressed by Virchow and thereafter determined to become, like him, a great physician and a teacher. Osler's education was especially comprehensive, but he was only one of thousands of North Americans to study medicine abroad. Returning to Canada in 1875 he was named professor of medicine at McGill University and, the next year, pathologist at Montreal General Hospital. With his education, his impressive teaching ability, and his personal magnetism, Osler soon acquired a considerable reputation.

In 1884 Osler moved to the United States, where he took a prestigious position as professor of clinical medicine at the University of Pennsylvania. He was not impressed by the "loose, slipshod way of conducting medical schools" in the United States. At "Old Blockley" of the Philadelphia Hospital, the oldest hospital in the country, a plethora of poor patients could be found, suffering from a host of different maladies. Osler initiated what became known as "ward walks." A large number of cases were terminal, and Osler had the opportunity to apply his European education as patients' symptoms were studied and evaluated in conjunction with what their bodies told the doctors postmortem.

Osler's most significant career move came in 1889, when he was named physician-in-chief at Johns Hopkins Hospital. Four years later, when the associated teaching school opened, he became professor of medicine. Recruited by the famous pathologist and microbiologist

William Welch, Osler was another of the hospital's principal intellectual architects; together with William S. Halsted and Howard A. Kelly, they constituted the "Baltimore four." Richly endowed, Johns Hopkins would be one of the forces to transform the teaching of medicine, combining in a single facility scientific research and clinical medicine. Osler developed an integrated program, with instruction in small groups. Johns Hopkins, writes sociologist Paul Starr, "radiated cultural as well as scientific assurance, especially in the person of Osler, whose learning and urbanity made him the profession's favorite doctor." Within a generation the influence of the school and hospital was felt throughout the United States.

As earlier they had impressed students at Old Blockley, Osler's daily ward rounds with interns at Johns Hopkins became famously emulated at hospitals everywhere. They also inspired some ghastly doggerel:

> Haste! Haste! ye clerks, make breakfast brief,
> And follow close your lord and chief:
> With paper blank and pen in fist,
> Let not a single note be missed,
> When William Osler, K. C. B., F. R. S., F. R. C. P.,
> Makes his rounds.

Although Osler made no profound discoveries, he undertook a good deal of research and made a number of original contributions. He was among the first to study blood platelets, and he also contributed to research on endocarditis and angina pectoris. His monograph *Cerebral Palsies in Children* dates to 1889. For the study of tuberculosis—then perhaps the most serious disease in the United States—he formed what he called "The Laennec," a study group named after the discoverer of the stethoscope. Osler's interest in tuberculosis was an aspect of his more general concern with hygiene and his activism as a sanitarian.

*The Principles and Practice of Medicine,* Osler's textbook of internal medicine first published in 1892, was exceptionally popular and influential. It was based on a scientific approach, incorporated the most recent advances in bacteriology, and was widely translated, with versions in French, German, Spanish, and even Chinese. Osler revised *The Principles* four times, and even after his death new editions continued to appear, the last being the sixteenth, in 1947. *The Principles* was subsequently revived as the *Hopkins Textbook of Medicine,* which remains in print today. The book so impressed Frederick Gates that in 1897 he advised John D. Rockefeller to underwrite an institute devoted to scientific medicine. This became the Rockefeller Institute, today Rockefeller University.

Osler was a driven man, and by 1903 he wrote, "I knew I was riding for a fall." Exhausted, he therefore decided to accept an offer from Oxford University to became its most prestigious Regius Professor of Medicine. (Indeed, his wife insisted, saying, "Better go in a steamer than go in a pine box.") Osler, who was British by culture in any event, would remain in England for the rest of his life. A bibliophile, he became curator of the Bodleian Library. (His own considerable collection was eventually bequeathed to McGill University, his alma mater.) Osler was greatly interested by the history of medicine and would eventually publish *Evolution of Modern Medicine* in 1921 as "an aeroplane flight over the progress of medicine through the ages."

In the last stage of his life, Osler came into great demand as a speaker. For medical students and for the public at large, he was full of good advice and aphorisms. "Soap and water and common sense are the best disinfectants," he once said. "Man should go out of this world as he came in—chiefly on milk." According to Charles S. Bryan, "Osler's aphorisms convey the image of a master teacher who knew his stuff, liked what he did, and made learning fun."

A number of Osler's addresses were collected and published, first in 1905, as *Aequanimitas*. In the title essay, one of the key inspirational texts in American medicine, Osler advises doctors to cultivate patience and to be sensitive, never callous or hard with patients, but also to keep an emotional distance. "Aequanimitas"—roughly, equanimity—is the virtuous mental attitude of calmly accepting what comes one's way. Another of his popular books is *An Alabama Student*, a collection of idealized biographical sketches. Overall, Osler wrote so extensively during the early decades of modern medicine that he has been compared to Hippocrates (p. 29) and Galen (p. 34). "To write the modern history of a disease," notes Michael Bliss, "you might begin by looking up what Osler said about it in the 1890s."

At age forty-two Osler married Grace Linzee Revere, a descendant of the American patriot Paul Revere, after whom they named their first child, who died soon after birth. A second child, Revere, was killed in Flanders during World War I. This was a tragedy for Osler, but he appeared to have recovered before he fell ill in the winter of 1919, perhaps having contracted the flu, which was then pandemic. He died within a couple of weeks.

When he died, on December 29, Osler was widely recalled as the most prominent physician in the world. Several years later Harvey Cushing (p. 227), one of his most eminent students, published an extensive biography that won the Pulitzer Prize. An "Osler revival" began in the 1960s and has not abated. More than eighty years after his death, he is still venerated. Charles S. Bryan published his *Osler: Inspirations from a Great Physician* in 1997. Osler has been the source of some fifteen hundred articles. Medals have been struck in his honor, and both a Pullman railroad car and a World War II liberty ship were named after him. He has been called greater than Hippocrates, not to mention Sydenham (p. 132). In a new biography, published in 1999, Michael Bliss could find nothing that would topple Osler from the pedestal he has occupied since his death. Osler, he writes, "may never be surpassed as English-speaking medicine's most inspirational father-figure, mentor, and role model."

# Elie Metchnikoff [1845–1916]

## Cellular Immunity

One summer's day in 1882—as he would tell it—Russian zoologist Elie Metchnikoff sent his family off to the circus while he observed, within the larvae of starfish, a specific type of cell that would be drawn to, surround, and carry off foreign particles. He concluded, in a major leap of scientific imagination, that these cells—phagocytes, he called them—were performing a defensive operation. Metchnikoff thereupon created a controversial theory of immune reaction that he defended vociferously until he died.

Although his account has elements of myth—his discovery was far from happenstance—time and science have proved Metchnikoff right. His concept of cell-based immunity represented a new and major stream of thought that would lead to a grasp of how the body recognizes and protects itself from foreign substances and organisms. In addition, Metchnikoff's work also introduced the view that the immune system distinguishes self from non-self. While a powerful understanding of the immune system would not arrive until the 1960s, Metchnikoff's theory represented an early glimpse, an insight gained by applying principles of evolutionary biology to pathology and to the newly minted germ theory of disease.

The youngest of five children, Ilya Ilich Metchnikoff was born on May 15, 1845, in Kharkov, in the province of Ivanovka in the Ukraine. His father, for whom he was named, was a genuine Russian noble, who liked nothing better than a game of cards and a day at the races. After dissipating a fortune in St. Petersburg, he moved his family back to the Ukraine, where he continued to entertain lavishly and to gamble. Elie was a sensitive, frail child far closer to his mother, Elilia, a woman whose beauty was attested to by Alexander Pushkin. The daughter of a converted Jew, she encouraged her curious, intelligent son. Elie began a herbarium, and importuned and bribed other children to listen to his botanical lectures. His early education was with a tutor; attending the lycée he learned elementary science and won a gold medal at graduation. He went on to the University of Kharkov, finishing the four-year program in two years and graduating in 1864. He studied at Giessen, in Germany, with a famous taxonomist, Rudolf Leuckart, and undertook field work in Naples, where he began work on the development of germ cell layers in the invertebrate sea creatures. Metchnikoff received his doctorate in 1867 from the University of St. Petersburg. He taught briefly at Odessa before being appointed to the zoology faculty at St. Petersburg at the young age of twenty-two.

Initially drawn to the field of comparative embryology of marine fauna, Metchnikoff had from the beginning of his career a philosophical inclination to theory building. He read Darwin while still a student but was not immediately—despite his later claims to the contrary—the enthusiastic convert he later became. As early as 1865 Metchnikoff discovered the first element in what would become his theory of phagocytosis when he observed intracellular digestion in a kind of flatworm. By 1872, when Metchnikoff returned to the University of Odessa—whose location on the Black Sea made it convenient to the study of ocean fauna—his interest in the simplest forms of life, the protozoa, was not narrow but formed part of his larger concern with understanding organisms in terms of evolutionary adaptations.

Metchnikoff's revelation concerning the cells he would call phagocytes emerged suddenly enough, but only on account of his vast fund of knowledge about the digestive system of invertebrates. His famous discovery took place in Messina in 1882—"one day," wrote Metchnikoff later, "when the whole family had gone to the circus to see some extraordinary performing apes." Studying digestion in starfish larvae, Metchnikoff noticed that certain cells surrounded and engulfed foreign particles. Importantly, these cells were not from the endodermic layer, which controls digestive processes, but from the middle, or mesodermic, layer of cells, from which the circulatory system arises in higher animals. He suspected that their function might be protective.

Metchnikoff's powerful insight was to recognize that he had discovered a basic function in the life of organisms. "A zoologist until then," he wrote later, "I suddenly became a pathologist." He viewed phagocytes as protecting the organism from invaders, but that was just one of their functions. He also credited phagocytic activity with tissue repair and surveillance of malignant cells. The phagocyte for Metchnikoff's system, writes Alfred I. Tauber, "defines organismal identity; that is, it determined what was not to be destroyed or eaten, whether foreign or native."

Skepticism greeted Metchnikoff's first paper on phagocytes, published in 1883, and it did not abate. He had the backing of the powerful and influential Rudolf Virchow (p. 8), but not of Robert Koch (p. 24). In general, the phagocytic theory clashed with several other notions concerning immunological response. According to one view, for example, white blood

cells indeed ingested bacteria, but they then served as convoys for the invaders, transporting them to other sites in the body.

Metchnikoff did not bow to this or other challenges, however, and the track of his career from 1883 is one of hard-fought battles. Although he returned to Russia in 1885 to head the Odessa Bacteriological Institute, he was limited by his nonmedical background, and he aroused the hostility of the local medical establishment. After only two years, he resigned and left Russia for Europe in search of a new appointment. In 1888 he visited Louis Pasteur in Paris. Pasteur was then at the height of his fame but was in physical decline. He lent his support to the phagocytic theory—he was no friend of German science—and offered Metchnikoff a laboratory at the newly founded Institut Pasteur. The next quarter century was to be the happiest period of Metchnikoff's life, as he became an eminence in one of the most vaunted institutions of medical research in the world, drawing students from France and abroad.

The most significant competition to a cell-based theory of immunity such as Metchnikoff proposed was the "humoral" theory advanced about 1890 by Koch, Emil von Behring (p. 195), and others. By this view, it was not cells but blood serum that was the key to the immune response. In this cell-less fluid, bacteria could be shown to undergo lysis, or degradation. Indeed, Behring showed that animals and human beings can produce substances that are toxic to bacteria and that circulate in the blood. Behring's great success, beginning in 1890 with diphtheria antitoxin, lent weight to the humoral theory. Metchnikoff, for his part, published *Lectures on the Comparative Pathology of Inflammation* in 1892, and ten years later, in 1901, *Immunity in Infectious Diseases*. Both were seminal works, controversial but respected.

In 1908, for his work in immunity, Metchnikoff shared the Nobel Prize with Paul Ehrlich, founder of chemotherapy. The award represented a partial rapprochement between the theories of cellular and humoral immunity. That the theories were not incompatible had been suggested in

1905 by Sir Almoth Wright, who employed them to devise his own broad theory. Ehrlich's concept of immunity—his "immunochemistry"—was prescient in its own way, foreshadowing, for example, the concept of cell receptors. The more profound aspects of Metchnikoff's biological theory, ignored in his day, were later recovered. The immune system, as it is understood today, includes both immune cells and antibodies, whose functions correspond, roughly but clearly enough, to phagocytosis and humoral immune response.

From about the turn of the century, as he himself aged, Metchnikoff began to study longevity. He developed a speculative view that senility might be due to chronic intoxication caused by intestinal bacteria. To support such a notion he offered a host of observations, creating an entire philosophy of nutrition and aging. He came to view the aging process as largely abnormal in modern man. Metchnikoff suggested the possibility of a normal life expectancy of about 120 years. To this end, taking his cue from long-lived Bulgarian peasants, he suggested people drink sour milk in the belief that the bacilli which produced lactic acid could inhibit intestinal pathogens. He drank it by the gallon himself, and for years afterward his name was used as a product endorsement for a brand of yogurt that was "sole provider of Professor Metchnikoff." After Pasteur's death in 1895, writes W. F. Bynum, Metchnikoff became the institute's "most visible adornment, a scientific guru whose ideas on diet, constipation, aging, and the biological future of man were eagerly sought and equally eagerly expounded." Metchnikoff published several books for popular consumption in the hope of advancing his philosophical ideas, including *The Nature of Man* and *The Prolongation of Life.*

Metchnikoff's extravagant personality seems to have combined charisma and an ability to make strong attachments with extreme sensitivity to criticism, eccentricity, and combativeness. He disliked the idea of having children, and as a young man liked to say that procreation in a feeling creature such as a human being was a crime. Described by Paul de Kruif (p. 401) as a "hysterical character out of one of Dostoevski's novels," Metchnikoff twice tried to commit suicide. His first wife died of tuberculosis, and he thoroughly dominated his second wife, Olga Belokopitova, "who was as clay in his hands." Nevertheless, the marriage was a success on its own terms. Metchnikoff became stepparent to two of his wife's younger siblings, and when Olga came into an inheritance, he became free of financial concern, an important advantage for a man of his temperament.

With all that he knew about growing old, Elie Metchnikoff hoped to live to an exceptional age himself. But his health began to decline in 1913, when he suffered a series of heart attacks. He kept a detailed diary of his illness, and in his last months he continued to work, writing the popular book *The Founders of Modern Medicine.* His death came on December 15, 1916, and while he awaited the end, he suggested to a friend, "You will do my post-mortem? Look at the intestines carefully for I think there is something there now."

# Willem Einthoven [1860-1927]

## Inventing Electrocardiography

After basic concepts of electromagnetism were established during the nineteenth century, a number of physiologists sought to visualize and record the heartbeat. The heart goes awry in various ways with different diseases, and a graphic recording of its electrical activity would constitute a diagnostic probe. One machine, invented around the turn of the twentieth century, became the tool that revolutionized the way doctors looked at cardiovascular disease. This was the electrocardiograph (ECG), which charts the heartbeat by measuring electrical potentials on the surface of the body. It was principally developed and perfected by the Dutch physiologist Willem Einthoven.

One of six children, Willem Einthoven was born on May 22, 1860, in Semarang, a seaport on Java, one of the Indonesian islands, then part of the Dutch East Indies. The family name was Dutch, but the Einthovens traced their ancestry to Jews who migrated to the Netherlands from Spain during the Inquisition. Jacob Einthoven was a military physician; his wife was Louise M. M. C. de Vogel. In 1870, several years after Jacob's death, Willem's mother brought the family back to Utrecht. Attending the university there, Willem was trained in physiology and medicine. He received his Ph.D. in medicine cum laude in 1885.

Einthoven's early work in the burgeoning discipline of physiology, it is interesting to note, was inspired by Franciscus Donders, a famous ophthalmologist. Donders, himself influenced by the invention of the ophthalmoscope, had done much to improve ordinary eyeglasses. By his mid-twenties, Einthoven's work in the field of eye research, with studies in stereoscopic vision, had established his reputation. He was appointed to the chair of physiology at the University of Leiden in 1886.

In 1889, at the First International Congress of Physiologists, held in Basel, Einthoven was present at a demonstration of the "electrogram," an invention of physiologist Augustus Waller. Using an instrument called a capillary electrometer, in which a column of mercury fluctuated with each beat of the heart, Waller traced the minute changes by recording them on photographic paper. Waller's demonstrations of the heartbeat—first with frogs, then a bulldog named Jimmy, and later with people—were

famous and won him applause from scientists all over Europe. Einthoven, too, was impressed. Returning to Holland, he told colleagues about "one of the most beautiful investigations" presented at the congress.

In search of a suitable project for his sophisticated laboratory, Einthoven recognized the limitations of Waller's machine and sought to improve it. Initially he too attempted to work with the capillary electrometer. But it consistently disappointed. As the mercury was displaced, the inertia of its mass defeated efforts to obtain precise measurements. Einthoven attempted to compensate for this distortion. He both developed extensive calculations to correct for the mercury's lag, and tried to improve the apparatus itself. He once attempted to stabilize the instrument by digging a hole in the floor of the laboratory and filling it with rocks. All these methods failed or were impractical.

Einthoven, familiar with instruments of measurement, was aware of a new "single string galvanometer" that had been developed by a French electrical engineer and aeronautics pioneer, Clement Ader. Creating a similar device—the thinnest possible needle suspended between poles of a horseshoe magnet—Einthoven attempted, eventually with some success, to establish the shape or form of the electrical waves generated by the heart. He finally obtained a fairly good picture of "das normale Elektrokardiogramm." He could show changes in the heart's activity when an individual exercised, for example, or with other variables. Making it a diagnostic tool, though, required further work.

Einthoven improved the string galvanometer by an ingenious adaptation. The galvanometer, in theory, could measure the most sensitive changes in the electrical field. But practically, to displace its wire needle required a fairly strong current. The electrical current stimulating the heart is quite weak. Einthoven eventually hit upon the idea of using a filament of silver-coated quartz as the machine's needle. He obtained it by attaching quartz to an arrow on a tightly strung bow. Heat was applied to the quartz, and the arrow was let fly across the laboratory. The quartz melted into a superfine string. This filament, so thin that a microscope had to be used to view the deflection caused by heartbeat, was the crucial innovation.

Although the primitive electrocardiograph was to be a triumph of delicate measurement, the instrument as a whole was cumbersome. To protect the string from environmental interference, Einthoven had to go to extravagant lengths. He was compelled to construct a machine that occupied two rooms and required five operators. The subject whose heart was to be measured was required to place hands or feet in tubs and bowls of saline solution.

But it worked. Einthoven viewed the heart as at the center of an imagined triangle. The apices of the triangle in the "Einthoven hypothesis" were the right and left shoulders, and the left groin. The heartbeat was recorded under several conditions: both hands in solution; right hand, left foot in solution; and left hand, left foot in solution. This enabled establishment of a measurable relationship between the action of the ventricles (the lower chambers of the heart) and the atria (the upper chambers), and so provided a means to detect both normal and disease rhythms. "From the nature of the case," Einthoven explained, "there must be a connexion between the curves obtained by the three different leads from the same person. If two forms are known, the third may be calculated from them."

Unlike earlier investigators, Einthoven pursued the prospects of the electrocardiograph for clinical use. Indeed, his success, it should be emphasized, was due to his clear-sightedness about the machine's potential value to medicine. In 1901 he published the first article on his new instrument. Two years later he provided some of the standards and nomenclature that would later be taught to all physicians. On an electrocardiogram, the P wave gives the activity of the heart's atria. The QRS wave complex and the T wave describe ventricular action. Although later modified, Einthoven's terminology and diagnostic descriptions were his enduring legacy to cardiology.

Manufacturers were soon interested in the electrocardiograph. Patent issues led Einthoven to make an agreement with the Cambridge Instrument Company, owned by Horace Darwin (youngest child of Charles Darwin [p. 3]). The first machines, available in 1908, were big, ungainly, and expensive, but models became progressively smaller and more affordable. A portable machine—albeit weighing eighty pounds—was introduced in 1926.

Meanwhile, over the first two decades of the twentieth century, Einthoven and others, notably English cardiologist Thomas Lewis, established electrocardiography as a discipline. By the time Lewis's text *Clinical*

*Electrocardiography* was published in 1913, an elaborate diagnostic classification scheme existed for "every form of cardiac irregularity." Although installed in a number of hospitals about the time of World War I, initially the machine was not really popular. But in 1918 the famous Chicago physician James Herrick used the electrocardiograph in a classic description of acute myocardial infarction, or heart attack. This work had considerable effect and helped clarify the full potential of the electrocardiograph. In 1924 Einthoven received the Nobel Prize in physiology or medicine.

Einthoven was "a man of regular, almost plodding habits, well suited to a quiet university town," writes Robert G. Frank. At the same time he was a sportsman, multilingual, with some traits that stereotypically characterize professors. Some have described his "childlike" humor and his absent-mindedness. He might forget about a lecture he had to give, or cancel it, because, as he explained, "I'm thinking." In the eyes of his students, Einthoven was nearly a saint. Generous with money, he determined to share his Nobel Prize award with his laboratory assistant, Van de Woerdt, but as the latter had died, Einthoven gave Van der Woerdt's share to his two surviving sisters.

In 1886, soon after receiving his doctorate, Willem Einthoven had married Frédérique Jeanne Louise de Vogel, a cousin from his mother's family. They had three daughters and a son. Willem Einthoven died on September 28, 1927.

For many years the electrocardiograph was cardiology's most valuable noninvasive diagnostic tool. By the 1970s, however, a variety of new technologies began to come to the medical marketplace, each of which possessed some advantage over the ECG. There was the safe and simple echocardiogram, for example, that employs sounds waves to create an image of the heart's activity. Among imaging techniques based on radioisotopes, which came into use about the same time, were myocardial perfusion scintigraphy and radionuclide cineangiography, both of which (unlike the ECG) could be employed during exercise.

But the electrocardiograph has proved a durable instrument, adapted in recent years to record patients' heartbeats while they go about everyday tasks. Today, writes cardiologist Jeffrey S. Borer, using the ECG in combination with computer-based technologies "can provide diagnostic and prognostic information, including direct guides to therapy, which were scarcely conceived only a relatively few years ago."

# Emil von Behring [1854–1917]

## Humoral Immunity

A dramatic story from 1891: On Christmas night, a young girl in Berlin is strangling to death from diphtheria. At the Bergmann Clinic she is injected with serum from the blood of experimentally infected sheep. This substance acts, as had been hoped, to counter the fatal diphtheria toxin. As though it were a miracle, the girl recovers. Diphtheria, one of the most feared diseases in history, henceforth has a cure.

To understand the popular impact of Emil von Behring's success, one needs to recognize that diphtheria was once a terrible scourge. It can spread easily through human populations, both via secretions from coughing and by touch. When encountered, the durable, club-shaped bacterium dwells in the upper respiratory tract. As a victim falls ill, the lymph nodes enlarge and the throat swells to a "bullneck" appearance, and suffocation may result. The bacteria generate a toxin, known as an exotoxin, that causes progressive heart damage, paralysis, and death. Diphtheria became especially virulent in the mid-nineteenth century, thriving in the crowded conditions of poor urban life. Its ravages were all the more poignant because its victims were often children. Many would agree with Edward Shorter: "To the extent that we can give any precise date to the crystallizing of the public's infatuation with medical science," he writes, "I think it would be the arrival in 1894 of the first diphtheria 'antitoxine.'"

The scientific significance of Behring's success was more ambiguous. It confused the basis of immunity. By demonstrating the immune properties of the cell-free blood serum, his work lent support to a "humoral," or chemical, theory at the expense of interest in cellular immunity. Humoral theory won the approval of the German "immunochemists" and became dominant for decades to come. It gave rise to what Arthur M. Silverstein once called "the dogma that circulating antibody would provide all essential answers to the problems of immunity and immunopathology." Cellular immunity, as discovered about 1882 by Elie Metchnikoff (p. 186), was neglected. Not until the mid-twentieth century, with the expanded development of the clonal selection theory of Macfarlane Burnet (p. 280), would the situation be appreciably clarified.

One of a dozen children, Emil Behring was born to August Georg Behring and Augustine Zech on March 15, 1854. His birthplace was a town in East Prussia, today Idawa, in Poland. His father was a schoolteacher of modest means who intended for his son either to become a teacher himself or to enter the ministry. In 1866, however, while attending the gymnasium at Hohenstein, Emil discovered an interest in medicine. With the help of a teacher, he was accepted in 1875 into the Friedrich Wilhelm University in Berlin, a state-run atmilitary medical school from which, after graduation, students agreed to serve in the military for ten years in exchange for a free education. Behring received his medical degree in 1878 and two years later, after passing state examinations, worked for a time at the Charité in Berlin before beginning service in the army as an assistant surgeon.

Behring entered medicine at a propitious moment. By the early 1880s, the work of Robert Koch (p. 24) and Louis Pasteur (p. 18) had led to early formulations of the germ theory of disease and had inspired a flurry of fruitful research. Behring was intrigued from the beginning. In 1881, while still serving in the army, he began to wonder about the possibility of treating infectious diseases with substances that would disinfect the body from within, much as carbolic acid was used for external wounds. Working with iodoform, a compound used as a wound dressing, Behring soon realized that the most serious problem was the substance's toxic effects—the cure was worse than the disease. However, Behring remained interested in the prospect of finding therapeutic agents, and he acquired experience in animal experimentation.

In 1889, after leaving the army to join the Institute for Hygiene at the University of Berlin, Behring became an assistant to Robert Koch. He also began a collaboration with Shibasaburo Kitasato, a Japanese microbiologist who, a year earlier, had isolated the bacterium responsible for tetanus. Like diphtheria, tetanus's deadly effects are produced by a toxin. This was consonant with recent discoveries by Émile Roux and Alexandre Yersin, who had demonstrated that even after all diphtheria bacteria had been filtered out of the laboratory broth culture, the remaining fluid could still produce the disease.

Behring and Kitasato worked to develop effective antidotes to tetanus and diphtheria, experimenting with animals that had survived the disease. The blood serum of such animals, they were soon able to show, could sometimes confer immunity on healthy animals. Within a year they had produced a serum for tetanus. On December 4, 1890, they published results of experiments that showed how the blood serum of tetanus-immune rabbits could be injected into other animals to counter or neutralize the toxins created by the tetanus bacilli. A week later, in another paper, Behring showed that the principle which held for tetanus also worked for diphtheria. "The foundation was thus laid," writes historian of medicine George Rosen, "for the specific serum therapy and prophylaxis of diphtheria as well as [certain] other infectious diseases." The great Christmas Eve trial came a year later.

After Behring had demonstrated its effectiveness, several years of work were required before the antitoxin could be employed on a large scale. During three years of clinical trials, some twenty thousand children received the antitoxin. Meanwhile, in 1893 Behring published both a history of diphtheria and *Die ätiologische Behandlung der Infections-krankheiten (Review of Etiologic Therapy of Infectious Diseases)*. After Émile Roux's great success with the diphtheria antitoxin at the Paris Hospital for Sick Children, his report to the Eighth International Congress of Hygiene and Demography in 1894 was widely viewed as a vindication of Behring's work. Henceforth the diphtheria antitoxin was produced worldwide. The great chemist Paul Ehrlich worked with Behring to standardize the dosage.

The original diphtheria antitoxin had a substantial rate of success, but it was not a cure-all and did not confer long-term immunity. It represented an example of short-term "passive immunity," in which, as we understand it today, antibodies are introduced into the system, but not the antigens that would provoke a more durable and active response from the individual's own immune system. In 1913, Behring introduced an active vaccine that combined neutralized toxins and antitoxins; so did others, about the same time. Immunization of children eventually became mandatory in most advanced industrial countries.

Behring's hopes for success in treating other diseases proved elusive. His relationship with Robert Koch had soured, and in 1894 he was named associate professor of hygiene at the University of Halle. The next year he accepted a more prestigious appointment as professor at the University of Marburg. Fabwerke Höchst, which was producing diphtheria antitoxin and in which Behring had a financial interest, built his laboratories. In the hope of finding an antitoxin, Behring studied the tuberculosis bacterium, but with less than spectacular results. Although he soon abandoned that work, his controversial assertion that bovine tuberculosis could spread to humans was correct. But his suggestion, in 1905, that cow's milk be disinfected by hydrogen peroxide and formaldehyde did not work.

After becoming a famous man, Behring was awarded a patent of nobility. As von Behring, he became known to popular journalists as the "children's savior." An institute was named after him, and in 1901, for having "placed in the hands of the physician a victorious weapon against illness and death," he received the first Nobel Prize for physiology or medicine. In 1904 von Behring founded the Behringwerke Company for research into infectious diseases and treatments. Von Behring consolidated his reputation during World War I, when tetanus immunization proved its real worth in protecting the wounded. He now became known as "Savior of the Soldiers," and was awarded the Iron Cross.

In 1896 Emil von Behring married Elie Spinola, with whom he had six sons. When he suffered from depression, which was fairly often, he would retire to his house on Capri. He was not a great teacher, and he quarreled not just with Koch but with Paul Ehrlich, whose work had done much to make his discoveries useful to medicine. As Ehrlich was being lowered down into his grave in 1915, von Behring appeared at the cemetery to ask pardon: "If we have hurt you," he importuned his old friend, "forgive us." Emil von Behring died of pneumonia on March 31, 1917.

# Alexis Carrel [1873–1944]

## Surgery, Science, and *Man, the Unknown*

The assassination of a French president by a knife-wielding anarchist in 1894 prompted a notable advance in surgery. Soon thereafter Alexis Carrel, a young French surgeon, set about developing new techniques for suturing blood vessels, including some such as might have been used to save the president's life. This work was a great success. Not only did Carrel learn to reconnect arteries and veins with unprecedented success, he also discovered how to accomplish surgical grafts of all sorts. "Between 1901 and 1910," writes Julius H. Comroe, Jr., "Alexis Carrel, using experimental animals, performed every feat and developed every technique known to vascular surgery today" (excepting the various technology-driven advances). For expanding the range of surgical procedures not long after asepsis made it possible, in 1912 Carrel received the Nobel Prize in physiology or medicine for his work "on vascular suture and the transplantation of organs."

The significance of Carrel's work extends beyond surgical technique. He possessed the mind of an inventor, and he performed a wide array of clever experiments and operations, including organ replacement. This work in turn involved him in basic research to preserve and even cultivate human tissue and organs. Organ transplantation would not become possible until the 1960s, but Carrel's demonstration of its plausibility at the turn of the twentieth century provided an important initial impetus. Finally, Carrel's philosophical and sometimes mystical temperament made him one of the most controversial figures of his generation, both in the United States and in France. He experimented with extrasensory perception, authored a visionary prescription for mankind, and flirted with ideas that one might call fascist. Carrel was a "scientist and mystic," wrote the aviation pioneer Charles Lindbergh, his friend, collaborator, and fellow reactionary, "...decorated and damned, often by the same people."

Alexis Carrel, baptized Marie-Joseph-Auguste, was born on June 28, 1873, the eldest of three children of Anne-Marie Ricard and Alexis Carrel-Billiard. His father was a prosperous textile manufacturer—intriguing in light of Carrel's preoccupation with silk sutures—and he died from pneumonia when Alexis was only about five years old. After an early education

with his mother, a highly religious woman with whom he was exceptionally close, Alexis attended the Collège de St. Joseph, a Jesuit institution. He went on to the University of Lyons, receiving a degree in letters in 1890, and he took a second baccalaureate in science in 1891 from the University of Dijon. He studied medicine for three years, and from 1893 to 1900 obtained experience in surgery in local hospitals. From 1899 to 1902 Carrel served as prosector at the University of Lyons. He received his medical degree from that university in 1900.

Carrel did not treat Sadi Carnot after the president was attacked on June 24, 1894, but he was deeply impressed that no medical intervention had been attempted. The fatal wound severed one of Carnot's large abdominal veins, and surgeons were of the opinion that such portal veins were too large to be successfully reconnected. Carrel wondered if improved techniques might have saved the president, and he began a series of investigations that would culminate, several years later, in a whole new toolbox of surgical procedures.

The principal problem in suturing vessels was that of causing injury to their interior lining, which could give rise to fatal blood clots. In this, as in much else, Carrel turned to his mother for advice. Anne-Marie directed him to a haberdashery, where he found very fine needles and threads. Carrel also took sewing lessons from a local embroideress. With improved dexterity, Carrel developed a technique that used three sutures as stays, allowing the round blood vessel to be treated as a triangle, thus enabling the surgeon to sew on a flat surface, one "side" at a time. This simple solution, "triangulation," is still used today.

In another innovation, Carrel coated his thin needles and sutures with Vaseline to protect fragile tissue from harm. He published a paper that described how surgeons could employ this technique in 1902. Although they were appreciated by his colleagues, his innovations did not win Carrel friends among the administrators of local hospitals, where he was not popular. For his part, Carrel appears to have found society in Lyons provincial and narrow. He also may have become embittered after he was passed over for a chair at the university.

Carrel's career prospects were also damaged, it appears, by his credulous attitude toward divine intervention. In 1903 he accompanied the sick and lame on their annual pilgrimage to Lourdes, the Catholic shrine famous for miraculous cures. Among them was the seventeen-year-old pilgrim Marie Bailly, said to be suffering from tuberculous peritonitis, a fatal disease that had already killed her parents. So ill she could not be immersed, she was only sprinkled with water. Remarkably, she appeared to "recover" almost on the spot. Although Carrel conceded that "no certain diagnosis could be made," he declined to discount a supernatural cure. This so dismayed his colleagues that he felt he could no longer hope for a future in academic medicine in France. Clearly distressed, for a brief time Carrel entertained the notion of raising cattle instead of working in medicine, and in 1904, after long discussions with his mother, he emigrated to Canada. But his farming plans came to nought, and soon he accepted an appointment at the University of Chicago.

Experiments in transplantation surgery became the new focus of Carrel's work. Within months, together with physiologist Charles Guthrie, Carrel was performing pioneer operations. With the opportunity to experiment on animals under aseptic conditions, his work flourished. Carrel and Guthrie explicitly intended to create a transplant revolution, and they essentially succeeded. Over a period of less than two years Carrel discovered how to graft veins into arteries and, spectacularly, to transplant kidneys and ovaries and replace thyroid glands. With Guthrie, he not only published nearly thirty articles in medical journals but won the attention of the popular press. An article soon appeared in the *New York Herald*, with the prediction that, one day, "If your heart is not in the right place, it will be transplanted."

Carrel's surgical success with grafts and transplants was limited by what would be understood, about forty years later, as an immune response that led to rejection. As Carrel understood it, more simply, "Cells are specific of the individual to whom they belong. This peculiarity of our body has so far prevented the wide use of the transplantation of organs for therapeutic purposes."

In 1906, Carrel moved to the Rockefeller Institute, where, provided with a laboratory and an operating room, he would remain until the beginning of World War II. A friend of Simon Flexner, Rockefeller's director, Carrel became an associate member of the institute in 1909 and a full member three years later. In a dramatic incident in 1908, Carrel was called on to perform what Douglas Starr calls the "first modern transfusion," in which he sutured a father's artery to a vein in the leg of his ailing baby daughter. Father thereby pumped blood into daughter and, because they had compatible blood types, the operation was a success. The Rockefeller reaped a public relations coup, reporting it in the press as "one of the most remarkable surgical successes ever achieved in this country."

Carrel's early work on heart surgery, using experimental animals, was both prodigious in output and influential. Among other things, Carrel discovered how grafting procedures could be applied to the coronary vessels that deliver oxygen to the heart. This involved using new methods of preserving grafts prior to transplanting them, and using paraffin tubes to keep the spinal cord supplied with blood during surgery. In all, Carrel's work was a great anticipation of the heart bypass operation that became plausible in the 1960s.

Another area of interest to Carrel was tissue culture and preservation. The prospect of inducing tissues to grow outside the body held great promise for medical research, and Carrel's own interest was prompted by a desire to understand how wounds heal. Impressed by Ross G. Harrison's demonstration in 1907 of in vitro cell growth, between 1910 and 1914 Carrel furthered techniques in his own laboratory. His most notable success was also the most enduring. In 1912 Carrel created nutritive conditions that immortalized—with appropriate care—a fragment of heart muscle from a chick embryo. One culture first produced this way was maintained for thirty-four years.* In the popular press this gave rise to the rumor that the tissue fragment had actually grown into a fully developed, ever-expanding organ. But Carrel's work represented a serious step toward cultivating viruses, and so was of great value to medical research.

With the onset of World War I, Carrel returned to France, where he served as a major in the medical corps of the French army. He helped popularize the suturing techniques he had developed for treating the wounded. And with biochemist Henry Dakin he developed a fairly effective, relatively mild disinfectant to irrigate wounds before closing them. Although its use was controversial for a time (like almost everything connected with asepsis), military physicians ultimately admitted its value. The Carrel-Dakin treatment became standard before the development of antibiotics such as penicillin. Carrel, more than most surgeons, was sensitive to the dangers of sepsis, and he insisted that bacteriologists work with surgeons to assess wound-healing progress.

After the war Carrel returned to New York and the Rockefeller Institute. Like many other scientists, he spent some of his time in cancer stud-

---

*The culture was cared for from its creation in 1912 by Albert H. Ebeling, then a technician in Carrel's laboratory. Ebeling took the culture with him when he began working at the Lederle Laboratories, and its cells were used to test germicides until 1946.

ies but produced little that was fruitful. More intriguing was his work with some twelve thousand mice of various strains. Although they have never been analyzed in detail, Carrel's studies apparently showed how easily the murine life span could be modified by diet, and, more generally, the importance of environmental factors in shaping genetic potential. On still another project, Carrel worked with pioneer aviator Charles Lindbergh to develop a perfusion pump for keeping whole organs alive outside the body. After meeting Lindbergh—who was self-taught in biology and engineering—in 1930, Carrel helped him to begin building an apparatus and subsequently to carry out nearly nine hundred experiments at the Rockefeller Institute. They appeared together on the cover of *Time* magazine in 1935, and published *The Culture of Organs* together in 1938.

During the 1930s Carrel also explored his growing interest in philosophical and social issues. A Catholic who believed in clairvoyance and the power of prayer, Carrel published popular pieces in *Reader's Digest*. He approved of certain aspects of National Socialism as it developed in Germany, praising what he thought were the "worthwhile features of Fascist education." Most extensive was his work *Man, the Unknown*, a bestseller when it was published in 1933. In it Carrel expressed his hope that scientific knowledge might be used to advance humankind's spiritual condition under the leadership of a group of intellectuals.

Beautifully written, *Man, the Unknown* was also highly reactionary. Carrel discusses the nature of society in light of discoveries in biology, physics, and medicine. The book is filled with insight cheek by jowl with bizarre speculation and hair-raising social prescriptions. Carrel was an enthusiastic supporter of eugenics. He also believed that not only murderers and armed robbers but also those who "despoiled the poor of their savings [or] misled the public in important matters" ought to be "humanely and economically disposed of in small euthanasic institutions supplied with the proper gases." For petty criminals Carrel favored the whip. Overall, *Man, the Unknown* reveals a genius at work in the shadow of fascist designs on the world, chiseling emblems of despotism with tools of science.

Alexis Carrel had an unusual personal life. At age forty Carrel married Anne de la Motte de Meyrie, and in 1914 her pregnancy was ended when a bee sting led to an anaphylactic reaction. They remained childless, although she had a son from a previous marriage. After about 1926 Anne, who was trained as a nurse, stayed most of the time in France, at their house on the island of Saint Gildas, off the Brittany Coast. Carrel remained in New York City, though he thought it "too fast, too noisy." He became a member of the Century Club, where once, martini glass in hand, he pronounced alcohol mankind's greatest invention. Characteristically, he also deplored alcoholism.

Just prior to World War II, Carrel retired from the Rockefeller Institute and returned to France, where he was to remain until the end of his life. Eminent and still active, he was an outsider well placed to receive a charter from the Vichy government to put some of his grander ideas into practice. In late 1941, funded to the tune of about $8 million, he created the Institute for the Study of Human Problems. Research conducted at the institute during its brief life concerned problems of childhood and also investigated subjects such as hypnosis, parapsychology, and telepathy.

Carrel declined in a variety of ways to actively conspire with the Nazis, but his support of General Pétain's government led to rank accusations of collaborationism. Weakened by heart attacks in 1943 and 1944, Carrel suffered in other ways as the German occupation ended and the Free French came to power. He was pilloried in the press, his home was searched, and he was nearly arrested. His death on November 5, 1944, did not come too soon for peace of mind.

# Frederick Banting [1891–1941]

## The Discovery of Insulin

**V**edic texts from India dating to 800 B.C. describe the signs and symptoms of diabetes mellitus. Aretaeus of Cappadocia, in the second century, called it "a melting down of flesh and limbs into urine." In modern terms, diabetes arises when the body cannot utilize sugar, its essential fuel. The discovery that insulin, a hormone of the pancreas, could be used to treat diabetes constitutes one of the first sensational tales of twentieth-century medicine. It is replete with false starts, chance discoveries, creative teamwork, and nasty disputes over priority. The central figure, who was helped on all sides and could not have done it alone, is the Canadian doctor Frederick Banting.

Of Irish and Scottish extraction, Frederick Grant Banting was born on November 14, 1891, in Alliston, Ontario. His father was a farmer, and as a boy Frederick developed a love of animals and of nature. In school he was an average but highly competitive student who excelled in sports. It is not surprising that, although his father encouraged him toward the ministry, he decided to study medicine. After graduating the University of Toronto in 1910, Banting remained for his medical studies, which he completed in 1916. He interned at Toronto's Hospital for Sick Children. In Banting's own opinion, his medical training, shortened by World War I, was "very deficient." Toward war's end Banting became an officer in the Canadian Medical Corps and was sent to England, where he treated wounds, saw action, and was awarded the military cross for bravery. Entering private practice after returning to Canada, Banting did not have a particularly auspicious future.

Physiologists in the nineteenth century, with a new grasp of digestion and metabolic processes, had provided the nub of a modern understanding of diabetes. In 1889, an accidental discovery with an experimental dog had shown that blood sugar levels soon run abnormally high if the pancreas is removed. The animal loses weight, becomes constantly thirsty and hungry, and eventually dies. The pancreas was known to produce digestive juice, but what did it have to do with regulating sugar metabolism? The situation became more complicated when further experiments showed that merely tying off the pancreatic duct did not produce disease. A dog with a degenerated pancreas would not develop diabetes—the organ had to be removed. Much research was done to try to explain these results. Pancreatic extracts were fed to people and animals with diabetes in the hope of reversing the course of disease. Such experiments proved unsuccessful, and a voluminous literature developed.

Meanwhile, a new context in physiology had emerged with the discovery at the turn of the century of the first hormones. The concept of these "chemical messengers" was crucial to a discovery in 1916 that was largely overlooked. A British researcher, Edward Albert Sharpey-Schäfer, found that groups of cells in the pancreas, the "islets of Langerhans"—named after Paul Langerhans, who had discovered them in 1869—remained intact when the pancreatic duct was tied off. It was plausible, Sharpey-Schäfer reasoned, that these cells manufactured a hormone responsible for regulating blood sugar. In fact, he went so far as to name the hypothetical substance "insuline." But he himself did not extract it from the islets of Langerhans. It was at this point that Banting entered the field.

Banting chanced to read an article about the islets of Langerhans on October 30, 1920. He was working as a part-time teacher and demonstrator in surgery and anatomy at the University of Western Ontario, and was preparing a lecture on carbohydrate metabolism. The article, by American pathologist Moses Barron, concerned a case of an obstructed pancreatic duct. At autopsy Barron had noted that, although the pancreas itself was shriveled, the islets were not. Barron thought this suggestive and noted that the patient had not been diabetic. In brief, his modest pathology paper—classic in its aim to link disease with findings at autopsy—supported the idea that the islets of Langerhans might be important to blood sugar metabolism.

According to Banting, reading Barron's article left him sleepless. In the early morning hours he wrote in his diary, "Ligate pancreatic ducts of dog. Keep dog alive till acini degenerate leaving Islets. Try to isolate the internal secretion of these to reduce glycosurea." Banting's original idea was essentially to repeat in the laboratory the natural occurrence Barron had reported. In a living dog he would force the pancreas to degenerate to discover whether the still-active islets of Langerhans would yield the substance thought to control blood sugar.

Banting did not have excellent credentials when, hoping to obtain the wherewithal for research, he approached John Macleod, chairman of the physiology department at the University of Toronto. Macleod, an expert in carbohydrate metabolism, doubted that the cause of diabetes was hormonal. But he recognized that the experiment Banting proposed was a sound one, even if it were to provide only a negative result. So he finally offered Banting laboratory space, some experimental dogs, and the assistance of Charles Best, a young graduate student. Moving to Toronto, Banting began work in May 1921.

The result was a medical fairy tale. Within a few months, and after initial efforts failed, Banting and Best developed an acceptable design for their experiments. In some dogs they left the pancreas in place but tied off the pancreatic duct, which caused the organ to shrivel but left the islets of Langerhans intact. From other dogs they excised the pancreas entirely. Weeks later, Banting and Best removed the degenerated organs from the first group of dogs, placed them in solution, ground them up with mortar and pestle, and finally filtered them through cheesecloth. They administered the pancreatic filtrate to the pancreas-less dogs, which by now had developed diabetes. The results were dramatic. Within hours, the diabetic dogs' blood glucose levels improved substantially. It was an encouraging result.

Banting was surprised, presenting his results to Macleod, that the latter was skeptical and raised questions about procedures. But when Banting demanded a dedicated laboratory and more help, he received what he wanted. With a view toward isolating the active substance, Macleod also assigned the laboratory the services of James Collip, an expert biochemist. Collip's contribution, developing a way to purify insulin, was crucial to creating a clinically useful product. By August 1921 the entire laboratory was set up to that end. After Banting realized that islets of Langerhans cells are especially numerous in developing animals, he used cow fetuses as the source of insulin.

Banting and Best first reported the findings of their research on December 28, 1921, at a meeting of the American Physiological Society. But the medical miracle, forever after associated with their names, occurred in January 1922, when Leonard Thomas, a fourteen-year-old boy dying from diabetes at Toronto General Hospital, was given insulin and improved dramatically. (Indeed, he would live for thirteen more years and die in a motorcycle accident.) Banting and Best published a summary of their work in April 1922 in a paper entitled "The Effect Produced on Diabetes by Extracts of Pancreas."

Over the next year, as the discovery of insulin was recognized as a medical triumph, the relationship between Banting and Macleod did not improve. Banting's suspicion that Macleod wanted some credit for the discovery was not unfounded—nor was such a demand too unusual in academia. Banting was further hurt when James Collip refused to reveal how he had discovered the active agent in the islets of Langerhans. But the final straw came in 1923, when Macleod was named to share with Banting the Nobel Prize in physiology or medicine. Banting was said to have flown into a rage. He made a point of giving part of the monetary award to Best. Macleod, for his part, divided his portion with Collip. The wisdom of giving Macleod a share of the 1923 award, as well as the question of Banting's scientific abilities, were issues debated long after. The simple story of Banting and Best was for many years the heroic tale for popular consumption, but Michael Bliss, in his richly detailed book *The Discovery of Insulin,* points out that the discovery of insulin was "a much more intricate, complex event than conventional accounts have suggested."

Frederick Banting became, over the next two decades, both a popular hero and a force in medicine in Canada. The Banting and Best Department of Medical Research, located at but separate from the University of Toronto, was said to be populated by a colorful group of hard-drinking scientists. (The affinity between Banting and Best did not endure, however.) Banting undertook research into heart disease and cancer; he was interested by the discovery of Peyton Rous (p. 261) of a filterable virus that seemed to cause cancer. There remained hope that he would follow his great success with insulin with other significant discoveries.

The whole world hoped insulin would be a simple, effective treatment for diabetes. It was considered, writes Richard B. Welbourn, "the greatest advance in medical therapy since the introduction of antisepsis fifty years earlier." As it turned out, however, the situation was far more complex. Thanks to greater opportunity to study diabetes after the discovery of insulin treatment, the disease underwent considerable scrutiny. Eventually two principal types were distinguished: type 1, or juvenile-onset diabetes, which insulin can control; and the more common type 2, or adult-onset diabetes, for which insulin, as it was eventually realized, is not an effective treatment. Another aspect emerging from insulin therapy was that as diabetic patients lived longer, they developed complications from the disease, some of them severe. Diabetes today remains a serious chronic condition. Although future prospects for treating type 2 diabetes are excellent, rising rates of obesity, at least in the United States, will make the condition more prevalent.

Frederick Banting's personal life was lively, with spice befitting a medical hero. As a young doctor he planned to marry Edith Roach. Her breaking off their engagement inflicted great pain and caused him to devote himself to what became his great discovery. After winning the Nobel Prize he became a sought-after bachelor. In 1924 he was lovestruck by the beautiful Marion Robertson, and the couple married and had one child before their sensational divorce eight years later. This did not prevent Banting from being knighted in 1934. In 1939 he was married again, to Henrietta

Ball. Banting always retained his sense of humor and his disarming, cheerful personality. It was difficult to dislike him. "Next person who calls me 'Sir,'" he is supposed to have said after receiving his knighthood, "will get his ass kicked."

Banting met a tragic end. During World War II he joined the army and served as a major with the medical corps. On one of many flights between Canada and England, his plane suffered a loss of power and went down at Gander, Newfoundland. Today the lake into which the plane crashed on February 29, 1941, is known as Banting Lake.

# Walter B. Cannon [1871–1945]

## The Wisdom of the Body

A pivotal figure in twentieth-century physiology and medicine, Walter B. Cannon left a trail of discoveries that belong to both scientific and everyday knowledge about the body. Early in his career, he made pioneer use of X rays to view the digestive system, and some of the things he learned about it are taught to every schoolchild. From his theory of the adrenaline-driven response to danger comes the mature concept of the "fight or flight" reaction. Cannon also hatched one of the main theories of the physiology of emotions. Cannon was a physiologist, not a biochemist. If he missed discovering today's concept of the neurotransmitter, it was because, as Henry Dale (p. 236) points out, he belonged "to a tradition which may possibly have passed... the peak of its influence." Nevertheless, at the distance of the best part of a century, his work still informs many fields — neurology and psychology, pharmacology, gastroenterology, and endocrinology.

Cannon's crowning achievement was his concept of *homeostasis*, by which the body is understood to maintain and regulate a stable internal environment. This a twentieth-century formulation of the *milieu intérieur* postulated by Claude Bernard (p. 14). Cannon coined the term in 1926 and discussed it at length six years later in a book both popular and sophisticated, entitled *The Wisdom of the Body*. Homeostasis, according to Cannon, ensures that "every change in the outer world, and every considerable move in relation to the outer world, must be attended by a rectifying process in the inner world of the organism." Although advances in understanding the sympathetic nervous system have changed certain of his formulations, this broad generalization remains today a cornerstone of biological thinking.

Walter Bradford Cannon was born on October 19, 1871, in the Mississippi River town of Prairie du Chien, Wisconsin. Of French-Canadian and Scotch-Irish descent, Cannon was a first-born son with three sisters. His father, Colbert Hanchett Cannon, was a railroad executive, ingenious and inventive but given to bouts of depression. His mother, Sarah Wilma Denio, a schoolteacher, was a sensitive and tender woman who told Walter to "be good to the world" before she died of pneumonia when he was ten years old. "That wish was most natural for her," wrote Cannon later; "it fixed deeply in her son a sacred and haunting memory."

While attending high school in St. Paul, Minnesota, Cannon became disenchanted with religion and aware—to his father's dismay—of the debates over Darwinian theory. He was encouraged to continue his education by one of his teachers, and in 1892, with the help of a scholarship, he entered Harvard University. Here he was interested in biology, but was also fascinated by philosophy and psychology courses with Hugo Münsterburg and William James. Although Cannon was inclined to go into philosophy, James, who had himself studied medicine, told him, "Don't do it. You will be filling your belly with the east wind." Cannon took this advice. After graduating Harvard summa cum laude in 1896, he entered the university's medical school. Cannon was awarded a master's degree a year later and received his MD in 1900.

Cannon was drawn to the laboratory from the beginning of his career, and he never became a practicing physician. Remaining at Harvard, he served as instructor of physiology from 1900 until 1902, when he was named assistant professor. He was named George Higginson Professor of Physiology in 1906, and would occupy that chair for the next thirty-six years.

Cannon's first important research began when he was a student in 1896. It was a direct consequence of the discovery of X rays by W. C. Röntgen the previous year. On a professor's suggestion, Cannon investigated the physiology of deglutition, or swallowing, by X-raying a small dog induced to gulp down some pearl buttons. He continued such experiments with other animals, observing the insides of frogs and geese made to swallow capsules of bismuth subnitrate. Cannon examined the stomach at work and the other organs of digestion, and reported in detail how food passed through the alimentary canal. He published these results and eventually, in 1911, his pioneering summary, *Mechanical Factors in Digestion.*

The physiology of emotion soon became a new focus of Cannon's research, due in part to the discovery of hormones at the turn of the century. Cannon was directly influenced by a series of important but little-known papers by British physiologist Thomas Benton Elliott. The hormone adrenaline, Elliott suggested, might affect the involuntary nervous system. The idea of a chemical acting on the nervous system—then not widely thought to be electrochemical—was quite novel, and Cannon brought it to bear on the physiology of strong emotion.* Adrenaline,

---

*Thus Cannon came close to discovering the chemical transmitters of nerve impulses. He showed that the sympathetic nervous system could accelerate the heartbeat without adrenal hormones, which operate through the bloodstream. Subsequently, experiments by biochemists Otto Loewi and Henry Dale (p. 236) led to the discovery of acetylcholine, the first of many neurotransmitters to be identified.

Cannon demonstrated in the laboratory, caused an increase in heart rate, raised blood pressure, and induced other reactions. All such changes he related to the notion (originated by psychologist William McDougall) of fear inducing a fight or flight response, and the basis of this notion lay in the Darwinian concept of survival of the fittest. Cannon published his research in 1915 in the landmark book *Bodily Changes in Pain, Hunger, Fear and Rage;* a second, more elaborate edition appeared in 1929.

Although Cannon did not venture far into psychology, his early work on nervous states led to a signal contribution. A theory devised in 1884 by William James, often called the James-Lange theory of emotion, holds that visceral changes are not mere manifestations of, but themselves constitute, the emotions. With his colleague Philip Bard, Cannon developed a contrasting theory in which the brain perceives and interprets events, and emotions arise as activities prepare the body for action. "We do not 'feel sorry because we cry,' as James contended," wrote Cannon, "but we cry because, when we are sorry or overjoyed or violently angry or full of tender affection...there are nervous discharges by sympathetic channels to various viscera, including the lachrymal glands." Today, both the James-Lange and Cannon-Bard theories retain a certain conceptual currency.

During World War I, Cannon went to France in 1917 as part of the Harvard Hospital Unit to study, and perhaps to help treat, soldiers affected by "wound shock." Cannon wrote that he had to "cease to be a laboratory hermit and go forth into the world for scientific study. I must turn from the observations on natural processes in lower animals to observations on grievously torn and battered human beings." "A Parenthesis of War," a chapter in his autobiography, *The Way of an Investigator,* is a harrowing introduction to the appalling battle wounds so common in the Great War. Cannon ultimately regarded shock as a reaction to the sudden drop in volume of circulating blood—essentially still a correct interpretation. In 1923 Cannon published a book on the subject, *Traumatic Shock.* When World War II renewed the carnage twenty years later, Cannon, as chairman of the National Research Council's Committee on Shock and Transfusion, would direct another series of research efforts on shock.

Cannon's concept of homeostasis, which was based on his earlier work with adrenaline, was first articulated in a 1926 paper, "Physiological Regulation of Normal States: Some Tentative Postulates Concerning Biological Homeostatics." He published a longer exegesis in 1929. He described how the body fluids remain in balance, and he explained hunger, thirst, and body temperature as examples of homeostatic functions. Cannon's concept of homeostasis represents an advance in understanding how the body functions, gained as a consequence of new discoveries about the nervous and endocrine systems. "Further research," wrote Cannon, "would probably prove that similar devices are effective in maintaining the constancy of other elements in the body fluids." Homeostasis both proved the idea of Claude Bernard's *milieu intérieur* and pointed toward new biochemical discoveries in the future. Norbert Weiner was influenced by the concept when he developed cybernetics in the late 1940s, and in 1975 Edward O. Wilson described homeostasis as an "elementary concept" in his construction of sociobiology.

A committed scientist, Cannon advanced some political statements that embroiled him in controversy late in his career. During the 1920s he became a friend of the Russian scientist Ivan Pavlov, which was not surprising in light of their shared interest in the nervous system, and in 1935 he visited the Soviet Union. Friendly remarks he made about the communist country, then in the midst of Stalinization, returned to haunt him, as did his term as president of the American-Soviet Medical Society. Cannon was also a member of the Medical Bureau to Aid Spanish Democracy, and at the end of the Spanish Civil War, he helped to find academic posts for physicians and scientists who had been forced to flee to the United States. These liberal actions were just that, done in the name of decency and a basic humanitarian outlook. Cannon himself was a Republican in politics and, by upbringing and inclination, a conservative.

Because of his eminence, Cannon was allowed to work at Harvard after the mandatory retirement age of sixty-six. He finally left the university in 1942, his health failing due to mycosis fungoides, a rare disease probably related to his overexposure to X rays four decades earlier. Walter Cannon died on October 1, 1945.

# Archibald Garrod [1857–1936]

## Genetic Disorders and Biochemical Individuality

K nowledge about genetic diseases has increased dramatically in recent years, and the role that genetics will play in the future of medicine is very great. By some estimates more than four thousand disorders and clinical syndromes—ranging from harmless to catastrophic and lethal—are genetically determined. In the final analysis, all such disorders are due to altered (or missing) enzymes produced (or not) by defective genes. As a group they constitute the "inborn errors of metabolism." This basic concept may be traced to the insights of the British physician Archibald Garrod.

Garrod developed this idea, and the allied notion of "biochemical individuality," at the turn of the twentieth century, just about the time the work of Gregor Mendel was rediscovered. Mendelian genetics was crucial to the development of a new and dependable grasp of heredity, but several decades were to pass before research would shed more light on Garrod's powerful insights. His reputation has since grown, and he is considered today, as Christopher Booth writes, "the great pioneer of biochemical genetics who...brought biochemistry to the bedside." American geneticist George Beadle, receiving the Nobel Prize in 1957, called Garrod the "father of chemical genetics."

Archibald Edward Garrod was born in London on November 25, 1857. He was the fourth and youngest son of Elisabeth Ann Colchester and Sir Alfred Baring Garrod. His father, a prominent physician, was the first to discover excess uric acid in the blood of patients suffering from gout. At Marlborough School, Archibald was interested in physical geography and science at the expense of the classics, and was encouraged by the school's headmaster. At Christ Church, Oxford, he was captivated by astronomy and graduated in 1880 with first-class honors in the natural sciences. He went on to medical school and trained at St. Bartholomew's Hospital, qualifying as a physician in 1884. During postgraduate studies in Vienna, he learned about the newly invented laryngoscope—the instrument for examining the larynx—and wrote an introduction to its use, published in 1886.

Garrod enjoyed clinical medicine and also had time for research. He presented the image of the handsome and personable young doctor and was able to coax detailed histories from his patients. Like his father, Garrod studied diseases of the joints, and in several original papers he illuminated the difference between rheumatism and rheumatoid arthritis.* Most significantly, Garrod became friends during this period with Frederick Gowland Hopkins, one of the influential founders of biochemistry. Through work with Hopkins, Garrod became intrigued by the pigmentation of urine, and this led to an interest in disorders of metabolism.

It had long been known that various diseases — diabetes is the most famous example — reveal themselves through urine. For centuries physicians tested urine using their five senses. By the end of the nineteenth century, however, new instruments were available and a new chemistry had emerged. Through the 1890s Garrod studied the color of urine, and in 1895 he published a paper entitled "A Specimen of Urine Rendered Green by Indigo." In 1896 Garrod began to employ spectroscopy to chemically analyze the composition of normal and abnormal urine.

One disorder that dramatically manifests itself through urine is alkaptonuria. It had been described in 1822 and was thought, by the late nineteenth century, to be due to a bacterial infection of the intestines. A rare and essentially harmless anomaly, alkaptonuria causes urine to darken dramatically when it meets the air. Garrod came across a case of it in hospital. Analyzing this case and over thirty others observed by him or his colleagues, he presented his findings in a brief article in *Lancet* in 1899. The parents of children with the disease, he wrote, were healthy. The disease could not be shown to be contagious but seemed to be congenital, coming to light soon after birth. More than one child in a family might be affected.

Garrod learned more over the next two years. In particular, he discovered that the parents of his original patient were first cousins — their mothers were sisters. He discovered the same pattern in other families of affected children. In an article in 1901, Garrod wrote that this consanguinity had clear significance: it "can hardly be ascribed to chance...." He added that "further evidence ... would be of great general interest."

Garrod's discovery gained its larger significance with the rediscovery of the work of Gregor Mendel and the publication, in 1902, of William Bateson's *Mendel's Principles of Heredity.* In general, Mendel's work on inherited characteristics of peas, originally published in 1866 and neglected for thirty-five years, provided a model for the new science of genetics. Garrod

---

*Garrod's classification was essentially correct. He saw rheumatism, a generic term today, as a specific disorder with various manifestations — rheumatic fever or rheumatic heart disease. By contrast, he saw rheumatoid arthritis as a disease of the joints; today it is known to affect other tissues and organs as well.

immediately understood that Mendelian laws also provided a basic explanatory mechanism for alkaptonuria. The appearance of the disorder among siblings at a ratio of 3:1 in families whose parents were closely related implied a recessive factor at work. With understated irony, Garrod wrote Bateson, whom he knew, "I do not see any way of introducing any marriageable alkaptonurics to each other with a view to matrimony."

Garrod was aware of the potential impact of his discovery. The same mechanism might explain a variety of diseases, several of which he could readily identify. Albinism (lack of skin pigment) was harmless, as was pentosuria (a disorder of sugar metabolism); more serious was cystinuria, which can cause kidney and bladder stones. Garrod realized that if some genetic diseases showed themselves dramatically, there would no doubt exist many others that probably would *not* present obvious signs. As he wrote Bateson, "Both alkaptonuria and cystinuria are conditions which advertise their presence, and it seems probable that there are other freaks of metabolism which do not do so." He soon published "The Incidence of Alkaptonuria: A Study of Chemical Individuality."

In 1908, when he gave the Croonian Lectures to the Royal College of Physicians, Garrod coined the term "inborn errors of metabolism." The next year these lectures were published as a book under the same title. Garrod "not only appreciated the medical importance of recessive inheritance," write Alexander Bearn and Elizabeth Miller, "but he also recognized the reality of the larger and ultimately more important concept of human chemical individuality." Indeed, Garrod wrote William Bateson, "I believe that no two individuals are exactly alike chemically any more than structurally. I fancy that monstrosities or rather malformations, vestigial remnants and individual differences all have their chemical analogues." No real modification of this view is necessary today.

Garrod's work was of fundamental importance to medicine and to the revolution in genetics research, but it was also long neglected. He became known for the concepts of biochemical individuality and inborn errors of metabolism, and a second edition of *The Inborn Errors of Metabolism* would be published in 1923. Garrod continued to expand and refine his ideas and in 1931 published *The Inborn Factors in Disease*. But for many years his work excited little interest among either physicians or researchers. Doctors seldom encountered rare conditions such as alkaptonuria, and geneticists were more occupied with the genetics of the fruit fly and still simpler organisms. Biochemists, meanwhile, could not produce evidence that would make physicians and geneticists sit up and take notice. Garrod predicted that alkaptonuria, for example, would eventually be shown to be due to an enzyme deficiency. So it was—but not for half a century.

Garrod was named full professor at St. Bartholomew's Hospital in 1912. In 1920 he took up the Regius professorship of medicine at Oxford, succeeding Sir William Osler (p. 181). Like Osler, Garrod was personable and well liked, and he also endured his share of personal tragedy. World War I was a brutal experience for him. Two of his three sons were killed in battle, and at war's end his third son died of Spanish influenza. He and his wife, Laura Elizabeth Smith, whom he had married in 1886, were consoled by the success of their daughter, Dorothy. She became a well-known archaeologist, distinguished for her work on the Pleistocene, and was the first woman professor at Cambridge University. Garrod died on March 28, 1936, after a short illness.

# Otto Warburg [1883-1970]
## Basic Discoveries in Biochemistry

I nasmuch as medicine today speaks the language of biochemistry, Otto Warburg's influence can scarcely be reckoned. He is best known for showing how cells use oxygen—an explanation that greatly clarified metabolic processes. But Warburg is also responsible for about sixty significant discoveries in basic research. If one considers Emil Fischer the greatest organic chemist, and Linus Pauling the most significant physical chemist, then the most original and productive biochemist in the twentieth century would be Otto Warburg.

Warburg, it should be said, was one of the first biochemists to possess a grasp of the new atomic physics as it developed in the early twentieth century. During the previous century, as modern chemistry suffered its protracted birth, scientists had to guess which of various chemical reactions might be involved in any particular biological process. But Warburg, working with a mathematically driven model drawn from physics, pioneered new measurement techniques and employed detailed in vitro studies of basic molecular reactions. This new approach proved enormously useful to medical research. It eventually yielded the whole panoply of pathways that characterize metabolism, the fundamental chemical activity of any organism. And it laid, in part, the basis for molecular biology.

Otto Heinrich Warburg was born in Freiburg im Breisgau, in Baden, on October 8, 1883. The Warburgs were an eminent Jewish family, and his father, Emil Warburg, was a renowned experimental physicist, known for his studies on the kinetic theory of gases. His mother, Elizabeth Gartner, came from a Christian family of scholars and bankers. When Otto was twelve years old, the Warburgs moved to Berlin, where Emil took a professorship at the university. As a child in this rich and scholarly home, Otto met some of the most important leaders of science, including Albert Einstein and Max Planck.

Warburg's university education embraced both biological and physical sciences. He studied chemistry at the universities of Freiburg and Berlin, where he came under the influence of Emil Fischer and adopted his high standards of scientific rigor in designing experiments. Moving between biology and physics, he also studied thermodynamics in living systems with the prominent chemist Walter Nernst. But Warburg was drawn to basic medical research. After receiving his doctorate in chemistry in 1906, he went on to study medicine at the University of Heidelberg and took his medical degree in 1911. He soon undertook research at the famous Zoological Station in Naples, where he became a disciple of Jacques Loeb, a well-known biologist with a penchant for materialist, chemical explanations of life processes. While in Naples, Warburg began experiments with sea urchins that would ultimately lead to an understanding of respiration on a cellular level.

Elected to the Kaiser Wilhelm Institute in 1913, at age thirty, Warburg had already developed a considerable reputation when World War I broke out. For the next four years he served as a cavalry officer with the Prussian Horse Guard. When he returned to the Kaiser Wilhelm Institute in 1918 — in part at the behest of Albert Einstein, then the leader of German physics — he thoroughly devoted himself to research. He neither gave lectures nor sat on committees, but served as head of a powerful laboratory and, in a sense, became an institution unto himself.

The significance of Warburg's studies of intracellular respiration — how cells use oxygen — is hard to overestimate. In providing a chemical explanation of a basic life process, this work united the historic aims of chemistry and biology and provided a basic model of the action of enzymes. As early as 1777, Antoine Lavoisier had recognized that respiration involves oxidation, which, for some years, was believed to take place in the lungs. After it became clear that the blood transported oxygen to the cells, the question arose: How do the cells use it? "If the combustible substances in the cell are not auto-oxidizable," wrote Warburg later, "and if the cell material itself is not, with what then does the molecular oxygen, which is absorbed by the respiring cell, react?" Presumably, some enzyme — a chemical catalyst — was at work.

Even before World War I, in 1914, Warburg noted that the crushed eggs of sea urchins absorbed oxygen faster when iron salts were added. Ten years later he was able to show that iron is the active ingredient, as it were, in the transfer of oxygen from the blood to the cell. He discovered the cell structure today known as the mitochondrion. And by 1930 he had identified an enzyme, eventually named cytochrome oxidase, as responsible for catalyzing the oxidative reactions in the cell. "The significance of Warburg's discovery," writes Garland Allen, "was that it identified a specific enzyme with a complex metabolic process such as respiration...." In 1931, Warburg won the Nobel Prize in physiology or

medicine "for his discovery of the nature and mode of action of the respiratory enzyme."

To this highly simplified account of Warburg's studies of oxygen use in cells it should be added that they involved a number of technical laboratory innovations. It is sometimes said that, first and foremost, Warburg regarded himself as a technician. To focus on enzyme action within the living cell, for example, he developed what came to be known as the *Warburg technique,* a method of collecting tissue samples that yielded sections of tissue so thin—ten to twenty layers of cells—that they could be kept alive in a nutrient-rich culture medium. Another invention was the *Barcroft-Warburg apparatus,* which enabled sensitive measurement of changes in gas pressure within a flask. Finally, to show the presence of various molecules—where quantities were too small to hope to isolate—Warburg adapted the venerable method of spectrophotometry, analyzing chemical composition through characteristic wavelengths of light.

Warburg's interest in plant metabolism paralleled his work in animal respiration. The pigment hemoglobin, found in red blood cells, is chemically similar to green chlorophyll, found in plants. The basic explanation of how plants, using chlorophyll, capture solar energy and convert it to chemical energy was developed over the course of the nineteenth century. Warburg's studies, beginning about 1920 and lasting decades, attempted to quantify this process according to the requirements of the new quantum theory of light and energy devised by Albert Einstein. Experimenting with green algae, Warburg was able to show that photosynthesis—the conversion of light into chemical energy—occurs with exceptional efficiency in terms of quanta of light required to produce individual molecules of oxygen. Warburg reacted bitterly when other laboratories could not replicate his numbers, and the controversy continued until the end of his life. Warburg apparently employed a plausible but invalid theory to arrive at his values, based on his view that photosynthesis is, "like the world itself, nearly perfect." Photosynthesis is an efficient process, but 8 to 12 quanta of light are needed to produce 1 molecule of oxygen, not 3 to 4, as Warburg maintained.

Far less fruitful was Warburg's extensive research into cancer. He theorized that tumors originated through respiration injury to cells, which led to the proliferation of cells characteristic of cancer. The root of all cancer, he proposed, was an aberration of oxygen uptake. He based this on the simple observation that cancer cells can live and reproduce without oxygen. "Cancer, above all other diseases, has countless secondary causes," wrote Warburg. "But, even for cancer there is only one prime cause."

Warburg made his arguments prominently and received a good deal of attention. He believed that adding the various respiratory enzymes to the diet, including iron and B vitamins, would help protect against cancer. This has never been shown to be the case. Today Warburg's theory holds purely historical interest. Subsequent research into the fundamental causes of cancer would be driven largely by discoveries in molecular biology and genetics. Nor does the wide variety of chemotherapeutic agents available today depend on Warburg's work.

Although Warburg was half-Jewish, his prominence protected him from anti-Semitism during the 1930s. Indeed, he decided to stay in Germany during the exodus preceding World War II. He had received the Iron Cross for his service with the Prussian Horse Guard, and in the Nazi era he was specially protected. Presumably this was because Adolph Hitler, a hypochondriac, had a great fear of cancer and believed he might benefit from Warburg's investigations. During the war Warburg continued his research at the Institute for Cellular Physiology, and when Berlin was bombed, his laboratory was moved out of the city. After the Russians invaded, his equipment was confiscated. But in 1950 he moved into a new laboratory, today the Max Planck Institute for Cell Physiology.

Famously, Warburg possessed a difficult and eccentric personality. He was stimulating to work with, straightforward, and honest—but he was also filled with resentment and quick to anger. He had detractors, writes Robert Weinberg, who "detested his style, his authoritarian voice, his imperial German certainty." Even Hans Krebs (p. 240) reproached Warburg directly for what he called "ghastly polemics" against a colleague. "There is really no reason," the equitable Krebs wrote to his old colleague, "for feelings of bitterness toward your fellow scientists who, all over the world, acknowledge you as one of the greatest of contemporary scientists."

Warburg, the former cavalry soldier, took early morning rides during which he did much of his thinking. On the last of these, he was thrown from his horse and broke his femur. He did not recover. Otto Warburg, a bachelor all his life, left a sole heir at his death on August 1, 1970—his companion, Jacob Heiss.

# Abraham Flexner   [1866–1959]

## Educating Doctors

By 1900 the United States, with a rapidly expanding urban middle class, had become an international power, an exemplar of capitalism, and an eager workshop of a new consumerism. For its many social and political failings, it was castigated from the podium, in the press, and on the soapbox by muckrakers, Progressives, suffragists, and socialists. This ferment, together with the growing alliance between science and medicine, ensured that traditional methods of medical education, notably out of step and antiquated, would have to be replaced. This reform became a significant turning point in twentieth-century medicine. The architect of the new and the trenchant critic of the old was Abraham Flexner.

An educator, not a physician, Flexner was hired by the philanthropic Carnegie Foundation to survey the medical colleges in the United States and Canada. Flexner's report, issued in 1910, set forth his empirical research and outlined his prescription for a progressive reorganization of the system of medical education. With the time ripe — forces for reform had been brewing since about 1870 — the effect was nearly immediate. Within a decade Flexner's views prevailed, and older methods of medical education folded and gave way. Ever since, the Flexner report has been a document of constant reference in the history of medical education.

Abraham Flexner was born in Louisville, Kentucky, on November 13, 1866, the sixth of nine children of Morris and Esther Flexner — "pious Jews," as he recalled them. Morris had taught school in Bohemia before coming to the United States in 1853. He developed a successful wholesale hat business and prospered during the Civil War, but he went bankrupt in the economic panic of 1873. Abraham, with the help of his brother Jacob, the proprietor of a profitable pharmacy, became the first in his family to obtain a college education. He entered newly founded Johns Hopkins University in 1884, studied classics, and graduated in two years to save the expense of a third. Abraham later encouraged his older brother, Simon, to attend Johns Hopkins. Simon Flexner went on to become as distinguished in the field of microbiology as Abraham was in education, and to serve as head of the Rockefeller Institute.

Returning to Louisville in 1886, Abraham Flexner taught at the Louisville Male High School. He was highly regarded by his students and soon developed unique ideas about education. After four years he set up his own preparatory school, aimed at helping pupils enter and succeed in college. His methods were radical: he did not believe in rules, gave no exams, and encouraged students to learn at their own pace. This system, which emphasized individual abilities and worked to the advantage of self-motivated students, won praise from Harvard's Charles William Eliot. Flexner soon visited Eliot and wrote an article for the *Educational Review,* "A Freshman at Nineteen," in which he expounded on his ideas and methods.

In 1905, his ambitions whetted by his local notoriety, Flexner closed his school and moved east to enroll in Harvard's master of education program. In this he was assisted financially by the success of his wife, Anne Crawford, a playwright. The system of teaching at Harvard did not impress him, and after receiving his master's degree Flexner traveled to Europe, where he spent a year at the University of Heidelberg. Published in 1908, his book *The American College: A Criticism* was an attack on higher education in the United States. Inasmuch as Flexner was already hoping for a position with the newly established Carnegie Foundation for the Advancement of Teaching, its greater significance was to lay the groundwork for Flexner's rise from relatively obscure educator to renowned educational reformer.

Through a friend, Flexner arranged for an introduction to Henry Pritchett, president of the Carnegie Foundation. Pritchett, whom Flexner had frequently cited in *The American College,* had just recommended that the Carnegie examine the state of medical education in the United States. When the two met, he proposed that Flexner undertake the task. At first Flexner believed Pritchett was confusing him with his already eminent brother, Simon, and he explained that he was not a medical professional. "That is precisely what I want," Pritchett replied. "I think these professional schools should be studied not from the point of view of the practitioner but from the standpoint of the educator. . . . This is a layman's job, not a job for a medical man." Flexner won the assignment because, in addition to being a good writer, he shared many of Pritchett's views on education.

In general, when Flexner began his work in 1908 medical education was in a period of significant transition toward higher standards. Johns Hopkins Medical School, recently founded in 1893, provided a positive model. This institution, Flexner thought, "adapted to American conditions . . . the best features of medical education in England, France and Germany." Johns Hopkins had become successful with a "learn by doing" approach that modified the older didactic teaching methods by integrating in-hospital training

with a sophisticated medical curriculum. Other universities—Harvard and the University of Michigan, for example—had also upgraded their medical schools.

However, the lesser universities and the private schools still accounted for a high proportion of the medical training institutions, and they became Flexner's target. These schools varied widely in the quality of education they offered, but most conspicuous were those at the bottom—the "proprietary" institutions. Most of these were essentially holdovers from the past, when a student could be graduated with a doctor's degree after two sixteen-week semesters spent listening to lectures from physicians who were out of touch with recent developments in medical research and practice. Many of these schools offered scant training in clinical medicine, and their laboratories were inferior or nonexistent.

Flexner amassed first-hand information through on-site inspections— he personally called on virtually all of the medical colleges in the United States and Canada. He was often welcomed by administrators who believed his association with the Carnegie Foundation might provide future philanthropic benefit to their school, and who were consequently especially forthcoming about their institution's shortcomings. Flexner was often able to scrutinize entrance requirements and to discover whether students were actually held to them. He looked into the laboratories, if the school possessed any, and examined the competence of teachers. With characteristic self-confidence he wrote that, "In half an hour or less, I could sample the credentials of students ... ascertain the matriculation requirements ... and determine whether or not the standards, low or high, set forth in the school catalogue were being evaded or enforced."

Flexner's report, *Medical Education in the United States and Canada,* was published in 1910 as Bulletin Number Four of the Carnegie Foundation. In an era of Progressive muckraking, it was a bombshell. Flexner's findings were widely reported in the press and created a demand for change. A favorable financial climate made this possible. Although some university administrators defended the status quo and charged Flexner with making "the worst of things," many accepted both his evaluations and prescription. But the lower-quality, more out-of-date schools did not survive. "Schools collapsed right and left," wrote Flexner, "usually without a murmur." Bad publicity drove some out of existence entirely; others merged with more viable institutions. The Flexner report reputedly sounded the death knell for nearly half the medical colleges in America at the time.

Flexner laid out an extensive and concrete plan for change. Above all, he recommended reducing the number of medical schools and, hence, the number of students. The country was producing too many doctors for the marketplace. Thirty-one good medical schools, Flexner suggested, could do a better job than the 155 schools of such widely varying quality that he had visited. He suggested that medical schools be attached to universities, and that entrance requirements include two years of science.

Flexner also attacked the idea that standards for a medical education should be low enough to enable a child from a poor background to become a doctor. It was no advantage, he pointed out, to have incompetent doctors practicing medicine badly in rural areas. Like many Progressives, Flexner would today be called to task for racism; his attitude was one of "benevolent paternalism." He believed that the number of Negro medical schools should be reduced from 7 to 2. Black doctors should be trained, he believed, because Negroes constituted a "potential source of infection and contagion."

Abraham Flexner had a long and distinguished career after the appearance of his famous report. In 1912 he followed his first report with a second, this on medical education in Europe. In 1913, he began working for the General Education Board of the Rockefeller Foundation, becoming its secretary in 1917. From this position Flexner solicited endowments and extracted philanthropic largesse to be funneled to the more successful institutions. Wealthy American capitalists and robber barons transformed themselves at Flexner's urging, as age crept upon them, into benefactors of all humankind. Department store magnate Julius Rosenwald supported Rush Medical College in Chicago. Robert S. Brookings gave a fortune to Washington University in St. Louis. "Flexner is the worst highwayman that ever flitted in and out of Rochester [New York]," said inventor George Eastman. "He put up a job on me and cleaned me out of a thundering lot of my hard-earned savings." Flexner himself would confess to having raised some $600 million for medical schools in the United States.

Flexner went on, in later life, to become director of the Institute for Advanced Study in Princeton, New Jersey. He saw the institute as a place where scholars should be able to pursue basic research without heavy teaching obligations. His 1930 book *Universities: American, English, German* was widely discussed among educators. He personally invited Albert

Einstein to leave the turmoil of an increasingly anti-Semitic Germany and join the institute in 1932.

Abraham Flexner married Anne Laziere Crawford in 1898; she was the first female student at his preparatory school. Anne's successful dramatic adaptation of stories by Alice Hegan Rice, *Mrs. Whiggs of the Cabbage Patch,* ran seven years in New York, was twice made into films, and provided her husband the wherewithal to embark upon his career. The couple had a companionable marriage and two daughters. Flexner's own *I Remember: An Autobiography* was published in 1940. Said to be good humored and charming when he wanted, and somewhat shy but affectionate, he was also regarded as an unyielding manipulator who was dogmatic and acerbic, and even a "prize academic snob." His death came on September 21, 1959.

Regard for Abraham Flexner's contributions has fluctuated considerably over the years. According to his front-page obituary in the *New York Times,* "No other American of his time has contributed more to the welfare of his country and of humanity in general." But he was an elitist, and by the 1980s his contributions were being reassessed. In 1984 historian of medicine Lester King called his famous report "probably the most grossly overrated document in American medical history." In general, Flexner is seen today, in a broader historical and social context, as the culminating figure in the reorganization of medical education in the United States. "While not entirely responsible for reforming American medical education," writes historian Susan Lawrence, ". . . Flexner gave a strong voice to the vision of scientific medical training and a profession with fewer but 'better' doctors."

# Harvey Cushing  [1869–1939]

## Arrival of the Brain Surgeon

B rain surgery is not easy or simple: the structure of the skull does not readily lend itself to be opened, and the brain is a self-contained unit not easily repaired. Nevertheless, from the time humans lived in caves, they practiced some kind of cranial surgery. Thousands of years later, at the dawn of modern medicine, pioneering brain operations often provided great harvests of useful knowledge, but the patient commonly died. Neurosurgery could not evolve as a specialty until the early twentieth century, and one of its great transformational figures was the American Harvey Cushing.

Great surgeons win immense admiration as a matter of course in medical affairs. Harvey Cushing, whose accomplishments extended beyond the operating room, operated where no one had gone before. He was also a neuropathologist whose research made possible new interventions to remove brain tumors and, most memorably, to treat pituitary disease. Over the course of about twenty years, Cushing, writes Ira Rutkow, "developed many of the basic techniques and procedures used in surgery of the brain and spinal cord." He did much to advance general surgical technique as well. The now standard practice of monitoring vital signs during operations and the use of suction are just two examples of Cushing's more general influence.

Cushing was a perfectionist. "He would emerge from an operation which had exacted extreme skill and attention for many hours—" wrote Walter B. Cannon (p. 210), "gay and eager if all had gone well, or toneless and depressed if the outlook for the patient was ominous." He drove his students mercilessly, and he himself suffered from gastric ulcer. The unparalleled surgeon was also a prolific and skilled author, an artist, historian, biographer, and bibliophile. No less than Charles Sherrington, founder of modern neurology, called Cushing "a personality of transcendent accomplishments and of singular charm."

Of patrician stock, Harvey Cushing was born on April 8, 1869, to Henry Kirke Cushing and Betsy Williams. He was the last child of ten, seven of whom grew to adulthood. Henry Cushing, a doctor who was himself a son and grandson of physicians, held himself aloof from family matters, but his wife preserved an atmosphere of warmth. In a classic picture of the nineteenth-century hearth, Harvey and the other children would sprawl on the floor on a Sunday afternoon, while their grandfather read aloud from Oliver Wendell Holmes's *The Autocrat of the Breakfast Table*. After taking a bachelor of arts degree at Yale in 1891, Harvey entered Harvard Medical School. He received his medical degree four years later and interned at Massachusetts General Hospital.

Cushing had the good fortune to enter surgery at a time when new scientific achievements were creating a climate of optimism. When news of the discovery of X rays reached the United States in early 1896, Cushing was enthusiastic. He wrote his father that "Dr. Röntgen may have discovered something with his cathode rays which may revolutionize medical diagnosis." After blaming himself unduly for the death of a surgical patient from an overdose of ether, Cushing took steps to remedy what he understood to be a larger problem in anesthesia. With a friend, he devised charts for recording temperature and respiration during surgery. These were adopted by Massachusetts General Hospital, and their use became widespread. This was Cushing's first contribution to medicine.

Cushing's residency under William Halsted, the eminent surgeon and renowned founder of Johns Hopkins, brought him directly into the high echelons of American medicine. Cushing learned from him even though, at the time, Halsted was suffering from a cocaine addiction and had largely withdrawn to his laboratory. Patients came to Johns Hopkins from far and wide, afflicted by all sorts of unusual disorders, and from 1896 to 1900 Cushing performed a number of unique operations. He became the first surgeon to remove a human spleen. He improved the use of cocaine as an anesthetic, using it for amputations. In 1898 his efforts to treat trigeminal neuralgia (tic douloureux), a painful neurological disorder, brought him considerable fame. Due in part to this work, Cushing became increasingly involved in neurosurgery.

To study with Halsted, Cushing had put off the training in Europe that was customary for scientifically minded American physicians. Finally in 1900, his residency completed, he journeyed across the Atlantic. In Switzerland he studied briefly with Emil Theodore Kocher, a famed surgeon who would win the Nobel Prize in 1909 for work on thyroid disease. Cushing soon moved on to England, where he worked with Charles Sherrington. Touring Italy, he stopped by Pavia to acquire a sphygmomanometer, a device for measuring the blood pressure, which had recently been improved for clinical use by Scipione Riva-Rocci. Its inflatable armlet was an important innovation, and Cushing brought it back to Johns Hopkins. It was soon employed widely (eventually universally) in clinical practice.

When he returned from Europe, Cushing effectively became the first full-time neurosurgeon in the United States. From 1903 he was associate professor of surgery at Johns Hopkins. In 1912 he was named Moseley Professor of Surgery at Harvard Medical School and surgeon-in-chief at Peter Bent Brigham Hospital in Boston. From these posts, which he would keep twenty years, Cushing became one of the most influential figures in modern medicine. Like William Osler (p. 181), with whom he became good friends, Cushing was stimulating and charismatic. He was an innovative teacher, in favor of exposing medical students to immediate clinical experience. In addition, Cushing established the Hunterian Laboratory for animal experimentation, named after John Hunter (p. 140), a surgeon and pioneer of comparative anatomy. The Hunterian played an important, widely emulated role in teaching and developing new surgical procedures by substituting dogs for human cadavers.

At a time when brain surgery was in all cases a last resort, Cushing strove for better survival rates. This was true both at Johns Hopkins and during World War I, when, posted to France, he performed surgery to treat numerous head wounds. The major problem presented by brain surgery was bleeding. Even eminent surgeons such as Victor Horsley frequently had success rates of only about fifty percent. Steve Lehrer, in his *Explorers of the Body,* recalls one of Cushing's own failures. Having excised a brain tumor, Cushing tried to cut off the stalk to which it had been attached, but this maneuver broke open the artery. Blood gushed forth, and the patient was doomed. Cushing laid down his instruments and told the patient, who was conscious, "You must not worry now. In a very few minutes you are going to feel better."

To avoid such fatal accidents, Cushing improved his skills through constant work in the operating room and made a number of innovations. In 1910 he devised a type of silver wire clip for controlling hemorrhage that allowed brain operations to be essentially bloodless. Fifteen years later Cushing learned about diathermy, in which an electric current could be applied nondestructively to tissue. He thereupon sought the help of a physicist, Dr. William Bovie, to devise a machine he could use to coagulate bleeding points in the brain during surgery. The "Bovie," for electrocoagulation, first put into use in 1926, would help Cushing operate on previously inoperable cases. He eventually performed over two thousand procedures, with an unheard of mortality rate of only about ten percent. The results of his work on intracranial tumors were detailed in his monograph *Meningiomas,* published in 1938.

One of Cushing's most significant accomplishments was to help elucidate the function (and malfunction) of the brain's pituitary gland. Located behind the nasal sinus, the pituitary became the focus of Cushing's interest as early as 1908. Such conditions as sexual infantilism, gigantism, and acromegaly (abnormal enlargement of the bones of the face, hands, and feet) had sometimes been linked to the pituitary by tumors found at autopsy. But the gland — "the most inaccessible and the most complex of all the glands of internal secretion" — was relatively little discussed in spite of the recent discovery of, and interest in, hormones and the endocrine system.

Indeed, Cushing's careful description of what was known as "polyglandular syndrome" was an important watershed for endocrinology. It helped illustrate the consequences of abnormal hormone production, whether reduced or excessive. In experiments with animals, Cushing found that removing the pituitary from dogs led them to become fat and sluggish. Cushing recognized that various conditions might be due to pituitary malfunction, whether from undersecretion or overproduction of hormone. In 1912, he published a famous study, *The Pituitary Body and Its Disorders.* Within a decade, the anterior lobe of the pituitary gland was found to secrete a growth-controlling hormone.

Cushing's interest in the pituitary extended over the next twenty years. In 1930 he was able to link a cluster of symptoms to basophilic cells in the pituitary gland, where an adenoma, a kind of tumor, can cause excess secretion of growth hormone. This abnormality became known as *Cushing's disease.* The related but more general term, *Cushing's syndrome,* describes the condition with or without tumor or tissue abnormality. In addition, Cushing was able to show that the functioning of the pituitary influences other aspects of the endocrine system. Not surprisingly, Cushing's 1932 report to the Johns Hopkins Medical Society is regarded as an exceptional work in modern medicine.

Cushing retired from surgery in 1931, after removing his two thousandth brain tumor. But he remained active. In 1933 he was appointed Sterling Professor of Neurology at Yale University. A bibliophile, he had collected some eight thousand books on medicine and physiology. He donated them to Yale Medical School, and today they form part of its historical collection. As a writer, Cushing matured over the years. His most famous book was a two-volume life of his mentor and friend Sir William Osler. Reverential and overlong, it won the Pulitzer Prize in 1926. Cushing's biography of Andreas Vesalius (p. 41) was published posthumously in 1943. Other of Cushing's historical contributions and literary pieces can be found in two volumes, *Consecratio medici,* from 1928, and *The Medical Career,* published in 1940.

"No eminent and inspiring leader ever had more devoted and affectionate admirers," wrote Walter B. Cannon in tribute to Cushing. But in reality, in spite of magnetism and charm, Cushing was domineering and ofttimes arrogant. He was so given to narcissistic rage as a young doctor that William Osler warned him about it. He was lucky to find in Katherine Stone Crowell a serene and charming wife. They were married in 1902, after ten years of courtship, and had three daughters and two sons. Cushing was a strict father and had better relationships with his daughters than with his sons. To say that he was not always readily in touch with his emotional core is an understatement. Learning that his eldest son, William Harvey Cushing, had been killed in an automobile accident in 1926, Cushing made several telephone calls and went on to perform that morning's scheduled operation. In the autumn of 1939, just as World War II began, Cushing's health began to seriously fail. He suffered heart block and died on October 7, 1939. Before he was cremated and his ashes were returned to the Western Reserve in Ohio, where he had been born, his body was autopsied. Harvey Cushing was found to have been suffering from a small but perceptible brain tumor.

# Hans Spemann [1869–1941]

## Embryology and the "Organizer"

In 1924 Hans Spemann arrived at a considerable generalization about the nature of embryonic development. The language may seem daunting, but he performed *dorsal blastosphere lip transplantation* on the embryo of a newt. By this means he discovered that a specific area of an embryo, at a specific point in development, will direct the structural development of surrounding tissue. The "organizer," as he called it, proved central to an enlarged understanding of growth and the mechanics of development. It engendered much research that eventually would be intersected by discoveries in biochemistry and molecular biology. Spemann was awarded the Nobel Prize in physiology or medicine in 1953, the only time the award would be bestowed for discoveries in what today may be termed classical embryology.

Hans Spemann was born on June 27, 1869, in Stuttgart, the eldest of four children of Johann Wilhelm Spemann and Lisinka Hoffman. The Spemanns were a cultivated family, and Johann was an affluent publisher. Hans was raised to appreciate art and literature, and he first intended to study classics. After graduating the Eberhard Ludwigs gymnasium in 1888, he worked with his father's firm for a year and fulfilled his military obligation with the Kassel Hussars. Not until 1891 did he enter the University of Heidelberg, where he initially intended to study medicine. But he was strongly influenced by Gustav Wolff, an eminent biologist who worked with the small semiaquatic salamanders known as newts. Wolff had shown that if the lens of a newt embryo's eye were removed, it would regenerate. Spemann became thoroughly intrigued. After studies at the University of Munich in 1894, he moved to the Zoological Institute of the University of Würzburg. There he worked under Theodor Boveri (p. 105); the two subsequently carried on an extensive correspondence. In 1895 Spemann completed his doctorate; three years later he began to lecture on zoology at Würzburg.

In general, with the advent of a mature cell theory in about 1880, the science of embryology entered a phase of rapid growth. A host of intriguing taxonomic and experimental programs got under way, and a voluminous literature developed. In 1896, having contracted a slight case of tuberculosis, Spemann spent some time at a sanatorium in Switzerland. There he read August Weismann's *The Germ Plasm,* the first great effort after Darwin to create a theory of heredity based on evolutionary principles. The concept that the embryo contains the complex information necessary for future development was a new and exciting idea. Spemann was highly impressed by the prospects for an experimental approach. "I found here," he wrote later, "a theory of heredity and development elaborated with uncommon perspicacity to its ultimate consequences...."

Indeed, Spemann developed his experimental program over many years, with the overall aim of discovering the fundamental dynamics of embryonic development. One line of research, from about 1901 to 1912, concerned the developmental mechanics of the eye. It was known that the eye of a newt would develop after the optic cup, growing out of the brain, reached the surface tissue, or ectoderm. Spemann burned off the tissue that the optic cup would ordinarily touch and grafted in its place epidermis from elsewhere in the animal. The eye still developed normally. This result, on which Spemann based the concept of "lens induction," would provide the basis for many of his experiments over the next three decades. These demanded extremely precise work, and part of Spemann's talent lay in his skills in microscopic manipulation of tissue. Spemann himself developed a number of microsurgical techniques and instruments.

Spemann's series of "split egg" experiments, dating to 1903, also became celebrated. Taking a newt's egg, Spemann wrapped it around with an infant's hair, compressing it into a dumbbell shape. The egg would then develop into either two separate embryos or one embryo and a useless mass of cells. The significance was clear: if a complete embryo can emerge from only half an egg, the fate of cells in the undeveloped egg has not yet been determined. Since in later stages this is not the case, Spemann termed the process that fixes the developmental fate of the parts as "determination."

In 1908 Spemann took a position at the University of Rostock as professor of zoology and comparative anatomy. He remained there for about six years, continuing his work on lens induction. In 1914, Spemann joined the Kaiser Wilhelm Institute for Biology (today, part of the Max Planck Institute) as its associate director. Spemann was by then too old to serve in the German military and so was able to continue working through the First World War. During this period, in fact, Spemann became widely known and his work was avidly followed by other researchers. In part, this was because his program, not easy to duplicate, strongly emphasized experimental manipulation of the embryo. He did

not share other embryologists' enthusiasm, rooted in Darwinian ideas, for comparative studies or classification; however, the kinds of basic discoveries he made were, implicitly, generally applicable to higher animals.

Spemann's work on structural development led him to transplant tissue harvested from specific sites on one embryo to other sites on another embryo. Transplantation was an exacting matter of excising tissue from a referenced point, fitting it into the right place, and holding it in place until it was accepted. Differences in pigmentation of tissues in the different organisms allowed Spemann to follow the path of embryonic development after transplantation. This was ingenious but highly exacting work, filled with opportunity for missteps.

Discovery of the organizer was an outcome of this research. By 1918 Spemann had been able to suggest that determination of the neural plate, which gives rise to the brain and spinal cord, begins during gastrulation, the critical growth stage during which the outer layer of cells folds inward, creating the cup-shaped "gastrula." But there was no known physical basis for this. Spemann and his coworkers performed tissue transplantations in the area of the gastrula known as the dorsal blastosphere lip. While tissue was simply absorbed in adjacent areas, something far more dramatic happened with tissue from the dorsal lip: formation of a second neural plate. The tissue from this specific area dramatically redirected the fate of tissue surrounding it.

Spemann published a famous paper, "On the Induction of Embryonic Primordia by Implantation of Organizers from Different Species" in 1924.* The discovery was dramatic—"the crowning achievement of this period." It lent the discipline a great deal of prestige. "What so far had been essentially [Spemann's] family enterprise,..." wrote Viktor Hamburger, "now,

---

*In this work, Spemann's collaborator was a graduate student, Hilde Mangold. Her contribution was so important that she might have shared the Nobel Prize with Spemann but for her premature death in a fire in 1924.

almost overnight became a cosmopolitan venture." Hamburger himself vastly extended Spemann's work on chick embryos, while the organizer intrigued other scientists; more were sought, and eventually found. They have been discovered in fish, amphibian, and bird embryos as well as, more recently, in the mouse embryo.

Spemann's *Organisator,* as he called it in German, had a certain intentional ambiguity, reflecting a kind of vitalism—the belief that life processes would be in some measure distinct from chemical processes. The organizer, Spemann wrote, "creates an organization field out of the indifferent material in which it lies." It was unknown at the time whether the specific area of tissue in the embryo represented some specific structure, or if its effect was chemical in origin. Spemann and his students tried repeatedly and unsuccessfully to degrade the "organizer" by crushing, heating, freezing, and drying it out. He refrained from asserting its chemical nature, while recognizing that advances in biochemistry would make such a determination likely.

With the exponential growth of biochemistry after World War II, Spemann's discovery of the organizer became less a dynamic path to the future than a great historical beacon. When he discovered it, scientists hoped the organizer would lead to a better understanding of cancer. In some measure this was borne out, for growth factors play a role in carcinogenesis. But such factors today are cast in terms of biochemistry and molecular biology. Rita Levi-Montalcini, for example, indirectly basing her embryonic work on Spemann's discoveries, teamed up with biochemist Stanley Cohen to discover nerve growth factor (NGF). An understanding of the relationship of cancer to growth factors is still emerging with insights from molecular biology. The organizer, as it would be understood today, owes its force to the expression of a group of architectural genes fundamental to embryonic growth and development.

Spemann is always remembered as being philosophical in outlook, just as he was artistic in temperament. He married Clara Binder in 1895, and they had two sons. When the Nobel Prize came to him at the end of his career, in the midst of a worldwide financial depression, Spemann wondered what to do with the money, which amounted to about $40,000. He retired from active work in 1937, and died on September 12, 1941.

# Henry Dale [1875–1968]

## Discovering the First Neurotransmitter

The nervous system, at least in its basic outline, was becoming a ponderable enigma by the turn of the twentieth century. Ramón y Cajal (p. 109) convincingly proposed that neurons were the system's basic units. Charles Sherrington developed the concept of the reflex arc and a model of excitation and inhibition as integrating and controlling the muscular apparatus. Anatomically, the system was mapped and known to be electrical. But what turned the switch—what was it made of? A number of scientists would help elucidate the chemistry of neural transmission and chemical mediation in the brain. Among them, one of the pivotal figures is Henry Dale.

Dale's work had far-reaching consequences in clinical medicine and pharmacology. A physiologist by training, like Claude Bernard (p. 14), Dale combined a broad conceptual reach with careful reasoning and experimental skills. He is a principal figure in the discovery of histamine, a key ingredient in the inflammatory response. Dale also outlined the chemistry behind anaphylactic shock and is responsible, in an important sense, for the standardization of dosages in the modern pharmacopoeia. But Dale's most famous discovery was that of the first neurotransmitter, acetylcholine. Moreover, he receives a large share of credit for explaining how such neural transmission works—how chemicals manage the complex web of signals that excite, enhance, delay, and block the action of neurons.

Henry Hallett Dale was born in London on June 9, 1875. His father was Charles James Dale; his mother was Frances Ann Hallett. As a boy his elementary school teachers nourished his interest in science, especially biology. His family was not prosperous, and Henry benefited from scholarships, first to the Leys School, then to Trinity College, Cambridge. He did exceptionally well at Trinity, winning first class honors in 1896 and 1898, and he remained there two years for further research with the neurophysiologist J. N. Langley. Dale eventually qualified in medicine, receiving his degree in 1902. He subsequently wrote a thesis and received a further "doctor of medicine" degree in 1909.

Dale's long and serious postgraduate education reflects the growing complexity of medical research at the turn of the twentieth century. At

University College, London, in 1902, he worked in the laboratory of Ernest Starling, the famous physiologist who, together with William Bayliss, had recently discovered and defined the first hormone, secretin. Dale also spent several months in Germany in the laboratory of Paul Ehrlich, the celebrated chemist, immunochemist, and bacteriologist. In general, Dale came of age at a propitious moment, when a cascade of developments in the nascent fields of endocrinology and neurophysiology provided a context that would, in time, give birth to a plausible neurochemistry.

The trajectory of Dale's career was changed in 1904 by a personal consideration. He wanted an acceptable income to marry his first cousin, Ellen Harriet Hallett. But university posts were poorly paid, while clinical medicine did not interest him. As a consequence, Dale accepted a position with the Wellcome Physiological Research Laboratories. Although friends had advised him not to work for a private pharmaceutical company, the association proved fruitful, and Dale became director in 1906.

Henry Wellcome, the laboratory's founder, suggested to Dale that he investigate the pharmacological properties of ergot. The product of a parasitic fungus that infects rye and other cereal grasses, ergot had been long used in folk medicine. It was known to make the uterus contract, and so was employed by midwives after childbirth. In conventional medicine ergot was also considered useful against headaches and other conditions. How it worked, though, remained a total mystery. "I was, frankly, not at all attracted," wrote Dale, "by the prospect of making my first excursion into [pharmacology] on the ergot morass." In spite of which, Dale's work on ergot would become the basis for his most significant discoveries.

Dale's first success with ergot came by chance. One day he was asked simply to test some adrenal gland extract to see whether it contained adrenaline, or epinephrine. (For historical reasons concerning trademark, epinephrine is known as adrenaline in Great Britain.) Testing the extract on a cat to which, by chance, he had recently administered ergot, Dale found that the animal's blood pressure did not rise as expected. The adrenal extract, Dale concluded wrongly, was inactive. A week later, however, when the same sequence of events occurred, Dale recognized the possibility of an interaction between ergot and adrenaline. Adrenaline administered to a cat would raise its blood pressure, but if ergot were given, adrenaline would make the blood pressure fall. Dale thus discovered the first substance to block the action of adrenaline. This work became a starting point for the development of antihypertensive drugs.

Ergot was also the source of a substance that Dale began to study in 1907 and identified, three years later, as histamine. Dale went on to extract histamine from animal tissue. Over the next decade he would show that it is widely distributed in almost all cells of the body, and he would outline its significance. Histamine, pretty much as Dale discovered and as it remains understood today, is an alarm signal substance emitted by injured cells that causes nearby blood vessels to dilate and capillaries to leak.

Some understanding of anaphylaxis—the severe, even life-threatening hypersensitivity response—also emerged from Dale's work with histamine. In 1911 Dale and his colleagues noted that the effects produced by histamine were similar to the conditions seen in anaphylactic shock. With characteristic caution, Dale refused to go further, and not until 1932 would histamine be definitively linked to anaphylaxis. Immunology has changed so drastically since Dale's investigations that some of his ideas are no longer relevant, but histamine does play a role in anaphylaxis.

Dale moved from the Wellcome laboratories to the Medical Research Committee (MRC) in 1914. During the First World War he worked on relevant issues—the biochemistry of gas gangrene and drugs to treat syphilis and dysentery. Afterward he returned to his prewar interests, and eventually became director of the MRC in 1928.

The discovery of acetylcholine as a chemical transmitter of nerve impulses, Dale's best-known and most influential discovery, was many years in the making: from 1913 to 1937. Equal credit should be accorded Dale's friend, the Austrian Otto Loewi. Dale's achievement was not simply to have isolated an important chemical substance. It was, rather, to have resolved a crucial question in twentieth-century neurophysiology. Considerable debate over the course of a century and more had failed to resolve whether nerve impulse transmission was simply electrical or whether it would be better described as chemical or electrochemical. After the work by Dale and Loewi, no serious doubt remained.

Acetylcholine was discovered and synthesized decades before it was known to exist in the body. When in 1914 Dale and colleague Arthur Ewins discovered it—first as occurring naturally in ergot—they reported that it causes reactions similar to those observed in response to the action of the parasympathetic nervous system: the pupils constrict, the heart slows, tears bathe the eyes.* There matters rested for years. In 1921, by an ingenious experiment, Otto Loewi solidified his hypothesis that chemicals can stimulate nerve transmission. This concept was on their minds when, eight years later, Dale and H. W. Dudley happened across acetylcholine in animal spleens. They immediately set out to investigate its action in nerve

---

*The parasympathetic system, a division of the autonomic nervous system, encompasses most functions for conserving and restoring bodily resources.

cells—a particular challenge, since acetylcholine, once activated, is almost immediately destroyed.

Between 1929 and 1936, a raft of papers on acetylcholine emerged from the National Institute for Medical Research, almost all bearing Dale's signature. Among other things, Dale and his colleagues discovered that acetylcholine was released by the vagus and splanchnic nerves, which lead from the brain to the structures in the thoracic and abdominal cavities. Dale also found acetylcholine to be released at ganglionic sites in the sympathetic nervous system, which prepares the body for flight, and in the nerve endings that reach voluntary muscles. He clinched the activity of acetylcholine with experiments that showed that muscle tissue contracts in its presence.

"Elucidation of impulse transmission in the muscles and organs," writes Roy Porter in a recent assessment, "was a remarkable breakthrough." In 1936, no one was surprised when Dale received the Nobel Prize in physiology or medicine, shared with Otto Loewi. Acetylcholine was the first of what today are counted as about fifty neurotransmitters. It provided a rudimentary but eminently useful model for a variety of phenomena in the nervous system.

Dale became one of the great eminences in British science. After the First World War, he served the League of Nations in the successful effort to create dosage standards for a wide variety of medications, from digitalis to newly discovered insulin, as well as vitamins. In 1936 he became a trustee of the Wellcome Trust and served as its chairman from 1938 until 1960. When invited to become president of the Royal Society in 1940, he decided he would have to give up some activity, and so he stopped smoking. Knighted in 1932, he joined the Order of Merit in 1944. His marriage to Ellen Harriet Hallett produced one son and two daughters.

Dale retired from active research in 1942. He subsequently served as chairman of the Scientific Advisory Committee to the War Cabinet from 1942 until 1947 and in other official positions. Much honored, he continued to be active through the 1950s. A collection of some of his most important papers was published as *Adventures in Physiology* in 1953. He also often addressed a wider audience, and some of these occasional pieces can be found in *An Autumn Gleaning,* from 1954. The title of the latter volume betokens old age, but Dale lived on for years, a revered figure in British science. Colleagues would visit even during his final days in a nursing home in Cambridge, where he died on July 23, 1968.

# Hans Krebs [1900-1981]

## The Krebs Cycle

As early as 1789 Antoine Lavoisier showed that chemical reaction with oxygen—in a word, combustion—is the underlying process that transforms food into life-sustaining energy. But understanding the complex chemistry of this process required another one hundred fifty years. Recognition that metabolism takes place within cells and is governed by enzymes came during the late nineteenth century. The field of intermediary metabolism, holding promise for medicine and pharmacology, advanced over complex ground during the next several decades. In 1937 came a crucial new theory, proposed by a German emigré to England, the biochemist Hans Krebs.

The Krebs cycle sets out the series of chemical steps involved in the breakdown of food molecules, after digestion, to produce packets of energy, water, and carbon dioxide. The culminating series of steps in the uptake of nutrients, the cycle takes place in aerobic organisms from bacteria to humans, and works for higher plants as well. Also known as the citric acid and the tricarboxylic acid cycles, its several names are an indication of its fundamental significance. The Krebs cycle, as taught in biology textbooks today, is a slightly modified but not substantially changed version of its original formulation. It was actually the second of Krebs's major discoveries; the urea cycle—the steps by which ammonia is detoxified in the liver—was the first. Krebs must receive credit for recognizing the vital significance of cyclic reactions in general in biochemistry.

Hans Krebs was born on August 25, 1900, in the lovely medieval town of Hildesheim, near Hanover, in Germany. He was the second of three children in a family of assimilated Jews. His father, Georg Krebs, was a physician with a strong personality and wide-ranging interests, including a love of nature and writing poetry. Indeed, he composed odes to Alma Davidson, a quiet and devoted wife and mother. The family was not demonstrative or outwardly warm, however, and Hans was shy as a child. Initially he planned on following his father into medicine. World War I ground to a halt soon after he was conscripted. When Hans's mother died in the postwar influenza epidemic, his inheritance amounted to just enough, with hyperinflation in Germany, to buy a copy of one book. He chose Hans Vaihinger's famous *The Philosophy of As If.*

Krebs attended the University of Göttingen for some months before transferring to the University of Freiburg in 1919, where he developed an interest in chemistry. He graduated in 1921 and went on to study medicine at Munich, passing his final exams in 1923. After a year's work in a clinic, in 1925 he received his medical license from the University of Hamburg. Immediately after completing his residency, Krebs entered the laboratory. He took a course in chemistry for doctors at Charité in Berlin and had already published several papers when, in 1926, he was hired as an assistant to Otto Warburg (p. 218).

At the Kaiser Wilhelm Institute, Warburg was at work on a variety of problems, including the nature of photosynthesis and the chemical composition of enzymes. Krebs published some sixteen papers over the next four years related to various aspects of Warburg's research. But in particular, he became interested in the chemistry of intermediary metabolism—the breakdown and synthesis of nutrient compounds. Warburg did not allow him to investigate it, however. Only after he left Warburg's laboratory in 1931, accepting a post at the University of Freiburg, did Krebs begin his landmark series of experiments.

Krebs's first signal discovery concerned urea, the nitrogenous waste product, as he understood it, of birds and mammals. Animal production of urea represents an evolutionary adaptation. Aquatic animals excrete ammonia, which is more toxic and requires plenty of water—not a problem in the ocean or a pond. Terrestrial animals, by contrast, convert ammonia into urea through a catalytic reaction or a series of reactions that, when Krebs began his research, was already known to take place in the liver. But the chemistry of this basic metabolic function remained a mystery.

The crucial phase of Krebs's research began with a technical innovation: he suspended liver slices in saline solution—a substitute for blood plasma—and supplied them with nutrients. In this way Krebs learned that if amino acids were added to liver in vitro, ammonia would be liberated and subsequently converted into urea. Two of the many amino acids that Krebs tested could cause large increases of urea—arginine and (when combined with ammonia) ornithine. Known to be produced in the presence of the enzyme arginase, ornithine led to the production of citrulline, another amino acid. Krebs recognized the cyclic nature of the process: In the presence of ornithine and carbon dioxide, the waste product ammonia will be detoxified by a series of reactions in which citrulline and arginine are intermediate stages. The final product is urea and, once again, ornithine. The presence of ornithine at both the

beginning and end renders the reaction cyclic. Some years later, in other laboratories, the cycle would be shown to include some five enzymatic steps.

In 1932 the urea cycle (sometimes called the ornithine cycle) was the first such metabolic reaction to be discovered, and it won Krebs considerable recognition. But his appointment at the University of Freiburg turned out to be brief. The Nazis came to power in 1933, and anti-Semitic laws were put into effect immediately. Krebs lost no time in contacting the famous biochemist Frederick Gowland Hopkins at Cambridge University. As a result, Krebs was in England several weeks before his position was officially terminated at Freiburg. Krebs initially took a position at Cambridge's school of biochemistry, and his research was supported by the Rockefeller Foundation. In 1935 he became lecturer in pharmacology at Sheffield University.

Discovery of the citric acid cycle, or Krebs cycle, took place over five years, from about 1932 to 1937. Krebs did not discover every component, but he brought together through theory and experiment several strands of isolated information to create a cogent and powerful whole. Both by conceptual complexity and historic significance, his work may best be compared to, say, a key advance in theoretical physics. The problem he had attacked was a basic conundrum. By the twentieth century chemists knew that, after digestion breaks down foodstuffs, there follows "combustion" of carbohydrates, amino acids, and fatty acids. But the pertinent chemical reactions, which occur within cells, were unknown.

Krebs took note of two sets of discoveries concerning several organic acids that are ubiquitous in cells. In 1935, the Hungarian biochemist Albert Szent-Györgyi had performed experiments with minced pigeon muscle, a tissue that, in order to support flight, has high energy requirements. Szent-Györgyi discovered that several dicarboxylic acids — succinic acid, fumaric acid, malic acid, and oxaloacetic acid — were all present when this muscle was active, or "burning" foodstuffs. Also, one of these products, succinic acid, could be converted into the other three.

Work with a tricarboxylic acid—citric acid—brought another part of the puzzle into place. In 1937 German biochemists Franz Knoop and Carl Martius discovered a series of reactions in the liver in which citric acid was converted into aconitic acid, and a sequence of reactions by which citric acid was converted to oxaloacetic acid. Products of this latter set of reactions included the substances that Szent-Györgyi had found—succinic acid, fumaric acid, and malic acid.

The findings of these isolated experiments formed the basis of what Krebs came to understand was an efficient and central series of metabolic reactions. The ready oxidation of the various organic acids suggested that they were "likely to be connected," Krebs later wrote, "with the combustion of foodstuffs." As an additional piece of information, Krebs learned that malonic acid would inhibit the oxidizability of succinate to fumarate, and the process of combustion would stop.

Although Krebs was not initially looking for a cyclic reaction, he eventually recognized it. He performed experiments that demonstrated how, in minced pigeon muscle, oxaloacetic acid and pyruvic acid reacted to form citric acid. He then demonstrated the rate by which citric acid is synthesized and degraded as a series of key reactions in which oxaloacetic acid is produced at the end. The "finer details" of the citric acid cycle remained unknown for some years. Krebs initially counted six steps in all. Not until 1951 did Fritz Lipmann show that a coenzyme—he called it coenzyme A—reacts with pyruvate to form acetyl coenzyme A (CoA). This proved to be the mysterious substance—formed from carbohydrates, fatty acids, and amino acids—that reacts with oxaloacetate to form citrate. Regeneration of CoA with the formation of citrate enables it to act as a catalyst so that very little is needed.

The discovery of the Krebs cycle may be offered as a prime example of the significance of basic biochemistry to medical research. Simply put, its relevance for research into metabolism and, more generally, the complex workings of the cell is difficult to overestimate. With Fritz Lipmann, Krebs shared both the Albert Lasker Award and the Nobel Prize for physiology or medicine in 1953. In 1954 Krebs moved to Oxford University, where as Whitley Professor of Biochemistry he headed the department until his retirement in 1967. His research in later years included investigations of errors of inborn metabolism—the biochemistry of genetics that Archibald Garrod (p. 214) had initiated at the turn of the twentieth century.

The quiet, reserved scientist Hans Krebs married Margaret Fieldhouse, an Englishwoman, in 1938. They had three children. Krebs wrote an eminently readable memoir, *Reminiscences and Reflections,* in collaboration with Ann Martin. He is also the subject of an extensive and much admired biography by Frederic Lawrence Holmes. In all, Krebs's good fortune, to have worked with Otto Warburg, his escape from Nazi Germany, and his innate optimism gave him the feeling that he had been exceptionally favored in life. "Because I have had more than my share of luck, and a lucky constellation of genes," he wrote, "life has felt special indeed." Hans Krebs died on November 22, 1981.

# Howard Florey [1898–1968]

## The Discovery of Penicillin

Penicillin, the refined byproduct of certain molds, naturally obliterates a wide range of bacteria. Because it can be tolerated by the body, it works as a lifesaving treatment for many potentially deadly systemic infections, from pneumonia to bacterial meningitis to blood poisoning. It can cure syphilis and is used in a large number of lesser infectious diseases as well, from gonorrhea to scarlet fever to sore throat. First manufactured during the Second World War, penicillin was the prototype for a whole series of potent antibiotics. It remains today, in spite of overuse and problems with resistant strains, the pharmaceutical juggernaut which practically defines modern medicine.

Penicillin's discovery is a weave of good and bad science, clashes of personality and culture, and old-fashioned and new-fangled research. It unfolds during World War II on two continents with scientists from Australia, Scotland, England, the United States, and Germany. Key aspects include fateful identification of the greenish mold, research to purify and amplify potency, and a campaign to manufacture it in bulk for delivery to the wounded and sick. From this tangled web the scientist who today receives chief credit for penicillin's discovery is the pathologist Howard Florey. With Alexander Fleming and Boris Chain, Florey received the Nobel Prize in 1945.

Howard Florey was born on September 24, 1898, in the city of Adelaide, in southern Australia. He was the youngest child and only son of Bertha Mary Wadham and her husband, Joseph Florey, a prosperous boot manufacturer. Howard attended elite primary and secondary schools, receiving the rough equivalent of a British public school education. Athletic and bright, he formed friends with difficulty and suffered from health problems, including dangerous bouts of pneumonia as a teenager. Persuaded by his family not to volunteer for military service during World War I, Howard attended the University of Adelaide beginning in 1916. In 1922, after receiving his bachelor of medicine degree, he began postgraduate work at Oxford University with the help of a Rhodes scholarship. He spent a year as a traveling fellow at the Rockefeller Institute in 1925, and when he returned to England, he took his doctorate from Cambridge

University in 1927. Florey had no interest in clinical medicine and found his place, from the beginning of his career, at the laboratory bench.

Even while a graduate student, Florey was recognized as an exceptional scientist with a promising future as an experimental pathologist. Soon after arriving from Australia, he came to the attention of Charles Sherrington, one of the founders of neurology, and through him met some of the major figures in British science, including Nobel laureates J. J. Thomson and Ernest Rutherford. Florey's acceptance by these older men is not surprising. Like them, he saw the value of a relatively new spirit of scientific teamwork, and he grasped the unity of nature through chemistry. Florey also was influenced by Frederick Gowland Hopkins, a founder of biochemistry. After several years of teaching at Cambridge, Florey moved to the University of Sheffield in 1932.

It is not easy to find substances that will destroy disease-causing organisms without harming the tissues and cells in which they reside and multiply. Adverse effects limited the usefulness of Salvarsan, for example, a harsh chemical remedy for syphilis that Paul Ehrlich discovered in 1910. An *antibiotic* that harnessed the bactericidal properties of certain microorganisms would offer a better solution.* Florey gradually became intrigued by the problem during the 1920s, and this led him to the work of Alexander Fleming, a Scottish bacteriologist at St. Mary's Hospital.

The careers of Florey and Fleming, who were interested in the same problems, would become curiously entwined, although the two would never work together. In 1921 Fleming had first noticed that mucus from his own nose was able to lyse, or kill off, a certain kind of harmless bacteria. Testing mucus from many sources and sites, he discovered that the protective substance was an enzyme he called lysozyme. It turned out to be a natural antiseptic, but lysozyme's protective effects did not seem to extend to dangerous bacteria. Fleming could not isolate the enzyme itself and soon lost interest. Florey, in the late 1920s, had no better luck. But he was impressed by a chance observation: he noticed that the presence of *E. coli,* bacteria normally found in the colon, clearly stopped the growth of other microorganisms. Florey knew about such antagonism—known as antibiosis—in which one kind of bacteria disabled another; it was "a very well known phenomenon." But its dramatic quality, viewed in the laboratory, seems to have made a singular impression on Florey's imagination.

---

*It should be noted that ancient and folk medical traditions held to the curative properties of various molds. Mayan Indians, for example, used green corn, and Ukrainians cultivated molds for wound dressings. But molds' potential as strong drugs remained unknown to scientific pharmacology.

Fleming also opened for Florey the door that would lead to penicillin. In 1928 he recognized, by the appearance of a contaminated staphylococcus culture on a petri dish, the work of what turned out to be a common mold, *Penicillium notatum*. To this day it remains unclear how a bread mold spore got into one of Fleming's petri dishes. His acute observation and identification of the mold were key events. However, being a somewhat old-fashioned scientist, Fleming was used to working alone and was fairly untrained in chemistry. He knew that the mold was nonlethal when injected into mice, but the idea of doing experiments to test it systemically apparently did not occur to him. When he could not readily extract the active bactericidal substance, Fleming did not persist. His basic insight into penicillin was thus at once both decisive and defective, a potential breakthrough thwarted by a failure of vision.

Lysozyme and penicillin represented two strands of research that merged in the late 1930s. In 1935 Florey accepted a position as head of the Dunn School of Pathology at Oxford University. He soon hired Boris Ernst Chain, a brilliant biochemist who had fled Nazi Germany. With a detailed knowledge of chemistry, and putting to use the new technique of freeze-drying to aid in purification, Chain succeeded where Fleming and Florey had failed: he purified and crystallized lysozyme. He showed that it was indeed an enzyme, and most importantly, he discovered how it might work. Lysozyme interfered with reproduction by breaking down the bacterial cell wall.

Success with lysozyme led Florey and Chain to the general idea that perhaps other antibiotic substances would work in a similar way. In 1937 they conceived a plan to study all the natural antibiotic substances then known. Chain unearthed about two hundred articles in the literature and found among them, published in 1929 in the *British Journal of Experimental Pathology,* Alexander Fleming's intriguing but sketchy paper on penicillin.

Florey and Chain determined to focus on penicillin near the end of 1938. Their decision, it should be added, was guided by scientific interest and imagination, not yet by any conviction that a miraculous drug was at hand. Unlike Fleming, who could only make of the penicillin mold a brownish-yellow juice that soon lost potency, Chain and Florey were soon able to extract and purify a more powerful, stable product. With the help of British chemist Norman Heatley, who made important contributions to the extraction process, they soon had enough penicillin to begin experimental research with mice.

In May 1940 Florey directed a simple animal trial known as the "mouse protection test." Eight mice were injected with lethal doses of streptococci. Four of these were then given penicillin. As Florey, Heatley, and Chain kept watch overnight, they saw the untreated mice all die while three of the four treated mice survived and flourished. The implication was unequivocal, and the next phase would clearly be to test penicillin in humans. The first case, in February 1941, was a policeman who had already lost an eye to a rampant streptococcal infection that had begun with a simple sore on the mouth. Near death, he made a dramatic recovery with penicillin—only to relapse and die when supplies of the extract were exhausted before treatment was complete.

With penicillin's promise apparent, drawing the attention of pharmaceutical companies and finding methods to manufacture penicillin now became crucial issues. But World War II had just begun, and in spite of penicillin's great promise for military medicine, British companies were all committed to other goals. Therefore, in June 1941, together with his colleague Heatley, Florey paid a visit to the U.S. Department of Agriculture's Northern Regional Research Laboratory in Peoria, Illinois. There they received support for the project and the help of Andrew J. Moyer, who discovered that corn steep liquor, a waste product of corn, could be used to greatly increase the yield of penicillin. Florey also solicited the interest of pharmaceutical firms, and when he returned to Britain, three companies were devoting time and money to developing ways to manufacture penicillin. The United States' entry into World War II in December 1941 only speeded matters up.

Clinical trials of penicillin took place during 1942, and by the end of that year some ninety cases had been treated. They confirmed penicillin's promise as a lifesaving drug in treating a wide range of infections. By the end of 1943, some twenty-one companies were involved in manufacturing penicillin. By war's end over 600 billion units were being produced monthly.

The original drug, known as "Penicillin G," was administered intravenously because digestive juices rendered it ineffective. Over the course of several years, a family of penicillins—as well as other antibiotics—came to market. Some of these could be taken orally, and they had a wide spectrum of use. The manufacture of partially synthetic penicillins, available before the end of the 1940s, accelerated production and lowered cost. *The Chemistry of Penicillin,* published in 1949, runs to 1,100 pages and describes the research of over four hundred scientists. But penicillin was only the first of an enormous number of similar drugs that would be developed over the next several decades.

Historically, Penicillin G represents the kickoff phase of the revolution in medicine that began at the end of the Second World War. On the whole, penicillin's tremendous impact has been to render virtually harmless many infections that were once life-threatening. But it has also had its

downside. Overuse of the penicillins has led to the emergence of dangerous, resistant new strains of bacteria, a problem that persists today with no
promise of a solution.

Great medical discoveries often provide fertile ground for disputes
over priority and patents, and penicillin was no exception. Howard Florey's
central role was not immediately clarified in the popular imagination.
Alexander Fleming, with the promotional efforts of his mentor, bacteriologist Sir Almoth Wright, took credit for the original discovery. This was not
literally false, but, with the active help of the British press, Fleming soon
became a hero out of all scale. With his implicit consent, extravagant articles overstated his actual contribution, and he was portrayed as having
been possessed by a vision of penicillin's potential during the 1930s, when,
for all intents and purposes, he had lost interest in it. Florey, normally tem-
pestuous and combative, initially bore the "Fleming myth" quietly, but
eventually he complained to colleagues. He never forgave Fleming, who
was both amused and gratified by the world's aggrandizement.

As an Oxford professor, Florey's decision not to seek patents related to
penicillin was common practice. But it rankled his collaborator, Boris
Chain, and led to their complete estrangement. The American Andrew J.
Moyer, who, with his corn steep liquor, had helped develop the techniques
of bulk production and extraction, was prevented by law from filing for
U.S. patents. But he could legally seek patent rights for foreign production.
This he did, with the result that British pharmaceutical firms were later
asked to pay royalties to an American for a discovery made in England.
The matter was eventually resolved.

A partial settling of discovery accounts came in 1945, when Florey,
Fleming, and Chain all received the Nobel Prize. From the beginning,
Florey had been recognized for his work by science and government. He
had been elected to the Royal Society in 1943 and was knighted a year
later. The French inducted him into the Legion of Honor in 1946. From
1960 to 1965 he served as president of the Royal Society, and in that year
he ascended to the peerage, as Baron Florey of Adelaide and Marston.

Florey had a complex but ultimately constricted emotional life. He
could be exceedingly blunt and was said to be ruthless in relations with
colleagues. Generally reserved, he was sometimes impatient and unable to
control his temper. He cultivated the image of a detached scientist and
professed no interest in "suffering humanity." But he also had a passionate
side and was capable of both self-scrutiny and speculation about morality
and society. His marriage to Mary Ethel Reed, who had been a medical
student when he met her in Australia, was a bitter disappointment to him
after a long courtship. Their relationship was unpleasant on both sides,

riven with conflict, and ultimately distant—in spite of some research they did together and two children. Over its four decades, Ethel suffered from a variety of disorders, including partial deafness, for which Florey reproached her. Shortly after her death in 1966, Florey wed Margaret Jennings, a coworker with whom he had been associated for some thirty years. That relationship brought Florey some tranquillity at the end of his life. He had long suffered from poor health, including angina, and when he married a second time, it was with the knowledge that he had not long to live. Howard Florey died on February 21, 1968.

# Wilder Penfield [1891 – 1976]

## Neurology: Mapping the Brain

As the field of neurosurgery opened up in the early twentieth century, it advanced both as a therapeutic intervention and, more dramatically, as a means of exploring the brain. In 1930, while operating on a woman for epilepsy, Wilder Penfield touched an electrode to a spot on one of the exposed temporal lobes. The patient, who was conscious during the operation, began to reexperience the birth of her child. She recounted the event as though it were occurring in real time — all the while aware that she was on the operating table. The richness of detail and the strong emotional charge of the experience were astonishing. Over years of surgery, Penfield evoked the same kind of detailed memories with other patients. "This is a startling discovery," he wrote. "It brings psychical phenomena into the field of physiology."

Indeed, the accomplishment of Wilder Penfield, in a broad sense, was to test upon tissue of the living human brain some of the hard-won insights of fledgling neuroscience. He was both an exceptional practical surgeon devoted to his patients and a careful investigator into brain function. It is not surprising to find that he studied with both Charles Sherrington, who had virtually founded the field of neurophysiology, and Santiago Ramón y Cajal (p. 109), who had revolutionized neuroanatomy. Penfield was the principal founder of the Montreal Neurological Institute, opened in 1934, which remains one of the leading brain research and treatment centers in the world.

Wilder Graves Penfield was born on January 26, 1891, in Spokane, Washington. A small settlement that had burgeoned in the wake of a gold rush, Spokane represented a final hurrah of the American frontier. Wilder was the last of three children born to Charles Samuel Penfield, a physician and surgeon, and Jean Jeffers. After some unhappy years together, his parents separated permanently in 1899. His father, although successful as a surgeon, would later undergo a mysterious midlife change, abandoning his practice for long hunting trips into the mountains, unable to resist "the call of the wild." His fate is intriguing in light of his son's explorations of the uncharted territory of the brain. But Wilder's greater and more immediate influence was his devoted mother. When she returned with her children to her hometown of Hudson, Wisconsin, Wilder attended Galahad School, from which he graduated in 1909. He went on to Princeton University, where he was turned toward medicine by Edward Grant Conkling. He received his bachelor of literature degree in 1913. A debater and all-around athlete, from age thirteen Wilder had been urged by his mother to aim for a Rhodes scholarship, which he in fact obtained. As a consequence he studied in England from 1914 to 1916, during the first two years of World War I. He was lucky to survive. In 1916, crossing the Channel to serve as a Red Cross volunteer in a French hospital, he was nearly killed when a German torpedo boat blew up his ship. He managed to escape with a mangled leg and recuperated in the home of William Osler (p. 181).

Penfield's interests were already in neurology. Returning to the United States, he studied at Johns Hopkins and received his medical degree in 1918. He interned at the Peter Bent Brigham Hospital in Boston, where Harvey Cushing (p. 227) was surgeon-in-chief and already celebrated for innovative procedures, including brain surgery. He then returned to England to complete his Rhodes scholarship, working (as he had from 1915) under Charles Sherrington, the transformational figure in the development of neuroscience. "I looked through his eyes," Penfield wrote later, "and came to realize that here in the nervous system was the great unexplored field, the undiscovered country in which the mystery of the mind of man might some day be explained." He decided to specialize in neurosurgery, then in its infancy. Oxford awarded Penfield his bachelor of science and master's degrees in 1920.

After returning to the United States, Penfield, committed to research, took a post at Columbia University, where he was named assistant professor in 1926. At nearby Presbyterian Hospital, he founded the laboratory of neurocytology in 1924. His background in neurological research and his academic credentials were impeccable, but Penfield's surgical skills remained limited. The relatively small number of operable neurological cases enabled him to hold several appointments simultaneously, and so he also worked at the Vanderbilt Clinic and New York Neurological Institute.

Penfield was already interested in treating epilepsy surgically, and he eventually came to realize that to gain a better understanding of the brain's neuroanatomy, he needed the help of the cell-staining techniques invented by Santiago Ramón y Cajal. The Spaniard's reputation was international—indeed, he had won the Nobel Prize—but he remained somewhat isolated from the mainstream of physiological research. As a consequence, Penfield learned Spanish and journeyed to Madrid, where he learned the methods that enabled him, as he later said, "to make a worthwhile contribution to neuropathology and to neuroanatomy and to clinical neurology."

Epilepsy presented both a human disorder to treat and, for Penfield, an opportunity for investigation and discovery. With its distinctive set of symptoms—transitory physical convulsion and sudden mental disturbance—epilepsy historically has been one of humankind's most bewildering disorders. Bromides were used with some success from the 1850s, and some patients obtained relief from a series of drugs beginning with phenobarbital in 1912. But there was also a tantalizing possibility that epileptics might benefit from surgery. The eminent neurosurgeon Otfrid Förster floated such a possibility during the 1920s. Just as he had gone to Spain to gain necessary knowledge, Penfield now traveled to Germany. There he became familiar with, and would later adapt, Förster's technique of probing the brain while the patient remained conscious.

In 1928 Penfield moved to McGill University in Montreal, Canada, and was appointed neurosurgeon at the Royal Victoria Hospital. A year later he took the opportunity to treat a young man, William Ottomann, for severe epilepsy. After much reflection and hesitation, he decided to operate. The operation would involve opening a "trap door" in the skull, peeling away layers of protective tissue, and probing the brain. Penfield later wrote of his patient, "It called for true heroism to lie there, looking out beneath the awning of cloth, hearing and sensing the grind and the thud of drill and Gigli saw as the trap-door is cut, hearing the crack of the bone when the skull door is opened." In this first operation, Penfield's electrode was able to provoke an epileptic attack, and he was able to locate and tie off an artery which, luckily enough, effected a cure.

During the 1930s Penfield consolidated his career in a variety of ways. In 1932 he edited a three-volume work, *Cytology and Cellular Pathology of the Nervous System,* a classic of neurology. His success in working with the other contributors to this book led Penfield to conceive of collaboration on an institutional level. The Montreal Neurological Institute, funded with help from the Rockefeller Foundation, opened in 1934 with Penfield as director. It had the ambitious aim of "understanding of the brain and the mind of man" and was explicitly dedicated, in fact, to "the relief of sickness and pain and to the study of neurology." Penfield would eventually perform over seven hundred fifty operations on epileptics. He would receive a wide variety of difficult and unusual cases, many of which were described in the 1941 volume *Epilepsy and Cerebral Localization*, written by Penfield in collaboration with Theodore Erickson. He would go on to write, with Herbert Jasper, *Epilepsy and the Functional Anatomy of the Human Brain* in 1954.

The great yield from Penfield's operations on epileptics was perhaps not so much any cures effected as a wealth of new knowledge about the brain. Epilepsy became Penfield's "teacher," as he called it, and he published reports concerning tumor formation, headache, and even the physiological basis of memory function. He eventually developed the famous "Penfield's homunculus," which indicates by caricature the relative proportions of cerebral cortex devoted to the various structures of the body. From today's perspective, Penfield's work was limited by a variety of features, most notably by a thorough lack of knowledge about brain chemistry. On a molecular and neurohormonal level, the brain remained largely terra incognita to Penfield.

Penfield retired from his academic position at McGill University in 1954, but he continued to perform surgery and publish reports of his work at the Montreal Neurological Institute until 1960. His last scientific book was *Speech and Brain Mechanisms*, written with Lamar Roberts and published in 1959. For years Penfield had been moving toward a role in the world at large as a wise man or what his grandson Jefferson Lewis called a "humanist-scientist-philosopher." This ambition turned him into a novelist.

Before her death, Penfield's mother had begun writing a fictional story based on the biblical figures of Sarah and Abraham. Penfield was inspired to recast and finish her work, which he published in 1954 as *No Other God*. A second novel, *The Torch*, from 1960, concerned the life and work of Hippocrates. He also authored several biographical works on significant physicians, including his associate Alan Gregg. He stressed the importance of family as the "first classroom" for shaping human values in *Man and His Family*, from 1967. His *The Mystery of the Mind*, a popular account of the brain, was published in 1975.

A Presbyterian in religion, strait-laced and sometimes domineering, Penfield could also be passionate. He was shocked when, on a visit to New York in 1955, he saw a Broadway performance of Tennessee Williams's *Cat on a Hot Tin Roof*. Penfield had a long, dutiful, but also somewhat painful marriage to Helen Katherine Kermott. They were wed in 1917, had four children, and remained together until the end of Penfield's life.

At age eighty-five, suffering from stomach cancer, Penfield decided he ought to die at the institute he had founded. He hoped to save his wife, herself in failing health, the shock of finding his body. The night before his departure, he and Helen dined together. He wore his red vest. Together they sat, playing records and singing old songs. Next morning he left home, deciding to take his cane, although he knew he would not need it long. Wilder Penfield died on April 5, 1976.

# Selman Waksman [1888–1973]

## Microbes from the Soil

D irt yielded its microcomposition to science and medicine in the twentieth century. Peat and humus are rife with microorganisms and all the products of their metabolism, dangerous and benign—coexisting, ordinarily, in a complex balance. Biochemistry and the promise of new pharmaceuticals made it possible to investigate the substances that naturally annihilate some of the "germs" that emerge from the soil to cause a number of human diseases. In 1943 the antibiotic streptomycin, discovered by Selman Waksman, stemmed the scourge of tuberculosis.

A Russian-born American soil microbiologist, Selman Waksman spent his life studying the wealth of microbes that inhabit the soil. "I have studied their nature, life processes, and their relation to man, helping him and destroying him," he wrote. "I have measured the growth of microbes and their multiplication, their feeding habits and the waste material they produce." He wrote some twenty-eight books and over four hundred articles. Streptomycin, one of a score of antibiotics to come from his laboratory, was the second "miracle drug," brought to market shortly after penicillin. Its different spectrum of action made it useful for treating such diseases as cholera and typhoid fever, in addition to tuberculosis. It was a second boon to medicine in the wake of the Second World War.

Zolmin Abraham Waksman was born on July 22, 1888, in a small Jewish village, Novaya Priluka, in the Kiev region of what today is the Republic of the Ukraine. His father, Jacob, was a textile weaver and a devout student of the Talmud. Zolmin was closest to his mother, who, he wrote, "loved me dearly, with an unselfish and devoted love." A somewhat timid child, Waksman nevertheless enjoyed *Robinson Crusoe* and the fantasy adventures of Jules Verne. His early schooling was in a *heder,* and he had private tutors. Although he desired a university education, this was not easy for Jews living in the so-called pale of settlement. Zolmin eventually journeyed to Odessa, where he graduated from the gymnasium in 1910. While still a student in the wake of the Russian revolution of 1905, Waksman became politically conscious, and he organized a Jewish defense group to fight the pogroms initiated by the czarist government. But with the death of his mother, Waksman resolved to emigrate, and he arrived in the United States in 1910. He lived at first with relatives in Metuchen, New Jersey, and worked on their farm.

Not prosperous enough to seek a medical education, in 1911 Waksman won a scholarship to attend Rutgers College to study agriculture. He received his bachelor of science degree in 1915 and a master's degree a year later. (About 1916 he changed his first name to Selman.) He went on to graduate studies at the University of California at Berkeley, which awarded him a Ph.D. in biochemistry in 1918. He then returned to join the faculty at Rutgers, and in 1921 he began work as a microbiologist for the New Jersey Agricultural Experiment Station. To augment his meager income, he also worked in private industry for a time. But by 1929 he would be appointed a full professor at Rutgers. In addition, in 1931 Waksman organized a laboratory of marine microbiology at the Woods Hole Oceanographic Institute. He worked summers there until 1942, and afterwards served as a trustee.

Early in his career Waksman saw serious flaws in the current theories of soil biology. The reigning "protozoan theory of soil fertility," wrote Waksman, "was reminiscent of the old idea of God and the Devil, Good and Bad, Light and Dark." In this view, protozoa and simpler bacteria were thought to be constantly at war, and the roles played by other significant components of the soil were largely ignored. By the late 1920s Waksman was prominently developing a theory that emphasized biological equilibrium. His aim eventually encompassed nothing less than a new and comprehensive understanding of soil microbiology.

Together with a growing number of his colleagues, Waksman provided new ways of evaluating bacterial populations in soil and their chemical properties and effects. Apart from basic research issues, improving soil fertility was an important aim. Waksman coauthored an important work, *Enzymes*, with Wilbur C. Davison in 1926. Still more significant was *Principles of Soil Microbiology*, first published in 1927. This volume, 900 pages long, was destined to became the bible of the discipline. Other early works included *The Soil and the Microbe*, which appeared in 1931, and *Humus*, from 1936.

Although Waksman's pursuit of antibiotics came rather late in his career, his interest in the pertinent microorganisms dated from his student days. Actinomycetes are a group of fungus-like bacteria. The "earthy" fragrance of rich dirt signals their presence, and most species are harmless. Discovered in 1875, the actinomycetes were recognized as a group in 1890 and were studied over the next quarter century. Waksman's first paper, in 1915, concerned actinomycetes, and he made a preliminary classification in 1919. Twenty years later, his early investigations intersected medical research.

Although in 1936 he compiled a study of antagonistic and interdependent relations among the soil microorganisms, Waksman had long avoided becoming involved in pharmacological research. A turning point came in 1939 after one of his former students, René Dubos, discovered tyrocidine and gramicidin, two soil-based antimicrobials. The latter proved promising for treating certain infections in animals, but it was too toxic for humans. But Waksman realized, he wrote later, that it was "relatively easy to isolate microbes which are able to kill disease-producing germs." Also in 1939 came news of a renewed attempt to develop penicillin, derived from a mold. Waksman set out to isolate and study the multitude of soil-based fungi and bacteria. He had long ago refined techniques to isolate and culture soil organisms, and to purify and crystallize soil-based substances. These served him well now.

The bacterium that causes tuberculosis is probably as old as any of the infective microorganisms. It originally thrived in primeval mud and afflicted humans in Neolithic times. The "white plague of Europe" that arose about the seventeenth century was due to growing urban populations. *Mycobacterium tuberculosis* was identified by Robert Koch (p. 24) in 1882. Usually affecting the lungs, the bacilli also could invade and colonize other organs of the body. The pasteurization of milk, establishment of sanitariums, and posting of "No Spitting" signs were all public health measures taken to control tuberculosis. But as to treatment, in the first decades of the twentieth century physicians were limited to such homespun remedies as cod-liver oil. Patients dosed themselves with everything from pig's pepsin to iodine and copper. Penicillin would prove ineffective against tuberculosis.

Waksman carried out his work with the help of graduate students, and one of them, the assiduous Albert Schatz, made the crucial discovery. In 1943 Schatz found that the actinomycete *Streptomyces griseus* seemed effective against *M. tuberculosis*. After Waksman reported on its antibacterial properties in January 1944, streptomycin was tested in the Mayo Clinic. Favorable results with guinea pigs led to human trials that were also judged successful. In October 1944, with the first human patients still in treatment, Waksman was introduced to senior staff at the Mayo as bringing "a very important message" about "a subject that is at the moment of great importance to medical science and clinical practice." Streptomycin had arrived.

The use of streptomycin to cure tuberculosis made Selman Waksman a medical hero, a "disease fighter" whose victory resonated with symbolic value in the wake of World War II. He toured the world, visiting Europe and the Soviet Union. He won the Albert Lasker Award and was featured on the cover of *Time* magazine. In 1952 Waksman alone was awarded the Nobel Prize for physiology or medicine. "Neither are you a physiologist nor a physician," noted the Nobel Committee, "but still your contribution to the advancement of medicine has been of paramount importance.... As physicians, we regard you as one of the greatest benefactors of mankind."

For his newfound fame, Waksman paid a price. In 1950, Albert Schatz, whose diligent laboratory work had first brought *Streptomyces* to Waksman's attention, sued for royalties as a codiscoverer. (He would also wage an unsuccessful campaign to obtain a share of the Nobel Prize.) Waksman reluctantly agreed to settle, and Schatz received $125,000 and a 3 percent royalty. Waksman shared 7 percent of his 17 percent royalty with the other laboratory workers at Rutgers. With some of the rest of the money he started the Foundation for Microbiology. The wrangling took its toll, and in his autobiography Waksman wrote, "As I look back upon the year 1950, I consider it the darkest one in my whole life." His autobiography, *My Life with the Microbes,* was published in 1954.

Waksman married Bertha Deborah Mitnik, the sister of a childhood friend who had also immigrated to the United States, in 1916. They had one child, Byron Halsted Waksman, who became a celebrated research immunologist. Waksman's death came suddenly, on August 16, 1973, from a cerebral hemorrhage. He is buried at Woods Hole, Massachusetts. His gravestone bears his own version of a biblical proverb: "Out of the earth shall come thy salvation."

Perhaps. Waksman's own popular book on the discovery of strepto-mycin, published in 1965, is poignantly entitled *The Conquest of Tuberculosis*. This reflects the optimism of the era and Waksman's own hopes for conquering infectious disease—it is not as history has unfolded. Within a generation of the discovery of streptomycin, tuberculosis made a spectacular comeback, in both industrialized and developing nations. In 1993 the World Health Organization declared its incidence a global emergency. Eight million people become infected with tuberculosis annually, and it currently claims about two million lives each year.

# Peyton Rous [1879–1970]
## Cancer: A Viral Theory

In 1909 a poultry farmer brought his sick Plymouth Rock hen to the Rockefeller Institute. Peyton Rous, a young researcher, diagnosed the animal as a victim of spindle cell sarcoma, a malignant and rapidly fatal cancer. He undertook some experiments. Among other things, he minced the tumor, extracted a cell-free solution, and passed it through the finest filter available. He injected the filtrate into other chickens. Some fell ill with the same disease. Rous suggested that the cancerous tumor had been due to an infectious "tumor agent." This idea, which implicated a "filterable virus," was rejected. But a half century later, as a new view of cancer causation evolved, Rous's concept gained impressive new relevance. Rous was still alive to receive the Nobel Prize in 1966.

In general, Rous is a key representative of the view that cancer may be environmentally induced—whether by viruses, chemicals, or other carcinogenic agents. Broadly, this is one of two general investigatory gambits that came to dominate cancer research in the twentieth century. The second concept, emerging about the same time, viewed cancer as caused by endogenous factors, most notably genetic mutations. Eventually, a marriage of these viewpoints produced what is essentially an evolving unitary theory. Today cancer is widely considered to be a genetic disorder, often but not invariably initiated by an environmental carcinogen.

Peyton Rous was born on October 5, 1879, in Baltimore, Maryland. He was the eldest of three children born to Frances Anderson Wood, daughter of a Texas circuit judge, and Charles Rous, a grain exporter who died when Peyton was eleven. From childhood Peyton was intrigued by the natural world, and by age twenty, while a college student, he was writing a column on flowers for the *Baltimore Sun*. He attended John Hopkins University, remaining there to study medicine after receiving his bachelor's degree in 1900. He suffered a brief bout of tuberculosis and took a year off from medical school to live and work in a hot, dry climate on a Texas ranch. Returning to the university, he came under the influence of one of its renowned founders, the pathologist William Henry Welch. Rous received his medical degree in 1905 and interned for a year at Johns Hopkins Hospital.

Deciding he was not suited to be a clinician, Rous chose to do research. He worked as an instructor of pathology at the University of Michigan from 1906 to 1908, with time off in 1907 to study morbid anatomy in Germany. A grant enabled Rous to work at the newly established Rockefeller Institute, and its director, Simon Flexner, invited him to remain there. An assistant in 1910, within two years Rous was an associate member; he would become a full member in 1920.

By the end of the first decade of the twentieth century, the concept of "filterable viruses" as causative agents in certain diseases already formed a tantalizing chapter in bacteriology textbooks. Since 1892 it had been known that a filtrate of sap from a tobacco plant afflicted with tobacco mosaic disease could pass through the pores of the best porcelain filter and remain infectious. Some extremely small agent seemed to be at work, one not visible with the light microscope. Filterable viruses were already held responsible for foot-and-mouth disease in cattle, for smallpox, rabies, measles, yellow fever, and several other diseases.

This was the context when, in 1909, a poultryman brought Rous his cancerous Plymouth rock hen. Rous's experiments were original because the sarcomas, as then understood, seemed to arise spontaneously. After obtaining a cell-free broth, Rous expected to rule out infection by injecting it into other hens, but instead he had intriguing results. One hen closely related to the sick bird fell ill, as did some other relatives. Distant relatives remained well. In another group of experiments, in which he kept the filtrate warm, Rous found that all the test hens—which were from the same stock—eventually developed spindle cell sarcoma. Rous reported his results in 1910, performed a second set of experiments, and published his "Transmission of a Malignant New Growth by Means of a Cell-Free Filtrate" in 1912 in the Rockefeller Institute's *The Journal of Experimental Medicine*. Rous's conclusion was that a cancerous tumor could be transmitted "by means of a cell-free filtrate."

Rous's work initially met with interest but not acceptance. "These revolutionary findings were generally disbelieved," Rous later recalled. "Either the growths were not tumors or the agents were tumor cells which the filters had let through." It should be added that the skepticism Rous met with was not dismissive. Edwin Oakes Jordan, in his *General Bacteriology*, for example, viewed Rous's studies as "especially interesting." But in general, the response was critical. None of the other viral diseases caused any such tumor; the effects of diseases such as smallpox were systemic. Moreover, Rous could not show that cancer was an invariable outcome of infection. This was, at the time, the accepted strong form of one of Koch's postulates. The work of Rous and his colleagues could not satisfy it.

The limitations of viral research led Rous to abandon his interest in spindle cell sarcoma and cancer generally. British researchers repeated and confirmed his experiments in the 1920s. Thereafter it was thought that the chicken sarcoma was indeed viral in origin, as Rous had shown, but not a cancer. Meanwhile, a novel idea came to the fore, first due to work by Theodor Boveri (p. 105) and, later, Hermann J. Muller: cancer was caused by genetic mutation. This avenue would be pursued with considerable vigor, but only limited success, for decades to come. In general, good working hypotheses about cancer causation awaited the electron microscope, the major discoveries of molecular biology, advances in biochemistry, and a better understanding of the immune system.

Over the next half century, Rous enjoyed a highly productive career at the Rockefeller. One technical achievement during World War I involved development of blood transfusion techniques. In principle, transfusions had been possible since the turn of the century, when the basic blood types were discovered; historically, blood banks would only appear during the Second World War. But Rous, together with J. T. Turner and Oswald H. Robertson, developed a citrate-sugar solution, known as ACD, in which whole blood could be successfully preserved for three weeks or more. In 1921 Rous became an editor of *The Journal of Experimental Medicine*, a position he would hold for many years. Rous was a careful editor and, as a writer, a stylist who nurtured his own prose carefully.

Liver function and the gall bladder occupied Rous during the 1920s. He demonstrated how bile, secreted by the liver, is stored in concentrated form in the gall bladder until it is used in the digestion of fats. He also showed how the arrival of acid in the duodenum stimulates duodenal cells to produce a hormone, cholecystokinin, that calls upon the gall bladder to discharge its bile into the intestine. And, in a demonstration of how hard things can get, Rous showed that if cholesterol is introduced into the gall bladder, a definite tendency to develop gallstones follows. Rous eventually investigated an array of pathological conditions such as cirrhosis, jaundice, and infectious hepatitis.

In the 1930s Rous returned to cancer research. Without giving up the viral-causation thesis, he demonstrated the involvement of environmental factors. At the instigation of his colleague Richard Shope, Rous began by investigating giant warts found on cottontail rabbits. The Shope papillomas, he discovered, were benign tumors that could progress to malignancy. Over the next three decades, Rous undertook a wide range of research into the influence of environmental factors in carcinogenesis. Rous advanced the view that cancer develops in stages and is induced by carcinogens. In strong words, he contested the widely held notion that cancer was an anarchic proliferation of cells induced by mutation. As has often been the case in cancer research, Rous had part of the story right and part wrong.

A shift toward integrating Rous's general ideas about cancer came about over many years, as technical advances again made it plausible to consider viral theories of cancer. At the same time, genetic factors became more prominent with the discovery of the structure of DNA and a growing understanding of its role in cell metabolism. By 1966, when Rous won the Nobel Prize (which he shared with another Rockefeller researcher, Charles Huggings), the way that viruses introduce themselves into cells without destroying them was becoming clear.

But there was more. The Rous sarcoma virus became the probe used to develop a broad theory of cancer causation. In 1970, using mutants of the same virus Rous had discovered sixty years earlier, Howard Temin and David Baltimore independently demonstrated that a virus composed of RNA could copy itself into a host cell's DNA. This led directly to the idea that "retroviruses" might be responsible for certain cancers. Three years later, Harold Varmus (p. 351) and Michael Bishop discovered a normal gene in animal and human cells that was essentially identical to what was now called the "src" gene in the Rous sarcoma virus. By 1976 this discovery had initiated a cascade of research based on the interplay of genetic, viral, and environmental factors that represents, at least *in statu nascendi*, a unified theory of carcinogenesis.

Peyton Rous was a much-admired figure in medical research. His integrity was apparent in his support of research by Ernst Wynder (p. 307) into the link between smoking and cancer at a time when he and other colleagues strongly doubted such a connection. Although he officially retired from the Rockefeller in 1945, Rous continued to work productively for years afterward. He worked morning and night according to a strict schedule throughout his career, until he was ninety years old.

On a personal basis as well, Rous was uncommonly well liked — "refined, gentle, exquisitely cultured," according to Paul de Kruif (p. 401), who used to lunch with him at the Rockefeller. In 1915, Rous married Marion de Kay, whose background was in the arts, and they had three daughters. The eldest, Marni, married the British physiologist Alan Hodgkin, who received the Nobel Prize for physiology or medicine in 1963. Hodgkin also recalled Rous fondly. His father-in-law's innate optimism, he wrote, often enabled him to hope he had just discovered the key to some aspect of the cancer puzzle. At such times, Rous would immediately go off and buy a painting or some beautiful object. "Later, when the new theory collapsed, he would console himself with the thought that at least he had the tea caddy or whatever it was." At the end of 1969, Rous retired from the *The Journal of Experimental Medicine* after nearly half a century with the review. He was suffering from abdominal cancer, and six weeks later, on February 16, 1970, he died.

# John Franklin Enders [1897–1985]

## Persuading Viruses to Multiply

The ability to grow pure cultures of microorganisms is crucial to research into infectious diseases. One of the great innovations from the laboratory of Robert Koch (p. 24) was the simple petri dish, for culturing bacteria. Viruses, however, are magnitudes smaller. To grow them presents a host of problems. They may measure only about two millionths of an inch across, and they replicate naturally only within living cells. Two centuries after the chance discovery of a smallpox vaccine by Edward Jenner (p. xxx), the promise of useful vaccines to combat numerous viral diseases, from herpes to AIDS, remains unfulfilled. Nevertheless, from the laboratory of John Enders, in 1948, came one of the most practical and well-timed discoveries in twentieth-century virology.

Polio had become an epidemic, frequently maiming for life the young victims it did not kill, when Enders discovered how to grow viruses easily and quickly in tissue cultures. This new technique "transformed virus production," writes Jane S. Smith, "the same way John Deere's plow and Cyrus McCormick's reaper transformed agriculture." Within a few years Jonas Salk was able to develop an effective vaccine, and the historic conquest of polio is recalled as a watershed in twentieth-century medicine. Over the long term, Enders's tissue culture method led to a cascade of new studies by which numerous viruses were isolated and identified. With colleagues Thomas H. Weller and Frederick Robbins, Enders was awarded the Nobel Prize for physiology or medicine in 1954.

John Franklin Enders was born into a wealthy and socially prominent family on February 10, 1897, in West Hartford, Connecticut. His father, John Ostrom Enders, was president of the Hartford National Bank, and his father before him had been president of the Aetna Life Insurance Company. His mother, Harriet Goulden Whitmore, was of Dutch and German ancestry. In 1914 Enders entered Yale. With time out to serve in the U.S. Naval Reserve Flying Corps during World War I, he graduated in 1920. Initially Enders had no career footing, but financial security was not a worry. After a brief stint as a real estate agent, he returned to graduate school at Harvard University, where he spent four years studying English and Celtic literature. By chance, however, his roommate was an Australian, Hugh

Ward, a graduate student in microbiology. Through Ward, Enders met the charismatic Hans Zinsser, author of the perennially popular *Rats, Lice and History* and also one of the great textbooks on bacteriology, still revised today. Enders's interest was aroused, and he entered Harvard's doctoral program in bacteriology, which he completed in 1930. Thus, Enders began what became a long research career at the relatively late age of thirty-two.

Enders's early work shifted focus from bacteria to viruses. Like many bacteriologists at that time, he first studied tuberculosis and pneumonia, diseases that were widespread and often fatal. But in 1937 Enders was drawn to investigate an epidemic of feline distemper that was killing off the experimental cats at Harvard. Together with a colleague, William Hammon, Enders soon showed that the agent responsible was a virus that attacked the bone marrow—a lymphatic cancer. Harvesting virus from the spleens and the lymph nodes of sick cats, Enders and his colleagues were also able to develop a useful protective vaccine.

Enders would spend the rest of his career in virology. During the 1930s he worked on typhus, a deadly febrile illness caused by one of the rickettsiae. Today regarded as belonging to a genus of rod-shaped bacteria, in the 1930s rickettsiae were thought to be one of the larger viruses, because they were found only within cells. In 1938 Enders began work on mammalian viruses, such as they were known. He studied the herpes simplex virus and made efforts to isolate the measles virus.

Promising results in Enders's laboratory on a variety of fronts were interrupted by America's entry into World War II. As a consultant to the military, Enders worked to develop practical diagnostic tests and immunization techniques, particularly against mumps. This disease did not become, as was feared, a serious problem for the wartime military. But Enders did manage to develop a skin test for mumps and, eventually, a vaccine from killed virus which conferred short-term immunity.

Polio represented a major challenge to modern medicine, and the search for an effective vaccine intensified after the war; some 50,000 new cases were reported in the United States in 1950. Although Enders received funding from the National Foundation for Infantile Paralysis, when he left Harvard University to become director of the Infectious Disease Research Laboratory at Boston Children's Hospital, he was initially not involved with polio research. Enders's mission, as he saw it, remained that of building basic virology. Neither he nor his two principal colleagues, Frederick Robbins and Thomas Weller, were specifically interested in joining the polio bandwagon. Consequently, their discovery of tissue culture technique is often lauded as a classic instance of scientific intuition combined with careful experiment leading to a medical breakthrough.

By midcentury a number of viruses had been identified and classified, and the inability to easily cultivate them had become a persistent and vexing problem. Using animals as reservoirs was cumbersome and had all sorts of limitations. In 1936 Albert Sabin and Peter Olitsky had demonstrated that the poliovirus could be made to grow in embryonic tissue of the central nervous system. This seemed like an advance for vaccine research. But brain tissue frequently provoked an allergic reaction, so a human vaccine could not be developed by this route. At the same time, there arose the belief that poliovirus would multiply only in nervous tissue, which was where, in disease, it did its damage.

Enders's accomplishment is often recounted with awe, which is perplexing inasmuch as it looks like fairly commonplace medical research entailing teamwork, a modest suggestion, and some luck. Early in 1948, Weller succeeded in growing the mumps virus within particles of chick embryo. His innovation was to replenish the nutrient medium surrounding the embryonic tissue every few days. Weller tried the same thing with the chickenpox virus and also—because "close at hand in the storage cabinet was the Lansing Strain of the poliomyelitis virus"—the poliovirus. Chickenpox could not be coaxed to grow in embryonic tissue. But the poliovirus flourished.

This result intrigued Enders. He was aware that the poliovirus had been harvested in large quantities from the gut. "It was in the back of my mind," he said later, "that, if so much polio virus could be found in the gastrointestinal tract, then it must grow someplace besides nervous tissue." Now Enders suggested an experiment to see whether the poliovirus would multiply in live human cells.

Unexpectedly, the effort was a success. The human cells were from muscle tissue taken from deceased infants. The poliovirus cultured in this tissue could be persuaded to multiply. Its presence was detected in monkeys who became paralyzed after being injected with a solution from the culture. Enders and his colleagues were able to dilute the virus by as much as one part in a quintillion and have it remain active and virulent. Their celebrated paper, "Cultivation of the Lansing Strain of Poliomyelitis Virus in Cultures of Various Human Embryonic Tissue," was published in *Science* on January 28, 1949.

The newfound ability to grow poliovirus initiated a series of rapid advances in polio research. Enders, Robbins, and Weller went on to show that tissue from the human intestine was a good host to poliovirus. They also developed techniques that revealed how the virus destroyed the cells it invaded. It was soon understood that the poliovirus enters the body, most often, through the mouth and is absorbed into the blood before finding its way to the brain and the parts of the spinal cord that affect muscles.

Developing a vaccine was a clear next step, but Enders did not take it. Weller and Robbins were interested, but the latter recalled, "Enders, in his thoughtful way, felt that this was not the kind of work our laboratory was best suited for." But, benefiting from Enders's techniques, by 1952 Jonas Salk was able to test a vaccine made from killed virus from the three known strains. Mass field trials, involving over two hundred thousand children, began in 1954. They proved the vaccine a success. The "Salk vaccine" became emblematic of the great advances of twentieth-century medicine.

Although Salk's work was more spectacular, for the scientific community the magnitude of Enders's accomplishment was judged to be greater. In 1954 Enders, together with Weller and Robbins, was awarded the Nobel Prize for physiology or medicine. Enders's insistence that his two colleagues share the award is widely cited as an unusual gesture of generosity in medical research.

Enders's later career was also fruitful. He helped develop a successful vaccine against measles and made technical innovations in cancer research. He formally retired in 1972, but during his last years he investigated ways to defeat the human immunodeficiency virus (HIV) that causes AIDS.

John Enders married Sarah Frances Bennett in 1927, and they had two children. Sarah died in 1943, and Enders married Carolyn B. Keane in 1951. Throughout his life he maintained the literary interests he had left behind for research. He had just completed reading a book of T. S. Eliot's poetry when he died, unexpectedly if not prematurely, of heart failure on September 8, 1985.

# Ernst Ruska  [1906 – 1988]

## Inventing the Electron Microscope

The electron microscope embodies the point at which twentieth-century physics and the biological microworld intersect. Within several years of their first incarnation in 1932, electron microscopes were providing access to a new molecular perspective from which eventually would emerge, among other things, a far more sophisticated topography of the cell, new taxonomies for microorganisms, and rational prospects for combating diseases. Although a practical version was long in the making and had many contributors, primary credit for its development is undoubtedly due to the German engineer Ernst Ruska.

Developing the "transmission electron microscope" was a demanding task, and it occupied Ruska for decades. He showed it was possible in 1931, and a year later he built a primitive model. He continued to improve on it during World War II, when he remained in Berlin and conducted research while bombs fell. After the war ended and Germany rebuilt its industry, Ruska directed the design and construction of a new generation of powerful machines. His work was successful in what had become a competitive marketplace, and he came to head the Institute for Electron Microscopy of the Max Planck Institute. He received the Nobel Prize in physics, after waiting many years, in 1986.

In its essential features, the electron microscope is analogous to an ordinary light microscope. Just as glass can be shaped and polished to act as a lens that will magnify an object by bending and focusing visible light, so too can electromagnetic coils be used to create a magnetic "lens" that focuses an electron beam. Visible light has a wavelength about two thousand times greater than the diameter of an ordinary atom. By contrast, electrons react to, and thus can be used to form images of, much smaller objects.

Ernst August Friedrich Ruska was born in Heidelberg, Germany, on December 25, 1906. He was the fifth of seven children born to Elisabeth Merx and Julius Ferdinand Ruska, an Orientalist who became well regarded for his work in the history of sciences and Islamic culture. The family background was learned, intellectual, and artistic; its atmosphere, austere. When he was ten years old, in the midst of World War I, his elder brother, Hans, committed suicide. That year Ernst began Heidelberg College, where his father taught, but within two years he was interested in electrical inventions—to his father's chagrin. No sooner had Ernst graduated the gymnasium than he tossed the contents of his school bag into the Neckar River as an act of rebellion. His father slapped him in the face.

Indeed, much to his parents' disappointment Ernst subsequently attended the Technical Universities of Munich, from 1925 to 1927, and Berlin, from 1927 to 1931. That year he was certified as an electrical engineer. He continued his studies at the University of Berlin and received his doctorate in 1933. Ruska's development of the electron microscope is directly linked to the work he did in physics while still a graduate student. His doctoral thesis concerned the "electron lenses" that were the key to inventing the electron microscope.

The transmission electron microscope was, in the final analysis, yet another innovation fostered—like X rays, television, and the computer screen have been—by the famous cathode-ray tube. Ruska's earliest work, from 1928, involved improving the cathode-ray oscillograph, an instrument that displays electrical variations on a fluorescent screen. He employed a new idea in electron optics that had been promulgated by Hans Busch, who had established that electrons passing through the magnetic field generated by a circular coil would obey the same laws as light passing through a glass lens. Ruska worked out experiments that showed how this might be engineered, using two coils to focus the beam of electrons. He and his teacher and colleague, Max Knoll, benefited from the fact that during the mid-1920s the Hungarian-born British physicist and inventor Dennis Gabor had developed—inadvertently—an ironclad magnetic lens. Ruska published results as early as 1929 that showed that a single such magnetic lens could focus an electron beam and create an optical image identical to that of a glass lens. The promise and practical possibility of inventing an electron microscope clearly emerged from this work.

The founding phase for the first actual instrument dates to the spring of 1931, and Ruska's initial sketches were made as early as 1929. In these he clearly demonstrated the basic elements of electron microscopy. The shape of the instrument was vertical and tubelike. The high-voltage cathode-ray source for the electron beam was at the top. Below, an aperture or wire grid served as a defined object for the electrons that passed through it and were then captured and magnified by two magnetic lenses. The image would be cast onto a fluorescent screen at the base of the instrument, and the microscopist would examine this screen through a viewing port. The distances between lens, grid, and screen could be varied to change focal length and magnification.

Working with Knoll, Ruska developed a primitive prototype. "We succeeded," Ruska later wrote, "on April 7, 1931 in taking the first two-stage image and photographic record...." Resolution, at a magnification of sixteen times, was quite low, and several innovations were needed before the electron microscope could be considered practical. Theoretically, there was concern that specimens could not withstand the heat intensity of a focused electron beam and would burn up — just as, for example, an insect under a magnifying glass can be ignited by focused sunlight. This turned out not to be the case, because electrons are scattered upon encountering the object, which must be extremely thin; they are not absorbed in the same measure as visible light. "The psychological hurdles that the pioneers of high resolution electron microscopy had to surmount," wrote Ruska later, "especially in the biological field, first of all within themselves and in their own ranks, later in others, were therefore extraordinary...." In 1935, electron micrographs of a biological specimen were refused for publication by an editor who believed they were of no interest.

The early phase of Ruska's career took place in the context of Germany's growing domination by Adolf Hitler, who came to power in 1933. That year, with the future of the electron microscope uncertain, Ruska moved from the university to the private sector. For several years he worked as an engineer at the Fernseh Corporation and was involved mainly in developing television tube technology. But during the mid-1930s, prospects for an electron microscope improved as scientists involved in basic research recognized its potential. Some of the first bacteriological images were developed in 1937 by Ladislas Marton. Ruska's own brother, Helmut Ruska, a physician, saw their potential significance for medicine and, indeed, obtained images of virus particles for the first time in 1940.

That the electron microscope was expected to benefit medicine was made clear to industry by 1936, when the firm of Siemens and Halske lent financial support to research efforts toward developing its commercial potential. At Ruska's suggestion, the firm allowed him to set up a laboratory of electron optics. Within two years the "Siemens Super Microscope" was ready for custom manufacture.

The onset of World War II did not change Ruska's preoccupation with the electron microscope. This was the case even though the House of Siemens was a large corporation heavily involved in radar and weapons research. (After the war, some of its officials would be charged with helping construct Nazi death camps.) Ruska appears to have worked on the microscope all through the war, corresponding with scientists in Japan and elsewhere in the restricted German scientific community. Apolitical, he did not subscribe to Nazism and, with some courage, took a Siemens official and his Jewish wife into his house outside Berlin during the bombardment of the city after they were refused entry into an air-raid shelter.* In 1946 Ruska, like many German scientists, was placed in detention in England for several months, but he soon returned to Berlin.

For a decade after the war, Ruska was a major force at Siemens during a period when demand for new and improved electron microscopes soared and competition among manufacturers increased dramatically. Provided with laboratories and workshops, "Ruska could always be relied upon to keep everybody on their toes," wrote British physicist T. Mulvey. The Siemens "Elmiskop-I" models developed around 1954 "set an extremely high standard in high resolution electron microscopy." Ruska's success with this microscope seems to have helped undermine his research role at Siemens, as the company now focused on production and sales rather than further research. Ruska began to feel underemployed, and he left Siemens in 1955.

Ruska made a simple transition to an academic environment. From 1949 he had spent part of his time at the Fritz Haber Institute (FHI), a division of the larger Max Planck Institute in West Berlin. In 1957 he accepted a position as director of FHI's Institute for Electron Microscopy. Here he would spend the remainder of his career, continuing to work even after he officially retired in 1974.

Toward the end of his life, Ruska began receiving recognition for his major role in inventing the electron microscope. The situation was complicated, in part because another German engineer with Siemens, Reinhold Rüdenberg, had filed a patent application some ten days before Ruska did. Rüdenberg had been inspired by Ruska's experiments, and his own ideas had been speculative; thus, Ruska's claim of scientific priority was solid. Later, Rüdenberg would work for the Radio Corporation of

---

*Some 4,700 Jews, protected because they were of "privileged mixed-marriages," are said to have survived the war in Berlin.

America (RCA) in the United States. He sued when RCA claimed its scientists had invented the electron microscope, and he finally won the U.S. patent for the invention. (It is unlikely that Rüdenberg would have received a portion of the Nobel Prize, but in any event he died in 1961.) In 1986 Ruska was awarded half the Nobel Prize for physics; the other half went to Gerd Binnig and Heinrich Rohrer for developing the scanning electron microscope (SEM). With this latter instrument, electrons do not penetrate, but rather scan the surface of a solid object, and a virtual image is developed. Scanning and transmission electron microscopes thus have different, complementary uses.

Ernst Ruska is remembered as a sober and serious scientist who was also absent-minded and somewhat eccentric. Absorbed by his work, he was reported to dislike weekends away from the laboratory. He wore neither hat nor gloves, and had problems wearing a wristwatch. Like some others of his generation, he never became competent using a telephone. Sometimes he would forget the name of a long-standing employee. Once, engaged in a discussion, he mistook an elderly cloakroom attendant for a colleague and vainly tried to assist him in putting on his own coat. Ruska did not have a military bent, and so he appreciated the irony when, in 1985, the governor of the Commonwealth of Kentucky made him a member of the Order of Kentucky Colonels—decidedly an honorary title. Ernst Ruska lived three more years and died on May 30, 1988, in West Berlin, shortly before that city's reunification.

Memoirs by friends of great scientists are often limited by a lack of candor, but this was not the case with Ernst Ruska. Ten years after his death, he was the subject of a fascinating, unusually honest profile by his secretary, Lotte Lambert, and colleague, Tom Mulvey. They recount that Ruska married Irmela Ruth Geigis in 1937, and they had three children. In addition, at the end of World War II Ruska began an affair with a woman identified as Ilse H., a Siemens employee. She became pregnant in 1946, bore Ruska one child, then another. Ruska confided in his wife, who accepted the situation with grace. The two families would come together each Christmas day, which was also Ruska's birthday—an arrangement that continued even after Ilse married in 1961.

# Willem J. Kolff   [b. 1911]

## Spare Parts Medicine

The pioneer of "spare parts" medicine is the Dutch physician Willem Kolff. During World War II, in occupied Holland, he invented the first successful kidney dialysis machine. In the United States after the war, Kolff went on to become the world's foremost bionics engineer. He headed teams that invented a wide variety of prosthetic devices, including machines to substitute for the kidney and the lungs. Although his role was not much publicized, he was one of the principal figures behind creation of the first artificial human heart. Kolff, who once asserted, "If man can grow a heart, he can build one," would live to see the first operation to replace a human heart with a fully implantable substitute, in 2001.

Kolff's landmark invention was the kidney dialysis machine, and this has, parenthetically, some nice ironies. For one thing, it took a Dutchman. The kidneys are nothing if not organs to maintain fluid balance throughout the body, and Holland's very existence depends on controlling sea level. In addition, the machine was developed during World War II, when the country was sorely afflicted by Nazi Germany. Indeed, the first patient to seriously benefit from it was a collaborator, a Dutch National Socialist. People begged Kolff to let her die, but with characteristic humanity, he saved her life. With the help of his jerry-built machine, this despised and unpleasant woman emerged from a uremic coma, was heard to say, "I am going to divorce my husband," and entered the annals of medical history.

Willem Johan Kolff was born in Leiden, Netherlands, on February 14, 1911. His mother was Adriana de Jonge and his father, Jacob Kolff, was a physician who directed a tuberculosis sanatorium. Growing up, Kolff once said later, "For me, there was never anything else but being a doctor." In fact, as a child, Kolff was reluctant to follow in his father's footsteps "because I could not bear the thought of seeing patients die." But he was strongly and positively affected by his father's sensitivity to suffering and death. "He would agonize over his frustrations in treating [his patients], and I recall seeing him weep on several occasions." As a student, Kolff persisted despite dyslexia. He attended medical school at the University of Leiden. An assistant in the department of pathological anatomy from 1934 to 1936, he received his medical degree in 1938. For a short time afterward, Kolff worked as a teaching assistant, an unpaid position, at the University of Groningen. In the medical service there, he became interested in treating kidney failure.

The basic science behind dialysis and the interest in building a machine to treat kidney disease dates to the mid-nineteenth century. Thomas Graham, a Scottish chemist, demonstrated liquid diffusion through a permeable membrane—a basic model of the kidneys at work. In the early twentieth century a small group of physicians developed what they called an "artificial kidney" and tested it on dogs with some success. World War I put an end to this research, however. Kolff's accomplishment was to develop—under adverse social circumstances—a machine that would work.

While at the university hospital at Leiden, Kolff first encountered a patient dying from a type of nephritis, or inflammation of the kidneys. The disease would be fatal if untreated, and the patient's death slow and painful. As his father had with tubercular patients, Kolff found renal conditions all the more distressing for being well understood. In principle, removing waste from the blood over a period of days or weeks would effect a cure. Kolff could seriously consider this prospect because a biochemistry professor at Groningen had recently discovered that the same cellophane used for sausage casing could be employed to determine osmotic pressure of various fluids and to concentrate blood plasma. Kolff soon performed experiments himself. He found that when cellophane casings were filled with blood and immersed in saline solution, the urea in the blood would leach through the permeable membrane. "I found that in five minutes," he explained, "nearly all the urea I had added to the blood sample, four hundred milligrams, had disappeared from the blood and entered the saline bath."

Kolff was already moving toward developing a machine when World War II interrupted. The Germans invaded the Netherlands in 1940, and the Nazi occupation proved a professional trauma, but also a fertile period of investigation and experimentation. In the wake of invasion, Kolff recognized that blood transfusions would be in demand, and he volunteered to establish one of Europe's first blood banks. But he could not remain at Groningen, especially after his mentor and head of the medical department, Polak Daniels, a Jew, took his own life. Kolff refused to work with his successor, a Dutch Nazi. Over the next five years, Kolff was consistently able to help and harbor fighters in the Dutch resistance. Toward the end of the war, at great personal risk, he directed a medical service that saved a large number of Jews and underground fighters from transport to Germany and certain death.

Kolff developed dialysis at a small municipal hospital in Kampen, an old town located on the Ijsel River, to which he moved after leaving Groningen. Solving a series of relatively uncomplicated problems, he constructed a machine that is easy to visualize. He wrapped about twenty meters of cellophane tubing around a slatted wooden drum that was suspended horizontally inside a tank filled with saline solution and connected to a motor. The tubing, snaked through the drum's hollow axle, shunted blood from and back to the patient. As the drum rotated, the blood was cleansed in the saline bath. Heparin, a naturally occurring substance, could be used to prevent clotting.

Kolff's cobbled-together machine, first put to use in March 1943, did cleanse the blood, but it was not immediately successful. Fourteen of the first fifteen patients died, and the survivor might have lived in any event. But Kolff was convinced the machine could be made to work. "I did not for one moment doubt that sooner or later a patient would come into our hands of whom it might be said, 'he is cured, and without the artificial kidney he would have died.'" A cure seemed especially possible for cases of acute reversible renal failure. Finally, at war's end in September 1945, the machine saved Maria Sophia Schafstadt. Imprisoned as a former Nazi collaborator, sixty-seven years old, she became the first person whose life was spared by dialysis.

Kolff consolidated his success in several ways. He had written articles for Scandinavian and French journals as early as 1944, and he soon wrote a book, *The Artificial Kidney*, that he published in both Dutch and English. In addition, after the war Kolff constructed and shipped kidney machines to researchers in England, Canada, and the United States. (He did not patent the machine.) At the same time, he continued work on a Ph.D. in internal medicine and received that degree summa cum laude from the University of Groningen in 1946.

Kolff made several visits to the United States before he immigrated in 1950, taking a research position with the Cleveland Clinic. With some difficulty, over the course of a decade he assembled a team of researchers. One of his hopes was to develop improved dialysis techniques; he was much in favor of home dialysis and foresaw the possibility of small, portable versions. But he also wanted to continue work on a heart-lung machine, to be used during various types of thoracic surgery.* Kolff built a "pump-oxygenator" that became an important factor in making open-heart surgery safer for many patients. He introduced this device, made from disposable polyethylene tubing, as early as 1955. Kolff and colleagues

---

*Work by Kolff and his colleagues on a heart-lung machine was one of many such efforts taking place at that time. The most famous heart-lung machine was invented by surgeon John Gibbon with help from International Business Machines, and was successfully demonstrated in 1953.

also created the first aortic balloon pump, introduced in 1961. An assist device for improving cardiac output in cases of cardiogenic shock, it became a widely used tool in emergency medicine.

The most ambitious project in Kolff's career, extending over a quarter century, was his work on the artificial heart. The possibility was broached in the mid-1950s by the American Society for Artificial Internal Organs, and within a decade it became a respectable area of research. As early as 1957, Kolff and his colleagues had tried to drive circulation in a dog using an air-driven pump, but the animal lived only ninety minutes. This gave a hint of the difficult task ahead. But with a workable heart-lung machine and with knowledge of the cardiovascular system expanding, the prospect for a bionic heart improved. Kolff tried several designs driven by electricity, including a self-cooling pendulum-driven model. But they were either weak or too heavy, and they often generated more heat than the body could stand. Kolff finally accepted the simpler concept of a silicone-rubber heart that operated with compressed air from an external power source.

Kolff was still at work on the artificial heart when, in 1967, he moved to the University of Utah, where he was professor of surgery as well as professor of engineering and bioengineering. To his research team he soon added Robert Jarvik, an ambitious physician and inventor, and William DeVries, a cardiothoracic surgeon. Over the course of the next fifteen years, Jarvik designed a number of models of the artificial heart, while DeVries developed the techniques of the heart replacement operation in animals. In 1982, Barney Clark became the first patient to receive an artificial heart. Clark, a sixty-one-year-old retired dentist, was subjected to a media circus the likes of which had not been seen since the birth of the Dionne quintuplets in 1934. He survived the operation and lived for 112 days before dying of complications unrelated to the beating of his Jarvik-7 heart. Kolff, who remained largely in the background, lamented that Clark's funeral took place with newscast helicopters flying overhead.

Willem Kolff continued to work through his ninth decade. At the University of Utah he oversaw development of a number of increasingly sophisticated and lightweight artificial hearts. His institute also looked toward developing an artificial eye and artificial ear, and improved the prosthetic arm. From 1979 Kolff was distinguished professor of surgery at the university's College of Medicine and also, from 1981, research professor of engineering and professor of internal medicine.

From all appearances, Kolff has enjoyed a relatively tranquil personal life. He married Janke Cornelia Huidekoper in 1937, and they had five children, three of whom became physicians. Widely admired by colleagues, Kolff's strong personality, which mingles perseverance and considerable social skills, has always been in evidence. He belongs to a generation of physicians that has held a high measure of optimism about the prospects of modern medicine along with a strong social conscience. Responsibility for treating the sick, not a wish to garner encomiums for technological progress, has guided Kolff's choices on the kind of inventions he engineers. He has always aimed, he maintains, not at merely prolonging life, but at improving its quality and prospects for happiness. "These are honest and good goals," according to Kolff, "and deserve to be pushed."

# Macfarlane Burnet [1899–1985]

## A New Theory of the Immune System

A grasp of how the body defends itself against microorganisms and various "nonself" invaders did not arrive with the advent of bacteriology in the late nineteenth century. In spite of fundamental discoveries by Elie Metchnikoff (p. 186) and ambitious theory building by Paul Ehrlich and others, immunology remained an immature branch of medical research. But in the 1950s there emerged a new and surprising theory: The body at birth possesses a biochemical system for self-protection that includes a great number of cells, each of which represents a preexisting snare for some specific invader, or antigen. When these cells, constantly in circulation, encounter antigens, they bind to them, clone themselves, and stimulate production of protective molecules known as antibodies.

"Clonal selection theory" is "overpowering in its simplicity," and crucial for understanding disease processes, the anaphylactic response, autoimmune disease, and the rejection response in transplantation. It was first proposed, and to some extent demonstrated, by Macfarlane Burnet. One of the most prolific medical researchers in the twentieth century, Burnet also made a host of advances in virology and bacteriology.

Macfarlane Burnet was born in Traralgon, a small town in the state of Victoria, Australia, on September 3, 1899. His father, Frank Burnet, was a bank manager; his mother was Hadassah Pollock Mackay. Shy as a child, "Mac," as he was known all his life, was not close to his father, and his mother was often occupied with caring for a retarded daughter, Doris. He developed a love of the outdoors and an interest in birds and insects, especially beetles. He was introduced to the theory of evolution via the Chambers encyclopedia, and Charles Darwin (p. 3) became an enduring influence. Burnet's aptitudes led a local minister to suggest that Mac obtain a university education. He studied biology, in addition to medicine, at Geelong College, and in 1917 moved to the University of Melbourne. There he received his bachelor of science in 1922, and his medical degree two years later.

Although he initially expected to practice clinical neurology, Burnet's talents for research were soon recognized. He began working as a resident pathologist at the Royal Melbourne Hospital and undertook research at the hospital's Walter and Eliza Hall Institute for Medical Research. Awarded a fellowship, in 1925 Burnet traveled to England to work for two years at the Lister Institute of Preventive Medicine, receiving a Ph.D. from the University of London in 1927. He returned to Australia and the Hall Institute in 1928, and in 1934 he was named assistant director. This institute would become his permanent base for the next thirty-five years; he was its director from 1944 to 1965.

Burnet's early work concerned the viruses that attack bacteria—the bacteriophages—discovered in 1915 by the French-Canadian bacteriologist Felix d'Hérelle. Viruses that shed their protein coats to invade their hosts, bacteriophages were basic components in experiments that culminated in the discovery of the structure of DNA. Burnet performed yeoman work with them, publishing some thirty-two papers between 1924 and 1937. His studies were in part taxonomic. He found phages in the excreta of various animals, and counted many distinct species and strains, which could be classified serologically. Indeed, Burnet is sometimes credited with initiating the "phage genetics" later advanced with great success by Max Delbrück and others.

Animal virology became one of Burnet's research interests about 1932 when a second appointment in England, at the National Institute of Medical Research, put him in touch with Henry Dale (p. 236). An easy method for culturing viruses was much desired, and Burnet discovered that the canary-pox virus could be made to grow on a type of fetal tissue found in the chick embryo, known as the chorioallantoic membrane. Burnet coaxed this tissue to host a variety of viruses, and his method became widely used in laboratories all over the world.

Burnet's work in virology with chick embryos had broader implications when, in the late 1930s, he developed a "pock counting" technique for assaying the presence and investigating the natural history of a whole variety of viruses. Burnet examined the ecology of infectious agents in *Biological Aspects of Infectious Disease,* published in 1940. It was the first of many such expositions and, although aimed in part at a general audience, was widely translated and had an impact on other scientists. Burnet's inclination to consider infectious diseases from the point of view of natural selection—the microorganism's strategies for transmission and survival—would become an influential stamp of his thinking.

Burnet also worked on the poliovirus, then causing outbreaks of epidemic proportions. As early as 1931 he showed evidence for a second, serologically distinct strain. Importantly, Burnet doubted the prevailing orthodoxy that the virus reached the central nervous system (where it inflicts its damage) via the olfactory bulbs in the forebrain. As early as 1940

he confirmed reports that it could enter the body via oral and intestinal routes. He also performed experiments that suggested that the poliovirus could be induced to grow in human embryonic tissue—but this he was unable to confirm. After 1949, Burnet abandoned research on polio, pessimistic as to the prospect for a vaccine. Within several years John Enders (p. 266) would prove him wrong with experiments that led to the Salk polio vaccine. Burnet's "near miss" with polio was one of several in his career. He also came close to discovering interferon, a cellular protein that protects against viral infection.

Burnet's investigations into viral diseases led to his revolutionary theory of immune response. It was shown—and Burnet replicated the experiment—that a chick embryo injected with a virus will not manufacture antibodies to that particular strain if reinfected after it has hatched. This discovery had weighty medical implications for tissue transplantation, and would draw the attention of both Peter Medawar and Jean Dausset (p. 321). But Burnet's perspective led him toward a broader realm: a general theory of the immune system.

At midcentury, the most plausible explanation of how the body recognizes and neutralizes foreign invaders was known as the "template theory." Antibody molecules were thought to cling to and neutralize invading antigens by changing shape; then, although the mechanism was unclear, they would direct synthesis of a large number of new, identically shaped antibodies. Although attractive to immunochemists, the template theory had several problems. It ran counter to recent developments in chemistry and molecular biology which suggested that contact with another molecule could not induce a protein to change its shape. Moreover, this theory could not easily explain why the immune system possesses a "memory" for antigens or, a related issue, how it distinguishes between "self" and "nonself."

These objections finally provoked Burnet to develop an entirely new theory. He was crucially inspired by Niels Jerne, who suggested in 1955 that antibody molecules might be preexistent in all possible configurations, ready to be "selected" to proliferate by an antigen of any shape.

Burnet recognized that, in biological terms, Jerne's theory required a cellular basis. It "would make real sense," he wrote, "if cells produced a characteristic pattern of globulin [antibody molecule] for genetic reasons and were stimulated to proliferate by contact with the corresponding antigenic determinant." Burnet suggested that an organism, while an embryo, produces a vast number of lymphocytes. Each possesses a specific receptor that will bind to a specific antigen. Once it encounters the antigen, the lymphocyte then initiates both antibody production and cell division, producing clones. Burnet outlined clonal selection theory for the first time in 1957, and *The Clonal Selection Theory of Acquired Immunity* was published in 1959.

Burnet's theory by no means found immediate acceptance; that required a decade of controversy and opposition. At first glance, nothing in human biology seemed similar to the colossal work of randomized immune cell production in embryonic development that Burnet suggested. But, as Niels Jerne had pointed out, the immune system may be compared to another recognition system, the nervous system. The idea that each of millions of lymphocytes is dedicated to producing a single antibody, based upon a potential encounter, may seem extraordinary, but clonal selection theory effectively integrated cellular immunity with the "humoral" theories of immunity that dated to the nineteenth century. In Burnet's theory, antibody molecules neutralize antigens found in the blood and lymph, outside of other body cells; specialized immune cells target and attack cells that are invaded.

Clonal selection theory was also rich in its implications for broader biological issues. In explaining self-tolerance, it provided the concept of autoimmune disease, today understood to comprise a large number of disorders, from insulin-dependent diabetes to rheumatoid arthritis. Clonal selection theory called for a revised understanding of allergy and the anaphylactic response (the catastrophic reaction to a bee sting, for example). In addition, clonal selection theory had significant implications for microbial genetics and for understanding bacterial resistance. Any complex organism must contend with invading organisms' capacity to mutate, and clonal selection theory provided an explanation that was logical but also properly imperfect in evolutionary terms.

Vast experimental support for, and theoretical extension of, Burnet's original clonal selection theory developed over the next thirty years. "Immunology after clonal selection," writes William R. Clark, "like the newly emerging field of molecular biology, seemed to move forward with a steady force that gradually swept everyone along with it." By 1961 the thymus gland, once thought to be a vestigial organ, was in fact found to be the central organ of the lymphatic system, crucial for the class of cells that mediate the cellular immune response, the "T cells." The spleen, another organ whose function had long baffled medicine, was discovered to be a major site for producing the "B cells," which bring about the humoral response by generating plasma cells that manufacture antibodies. The two major classes of lymphocytes, T cells and B cells, represent elaboration on a functional plane of Burnet's clonal selection theory. Today immunology, for all intents and purposes, is a unified science.

Burnet was covered with honors through much of his later career. Knighted in 1951, he also won the Albert Lasker Award and the Copley Medal of the Royal Society. In 1960 he shared the Nobel Prize with Peter Medawar for their efforts to understand acquired immunological tolerance. As an elder eminence of Australian science, Burnet was a prolific author and wrote a number of books for a popular audience, including *Viruses and Man*, published in 1953; *Changing Patterns*, his 1968 autobiography; and *Dominant Mammal: The Biology of Human Destiny*, from 1970. In 1979 Burnet also wrote a philosophical text, *Credo and Comment: A Scientist Reflects* and a textbook on genetics, *Endurance of Life*. It is interesting to record that Burnet was a serious skeptic as to whether discoveries in molecular biology would lead to great advances in medicine, and he doubted that genetic diseases would someday be preventable.

Burnet had a complex personality. He could be timid in social situations, but at the same time he possessed considerable self-confidence and was said to be an inspirational teacher. Not overly self-effacing, his achievements showed "that I have the sort of intelligence, drive and 'creativity' appropriate to an experimental scientist," he wrote, "plus a taste for, and some competence in scientific generalization about biological matters." Burnet married Edith Linda Marston Druce in 1928. They had three children; she died in 1973. His second marriage was to Hazel Jenkin in 1976. Two years later he retired. He continued to work until shortly before his death, on August 31, 1985.

# Part V  Recent and Contemporary

# Rosalyn Sussman Yalow [b. 1921]

## Radioimmunoassay

R adioimmunoassay probes the complex chemical makeup and dynamics
of the human body. Developed in the late 1950s, it enables sensitive
measurement of concentrations in the blood of various proteins, antibodies, and antigens. A prepotent tool used in both research and diagnosis,
radioimmunoassay is an aspect of nuclear medicine. It is the principal
discovery of Rosalyn Sussman Yalow, a physicist, in collaboration with
Solomon Berson. In 1977 Yalow became only the second woman to win the
Nobel Prize for physiology or medicine.

The daughter of Jewish immigrants from Eastern Europe, Rosalyn
Sussman was born on July 19, 1921, in the South Bronx, New York. Her
mother, Clara Zipper, had come to the United States from Germany at age
four, and had received a rudimentary education. Rosalyn's father, Simon
Sussman, worked as a streetcar conductor and later owned a small business. Rosalyn was a bright, independent, and determined child who
learned to read early. Close to her father, by age eight she was considering
a career in science; in middle school she envisaged a career in medical
research. Skipped ahead, Rosalyn graduated high school at age fifteen.
She was fascinated by the twentieth-century revolution in physics, and in
1939 she attended Enrico Fermi's famous lecture on the recent success in
splitting the atom. She recalled "hanging from the rafters" in the crowded
lecture hall at Columbia University.

Yalow's higher education and early career recall that of another Nobel
laureate, Gertrude Belle Elion. Both attended the same university, endured
a measure of institutionalized anti-Semitism, and encountered gender
bias. Yalow expected she would not easily gain admittance to medical
school, and so did not try. Rather, she studied physics and chemistry at
Hunter College, graduating with honors in 1941. She briefly attended sec-
retarial school, but by then the military draft was drawing young men into
the army prior to the United States' entry into World War II. As a result of
this student drain, Yalow was offered a teaching assistantship at the University of Illinois, where she became the only woman among a faculty of
four hundred. In 1942 she received her master's degree in physics, and for
a time she taught in the engineering school. The next year she married

Aaron Yalow, also a physicist, and in 1945 the couple returned to New York, shortly after Rosalyn received her doctorate.

Medical applications of nuclear physics interested Yalow from the beginning of her career, a time when the biological sciences were poised to make broad advances based on molecular research. Yalow was influenced by George Hevesy, the Hungarian chemist, who as early as 1923 had placed bean plants in a solution containing a radioactive isotope of nutrient lead. He was able to measure the radioactivity as the lead was absorbed, rising through the roots to the stems and leaves. Further work had won Hevesy the Nobel Prize in 1943, and by the late 1940s radioactive isotopes were generally recognized as holding great potential as biochemical probes. But putting them to practical use in medicine met with resistance and posed a series of theoretical and technical problems.

Yalow managed to find a durable berth for research early in her career. When she taught at Hunter College, from 1946 until 1950, no laboratory facilities were available to her. But in 1947 Yalow received help from Gioacchino Failla, known as the dean of American medical physicists. Through his offices, Yalow was offered a part-time position at the government's Bronx Veterans Administration Hospital, which, at the end of the Second World War, was committed, in principle at least, to research in nuclear medicine. Funding for Yalow's research was initially limited, however, and she was offered a refitted janitor's closet for a laboratory.

Soon Yalow found a research partner in Solomon A. Berson. An internist who also had surmounted academic anti-Semitism, Berson had intellectual ambitions and accomplishments similar to Yalow's. They possessed complementary styles. Yalow was a logical, orderly thinker. Berson, an accomplished violinist and expert chess player, tended to think in broad terms. According to Yalow, Berson "wanted to be a physicist, and I wanted to be a medical doctor." They were to work together closely for twenty years.

Diabetes provided the context for the development of radioimmunoassay. For years, an insufficiency of insulin that caused disruption of blood sugar levels was thought to be responsible for both juvenile and adult-onset forms of the disease. But by the 1950s it had become clear that diabetics with the adult-onset form of the disease did, in fact, produce insulin. This was surprising. For a time researchers surmised that, although production might be more or less normal in these cases, the insulin hormone—one of the smallest proteins—was probably destroyed by a liver enzyme. This was the plausible hypothesis Yalow and Berson were able to test when, beginning in the mid-1950s, they radioactively tagged insulin and injected it into diabetics with adult-onset disease. Taking blood samples over time, they measured how quickly the insulin was broken down. To their surprise, they found that injected insulin remained longer, albeit uselessly, in the bodies of diabetics than in healthy individuals.

This unexpected finding was of great interest. Yalow and Berson suggested that insulin might be more slowly metabolized by adult-onset diabetics because it was treated as a foreign antigen to which antibodies became attached. Antibody molecules that sought out and bound to insulin, they reasoned, would prevent it from entering cells and metabolic pathways. As a consequence, the common treatment for adult-onset diabetes—daily injections of animal insulin—could be doing more harm than good. The range of individual response to injected insulin, which included a number of adverse effects, lent suggestive support to this view.

Yalow and Berson encountered considerable skepticism to the idea that insulin could provoke an immune reaction. Most researchers believed that the insulin molecule was too small to attract an antibody; an "insulin antibody" was considered an impossibility. After the prestigious American journal *Science* rejected their key paper, Yalow and Berson turned to the *Journal of Clinical Investigation,* publishing "Insulin-I131 Metabolism in Human Subjects" in 1956. Even there they were compelled not to use the term "insulin antibody" in the paper's title.

Yalow and Berson also explored the broader applications their radioactive labeling method might have as a molecular probe. The smallest concentrations of a great many substances inside the body—down to a billionth of a gram—might now be measured. Radioactively labeled molecules would compete for attention with essentially identical but unlabeled molecules. To test for various substances, baselines could be established, showing ordinary and abnormal values. Yalow and Berson spent several years developing radioimmunoassay as a practical technique and expanding its range of applications. Although it continued to encounter resistance for about a decade, by the late 1960s radioimmunoassay constituted a vibrant field for research, with great potential in diagnostic medicine and much to say about how the body works on a molecular level.

Adhering to long tradition in basic research, Yalow and Berson did not patent radioimmunoassay. As its value was recognized, it was taken up by a number of commercial laboratories, underwent considerable technical elaboration, and today is used to measure the concentrations of hundreds of substances in the body, including drugs, viruses, and proteins. It is a staple of medical research, most especially in endocrinology, but it has many other uses. It can be used to screen blood in various ways — to detect hepatitis virus, for example — and to determine drug dosage levels. For diabetes and many other diseases, radioimmunoassay has become a diagnostic tool.

Yalow and Berson were aware that their research made them candidates for the Nobel Prize. Solomon Berson's sudden and premature death from a heart attack in 1972 came before much of the adulation that Yalow later received. (Yalow, who was personally and uncharacteristically crushed by his death, would rename her laboratory the Solomon A. Berson Research Laboratory in his honor.) In 1976 Yalow won the Albert Lasker Award. A year later came the Nobel Prize in physiology or medicine, shared with the Polish-American biochemist Andrew V. Schally and the French-American physiologist Roger Guillemin, for basic advances in endocrinology.

As a Nobel laureate and a woman, Yalow became eminent in the scientific and medical worlds, and also in the popular imagination. She held academic appointments at Albert Einstein College of Medicine and the Mount Sinai School of Medicine, where she was Solomon A. Berson Distinguished Professor-at-Large. Yalow won the National Medal of Science and many other awards and honorary degrees. She was also the subject of inspirational biographies for children and even hosted a dramatic presentation of the life of Marie Curie on public television. The popular press emphasized her ability to manage both a scientific career and a family, and to some extent obscured an impressively difficult personality.

Yalow retired to emeritus status at Veterans Administration Medical Center in 1992. She lived with her husband — they raised two children — until his death in 1993. That year she suffered a minor stroke, and another more debilitating event in 1995. She recovered to some extent, however, and after rehabilitation, returned to work in 1997.

# Benjamin Spock [1903–1998]

## Raising Children in a Complicated World

In *The Common Sense Book of Baby and Child Care,* Benjamin Spock provided parents with a wealth of information and practical advice undergirded by a fundamentally new perspective on raising children. First published in 1946, just after the end of World War II, Spock's manual was written with great clarity in a friendly and congenial tone. He rejected corporal punishment and an older disciplinarian stance and urged parents to cultivate affectionate relationships with their children and to understand their behavior. Spock's underlying views strongly represented the influence of Freudian psychoanalysis wedded to his own Yankee optimism and, to some extent, the liberal educational philosophy of John Dewey. By the end of the twentieth century, *Baby and Child Care* had been revised and expanded seven times, translated into thirty-nine languages, and had sold about fifty million copies.

Benjamin Spock ultimately became a controversial figure. He was accused, beginning in the 1960s, of advocating "permissiveness." Responsibility for a whole generation of rebellious children was laid to his pen. The Reverend Norman Vincent Peale accused Spock of encouraging parents to "Feed 'em whenever they want, never let them cry, satisfy their every desire." This was not the case, but Spock's views meshed with parents' needs. For the first time, in large part due to advances in public health and medicine, most children survived to adulthood. Many received more than a rudimentary education and would grow up to value emotional and sexual relationships. "The political message from [Spock's] writing, just as powerful as any tract by Locke or Rousseau," writes Thomas Maier, "underlined the capacity of good intentions and common sense to form a better child, improve human nature, and perhaps inspire a better world."

The eldest of six children from an upper-middle-class background, Benjamin McLane Spock was born in New Haven, Connecticut, on May 2, 1903. His father, with whom he a had a friendly but distant, "grave but just" relationship, was Benjamin Ives Spock, a corporate lawyer and general counsel for the New Haven Railroad. Benjamin was much closer to his mother, Mildred Louise Stoughton Spock, a devoted but frequently stern and domineering parent. After attending Hamden Hall Country Day

School, from tenth grade Benjamin was sent to Phillips Academy. In 1921 Benjamin entered Yale, the university his father had attended. A strapping youth, he was an oarsman on the college's laureled rowing team, which was awarded a gold medal at the 1924 Olympics in Paris. He majored in English, was an average student, and received his bachelor's degree in 1925.

Although Spock initially considered a career as an architect, a summer as a counselor at the Newington Crippled Children's Home convinced him to turn to medicine. He remained at Yale for two years of medical school, then transferred to the Columbia University College of Physicians and Surgeons, receiving his medical degree in 1929. Spock undertook two residencies, one in pediatrics at the New York Nursery and Child's Hospital, and another in psychiatry at New York Hospital. In addition, beginning in 1933, Spock trained at the New York Psychoanalytic Institute. He was psychoanalyzed himself, first for several years with Bertram Lewin, then briefly but productively with the Hungarian analyst Sandor Rado. Spock considered becoming a psychoanalyst. "But having discovered how difficult that is," he later wrote, "and also how grateful mothers were to have a pediatrician who was willing to spend any amount of time discussing everyday problems of child care, I had no trouble deciding in the end to remain in pediatrics."

Spock's early career prepared him to understand the problems of raising children in a newly urbanized society. In spite of the Great Depression, his practice flourished. He enjoyed house calls, and parents appreciated his kindly manner and rapport with children. At his office, patients reached the examining table through a special stairway and trap door. The parents of his patients included psychoanalysts, social workers, and psychologists. Although the locus of psychoanalysis was childhood experience, child therapy was just beginning, and Spock's practice became a unique site of inquiry and referral. Psychoanalyst Margaret Mahler, who became the principal architect of the influential theory of "separation-individuation," received her first referral from Spock after immigrating to the United States in 1939.

Spock began writing *Baby and Child Care* in 1943 while serving as a psychiatrist with the U.S. Naval Reserve medical corps. He aimed, he explained, to "cover the emotional as well as the physical aspects of child care in a tone which would support rather than scold parents." Although a number of manuals provided parents with basic information, psychological development was generally given short shrift. John B. Watson's *Psychological Care of Infant and Child* dominated the field. A strict behaviorist who was convinced his approach was scientific, Watson firmly believed in treating children in specific ways to elicit desirable behavior. His techniques were authoritarian, prescriptive and much discussed, but they never led to a medical consensus. Famously, he told parents not to kiss their children or even hold them excessively, for fear of spoiling them.

By contrast, Spock spurned rigidity. "My purpose was not to advocate a theory," he wrote in his autobiography, "but primarily to tell parents what children are like, including descriptions of their unconscious drives." *The Common Sense Book of Baby and Child Care* was written in a conversational tone—Spock actually dictated it to his wife—and reflected his own self-confidence. "You know more than you think you do," he told parents in the book's famous first sentence. Spock's ability to communicate congenially in print while at the same time transmitting fairly complex information, clear guidelines, and pertinent asides and qualifiers was a key factor in the book's success.

Published simultaneously in softcover and hardcover editions in 1946, Spock's guide soon became a bestseller. Contributing to its success was the postwar baby boom, initiated by returning veterans and their wives. The book received no advertising, but word of mouth quickly multiplied sales. In 1953, comedians Lucille Ball and Desi Arnaz added to the book's reputation when, in an episode of their enormously popular television show, they said repeatedly, "Well, let's see what Spock says," and consulted the book. "They never sneered at the book's advice," wrote Spock years later. "I always credit them with helping greatly to popularize the book."

Historians and scholars of the family have often tried to analyze the success of *Baby and Child Care*, with mixed results. In a polemical article in 1975, Michael Zuckerman found Spock's book "part of a sustained onslaught on the structures of conscience, and on the family in which they are formed." This dire assessment was not echoed by William Graebner, who traced the influences on Spock to the work of intellectuals such as anthropologist Margaret Mead, psychoanalyst Erik Erikson, and child development theorist Lawrence K. Frank. The latter had characterized American culture as a whole as "sick, mentally disordered, and in need of treatment"—and much of this as a consequence of poor child rearing. "Spock was nothing less than a social engineer," writes William Graebner, "and an important one at that, for his democratic methods could be found in many areas of American life...."

After World War II Spock took a teaching position at the University of Minnesota, and from 1947 to 1951 he served as a consultant with the Mayo Clinic. From 1951 until 1955 he was professor of child development at the University of Pittsburgh. He moved to Western Reserve University in Cleveland, and he retired in 1967 at age sixty-four. Spock wrote a column for the *Ladies Home Journal* from 1954 to 1963 and would continue to write for the popular magazine press for the rest of his life.

Growing older and disturbed by the Vietnam War, Spock became political. Raised in a Republican household, he had begun voting Democratic with the advent of Franklin Roosevelt and the New Deal. Not until the early 1960s, though, did politics take first place in his thoughts. He aligned himself with the left. In 1962 President John F. Kennedy's decision to resume nuclear arms testing after he had promised otherwise led Spock to join the National Committee for a Sane Nuclear Policy, SANE, of which he became cochairman in 1963. Spock felt betrayed again when, after he had supported Lyndon B. Johnson for president, Johnson escalated American military involvement in Vietnam.

As a symbol of establishment opposition to the war, Spock was widely criticized. Indeed, he was sometimes held responsible for helping to raise a generation of heretical youth unwilling to love their country or to die for it. His most significant antiwar activity was to circulate "A Call to Resist Illegitimate Authority." This antidraft provocation led to Spock's being charged, along with poet Allen Ginsberg and others, as conspiring to aid and abet violators of the Selective Service Act. At a celebrated trial in Boston, he and his defendants were initially found guilty. The conviction was reversed on appeal in 1969.

One result of Spock's political and courtroom battles was his conversion to socialism. In 1972, at the urging of Gore Vidal and Marcus Raskin, he ran for the presidency as the nominee of the People's Party, a coalition of left-wing groups. The party platform included a call for socialized medicine and the legalization of marijuana and promised a tax policy that would not favor the rich. Spock received about seventy-nine thousand votes in ten states, which he reckoned "not impressive, but at least it's visible." In 1976 Spock ran again, this time as the party's vice-presidential candidate.

Spock continued to revise *Baby and Child Care* — "B&CC," he came to call it — time and again. He not only integrated new findings in pediatric medicine but also reshaped the book against a changing social background. Accused of sexism — Gloria Steinem, for one, counted him a terrible male chauvinist — in 1976 Spock, for the fourth revision of his book, rendered it gender sensitive. Spock also wrote some sixteen other books, including *Dr. Spock Talks with Mothers, Problems of Parents, A Baby's First Year, Feeding Your Baby and Child,* and *Caring for Your Disabled Child.*

Benjamin Spock had a complex, sometimes painful family and emotional life. He married Jane Davenport Cheney in 1927, and they had two sons. As a father, Spock was not so much permissive as demanding, and at the same time he found it difficult to express strong emotions. Jane suffered from alcoholism, was institutionalized for a time, and was diagnosed as a paranoid schizophrenic. Their difficult but long marriage ended in separation and then, in 1976, divorce. That year Spock married Mary Morgan, an Arkansas-born woman transplanted, as a hippie, to California. Although this marriage was not without tension, it was marked by strong bonds of fidelity. When he and his stepdaughter could not get along, Spock underwent family counseling. Spock and Morgan collaborated on a superficial autobiography, *Spock on Spock,* published in 1989. Far more trenchant was the comprehensive *Dr. Spock: An American Life,* written by Thomas Maier and published in 1998.

For the last two revisions of *Baby and Child Care,* Spock acquired a coauthor. The collaborator on the eighth, most recent edition of the book is pediatrician Steven J. Parker. Consonant with earlier revisions, this edition reflects the evolving diversity in American culture. It addresses, for example, issues specific to gay and lesbian parents. Also new is Spock's nutritional counsel. At Morgan's urging, Spock had himself adopted a "low-fat, plant-based diet"—an echo in his old age of his mother's largely vegetarian fare—and he brings this prescription to the last edition of his book.

Spock was well known as charming, gracious, and serene. By the end of his life he had also cultivated some of the tastes of his younger wife, including, in addition to diet, a passion for kundalini yoga and meditation. Although mentally alert well into his nineties, Spock's health eventually deteriorated. At the end he required round-the-clock nursing, the cost of which depleted his financial resources. Benjamin Spock, his life having nearly spanned the century in which he made an impact on millions from cradle to grave, died at home on March 15, 1998.

# Arthur Kornberg [b. 1918]

## The Enzyme Hunter

Enzymes are microworld machines of diverse molecular shape and construction, ubiquitous in every organism down to the simplest bacteria and viruses. Only with enzymes can life processes be described in biochemical terms; they put ordinary chemicals to biological use. Enzymes are proteins, comprised of amino acids. They were glimpsed in various ways during the nineteenth century, but as a class their structure and breadth of function came into focus only with improved techniques for chemical purification and crystallization, from about 1925. Not surprisingly, enzyme chemistry played a central role in the development of molecular biology. And among the welter of enzymes identified and studied over the past half century, none stands out more, perhaps, than DNA polymerase, discovered in 1959 by Arthur Kornberg.

DNA polymerase is the indispensable catalyst for assembling the units that constitute the double helical strands of deoxyribonucleic acid (DNA), the master molecule that controls cellular activity at the genetic level. Kornberg's discovery of DNA polymerase—a "remarkable copying machine"—lies at a historical crossroads in the intellectual affiliation of molecular biology with biochemistry. "High adventures in enzymology lie ahead," said Kornberg in 1959, when he received the Nobel Prize. Kornberg himself would go on to synthesize DNA outside a living cell in 1967. A host of other crucial enzymes that operate on DNA have since been discovered. To enzymes, and to the chemical imaginations that unveiled their significance, are owed many of the current and pending transformations in medicine and genetics.

Arthur Kornberg was born on March 3, 1918, in Brooklyn, New York, to Lena Katz and Joseph Kornberg. His father worked as a tailor—a specialist "in cloaks," as they used to say in the garment trade—and for a time he operated a hardware store. Joseph was curious about the world, multilingual, and largely self-taught. Kornberg's parents economized to advance his education while he skipped grades, and soon after turning fifteen he graduated from Abraham Lincoln High School. He attended City College of New York, majoring in biology and chemistry, and graduated with honors in 1937.

In spite of Kornberg's scholastic record, as a Jew from Brooklyn his prospects for being accepted at an upper-echelon medical school were slender. Institutional anti-Semitism ensured that he was summarily rejected from a number of East Coast schools, including Harvard, Cornell, and Columbia University. But he was accepted at the University of Rochester, New York, which possessed a well-regarded school of medicine. He received a scholarship, graduated in 1941, and went on to an internship at Strong Memorial Hospital. As the United States entered World War II, Kornberg served as a commissioned officer with the United States Public Health Service. He was transferred from the U.S. Coast Guard to the National Institutes of Health (NIH) in 1942 and remained there through 1945. By this time, he had decided against clinical medicine in favor of research.

Kornberg's decision to focus on the chemistry of enzymes emerged from his work at NIH in the nutritional section of the division of physiology, where much research was done with animals, an approach especially valuable for investigating nutritional deficiencies. But by the end of World War II, as Kornberg recognized, the major vitamins had already been discovered, isolated, and purified. "It was clear...that the vitamin hunters had about exhausted their prey and that the enzyme hunters would soon command the field." Kornberg developed great enthusiasm for biochemistry. On a year's leave from NIH, he worked in laboratories at New York University Medical School and, briefly, at Washington University in St. Louis. "Instead of waiting four to six weeks for a rat to develop a nutritional deficiency," Kornberg later recalled, "I was doing spectrophotometric assays that were complete in a minute." Returning to NIH, Kornberg set up an enzyme section there, serving as its chief from 1947 to 1952.

The field of biochemistry was still rather small in the late 1940s. Kornberg soon became an authority on coenzymes, the nonprotein molecules that participate with enzymes in catalytic reactions. Given his early work in nutritional research, this was not too surprising, since many vitamins are precursors of coenzymes. In 1953 he moved to Washington University School of Medicine, where he became chairman of the department of microbiology. The same year, discovery of the structure of DNA by Francis Crick and James Watson became the scientific watershed that determined the trajectory of Kornberg's subsequent career.

The double-stranded DNA molecule is comprised of paired nucleotides that each consist of a sugar bonded to a phosphate group and one of four nitrogenous bases: adenine (A), thymine (T), cytosine (C), or guanine (G). Once it was suspected that DNA encoded genetic information, the dynamics of its composition acquired great significance. As Kornberg put it, "What is the chemical mechanism by which this super molecule is built up in the

cell?" This was the question he set out to answer in 1956, with the help of several colleagues and graduate students, in his laboratory at Washington University.

In spite of technical obstacles, Kornberg made fairly rapid progress at first. It was clear that the DNA molecule would not arise spontaneously simply by mixing its constituent bases. But by working with large quantities of proteins harvested from *E. coli*—which reproduces rapidly and often—Kornberg used a method of radioactively tagging and tracking a DNA building block that would be incorporated into a DNA chain. Within six months Kornberg could report on three fractions that appeared to play a role in the biosynthesis of DNA. Of these the most significant was "fraction P," which contained an enzyme that assembled the bases into a DNA chain. Kornberg, while attempting to purify it, named it "polymerase."

The activity of DNA polymerase, as Kornberg began to understand it, was consonant both with what was known and suspected about the DNA molecule. For one thing, synthesizing DNA required the presence of all four bases (A, C, G, and T), as would be expected if the molecule's base sequences coded for genes. But moreover, some DNA was required as a "template." No reaction at all would take place without DNA. The enzyme was "unique in present experience," as Kornberg would later explain, "in taking directions from a [DNA] template."

Moreover, these directions were specific. In an era before it was possible to unravel specific base sequences, Kornberg would show that the template was reproduced by DNA polymerase in the same proportion as its base components. The ratios of the constituents adenine (A) and thymine (T), and cytosine (C) and guanine (G) were equal—consonant with the fact that A always links to T, and C to G. By mid-1958, Kornberg showed that the DNA from different sources gave different ratios of base pairs. DNA, with the help of DNA polymerase, was clearly a self-replicating molecule.

A certain amount of skepticism initially greeted Kornberg's work, but it soon vanished. Two papers submitted to the *Journal of Biological*

*Chemistry* were initially rejected by that review before being published in May 1958. By the end of that year, however, further experiments, both in his laboratory and elsewhere, were conclusive. The synthesis of DNA "by the 'polymerase' of *E. coli*," reported Kornberg, "represents the replication of a DNA template."

The potential represented by Kornberg's work was not lost on medicine. Pharmacologists had been guessing at the significance of the nucleic acids for years; discovering their enzymatic pathways would prove to be of value in designing drugs for treating cancer and autoimmune diseases, and eventually, viral infections from herpes to AIDS. Almost immediately, in 1959, Kornberg received the Nobel Prize for physiology or medicine, the first to be awarded specifically for work on DNA. Kornberg shared the award with the Spanish biochemist Severo Ochoa, who had discovered a powerful enzyme associated with ribonucleic acid (RNA). (Francis Crick and James Watson, together with Maurice Wilkins, would receive the Nobel Prize in 1962.) In 1959 Kornberg moved to Stanford University, where he founded the department of biochemistry. He would remain its chairman until 1968.

Although they had synthesized DNA, Kornberg and his colleagues had not shown that the synthetic molecule was biologically active and operated like genetic material. This became Kornberg's central objective from 1957, and it occupied him for more than a decade. In general, early efforts with bacteria came to naught. Kornberg had better luck after turning to the bacteriophages, a class of viruses that invade and replicate within bacterial cells. Due to their relative simplicity and the fact that their presence can be easily visualized via the bacteria they attack, the bacteriophages had performed yeoman service in molecular biology and had been extensively studied and classified.

One species, discovered in Parisian sewage and named "phage φ174," possessed several unique characteristics. Exceptionally small even for a phage, it possessed only about five genes. Unusual proportions of its bases suggested that its DNA molecule was single-stranded rather than double-stranded, and circular in shape. Indeed, the phage's strategy is to enter the bacterial cell and use a cellular enzyme to convert itself from single-stranded to double-stranded DNA for purposes of replication. In 1967 several research groups independently discovered in *E. coli* an enzyme — to be called DNA ligase — that joined the ends of DNA to form a circle.

With a grasp of how φ174 worked, Kornberg's laboratory — as well as several others in competition — recognized the prospects for synthesizing the phage's DNA, then showing it to be infectious and, therefore, biologically active. After synthesizing a matching strand of φ174 DNA, Kornberg and his group radioactively labeled it to distinguish it from the original chain, and used DNA ligase to link the ends and form a circle. Isolated and harvested, these synthetic chains proved to be not only indistinguishable from the original under the electron microscope but also just as infectious. For the first time, using DNA polymerase, a synthetic DNA chain was shown to be the same not only in composition, but also in action, as the original DNA from a natural virus.

This result represented a landmark in biological research. "The way was open to create novel DNA and genes by manipulating the building blocks and their templates," wrote Kornberg in his memoir, *For the Love of Enzymes.* He added, without false modesty, that "In a very small way, we were observers of something akin to what those at Alamogordo on a July day in 1945 witnessed in the explosive force of the atomic nucleus."

Indeed, although the popular press had trumpeted the concept of "life in a test tube" several times during the twentieth century, Kornberg's demonstration had real consequences throughout the world of medicine and biology. It would form an integral part of a fund of basic research that gave birth to a powerful biotechnology industry. Cloning of genes and recombinant DNA, rapid sequencing, and a host of technical advances all emerged with fresh and tantalizing objectives in medicine and allied domains, from pharmacology to agriculture.

Kornberg played a modest but significant role in the early years of the biotechnology industry. Relinquishing his chairmanship at Stanford in 1968, he sat on scientific advisory boards of several companies and was a founder, notably, of DNAX Research Institute of Molecular and Cellular Biology, which was eventually acquired by Schering Plough. Although generally positive about biotechnology, Kornberg's *The Golden Helix,* published in 1995, was critical of the widespread practices that sought to profit from the same kind of basic research that had given birth to the industry itself.

Arthur Kornberg's personal life, as he recounts it, was as congenial and successful as his scientific career. He married Sylvy Ruth Levy in 1943, and they had three sons. Also a biochemist, Sylvy played a role in Kornberg's laboratory and made significant contributions of her own. Two years after her death in 1986, Kornberg married Charlene Walsh Levering, who died in 1995. He married Carolyn Dixon in 1998.

Since 1988 Kornberg has been professor emeritus at Stanford University, on active status. In recent years he has shifted the focus of his research to inorganic polyphosphate, known as "poly P." This molecule, found in volcanic matter and deep-ocean steam vents as well as in every living thing from bacteria and fungi to plants and mammals, has been generally ignored by biochemists. But Kornberg has suggested various functions for poly P. It may play a role, he thinks, as an energy reservoir and, even more profoundly, may affect physiological growth and development and the virulence of pathogenic bacteria.

In fact, Arthur Kornberg toward the end of his career sought to discover the function of poly P according to the broad design of his earlier research — by seeking the enzymes that create it. Kornberg remains a partisan of enzymes in an age when students frequently consider them "as faceless as buffers and salts." He argues the significance of understanding their chemistry. For lack of attention to enzymes, writes Kornberg, "the true molecular basis of biology will remain obscure; profound questions of how cells and organisms function and develop will not be answered."

# Carleton Gajdusek  [b. 1923]

## A New Agent of Disease

A new frontier in microbiology opened in 1957 in an obscure corner of the world with the discovery of a fatal disease initially known as kuru. The Fore, a small tribe in New Guinea with a Stone Age culture, had fallen prey to an epidemic apparently spread by cannibalism, in which an infectious agent passed from the dead to the living. The disease did not seem to be a result of either bacterial or viral infection. But kuru was a fatal neurological disorder. Recognition in the mid-1980s that a closely related disease was killing British cattle—and potentially human beings—led to an ongoing contemporary public health crisis of unknown potential magnitude.

The original, and for long the most prominent, scientist at the heart of the investigation into kuru and related disorders was Carleton Gajdusek. On his initial encounter with the disease in 1957, Gajdusek had recognized its potential significance. Through his association with the National Institutes of Health in the United States, he led the effort to understand the nature and discover the cause of what have since come to be known as the transmissible spongiform encephalopathies (TSEs). Trained as a pediatrician and devoted to children, Gajdusek worked for decades as an ambitious medical explorer with a grasp of epidemiology, virology, neurology, and anthropology. He was "at the hub of what has been called an empire of two hundred laboratories worldwide," wrote Roger Bingham in 1984. Gajdusek was awarded the Nobel Prize for physiology or medicine in 1976 for his work with a "new class of human diseases caused by unique infectious agents."

Daniel Carleton Gajdusek was born on September 23, 1923, in Yonkers, New York. He was the eldest son of immigrants Karl Gajdusek, a butcher originally from Slovakia, and Ottilia Dobroczki, from Hungary. The family was prosperous and, on his mother's side, cultivated. Ottilia read to him and his younger brother the poetry of Homer and Virgil, and enrolled him in after-school courses at the American Museum of Natural History and the Metropolitan Museum of Art. With the inspiration of his Aunt Irene, an entomologist, Carleton studied insects. He was so affected by reading *The Microbe Hunters* that he stenciled the names of the famous scientists profiled by Paul de Kruif (p. 401) on the stairs leading to his attic laboratory. As early as age ten, Gajdusek recalls, he claims to have understood that mathematics, physics, and chemistry would shape the biology of the future.

Gajdusek's university education left nothing to be desired and is remarkable for the number of Nobel laureates—no fewer than five—with whom he studied. He entered the University of Rochester at age sixteen and graduated summa cum laude three years later with a degree in biophysics. He finished Harvard Medical School, again in three years, and, fascinated by children, took his internship and residency in pediatrics. But he also wanted to pursue basic research. From 1948 to 1949 Gajdusek was a fellow at the California Institute of Technology, where he worked with chemist Linus Pauling and biophysicist Max Delbrück. He was also influenced by the biochemist and geneticist George W. Beadle. He undertook research at the National Foundation for Infantile Paralysis from 1949 to 1952, then went to Harvard to work with John Enders (p. 266).

Gajdusek pursued his interest in infectious diseases all over the world. Drafted during the Korean War, he investigated viral and rickettsial disease at the Walter Reed Army Hospital. After his military discharge, he worked on various infectious diseases and epidemics in the Middle East at the Institut Pasteur in Teheran, Iran. Here he became intrigued by the potential significance of unusual diseases found among isolated populations. To study them he journeyed to India, South America, and Malaysia. In 1955 in Melbourne, Australia, Gajdusek worked with Macfarlane Burnet (p. 280). And in nearby New Guinea he encountered the illness that would provide the substance for his life's work.

The Fore, living in the Eastern Highlands of New Guinea, were by the 1950s in the grip of the epidemic they called "kuru." The symptoms were frightening: loss of muscular control and coordination followed by dementia and, after about a year, death. At first Gajdusek could only describe the disease as a neurodegenerative disorder. Autopsies did not reveal any sign of a toxin or of an inflammation that would indicate a reaction to an invading organism. Thus, initially Gajdusek suspected that kuru was a genetic disorder.

Gajdusek's descriptions of the disease brought him professional recognition. In 1958, with the help of a mentor, Joseph Smadel, he was appointed to a unique position as visiting scientist at the National Institute of Neurological Diseases and Blindness, a part of the National Institutes of Health. In this capacity he continued his work in New Guinea, tracking kuru with considerable devotion, while at the same time raising awareness of the disease in the popular press and among colleagues.

Two years after he began his research, in 1959, Gajdusek received a clue to the actual nature of kuru. He learned from a veterinary scientist, William Hadlow, that the symptoms strikingly resembled those of scrapie, a disease of sheep. Moreover, scrapie's hallmark at autopsy, like kuru's, was a characteristic sponginess in the brain. Gajdusek further learned that this degeneration of the brain also characterized another human illness, Creutzfeldt-Jakob disease (CJD), first described in 1921. Extremely rare, CJD was thought to run in families. As would eventually become clear, the same causative agent was at work in all three diseases: kuru, scrapie, and CJD.

Because scrapie was known to be transmissible from sheep to sheep, the prospect that kuru was similarly transmissible led to further animal research. In 1963 Gajdusek and his colleagues injected chimpanzees with brain material taken from human victims of kuru. By 1965, the first chimp so treated developed signs of the disease. In this way science finally caught up with gossip in the taverns of Goroka, capital of the Eastern Highlands — where for years local prospectors had been saying the disease was transmitted by cannibalism. Gajdusek's experiments with chimpanzees also confirmed work by anthropologists Ann and J. L. Fischer, who in 1961 had suggested that kuru was spread by cannibalism among the Fore.

A new phase of basic research commenced about 1968, aimed at identifying the cause of kuru. The absence of inflammation in the degenerated brains of kuru victims remained puzzling. In addition, although researchers could demonstrate the presence of an infective agent, they could not easily destroy it. Gajdusek initially suggested the concept of a "slow virus" that invades cells but does not immediately cause disease or damage. But this idea was dogged by the fact that it was impossible to elicit evidence of nucleic acids, which are the fundamental substance of all viruses. The actual composition of the disease-causing agent remained unknown and a considerable and tantalizing mystery.

At Gajdusek's Central Nervous System Studies Laboratory, from 1970 the transmissible spongiform encephalopathies (TSEs), as the kurulike diseases became known, were experimentally induced in a large number of animals, from hamsters and mice to mink and various species of monkeys. The importance of this work was underscored when, about 1971, it became evident that some cases of Creutzfeldt-Jakob disease could be passed to humans by such procedures as corneal transplantation and hormone replacement therapy. One woman apparently contracted the fatal disease from electrodes implanted in her brain to treat epilepsy; the electrodes had previously been used on a patient suffering from CJD.

The infectious kurulike diseases did not initially appear to present a public health danger outside of New Guinea, where, in fact, cessation of cannibalism ended the epidemic by the mid-1970s. But this changed dramatically when, in England in the 1980s, cattle began dying from a mystery ailment that the British press began to call "mad cow disease." The symptoms resembled sheep scrapie and kuru, and a small number of cases soon mushroomed into a full-scale epidemic. Bovine spongiform encephalopathy (BSE) afflicted thousands of cattle. Epidemiologists traced the cause to animal protein supplements that contained the offal of sheep, cattle, and pigs. By this route the agent that causes scrapie in sheep had jumped species. From 1986 to 2000 some 180,000 cases of BSE were reported in England, where huge numbers of cattle were slaughtered, and the disease had spread to other countries.

Still more significantly, BSE also passed the species barrier to infect humans, with the first cases reported in 1996. Although relatively few people died over the next several years from what has come to be known as variant Creutzfeldt-Jakob Disease (vCJD), public concern has intensified as governments face a potential epidemic of unknown proportions. The disease's long incubation period, its lethal neurodegenerative symptoms, and its provenance from an everyday source of nutrition have all contributed to the anxiety. Much as the rapid spread of AIDS has been linked to travel and mobility in the contemporary world, should vCJD become epidemic, it will owe its spread to the global nature of commerce.

The agent that causes TSEs has remained uncertain. Gajdusek advanced his early theory of a "slow virus" to suggest an agent that reproduces by a nonbiological method similar to crystallization. A virus remained a possibility, but a theory of "prions" came into favor due to work by Stanley Prusiner. Prions are protein-like particles that exist in both normal and pathological forms. The two forms are isomeric—that is, they have the same amino-acid sequence but different properties. Although the role that prions play in normal cell metabolism remains unknown, it is clearly subverted after invasion by the pathogenic form. How infectious prions convert the normal form remains a mystery. Prusiner's theory, however, was plausible for both infectious and inherited forms of the spongiform encephalopathies.

Carleton Gajdusek has often been described as a voluble nonconformist, possessed of a charming and sometimes extravagant personality. Macfarlane Burnet described him as someone with "an intelligence quotient up in the 180s and the emotional immaturity of a fifteen-year-old. He is quite manically energetic when his enthusiasm is roused and can inspire enthusiasm in his technical assistants. He is completely self-centered, thick-skinned, and inconsiderate, but equally won't let danger, physical difficulty, or other people's feelings interfere in the least with what he wants to do."

Although he never married, in 1963 Gajdusek began adopting children from New Guinea and Micronesia, bringing them to the United States to be educated, and raising them at a beautiful manor near Baltimore.

While his scientific life's work was invaluable, Gajdusek's career moved toward its close with a counterpoint of personal tragedy. He was suspected of pedophilic practices, partly on the evidence of his own published journals (eighteen volumes, five thousand pages, published by the National Institutes of Health), which contained alarmingly personal information. He was investigated by the Federal Bureau of Investigation, and agents succeeded in finding one of Gajdusek's charges who was willing to snare him, in a taped telephone conversation, into confessing to their sexual relations while the young man was still a teenager.

Gajdusek was arrested in 1996 at age seventy-three. Colleagues helped post his $350,000 bond. He pleaded guilty to charges of child abuse on February 18, 1997, the day after he officially retired from the National Institutes of Health. Neither his age nor the letters of support from many colleagues, including Robert Gallo (p. 365), and from some of his adopted children, could save him from a year's prison sentence. "However troubling his personal life," wrote Richard Rhodes in *Deadly Feasts*, his compelling account of the TSE epidemics, "his authority as a scientist was never in doubt." Immediately after his release from prison in 1998, Gajdusek left the United States to live in Europe.

# Ernst Wynder [1922–1999]
## Smoking, Health, and Preventive Medicine

With the advent of a new consumer market and the rise of the advertising business, cigarette consumption in the United States and Europe surged in the twentieth century. Contributing social factors included two world wars and a severe economic depression. Tobacco had long been suspected to be unhealthy, and in 1927 a British investigator had written that in almost every case of lung cancer "the patient has been a regular smoker, generally of cigarettes." But not until after midcentury did the growing numbers of cancer patients evoke alarm. Doctors were not trained to practice preventive medicine, and so perhaps were not quick to recognize the dangers of an activity popularly considered relatively harmless, at least for adults. In 1950, however, smoking and cancer were linked by a landmark study conducted by a young, German-born American physician, Ernst Wynder.

Set against the larger history of the tobacco wars, Ernst Wynder is a much underappreciated figure in a debate that has obscured clear thinking. He developed a "chain of evidence," he wrote, "that led us to conclude that cigarette smoking and, for that matter, tobacco use in general is indeed carcinogenic to humans." Wynder persisted in the face of considerable opposition from physicians, and throughout the 1950s his research was consistently supported by other studies. In 1962 and 1964 his anti-smoking message was vindicated when, with the health disaster he foresaw coming to pass, first the Royal College of Physicians in England and then the surgeon general of the United States issued reports on smoking and health. However, Wynder was also a realist who doubted that people would or could stop smoking en masse simply because they learned it was unhealthy. Again he was right. Although doctors and other health care professionals eventually accepted the message, millions continued to smoke, not with great moderation, and eventually to pay the price in terms of cancer and heart disease.

Ernst Ludwig Wynder was born on April 30, 1922, in the city of Herford in Westphalia, Germany. His father, Alfred Wynder, a physician, and his mother, Therese Godfrey, were prosperous members of the middle class, but Jewish, and they fled the country after the Nazis came to power, immigrating to the United States in 1938. (Reflecting ambivalence over his German heritage, Wynder would sometimes anglicize his first name as Ernest.) With the family fortunes reduced, Ernst worked his way through New York University by waiting on tables and selling newspapers, among other jobs. He received his bachelor's degree in 1943 and immediately entered the armed services. He was assigned to a psychological warfare unit, monitoring and analyzing German newscasts. After the war ended, he entered medical school at Washington University in St. Louis, graduating in 1950 with both a medical degree and a bachelor's degree in medical sciences. He interned at Georgetown University Hospital in Washington, DC, and returned to New York for his residency, from 1951 to 1954, at Memorial Hospital for Cancer and Allied Diseases.

Wynder's investigation of the link between smoking and cancer began while he was still a medical student, during a summer's internship at New York University. After observing a case of lung cancer at autopsy, he found it curious that no mention was made as to whether the patient was a smoker. He sought out the dead man's widow and learned that the patient had consumed two packs of cigarettes per day for thirty years. This was suggestive, as were several other cases. Returning to St. Louis, Wynder approached Evarts A. Graham, an eminent thoracic surgeon well situated to notice the growing number of deaths due to lung cancer. Graham was dubious of the connection, however, and raised a variety of objections. But he approved Wynder's proposal to continue statistical research.

Wynder's approach was straightforward. His discovery that smoking can cause lung cancer was a textbook example of tracing the cause of a disease from findings at autopsy. With the help of a small grant from the American Cancer Society, Wynder investigated hundreds of cases of lung cancer. Together with Graham, he published his first article on the effects of smoking in 1950 in the *Journal of the American Medical Association.* They reported on nearly seven hundred cases, and showed that 94 percent of lung cancer patients were cigarette smokers. Comparing the rates of cancer among cigarette smokers with pipe smokers and cigar smokers, Wynder suggested that the cigarette smoker's tendency to inhale the smoke was particularly noxious. "[S]moking," he concluded, "especially in the form of cigarettes, plays an important role in the etiology of lung cancer."

From an epidemiological point of view, Wynder's study was solid if preliminary. He had used personal interviews and a questionnaire rather than simply gathering information from hospital records; he had excellent controls and considerable geographic spread. But physicians greeted Wynder with silence when he presented preliminary data at a meeting of

the American Cancer Society as early as 1949. Nor did his article in *JAMA* create a groundswell of opposition to smoking. Wynder, not tobacco, was suspect. Some thought he had manipulated his data, even though a British study by Richard Doll and Austin Bradford Hill, published about the same time, also showed the link between smoking and cancer. Wynder's work made some suspicious, but few were convinced.

Wynder did not back down or give up. By 1953 he brought forward evidence that painting the backs of mice with tar distilled from Lucky Strikes, a popular cigarette brand, could lead to an epidermoid cancer. This work brought him to the attention of a wider public, as *Time* magazine publicized his results. At the Sloan-Kettering Institute, where Wynder became assistant professor of preventive medicine in 1954, he undertook a number of studies, both epidemiological and experimental. He also studied smoking in relation to other cancers—of the mouth, larynx, and esophagus, as well as the kidney and pancreas.

By 1957 Wynder had won the official support of the National Cancer Institute. In 1958, together with Frank R. Lemm, he published a study on cancer, coronary artery disease, and smoking among the Seventh Day Adventists, a religious group that forbids its members to use tobacco. Wynder and Lemm found 90 percent fewer cases of lung cancer and 40 percent fewer cases of heart attack in this population as compared to the general population.

The medical community remained skeptical of Wynder's results through the 1950s. In the United States, where television had rapidly become a dominant advertising medium, Americans were inundated with positive messages about smoking. People who might otherwise never have touched tobacco began to smoke, and doctors were disinclined to blame tobacco for disease. Memorably, in 1960 Wynder debated Clarence Cook Little, a respected researcher who in 1954 had accepted a post as scientific director of the Tobacco Industry Research Commission. Little's defense against Wynder's impressive epidemiological data is a vivid illustration of the power of rhetoric and wishful thinking in evaluating diseases. Among Little's points of rebuttal was the fact that precancerous growths can be found in the lungs of some infants. He added that there was no good animal model for lung cancer and all the diseases Wynder associated with smoking had been known long before cigarettes were invented. At a convention of pulmonary physicians shortly thereafter, Little's arguments were taken seriously, in spite of Wynder's epidemiological evidence.

Although Wynder did introduce his colleagues to the debate over smoking, it is often said that they found his style unappealing. "Scientists and physicians," writes Robert Weinberg in his *Racing to the Beginning of the Road*, "were offended by Wynder's strident style, his incessant public preachings, his frequent appearances in *Time* magazine, and his statistical analyses and experimental protocols, which they found less than rigorous." These responses were contrived. Indeed, Wynder was criticized for the same style and attitudes that physicians would praise and adopt themselves a decade later.

The most egregious challenge to Wynder's authority came from Frank Horsfall, an eminent scientist who was named director of research at the Sloan-Kettering Institute beginning in the early 1960s. He cut Wynder's research budget, called his claims about the dangers of tobacco and smoking irresponsible, and demanded to review his manuscripts before they were submitted for publication. Meanwhile, Horsfall had accepted, on behalf of Sloan-Kettering, the promise of annual cash gifts from Philip Morris, the tobacco company. Although Wynder appealed to colleagues, he received no help until he approached Peyton Rous (p. 261). Rous, formerly Horsfall's colleague at the Rockefeller Institute, did intervene for Wynder, on behalf of scientific integrity.

It is doubtful that any one person could have brought about a decisive shift in the debate over tobacco, but the rules of the game changed dramatically in Great Britain and the United States in 1962 and 1964, respectively, when the Royal College of Physicians and the surgeon general issued their reports. These essentially vindicated Wynder's research. Warning labels were mandated for cigarette packs in 1968, and in 1971 tobacco advertising would be banned from television and radio.

Over the next three decades tobacco use became a monumental public health issue without a satisfactory resolution. Wynder himself continued to crusade against tobacco use throughout the 1960s and 1970s. In the laboratory he conducted numerous studies on the constituents of tobacco smoke, many in conjunction with his colleague Dietrich Hoffmann, a leading authority on the chemistry of tobacco products.

Although he considered tobacco a scourge, it is important to note that Wynder was a realist who recognized that people would not readily stop smoking cigarettes—and indeed they did not. In the early 1970s he was a proponent of research for a safer cigarette, and he supported the work of the Less Hazardous Cigarette Working Group of the National Cancer Institute. This work was not successful, in great part because tobacco smoke puts so many carcinogens in direct contact with lung tissue, and most smokers smoke constantly over the course of years. Such an effort also became implausible, at least in the near term, for other reasons. A snowballing legal war against the tobacco companies increased their liability relative to any health claims about cigarettes, and the idea of a "safe cigarette" became a legal oxymoron.

In 1968, Wynder left Sloan-Kettering to found the American Health Foundation (AHF), becoming its president and medical director. This was in part because at Sloan-Kettering Frank Horsfall had kept him on tight budget constraints, but also because Wynder saw his mission as belonging to the larger realm of preventive medicine. Wynder had little difficulty acquiring philanthropic support, and the AHF became a thriving research center with concerns that went beyond smoking.

Wynder was a harbinger of the physician committed to the benefits of optimal nutrition, exercise, and a healthy lifestyle. He was the founder and editor-in-chief of *Preventive Medicine,* one of a number of magazines published under the auspices of his foundation. Like other researchers, he recognized the relationship between smoking and various cancers as well as heart disease and certain environmental factors. In his more than seven hundred fifty published articles, Wynder discussed a wide range of issues, including: the role of dietary fat in various cancers, the carcinogenic effects of automotive air pollution and asbestos, occupational risk factors, the use of vitamin supplements, and the protective effects of dietary fiber.

Wynder's "very versatility and virtuosity invited much skepticism and envy," writes Richard Kluger in his account of the tobacco wars, *Ashes to Ashes.* His personality unnerved the scientific establishment. Though energetic and self-confident, he was considered a self-aggrandizing egoist by his detractors. Almost a lifelong bachelor—he married Sandy Miller in 1993—Wynder was known for driving sports cars and dating attractive women. In the last phase of his career, he seemed in some ways an old-fashioned presence in a world of medicine dominated by molecular biology. Wynder wrote in 1988 that, in his view, "the human body is a nearly faultless organism if we do not overfeed it with toxic and carcinogenic burdens." His basic message was the ironic motto of his health foundation and underscores the broader aims of medicine: to "help us to die young, as late in life as possible." Wynder himself died on July 14, 1999, at age seventy-seven, of thyroid cancer.

# Melanie Klein [1882–1960]

## Psychiatry: New Trends in Psychoanalysis

**B**eginning in the 1920s, Melanie Klein developed a model of human psychological development based on the relationship between mother and infant. Today her influence on psychoanalysis and psychotherapy remains at once direct and diffuse, controversial but undeniable. Kleinian concepts, such as introjection and projective identification, significantly clarify some the most puzzling interactions between patient and therapist in psychoanalysis and psychotherapy—or, indeed, between people in everyday life. Klein's work broadened the scope of psychoanalysis and was crucial in founding the field of child therapy. Specifically, it laid the groundwork for "object relations theory"—arguably the most fruitful turn in psychoanalytic thinking since the work of Sigmund Freud (p. 173). "The influence of [Melanie Klein's] theories and her techniques," writes Hanna Segal, "has spread well beyond those known as 'Kleinians.'"

The influence of Melanie Klein, however, has been negative as well as constructive. In illuminating the formative and strongly emotional aspects of interactions between mother and child, Klein's work redressed the imbalance of patriarchal biases in Freudian theory. At the same time, her theories, and the language in which they were couched, helped move psychoanalysis further away from scientific thinking. In Klein's writings, as Pearl H. M. King has observed, "the language of phantasy was mixed with abstract terminology."

The youngest of four children, Melanie Klein was born in Vienna, Austria, on March 30, 1882. Her mother, Libussa, was a strong personality from a family with a commitment to learning. Her father, Moriz Reizes, had deserted his Orthodox Jewish roots to study medicine. When Melanie was born he was about fifty years old, and she recalled him as a relatively ineffectual, distant parent. As a child and adolescent, Melanie was attractive and self-confident but prone to depression. Although she had an early ambition to study medicine, she let these plans drop at age seventeen when she was betrothed to Arthur Klein, a young chemical engineer. She had misgivings about her husband-to-be, and her marriage night left her disgusted. Nevertheless, she soon had two children, Melitta, born in 1904, and Hans, born three years later.

Klein's entry into the field of psychoanalysis was driven by both intellectual ambition and emotional distress, not an uncommon combination. Her difficult relationship with her husband was probably exacerbated by her mother, who was invasive and domineering. Klein became depressed and spent time in a Swiss sanatorium in 1909. When she moved to Budapest, her interest in psychoanalysis was sparked by reading a popular essay of Freud's, "On Dreams." In 1912 Klein began psychoanalysis with Sandor Ferenczi, the original and ingenious Hungarian analyst. Ferenczi recognized Klein's potential talents. He encouraged her to attempt to psychoanalyze children, then a topic of nascent interest. Her first patient would be her young son—her third child, born in 1914—Erich.

When Klein entered psychoanalysis, the field was in transition. Since its founding at about the turn of the century, the aim of psychoanalysis as a therapy had been chiefly to undo or clarify the repression of unconscious wishes. The paradigm was the "oedipal conflict," in which a young boy's ardent desire for his mother and envious hatred for his father must be repressed. However, this basic model would undergo much modification as Freud developed a more useful "structural theory," in which a psychological "ego" adapts to the real world while defending itself from, and integrating the demands of, a primitive and unconscious "id" and a punishing "superego." How these functionally defined structures developed, and how the ego employed psychological "defense mechanisms" to protect itself from discomfort and perceived dangers within and without, would become questions of increasing concern and clinical importance. Klein was to provide a potent, sometimes speculative, and highly provocative exegesis.

Analysts were beginning to explore the possibility of treating young children in the years after the First World War. Though intrigued by the prospect, they initially had considered it potentially dangerous and were uncertain of its ethical implications. Freud's pocket analysis of "Little Hans" in 1904 took place through the intermediary of the boy's parents. Viennese analyst Hermine von Hug-Hellmuth had attempted to treat children somewhat earlier than did Klein, but she was murdered by her own nephew, whom she had tried to analyze. In the 1930s Anna Freud, Freud's youngest child, would become an influential child analyst, and, in terms of theory and techniques, Melanie Klein's rival.

Klein read her first paper, "The Development of a Child," about her analysis of her son, before the Hungarian Psychoanalytical Society in 1919. It represents the first serious attempt to psychoanalyze a child. While with adults analysts were learning to use interpretations sparingly, Klein came to believe that a child's anxieties could be addressed directly. She provided her young analysands with a drawerful of toys for activities to be interpreted symbolically, and her method marks the beginning of play therapy. First with Erich, later with other children, Klein also encouraged her young patients to talk about fantasies, whether aggressive or sexual. Interpretation, she claimed, led to symptom reduction. Later, Klein would analyze adults in a conventional setting, but, while using many of the same methods as orthodox Freudians, she often tried to immediately interpret unconscious anxiety. In general, Kleinians emphasized the primitive aspects of "phantasy"—their preferred term for unconscious mental processes. "Freud acquainted us with the child in the adult," Hanna Segal once explained, "and Klein with the infant in the child."

From the beginning Klein's ideas were controversial, and she won as many enemies as friends. In 1921 Klein moved to Berlin, where she soon came into the orbit of Karl Abraham, another of Freud's close colleagues. Importantly, at a psychoanalytic congress in 1924, Klein impressed Ernest Jones, the famous British psychoanalyst. Two years later, when Abraham died, Klein moved to London, where she became the first European psychoanalyst to be elected to the British Psycho-analytical Society. In 1932 she published her first important book, *The Psychoanalysis of Children.*

In general, Kleinian theory centered on observationally based specu-lation. She believed that an infant's early mental life is "psychotic"—dom-inated by fantasy and magical thinking—and she inferred complex mental processes from early behaviors. She developed concepts to explain neurotic, even schizophrenic, conflicts in both children and adults. Klein emphasized the psychologically archaic character of anxiety and devel-oped the idea of emotionally driven psychological "positions" that shape the infant's view of the world. The "paranoid" position (later called the paranoid-schizoid position), according to Klein, characterizes the earliest mental life (to about four months) and is associated with feelings of greed, deprivation, gratification, and anxiety. It is centered initially on the mother's breast—by turns a "good" and "bad" object or, as she phrased it, experienced in a "split" manner, as both simultaneously. This primal viewpoint is succeeded by the "depressive" position, in which the infant is able to view the all-important mother as a "whole object," but not without fears of repudiation and abandonment.

As endlessly contestable and contentious as Klein's stage theory would be, the associated psychological defense mechanisms she described proved eminently useful to psychoanalysis and psychotherapy. "Splitting" is a primitive psychological effort to simultaneously retain a good, loving psychological object while expelling the object invested with violent and punishing feelings. Similarly, "projective identification" involves the fantastical relocating and manipulating of dangerous parts of the self within another person, as well as safekeeping "good" parts of the self from one's own destructiveness. All sorts of extreme psychological conflicts—from claustrophobia to schizophrenia—derive explanatory benefit from these concepts.

Given the powerful but highly speculative character of Klein's theories, the debate they caused is not surprising, and it intensified with the migration of a number of psychoanalysts, including Sigmund Freud and Anna Freud, from Nazi-occupied Europe to Britain at the beginning of World War II. In general, Klein emphasized the early infant-mother relationship at a time when Freudian analysts, using a more biologically oriented model, possessed relatively vague concepts concerning "pre-oedipal" development. She viewed the child as, nearly from birth, in a state of great vulnerability to cognitive alarm and emotional distress—in which mothering played a significant role. Freudian theory focused on the development of a psychological constellation from innate, biologically determined instinctual drives. Kleinian theory also investigated these drives, but it paid special attention to the interactive aspects of the associated unconscious fantasies—principally, the relation between mother and infant.

Klein's immigration to England, it should be added, proved pivotal to the development of her ideas. There she encountered the fundamental rationality of English philosophical discourse. Without this favorable development, Kleinian thought would probably have become sterile. But Freud himself (who died in 1939), although cool to many of Klein's ideas, was aware that they represented extensions of, and not rejection of, his fundamental ideas. In this context British analysts engaged, during 1943 and 1944, in a series of "controversial discussions." Although these resolved little theoretically, they led to a tripartite division of psychoanalysis in Britain. "Group A" accepted Klein's theory, with all its speculative generalizations; "Group B," led by Anna Freud, represented a repudiation of this viewpoint. The "Middle Group" accepted certain aspects of Klein's theory while rejecting others.

In significant papers and books after World War II, Klein continued to refine her theoretical views. Her *Contributions of Psycho-Analysis* was published in 1948. *Envy and Gratitude*, published in 1957, represented the culmination of her work. Here she stressed the significance of the controversial "death instinct"—a speculative concept to explain aggression that Freud had developed after World War I, and which mainstream analysts tended to reject. *Narrative of a Child Analysis* appeared in 1961.

The influence of Melanie Klein is not easy to summarize, but it recalls that of evolutionary biologist Ernst Haeckel, whose impact on Darwinism was basic and immediate, not long-lasting in the forms he proposed, and in some ways often considered negative. Most importantly, Klein's ideas generated the "object relations" school of psychoanalysis developed by W. R. D. Fairbairn and others during the 1950s. Klein in this way became principal inspiration for a distinguished and highly influential list of analysts, including Hanna Segal, D. W. Winnicott, R. E. Money-Kyrle, and Wilfred Bion. Her work became known throughout the world. It was especially popular in Latin American countries and was a strong influence on the French followers of Jacques Lacan.

Although American psychoanalysts were programmatically hostile to Melanie Klein through the 1950s, many eventually accepted some of her ideas, at least in modified form. Most particularly, the theory of "separation-individuation" proposed by Margaret S. Mahler adapted and incorporated aspects of Kleinian thinking, as did Otto Kernberg's effort to delineate the more severely neurotic "narcissistic" and "borderline personality" disorders. Mahler and Kernberg came to the forefront of American psychoanalysis with the passing of an older generation whose rigid adaptation of Freud's ideas had done considerable and lasting harm to the standing of the profession in the United States.

Melanie Klein, beautiful when young, still vain in old age, could be the life of a party. She was affectionate toward friends until crossed; then she would become hostile and bitter. She became alienated from her daughter, psychoanalyst Melitta Schmideberg, in the early 1930s, and had a rift with her devoted disciple Paula Heimann later in life. In old age Klein became increasingly dogmatic, which apparently caused her to end relationships with some of her most devoted followers. While dying of cancer, she made elaborate preparations for her own funeral. Her death came on September 22, 1960, in London.

# Godfrey Hounsfield [b. 1919]

## The Revolution in Diagnostic Imaging

Within weeks of the discovery of X rays by Wilhelm Conrad Röntgen (p. 100) in 1895, machines were designed and built to examine the interior of the human body. X rays were a clear boon to medicine, used to detect broken bones, bullets, and even certain significant tumors, and radiology developed as a medical specialty and field of expertise.

But the X-ray image is decidedly limited. The body is filled with substances the densities of which differ only slightly. The ordinary X-ray image is essentially taken through the width of the body. Images of the heart and lungs, for example, fall on top of one another and cannot be seen individually. Nor can an X ray distinguish between types of tissue. These drawbacks were first overcome in the early 1970s, with the development of the CAT scan.

A machine that extracts the maximum amount of information from an X ray using the calculating speed of a computer, the CAT, or CT, scan (for computerized axial tomography or, simply, computed tomography) soon transformed diagnosis in various branches of medicine. A simple procedure for the patient, the CT scan often obviated the need for more invasive procedures, including exploratory surgery. Since its introduction in the 1970s, there have been a whole array of increasingly sophisticated imaging technologies brought to market, including positron emission tomography (PET scan), improved ultrasound machines, and magnetic resonance imaging (MRI). But the CT scan represents the first major use of information-processing technology in medicine. It was the invention that inaugurated advanced biomedical engineering, and it is the principal achievement of British inventor and engineer Godfrey Hounsfield.

The youngest of five children, Godfrey Newbold Hounsfield was born in Newark, a town in the county of Nottinghamshire, on August 28, 1919. His father was Thomas Hounsfield, an engineer who had worked in the steel industry before turning to farming due to poor eyesight. A relative, Leslie Hounsfield, had designed the Trojan, a British automobile, in 1910, and invented the Hounsfield tensometer. Godfrey was himself a tinkerer as a child, constructing radios and building a recording machine from spare parts. He was not, however, an excellent student, and after finishing

secondary school he worked for a short time as a draftsman. With the outbreak of the Second World War, Hounsfield joined the Royal Air Force. Initially assigned to be a radio mechanic, he attended the Cranwell Radar School. His talents were noted, and he finished school as a lecturer not a student, known for his innovative teaching methods. After World War II, he went on to study electrical and mechanical engineering at Faraday House, a polytechnical college, from which he graduated in 1951.

Beginning his professional career at age thirty-two, Hounsfield took a position with Electric and Musical Industries (EMI), a British corporation that had grown from being a manufacturer of record players to a conglomerate with various entertainment and communications divisions. Hounsfield's early years at EMI soon found him working on computers, which were then being redesigned to replace bulky vacuum-tube technology with transistors. Hounsfield's innovative work helped create the EMIDEC 1100, the first large solid-state computer manufactured in England. Success for the EMIDEC was limited, however, by the company's lack of experience in manufacturing complex machines or in competing in a rapidly changing marketplace.

Given his choice of projects in the early 1960s, Hounsfield took up another computer-related concern: automatic pattern recognition. This was a key area of research, because a computer able to recognize and input information without human operators would have commercial value. Although pattern recognition was frequently the province of mathematicians, Hounsfield was undeterred. As in other research, he followed an approach that used mathematical reasoning in only a limited way, relying first on basic principles. Hounsfield's perspective was that of a practically minded engineer: "I think at the start you use the minimum of maths but have a lot of intuition." Confirmation by mathematics could come later.

In 1967, while on a "ramble" in the English countryside, Hounsfield had the insight that led to the development of the CT scan. He recognized that if X rays were scanned across the body, readings taken at all angles to it would provide sufficient information to "mathematically reconstruct a picture of what was inside the body." He recognized the prospects this held for radiology and medical diagnosis. "Once I realized that my method was considerably more efficient," Hounsfield explained, "I hoped to see things which conventional X rays could not possibly see."

EMI initially refused to give Hounsfield the money he needed to further develop his idea, but health officers at the government's Department of Health and Social Security agreed to fund half the cost of feasibility studies and, later, to support the laboratory experiments. Neurology stood most clearly to benefit, and so the first scanners were designed for the brain.

As Hounsfield conceived the machine, it would consist of four basic components: an X-ray generator and detectors, a scanning unit, and a computer. The scanning unit would physically move the detectors across and around the object being examined, and the computer would process and display pictures from the information they gathered. Hounsfield began experiments toward a working model in 1968. Initially it took over a week to record 28,800 readings and to integrate and process the information. In spite of fuzziness in the original images, the idea was clearly sound. Brains of cows and bodies of pigs were the first subjects, and after technical improvements were made, good pictures were obtained. "The diagnostic implications were awesome," writes Charles Susskind in his history of the CT machine. "Abnormalities of bodily organs would become clearly discernible, as would many malignancies, whose absorptivity in most cases differs only slightly from that of normal tissue."

In late 1971 a prototype of the CT scanner was installed at Atkinson Morley's, a small hospital in Wimbledon. The first patient was a woman with symptoms that suggested a brain tumor, and the scan confirmed the diagnosis. Success in early trials led EMI to announce that it would produce the machine itself, although the company had little experience in marketing medical products.* In addition, the major market for the machine would be in the United States. EMI soon faced stiff competition and—as is common with breakthrough technology—a number of patent battles.

Success for the CT scan, when it was brought to market, was immediate, and Hounsfield's role was given center stage. The machine's diagnostic

---

*One boon to the CT scan's development was the success of the singing group the Beatles. Their recordings netted EMI a fortune. Eventually the belief became widespread that the CT scan "was grubstaked by the Beatles."

capabilities were comparatively so great that in 1972 neurologist Fred Plum announced on American television, with Hounsfield present, that it would soon be unethical for neurologists to treat certain cases without using the CT scan. In 1973, at a meeting of the Radiological Society of North America, Hounsfield's display of the CT scan generated tremendous interest. Sales to hospitals were enormously profitable to EMI over the next several years, and the machine was constantly improved. In 1975, the year EMI introduced a whole-body scanner, radiologists at a meeting in Bermuda gave Hounsfield a standing ovation.

The invention of the CT scan serves as a good illustration of the importance of timing in technological advance. In 1979 Hounsfield was awarded the Nobel Prize for physiology or medicine, shared with Allan MacLeod Cormack, a South African–born American physicist who taught at Tufts University. In the 1950s Cormack had recognized how the limitations of X rays might be overcome with the help of a computer. He had worked out a complex differential equation to demonstrate as much and published his work, but its significance went unnoticed. Similarly, William Oldendorf (who did not share the Nobel Prize) had conceived aspects of the CT scan as early as 1958 and received patents for an apparatus in 1963. But he had not worked out the computerized aspects, and his efforts to interest X-ray manufacturers were rebuffed out of hand.

Any account of the CT scan must come with an important footnote. The machine was the first, and for a time the most visible, of many new instruments which have made contemporary medicine burdensomely expensive. Early models cost $300,000; with later improvements, the cost rose to over $1 million. In the 1970s the *New England Journal of Medicine* called the rage for scanners "CAT fever"—but it could not be stopped. The capabilities of computerized tomography were irresistible.

Godfrey Hounsfield has remained a bachelor throughout his life. A pianist, he is devoted to classical music. Courteous, soft-spoken, and introverted, he was described by Charles Susskind as "sitting at his usual desk that almost entirely filled his modest cubicle," at EMI's Central Research Laboratories, "hoping the world would forget him so he could get on with his work." He has been showered with many honors over the years in addition to the Nobel Prize. In 1975 he was elected a fellow of the Royal Society and also received the Albert Lasker Award for basic medical research. In 1976 was named a companion of the Order of the British Empire. He continued to work at EMI and remains a consultant to its Central Research Laboratories.

# Jean Dausset [b. 1916]

## Molecular Self and Nonself

The self is not just a narrative fiction born of language and mind, nor is a physical structure its only boundaries. The self may also be said to exist on a molecular level, comprised of a group of antigenic proteins found in all cells in the body. The specific complexion of these antigens is configured by a set of genes known today as the "major histocompatibility complex" (MHC). A component of the cellular immune system, the MHC varies among all individuals save identical twins.

The medical implications of the histocompatibility complex have been recent but exceptional. The MHC figures as a crucial aspect of transplantation technology, enabling favorable tissue grafts and reducing the chances of rejection of donated organs. In addition, undergirded by a wealth of recent genetic research, discovery of the MHC has greatly illuminated and enlarged knowledge of autoimmune disorders. A wide variety of diseases, from allergies to arthritis, are now recognized as resulting from egregious genetic mismatches that render some part of self "nonself."

Unraveling the MHC came about through an improved grasp of the immune system, achieved in the last half of the twentieth century. The problem of tissue rejection in transplantation was linked to immunologic intolerance and was plugged into the clonal selection theory of immunity suggested by Macfarlane Burnet (p. 280). Important work carried out by George Snell and Peter Gorer led to the concept of a genetic locus responsible for what Snell was the first to call "histocompatibility." All these scientists eventually were awarded the Nobel Prize, but, arguably, the central figure to discover how the system works in human beings is the French physician, immunologist, and hematologist—and also Nobel laureate—Jean Dausset.

Jean Baptiste Gabriel Joachim Dausset was born in Toulouse, France, on October 19, 1916. His father was Henri Dausset, an eminent French physician and radiologist. His mother was Elisabeth Brullard. Jean was one of three children. He was introspective and recalled a happy childhood. He attended the prestigious Lycée Michelet in Paris, and decided, not surprisingly, to study medicine. He attended medical school at the University of

Paris, but before Dausset actually obtained his degree, World War II broke out. Briefly mobilized to join the medical corps, he subsequently volunteered with the Free French in North Africa and took part in the Normandy campaign. Dausset gave away his identification papers to enable a Jewish colleague at the Institut Pasteur to remain in occupied Paris throughout the war.

Returning to France at war's end, Dausset received his medical degree in 1945. He served his internship and residency from 1946 to 1950 at the Paris hospitals. During the war Dausset, working in the resuscitation service, had become fascinated by the biological aspects of blood transfusion, and so he trained in both internal medicine and hematology. He was appointed to the National Blood Transfusion Center in 1946 and soon began to publish widely. One of his papers, from 1951, discussed problems in screening universal donors. In principle, such donors could give blood to anyone; in practice, however, some carried antibodies for blood type A. Dausset showed how testing for anti-A antibodies could eliminate the dangerous transfusion reaction.

In general, Dausset's early papers reflect postwar advances in hematology (the study of blood and the blood-forming tissues). He followed his work on hemolytic anemia (destruction of red blood cells) with studies on agranulocytosis (a condition marked by a severe drop in the white blood cell count). This research brought Dausset to pose a question that led, in 1952, to a discovery of fundamental importance.

It had been known for several decades, since the work of Karl Landsteiner, that human blood could be classified into four groups by red blood cell types—familiarly A, B, AB, and O. (Rh factor, an additional typing mechanism, was identified in 1940.) "If there existed individual differences carried by red blood cells," asked Dausset, as he later recalled, "why wouldn't there exist others, carried by white blood cells, or leucocytes?" To test this idea, Dausset placed white blood cells from a donor into the blood serum of an individual who had already received several transfusions. "With the naked eye, I saw the formation of enormous clumps of agglutinins." This result—not inevitable but predictable—meant immediate recognition of nonself cells. (As would soon be understood, the agglutination was due to antibodies in the serum reacting with antigens detected on the white blood cells.) It suggested to Dausset that, as with Landsteiner's blood groups, there existed a genetically based recognition system with a much finer level of discrimination. Since blood transfusion is comparable to other efforts that introduce foreign tissue into a host, Dausset also recognized the affinity of his experiments with ongoing research in tissue compatibility.

The concept of tissue compatibility had been developed in the 1930s, most especially by the American George Snell, in his work with congenic mice—that is, mice bred as identical twins save for one genetic region, or locus. Snell had been able to demonstrate that among ten possible genetic regions one was prepotent in determining whether a mouse would accept tissue grafts. Snell, together with Peter Gorer, called this most significant locus "H-2," designating the surface antigens that would indicate tissue compatibility. It was plausible to suppose, and evidence soon suggested, that an analogue of the H-2 complex existed in humans. In 1958 Dausset described the first of these human antigens, which he called "Mac."

Dausset undertook a long series of fairly simple experimental operations. About 1962, he learned of skin graft studies made by Felix Rapaport at New York University, including an effort to classify human tissue groups. Within weeks, at the Hôpital Saint-Louis in Paris, Dausset and Rapaport began tissue graft studies, performing skin grafts on a wide variety of volunteers. Donors and hosts were both unrelated and related (and included Dausset himself). Some nine hundred operations would be performed over the course of fifteen years.

Through this work the significance of using leukocyte groups to distinguish between self and nonself soon became clear. Dausset's graft studies inspired a cascade of research, and much competition; for a time during the 1960s matters became exquisitely confused. It had been hoped that just one "supergene" would be responsible for the histocompatibility complex. But, as Dausset and a number of others began to realize, the complexity of the self/nonself boundary was very great. It became necessary to standardize procedures and techniques, and a series of international workshops and conferences took place.

The most significant of several breakthroughs came in 1965, when Dausset, together with two Czech researchers, brothers Pavol and Dagmar Ivany, identified the genetic region that seemed to code for the entire system of antigens. They called this the Hu-1, and showed how its several sub-loci would determine the appearance of a small number of specific antigens on the surface of human cells. The simple mathematics of the system ensured that, with odds of 20 million or so to one, no two individuals, save identical twins, would carry the same set of histocompatibility antigens. Eventually, Hu-1 was renamed HLA (for *human leukocyte antigen*), of which there were discovered various subgroups (HLA-A, HLA-B, etc.). In tissue and organ transplantation, finding close genetic matches could reduce if not eliminate the rejection response.

Dausset eventually sought to classify tissue compatibilities in groups beyond France. He organized an international cooperative study that examined the immunogenetic complements of some fifty-four populations from all over the world. "Disguising ourselves as explorers," wrote Dausset later, "we penetrated the thickest jungles, climbed the highest mountains, and sailed to the most forsaken islands to collect samples of blood."

Repercussions from the discovery of the major histocompatibility complex coursed through the related fields of immunology and transplant medicine. Equally significant for general medicine, the MHC shed new light on what came to be known as the "autoimmune" diseases. As now understood, in these disorders the immune system recognizes as "nonself" groups of cells that do in fact belong to the individual. Incompletely understood and imperfectly classified, examples of autoimmune diseases include insulin resistance and insulin-dependent (juvenile or type 1) diabetes, multiple sclerosis, certain types of anemia, ulcerative colitis, and Graves' disease—but there are many others, associated with all types of tissue and cells of the body.

No one was surprised when Jean Dausset was awarded the Nobel Prize for physiology or medicine in 1980, which he shared with George Snell and Baruj Benacerraf. Dausset was joined to the French Legion of Honor and is also a commander in the National Order of Merit. He served as chief biologist for the Paris hospitals from 1963 to 1978. He was cochairman of the Institute for Research into the Diseases of Blood from 1963 to 1968. In 1968 he became director of research at the National Institute of Health and Medical Research. He is professor of immunohematology at the Lariboisière-Saint Louis Medical Faculty and professor of experimental medicine at the Collège de France. In 1984 he was a founder of the Center for the Study of Human Polymorphism, dedicated to research in human genetics—today known as Fondation Jean Dausset.

Dausset married Rose Mayoral in 1962, and they raised two children. Characterized by colleagues as generous and modest, he cultivated a sophisticated life outside the laboratory. With his wife he owned an art gallery, and they became friends with Yves Tanguy, Victor Brauner, and other celebrated artists. In later life, as a Nobel laureate, he was well known to the French public; his autobiography, *Clin d'oeil à la vie,* was published in 1999. Like many of his generation, Dausset is strongly optimistic about the future of mankind in general and most particularly of medicine, which, he predicts, "will be tailored to the individual and will prove less costly and more effective." At the same time, he has taken his own measure, in contrast with learned men of the past. "There are no longer any scholars but those who know everything about almost nothing," he wrote, in reference to his molecular research. "I am one of them."

# James Black  [b. 1924]

## The Rational Search for New Drugs

A s heart disease became increasingly common in the first half of the twentieth century, the drugs to treat it were mostly old news. Digitalis, used to regulate the heartbeat, dates to the sixteenth century. Nitroglycerin, used to relieve the painful attacks of angina pectoris, has been used therapeutically since the mid-1800s. By the 1950s, though, with an improved understanding of the chemical mechanisms that regulate the cardiovascular system came the prospect of new drugs. The advent of beta blockers, used to treat a variety of heart disorders, is owed to the work of the Scottish physician and pharmacologist James Black.

The significance of beta blockers, however, extends beyond their use in heart disease. Their identification represented a new approach to selecting and testing potential drugs by analyzing molecular action. Beta blockers, for example, replace and forestall action of the hormone adrenaline on the heart. Their discovery came about not through chance in the course of testing a host of compounds but through a search for a specific complex molecule. This approach, after a host of technical refinements, underlies the contemporary search for new pharmaceuticals; many future discoveries, with the advent of genomics and proteomics, will be based upon it.

The fourth of five sons in a working-class family, James Whyte Black was born on June 14, 1924, in Uddingston, Scotland, a town in the Lanarkshire coal district, near Glasgow. His father was a coal miner who advanced to become a mining engineer. As a child James enjoyed music and mathematics. His leanings toward medicine were influenced by his older brother, a medical student. At age fifteen, James won a residential scholarship to St. Andrews, Scotland's oldest university. He received his degree in medicine in 1946.

From the beginning of his career Black wanted to work in applied science. He did not enjoy clinical medicine. "I found the way patients were treated unacceptable," he said of his hospital experience. "Not cruelly or sadistically but insensitively. They were just classes: a heart, a liver, a lung. They were not even patients, because patients have individuality." Black remained at St. Andrews for a time, studying how various drugs affect blood pressure. But in 1946, after marrying Hilary Vaughan, he needed to make money. He moved to Singapore to teach from 1947 to 1950. Returning to Scotland about the time his daughter was born and still financially insecure, he accepted a lectureship in physiology at the veterinary school of the University of Glasgow. One of his colleagues was James Stephenson, the chemist with whom Black would make his major discovery.

The development of beta blockers must be traced to 1948, when the American pharmacologist Raymond Ahlquist proposed a theory to explain the famous "fight or flight" reaction by which the body, executive of the sympathetic nervous system, responds to danger. The stress hormone adrenaline (known in the United States as epinephrine) increases heart rate and at the same time causes certain vessels to dilate, making more blood available to the heart, brain, and skeletal muscles. These reactions are perplexing. How can different tissues react to the same hormone, adrenaline, in such divergent ways? How can the heart be excited to beat faster, while certain blood vessels relax? Ahlquist suggested mediation by cell-based chemical receptors of different types he called "alpha" and "beta." Adrenaline inhibits the action of most organs by acting on alpha receptors, but distinct beta receptors located in the heart respond by speeding up the heartbeat. Ahlquist's theory, elegant and relatively simple, met resistance for a decade. But when Black came across it in the mid-1950s in a textbook he was preparing to teach, it became the influential basis for his subsequent research.

Much attention was being paid to treating certain types of heart disease by the 1950s, especially in the United States and other industrialized countries. For the painful disease angina pectoris, researchers widely assumed a good drug would be a vasodilator that allowed more oxygen to be delivered to the heart. Black, however, wondered on the basis of Ahlquist's theory whether it might not be better to reduce the heart's oxygen demand instead. A drug that blocked the heart's beta receptors from taking up adrenaline might constitute a more effective treatment.

In 1958 with this as his goal, Black began working for the British pharmaceutical firm, Imperial Chemical Industries (ICI). Together with chemist James Stephenson, Black searched for three years to find the appropriate "false key"—an emasculated form of adrenaline that would bind to the beta receptor. A substance developed in 1958 looked promising, but it was too toxic to be marketed. Two years later a similar compound, pronethalol, could be shown to work in human beings by decreasing the heart rate, but safety was still a problem. Chemists at ICI soon found a similar but still safer drug, propranolol. This was the drug launched under the brand name Inderal in 1964. It quickly proved its worth as death rates from heart attack for patients taking beta blockers dropped significantly. Some studies found that the incidence of fatal heart attacks in patients taking Inderal was four times lower than among patients not given the drug.

Although introduced for treating angina pectoris, propranolol also proved useful for other cardiac conditions, including arrhythmias and essential hypertension. In addition, it improved survival rates among patients who had already suffered a heart attack. The drug became, and remains, a treatment mainstay. Its impact was all the greater because it helped lead to an improved understanding of the sympathetic nervous system, and, for better or worse, it helped create a highly competitive drug bazaar for new and slightly differently acting compounds.

By 1963, Black was anxious to begin a new program. He moved to the pharmaceutical firm of Smith, Kline and French in 1964, as head of pharmacology research. Early in his career he had been interested in the interrelated problems of excess gastric secretion, peptic ulcer, and the role of histamine, and now he returned to them.

Peptic ulcer is the painful and sometimes malignant inflammatory disease of the mucous membrane that lines the stomach. One reason that an ulcer becomes chronic is that the constant presence of gastric acid prevents it from healing. (Black's work came before the theory implicating a bacterium, *Helicobacter pylori,* in peptic ulcer.) In the 1960s the time-honored remedy was nothing more than rest and a bland, milk-based diet. But it was also known that histamine, the substance released during allergic reactions, also promotes the secretion of gastric acid. If antihistamines, developed about 1950, could prevent the discomfort of allergy, why couldn't they shut down gastric acid secretion?

Black recognized—he was not the only one to suggest it—that histamine's role in peptic ulcer might be analogous to that of adrenaline in angina pectoris. The fact that the popular antihistamines did *not* affect gastric secretions was significant and had to do with the composition of tissue. Black wondered if, just as beta receptors in the heart control the effect of adrenaline, specific receptors in the stomach lining might react to histamine—but not to antihistamines. In 1964 Black's analysis of the situation led him and his colleagues to develop a test to identify chemicals that inhibit histamine release in the stomach.

Although Black hoped that finding the right antagonist would be easy, it took a number of years and, like many scientific projects, involved much wasted effort. Chemists working with Black developed a variety of histaminelike substances. But histamine is a lively molecule and difficult to pin down as to which aspects of its chemical behavior are biologically important. Indeed, its central role was not evident to everybody. Some believed that histamine was probably of little significance in regulating gastric acid secretion. Black's approach was one among several, and during the 1960s considerable pressure mounted at Smith, Kline and French to abandon the project.

But in 1968, after some two hundred compounds had been tested, one showed promise. Four years more passed before Black and his colleagues published their first article on the "H2" receptor and its blocker, burim-amide, in 1972. This compound had potential toxicity problems, but the similarly structured cimetidine proved safe. Cimetidine was brought to market as Tagamet in 1976. It went on to become the world's most pre-scribed drug and was enormously profitable. Tagamet was soon prescribed not only for gastric ulcer but also for gastric reflux disease and heartburn. In 1995 it was launched with great fanfare as an over-the-counter drug.

But by 1973, several years before cimetidine was actually marketed, Black had left the private sector for an academic post as professor and head of the department of pharmacology at University College in London. In 1978 he became director of therapeutic research at Wellcome Research Laboratories. Six years later he moved to King's College, and there, with the help of the private pharmaceutical firm Johnson and Johnson, he assembled a small research group, the James Black Foundation. Drugs to treat common and debilitating diseases often win honors for their makers, and this was true for Black. He was knighted in 1981 and seven years later was awarded the 1988 Nobel Prize for physiology or medicine, sharing the award with George Hitchins and Gertrude Belle Elion.

Black's first wife, Hilary, with whom he had one daughter, died of cancer in 1987. In 1994 he married Rona Mcleod Mackie. Greatly admired by colleagues but famously private, Black, like many chemists, does not dwell on personal motivation concerning his research and resents intru-sive speculation. "Are you trying to analyze me?" he asked an interviewer contentiously. "Am I on your couch to be dissected and poked?" He told Thomas A. Bass, "I have absolutely no idea where my ideas come from. For all I know they come from comets. They creep up on me." In an echo of the great chemist August Kekulé, who discovered the central importance of the carbon atom while dozing aboard a London bus, Black added, "The most creative thing your brain does is dream."

# Walter Gilbert [b. 1932]

## Molecular Biology Takes Command

Genes are embedded in molecules of deoxyribonucleic acid (DNA). They are the physical units of heredity and govern protein synthesis, which is fundamental to all metabolic functions. Since Francis Crick and James Watson discovered the structure of DNA in 1953, a host of researchers could be cited for their generative influence on molecular biology and its growing importance to medicine. One of them, whose work ranges from basic science to the business of gene hunting and drug development, is Harvard professor and Nobel laureate Walter Gilbert.

Trained as a physicist, Walter Gilbert moved into molecular biology in the early 1960s. His discovery of the "lac" repressor molecule, about 1966, was crucial for understanding the control mechanisms by which individual genes are activated. A decade later, soon after the genetic code was deciphered, Gilbert developed a technique for reading the precise sequence of DNA bases comprising any gene. Gilbert then moved into one of the earliest ventures in bioengineering and for a time directed a private pharmaceutical corporation. He was a strong and early proponent of the massive effort to map the entire human genome, which was effectively completed in 2000. The ability to manipulate genes to medical ends, which is perhaps the most practical outcome of all this work, virtually defines future shock.

Growing up in a cultivated, middle-class home with highly educated parents, Walter Gilbert had a paradigmatic background for a great scientist. He was born on March 21, 1932, in Cambridge, Massachusetts. His father, Richard V. Gilbert, was professor of economics at Harvard University. His mother, Emma Cohen, was a child psychologist. Both his parents were of Russian Jewish descent, and Walter's maternal grandfather was the founder of an anarchist community at Stelton, New Jersey. When he was about seven years old, his parents moved to Washington, DC, where Richard Gilbert became part of the "brain trust" in the administration of Franklin D. Roosevelt. Interested by science throughout his childhood, Walter was distinguished by his wide-ranging curiosity. Early on he became a mineral collector and young chemist—who once blew up the kitchen pantry. But he was also interested in astronomy and, by the end of high school, physics. He attended Sidwell Friends High School, a Quaker institution, and in spite of sometimes cutting classes, he won the Westinghouse Science Talent Search in 1949.

The initial trajectory of Gilbert's career was not toward medicine or biology, but physics. He majored in chemistry and physics at Harvard and earned a bachelor's degree summa cum laude in 1953—the same year that James Watson and Francis Crick discovered the structure of DNA. Gilbert continued at Harvard in theoretical physics before moving to Cambridge University, where he worked with Nobel laureate Abdus Salam. For his thesis on elementary particle scattering, Gilbert received his Ph.D. in mathematics from Cambridge in 1957. (Theoretical physics would be the equivalent degree in the United States.) He returned to Harvard as a postdoctoral fellow and, from 1959 to 1964, served as assistant professor of physics.

Gilbert's move to molecular biology came about in consequence of his acquaintance with James Watson, whom he had initially met at Cambridge. Now at Harvard, Watson suggested that Gilbert consider switching to biology, telling him, "There's something very exciting going on." Gilbert began visiting Watson's laboratory and familiarized himself with the current research in nucleic acids. Soon he was performing experiments himself. By the time the last of his papers in theoretical physics was published in 1964, Gilbert was already winning acclaim for work in molecular biology.

In the course of unraveling the chemical mechanics of DNA in the 1950s, researchers clarified key aspects of its composition. The same complement of DNA, it was found, exists in every nucleated cell of a living organism. Genes, comprised of specific sequences of DNA bases, control the production of amino acids and proteins. These in turn account for the whole gamut of metabolic activities of cells and organisms. Thereupon arose a central problem: What molecular mechanism controls—that is, turns "on" and "off"—a particular gene in accordance with metabolic requirements? How are needs met inside the cell?

Gilbert took up this issue in the mid-1960s. By this time it had been nicely framed for molecular biology by the French scientists Jacques Monod and François Jacob, who proposed that a "repressor" molecule would by its presence halt (or by its absence enable) transcription of a particular stretch of DNA, the basic first step in protein synthesis. The simple model employed to search for such a molecule was the *E. coli* bacterium. Directed by its DNA, *E. coli* produces and uses an enzyme, beta-galactosidase, to break down nutrient lactose into simpler sugars that serve as its source of energy. It was known that when no lactose is available, this enzyme is not produced; it is, in a word, repressed. A "lac" repressor was thus initially a hypothetical entity—much in need of being discovered. Not only was it infinitesimally small, but also its basic composition—as a protein or some other molecule—was unknown. "The problems," wrote Gilbert later, "were both scientific and psychological."

Indeed, Gilbert worked for months without progress. Eventually he developed a method by which he introduced radioactively labeled, lactoselike molecules into cells of *E. coli*. These impostors, he discovered in collaboration with Benno Müller-Hill, would indeed draw to themselves the lac repressor, the absence of which would in turn set into motion the production of lactose. The announcement of the discovery of the lac repressor came in 1966 in articles in the *Proceedings of the National Academy of Sciences*. "In light of subsequent milestones in molecular biology, it is difficult now to convey the historic importance of this work…," writes Stephen S. Hall. "What began as rather forlorn and lonely scientific paths opened up broad avenues of research that…are still among the most heavily traveled of the biological sciences: the control and regulation of gene expression." Four years later Gilbert identified the gene to which the lac repressor binds. This gene, known as the lac "operator," set the stage in turn for another important discovery.

Broadly speaking, molecular biologists had learned by the mid-1970s how essentially two-dimensional DNA is translated into three-dimensional proteins—how, that is, the "genetic code" of DNA bases determines the amino acid sequence of any protein. If genes could be located and isolated, they could be also cloned by inserting them into bacteria, which multiply exponentially, and used in test-tube experiments. Now, for the first time, the precise sequence of DNA bases—adenine (A), cystine (C), guanine (G), and thymine (T)—became of interest. Gilbert, together with biochemist Allan Maxam, set out to unravel the string that constituted the lac operator. In doing so, they stumbled upon, and developed, a technique for sequencing any stretch of DNA.

Sequencing DNA was essentially a problem of sophisticated chemistry. First, Gilbert and Maxam would multiply a strand of DNA a millionfold in bacteria. One end of each strand would be radioactively labeled to indicate directionality, much like a caboose added to a string of freight cars. The sample would then be nested into four groups. A reagent, dimethyl sulfate, would selectively separate DNA at two of the four DNA bases, adenine and guanine. Maxam found another chemical, hydrazine, that would separate the other two bases, cytosine and thymine. Running these reactions in order and careful dosing with the reagent would produce fragments of all possible lengths, each terminating at a known base. Gel electrophoresis, a fractionating technique, would range the fragments in order by length. The sequence of bases, visible as dark bands of contrasting intensity, would appear in the order corresponding to the original strand of DNA.

Historically, the time was ripe for a technique to sequence DNA base by base, and when Gilbert and Maxam published the first paper detailing their method in 1977, it was an instant landmark. Together with Frederick Sanger, the British chemist and Nobel laureate who had developed a similar technique about the same time, Gilbert was awarded the Albert Lasker Award in 1979. Gilbert and Sanger shared the Nobel Prize for chemistry in 1980, together with another American molecular biologist, Paul Berg, whose work had also played a critical role in founding genetic engineering. DNA sequencing would eventually become automated and applied throughout molecular biology. It is fundamental to the new science of genomics and also central to associated practical sciences, such as forensics.

Indeed, with this and other discoveries, Gilbert was at the forefront of a historic shift that put the ability to manipulate genes to industrial use. Genetic manipulation held enormous promise for medicine, and the most immediate prospects lay in synthesis of useful proteins by cloning. In 1978, Gilbert and several colleagues met with investors and hatched an agreement to found a company, Biogen, to develop genetically engineered pharmaceuticals. Over the next seven years Gilbert served as chairman of Biogen's scientific board of directors, and in 1981 he left Harvard to become the company's principal executive officer. His tenure was controversial, and Biogen was handicapped as an early player in a high-stakes game. The company's synthesis of alpha interferon, for example, was expected to lead to important new gains in cancer therapy, but its initial promise went unfulfilled. Gilbert left his position at Biogen in 1984 and the next year returned to Harvard.

Gilbert's authoritative presence in molecular biology was also evident in his role as an early advocate of the massive effort to decipher the entire complement of human DNA—the human genome. By 1987 Gilbert had become a self-appointed spokesman urging the development of a "genome project." He even made plans to set up a private corporation, with the idea of eventually publishing a genetic atlas. Although he did not succeed in starting a company, his high profile in the debate constituted a green light for the research world of molecular biology. The Human Genome Project eventually developed as the work of an international consortium. It initially looked to complete a basic sequence by 2005, but with the help of a host of new techniques, including computer-based sequencing machines, and with competition from the private sector, a "first draft" was completed some five years ahead of schedule.

As many of the technical problems in DNA research moved toward resolution, Gilbert turned to broader issues of evolutionary biology. In the 1970s Gilbert had distinguished two kinds of base sequences of genes: relatively short "exons," which convey information, and longer "introns," which seemed to be useless stretches of base pairs. Exons and introns are not found in the DNA of bacteria but are abundant in DNA in higher animals. As early as 1979, Gilbert had suggested that the apparently dispensable introns actually play a crucial evolutionary role in assembling new genes. He returned to this concept in the late 1990s.

Today Walter Gilbert remains at Harvard, chairman of the Department of Cellular and Developmental Biology, and the department's Carl M. Loeb University Professor. Since 1992, he has been vice chairman of Myriad Genetics, a corporation that has combined significant information from research in genealogy and DNA research. He is married to Delia Stone, a poet, and they have two children. Sometimes described as aggressive and arrogant, Gilbert's dominating personality covers a quieter temperament, blending optimism with impatience for new knowledge. He possesses, writes Stephen S. Hall, "an intellectual self-confidence so immense that it seems to suffuse his consciousness like a drug."

# Solomon Snyder [b. 1938]

## Advances in Neuroscience

Neurology and neurosurgery became specialized fields of medicine beginning in the mid-nineteenth century, as clinicians attempted to link symptoms and signs of illness with pathological findings in the brain at autopsy. Santiago Ramón y Cajal (p. 109) revolutionized the era's limited grasp of how the brain works about 1900, with the concept of the neuron. A broadly electrochemical view of the brain was at hand by 1924, when the first electroencephalograph (EEG), a device for measuring brain waves, was invented. But truly powerful techniques for investigating the nervous system and developing new therapeutics awaited a mature biochemistry. That knowledge was in place by the 1970s, and one of the first to exploit it was Solomon Snyder.

Director of a powerful research laboratory at Johns Hopkins University, Snyder has a long series of fundamental discoveries to his credit. Most memorably, with graduate student Candace Pert in 1973, Snyder discovered the opiate receptors, which initiated a flood of research in brain chemistry. Snyder himself went on to identify and characterize other neurotransmitters. He linked much of this research to potential advances in medicine. His work was crucial to the development of new psychotropic medications as well as the prospect for new drug therapies for cerebral hemorrhage and other brain diseases. Most recently, Snyder showed that a gas, nitric oxide (NO), may play important roles in neurotransmission. In brief, much recent research in neurology and neuropharmacology derives from Snyder's work.

Solomon Halbert Snyder was born on December 26, 1938. He was the second of five children of Samuel Simon Snyder and Patricia Yakerson Snyder. His father was an expert cryptanalyst, pioneering the use of computers in code breaking, and the author, with Ashley Montagu, of *Man and the Computer*. Growing up in Washington, DC, though the family was not religious, Solomon attended an Orthodox Jewish elementary school. As an adolescent he was intrigued by philosophy rather than science. He read Freud (p. 173), viewing psychoanalysis as "a practical form of philosophy." After graduating Calvin Coolidge High School in 1955, he went on to Georgetown University. Here he followed a premed program, but after his third

year he was admitted to Georgetown Medical School, bypassing the baccalaureate. Snyder received his medical degree cum laude in 1962 at the age of twenty-three.

Snyder had been drawn to neuroscience and brain chemistry throughout medical school. While working as a technician at the National Institutes of Health (NIH) one summer, he was seduced by the creative side of research. "Research in a laboratory at the forefront," he once recalled, "was vastly different from the boring science of classes and textbooks." Snyder's interest in the actions of drugs on the brain arose when, while interning at the Kaiser Foundation in San Francisco, he happened to take lysergic acid diethylamide (LSD), the hallucinogenic agent then coming into use as a powerful recreational drug. He has described in his book *Drugs and the Brain* how, after taking LSD, he was overtaken by synesthesia, a mingling of the senses, and later "the powerful feeling of oneness with the universe was followed by a loss of awareness of just who I was."

Snyder subsequently became an authority on hallucinogenic drugs. He returned east in 1963 to work at the National Institute of Mental Health (NIMH) with Julius Axelrod, the eminent scientist who, several years later, would become a Nobel laureate for his work in psychopharmacology. Snyder was strongly influenced by Axelrod's intellectual approach to neuroscience, which was strongly conceptual and creative in the design of experiments. In 1965 Snyder became assistant resident in the department of psychiatry at Johns Hopkins Hospital, a post he held for three years. Although he enjoyed treating individual patients in a therapeutic setting, he became committed to research. In 1966, he established a durable base when he was named assistant professor of pharmacology and experimental therapeutics at Johns Hopkins University. He was a full professor by 1970.

Snyder's interest in molecular aspects of brain chemistry emerged from his drug research. Both scientific advances and the social context of the 1970s made such work possible. The population of heroin addicts in the United States had increased dramatically, largely due to the country's military involvement in Vietnam, and in 1971 President Richard Nixon declared a "war on drugs." Snyder became aware of the tremendous gap that existed between the then-current treatments for addiction—such as the use of methadone as a substitute for heroin—and any basic understanding of how drugs act on the brain. The NIH was skeptical when he proposed to look for the molecular target of opiate action, but Snyder was able to obtain funding for research into the action of amphetamines, another group of frequently abused pharmaceuticals. He could then use those funds for opiate research. Such a ruse to acquire money for basic research in unpopular areas was not uncommon, and in Snyder's case, it was productive.

By the 1970s the idea that drugs affected the brain via cell receptors and chemical neurotransmitters had become a plausible hypothesis. The receptor concept dated to the turn of the twentieth century but was long in coming to fruition, in part because many of the associated molecules are small and volatile. All the known neurotransmitters carried electrical charges that ensured they would remain outside the target cell, where they could bind to presumed receptors on the cell membrane. But the actual presence of receptors in the brain remained to be demonstrated.

Snyder's success in seeking the opiate receptors came in part from a decisive innovation that adapted a technique, previously used in looking for hormone receptors, known as "reversible ligand binding." In 1972, in experiments in collaboration with Candace Pert, a graduate student in neuropharmacology, Solomon employed a powerfully addictive opiate (levorphanol), a nonaddictive isomer (dextrorphan), and an opiate antagonist, naloxone. The naloxone was radioactively labeled to permit detection of even the most minuscule amounts. Pert and Snyder showed that the potent opiate, levorphanol, would compete with naloxone to bind to brain tissue, while its nonaddicting, nonanalgesic isomer dextrorphan had no such effect. "We have shown," they wrote, "that a component of nervous tissue can selectively form complexes with opiate drugs at very low concentrations." This strong presumptive evidence for the existence of the opiate receptor was published in a landmark paper in *Science* on March 9, 1973: "Opiate Receptor: Demonstration in Nervous Tissue."

Viewed with the perspective of a generation, discovery of the opiate receptors was a watershed in neuroscience and pharmacology. The technique of reversible ligand binding subsequently became widely employed in screening potential new pharmaceuticals. A flurry of research ensued, aiming to discover other neurotransmitters and receptors. From Snyder's own laboratory came evidence of receptors for acetylcholine, glycine, and serotonin. In the mid-1970s Snyder and his laboratory showed that the neuroleptics, a class of antipsychotic drugs which can sometimes relieve symptoms of schizophrenia, act by blocking dopamine receptors in the brain.

Snyder's work had further implications for understanding the molecular mechanics of both normal and pathological brain function, and for developing improved treatments for stroke, psychosis, and other mental disorders. The very fact that opiate receptors existed, for example, strongly suggested that the body produced its own "natural opiates." These neurotransmitters, now known as the enkephalins, were discovered in 1975 by Hans W. Kosterlitz and John Hughes at the University of Aberdeen in Scotland. Snyder shared the Albert Lasker Award with these scientists in 1978.

Although his laboratory was devoted to molecular research in neuroscience, Snyder retained his interest in medical applications of research. The potential for basic research to bring new tools to clinical psychiatry and to the broader problems of drug abuse especially concerned him. His first book, *Uses of Marijuana*, published in 1971, was followed three years later by *Madness and the Brain*. In this volume he analyzes the current treatments for schizophrenia and other mental disorders, and also discusses the actions of a variety of drugs, from LSD to cocaine. His *The Troubled Mind: A Guide to Release from Distress* was published in 1976. In 1980 came *Biological Aspects of Mental Disorder*, a guide to a wide variety of psychiatric and neurological diseases, from epilepsy and age-related mental decline to affective disorders and problems such as suicide and alcoholism. His *Brainstorming: The Science and Politics of Opiate Research*, is in part a scientific autobiography, and it also discusses the frustrating inability of such basic scientific advances as Snyder has made to substantially affect the problems of drug abuse. In this volume, published in 1989, Snyder's social, historical, and psychological insights into drug use reflect the flexibility and range of his thought.

Even when he wrote for a professional audience, Snyder's longer works were readable, free of jargon, and seemed to represent his way of thinking out loud about the ultimate concerns of neuroscience. It was not surprising that in 1982 Snyder cofounded, with venture capitalists, a biotechnology firm, the Nova Pharmaceutical Corporation. Meanwhile, his laboratory at Johns Hopkins conducted research in a variety of areas. By the mid-1980s Snyder had mounted a challenge to the idea, born of observation, that brain cells would not reproduce. In 1990 he announced that his laboratory was nurturing colonies of them that were multiplying and producing neurotransmitters. A patent for a human cerebral cortex cell line was issued in 1993, with prospects for its medical use in brain injury or disease.

Snyder was aware that, as he expressed it, "some of the finest advances come from jumping fields." In the late 1980s new interest arose in the biological properties of nitric oxide (NO), a gas first discovered in the eighteenth century. Nitric oxide eventually provoked a torrent of research, based on its apparently fundamental significance as a regulator. Still regarded with skepticism by many in 1990, ten years later nitric oxide was implicated as having a role in blood circulation, immune system function, the action of nearly every orifice in the body, and pathological conditions from rheumatism to depression.

Snyder examined the role of nitric oxide in brain chemistry beginning in the late 1980s and initiated one of its major lines of research. Working from hints that nitric oxide is produced in the brain, Snyder, together with graduate student David Bredt, discovered the enzyme necessary for its synthesis, nitric oxide synthase (NOS). Its action in the brain is evanescent, but nitric oxide behaves like a neurotransmitter. Snyder has suggested a variety of implications for its use in neuromedicine, showing that it regulates aggressive and sexual behavior and mediates penile erection. The recent drug to combat impotence, sildenafil, enhances the effect of nitric oxide on vascular smooth muscle, facilitating blood flow to the penis. Nitric oxide also holds promise for advances in treating stroke, Alzheimer's and Parkinson's diseases, and other neurological conditions.

Snyder has frequently been described in attractive terms in the American popular press. "There is warmth about Snyder—reflected in his softness of voice, his thoughtfulness, his humor," writes Denise O'Grady, "a seemingly genuine interest in others." His marriage to Elaine Borko in 1962 produced two daughters. In spite of renown, he remained close to his home base and did not want to become, he once wrote, a "jet-set" scientist.

Since 1980 Snyder has served as director of the Department of Neuroscience and Distinguished Service Professor of Neuroscience, Pharmacology and Psychiatry at Johns Hopkins University. His participation in laboratory research continued to be profound but indirect, with all the bench work performed by his graduate students. After years in research, "I am still unable to dissect the major regions of a rat's brain," he has written, "a skill most of my students acquire during their first week."

# William Masters [1915–2001]

## Sex Research and Therapy

At the turn of the twentieth century, Sigmund Freud (p. 173) illuminated the fundamental role of sexuality in human psychology, the British physician Havelock Ellis wrote best-selling books about sex in the modern world, and Iwan Bloch in Germany penned huge tomes concerning the sexual life of humankind through the ages. In the United States, how married couples ought to copulate was the subject of books like Theodore Hendrik van Velde's *Ideal Marriage.* A modern taxonomy of the bedroom behavior of men and women was the accomplishment, at midcentury, of Alfred Kinsey.

Despite all this work, knowledge about the sexual act remained fairly rudimentary in scientific terms, known only through intriguing but unsystematic studies. A more detailed view, leading to new therapies and much discussion and controversy, emerged from the work of William Masters and his collaborator, Virginia Johnson.

Beginning in the mid-1950s Masters and Johnson studied the physiology of sexual intercourse in a laboratory setting. They subsequently focused on therapy, developing an approach, based on their findings, for classifying and treating sexual problems among couples. "By making the study of human sexuality respectable—and big business—Masters and Johnson set an inspiring example for countless others," writes John Heidenry, "and the decade [of the 1970s] was to witness the greatest blossoming of sexual research, experimentation, and activism in history." A generation later, they are still the figures of reference who helped enlighten a whole culture eager for a new openness about sexuality. In creating a new therapeutic modality, their influence was exceptional. At the same time the complexity of human sexuality, with its strong relationship to culture and subjective experience, resists reductionist incursions. As the story of Masters and Johnson illustrates, sexuality in the Western mind is durably confusing.

William Howell Masters II was born into a prosperous family in Cleveland, Ohio, on December 27, 1915. His father was Francis Wynne Masters, and his mother, Estabrooks Taylor. After elementary school in Kansas City, Masters went on to prep school in New Jersey before attending Hamilton College, where he studied science. He was on the debate team and was also an all-around athlete who played football, baseball, and basketball. After receiving his bachelor's degree in 1938, he went on to medical school at the University of Rochester. Here Masters came under the influence of George Washington Corner, a prominent anatomist who was studying the reproductive tracts of humans and animals.

Masters became aware of the paucity of information on human sexuality through early experimental work on the estrous cycle of the female rabbit. When Masters suggested studying the physiology of sexuality in men and women, Corner thoughtfully advised him to wait until he was forty years old and had established academic credentials. After taking his medical degree in 1943 from the University of Rochester, Masters served his internship and residency in obstetrics and gynecology at St. Louis Maternity and Barnes Hospital of the Washington University School of Medicine in St. Louis. Here he became an instructor 1947, and soon thereafter, associate professor of clinical obstetrics and gynecology.

Although Masters's early research focused on hormone replacement therapy, his interest in human sexuality abided. In 1954, the same year that Alfred Kinsey died, he undertook to study sexual response with the help of a small grant from the United States Institute of Health and with support, based on the principle of academic freedom, from Washington University. To avoid charges of immorality, Masters sought advice and consent from several local leaders, including the St. Louis police commissioner, the head of the local Roman Catholic archdiocese, and the publisher of a conservative newspaper.

Masters began his research with a program in which, over a period of about eighteen months, he observed all forms of sexual intercourse. He also interviewed a large number of prostitutes, from whom he gained considerable knowledge about techniques used to stimulate detumescent clients. Some of these modalities would later prove useful for therapeutic purposes. One further outcome of his research was that Masters became aware that he would need a female collaborator to better understand female sexual response. In 1956 he hired Virginia Eshelman Johnson. Born in 1925, Johnson was ten years younger than Masters. She had studied music at Drury College and had worked as a journalist and a band singer, but she held no university degree. She also had been married twice and was the mother of two children.

In 1957 Masters and Johnson began what turned out to be eleven years of research in a small laboratory. Their subjects were volunteers, drawn to the study mainly out of curiosity and, sometimes, sexual dysfunction. In the famous "Green Room," a diverse group of some seven hundred men and women ranging in age from eighteen to eighty-nine experienced in excess of ten thousand orgasms. Masters and Johnson observed at close range the various positions of intercourse as well as masturbation and extracoital forms of stimulation. In addition to filming the sexual act, they employed a variety of instruments to measure and record the physiology of sexual response. A recording drum could trace vaginal contractions and an electrocardiograph recorded heart activity. Blood volume change in the penis was measured. The physiological response of women during intercourse was viewed through a clear Lucite phallus equipped with a camera lens.

It should be said that Masters and Johnson were not the first to measure some of these variables. Robert Larou Dickinson, for example, in his *Atlas of Human Sex Anatomy,* published in 1933, also used a transparent phallus to illuminate the physiology of sexual intercourse. As in other aspects of Masters's sexual research, it was not originality but systematic pursuit and statistical analysis that were the key elements in creating a new authoritative view of sexuality.

As Masters and Johnson accumulated data, they developed a cycle of sexual response comprised of four stages: excitement, plateau, orgasm, and resolution. This basic four-phase cycle was not much different from a classification proposed by Albert Moll in 1912, but it was far better informed. Within this framework Masters and Johnson compiled a basic physiology of sexual response. Overall, they found a great deal of similarity between men and women. In their effort to overcome what they called "a massive state of ignorance,"—especially concerning female sexuality—they provided considerable demystification by linking physiologic response to behavior. One of Freud's ideas, for example, had been that orgasm was either clitoral or vaginal, with psychological implications. This proved a false dichotomy, however, at least from an observable distance. In addition, Masters and Johnson found that the clitoris is not stimulated directly by the penis—a "phallic fallacy"—but via the inner labia that are attached to the clitoral hood.

*Human Sexual Response* was published in 1966. In spite of its technical prose and fairly turgid style, the first printing sold out in a single week. The popularity of the book was due in great part to Masters and Johnson themselves, who were not wary of fame. With a dedication to sexual enlightenment, they actively sought venues in popular culture. Articles in major magazines predated the appearance of their book, and they readily took to television, radio, and other public forums to discuss their work. The reason for this was essentially that, unlike Alfred Kinsey, who was more or less content to describe sexual behavior, Masters and Johnson maintained a clinical perspective and sought to develop a therapeutic dimension.

Indeed, the more significant and most influential outcome of Masters and Johnson's work was a therapeutic approach specific to problems of sexuality. They began this work in 1959, when couples began arriving for treatment at their foundation in St. Louis. Masters and Johnson provided innovative therapy, with daily sessions and couples treated by both a male and female therapist. The therapy was strongly directive and aimed at modifying behavior, changing attitudes, and replacing an antagonistic sexual relationship with one that was more cooperative. First and foremost, the focus was not the impotent man or frigid woman, but the couple. In 1970 *Human Sexual Inadequacy* embodied their therapeutic ideas. Like their first book, it was well received and influential.

Not everyone approved of Masters and Johnson. They were "lambasted and lauded, lightning rods for controversy and criticism," writes Enid Nemy. Their early work was criticized by such figures as psychoanalyst Lester Farber and anthropologist Margaret Mead. The latter, who had years earlier objected to the work of Alfred Kinsey, denigrated Masters and Johnson for obtaining "a little not very exciting data on such matters as the circulatory and respiratory of sex arousal and the subsidence of sex excitement." Later, as icons of popular culture, Masters and Johnson became the subjects of journalistic irony and broad critiques. More significantly, few therapists could replicate the high rates of success reported by Masters and Johnson. Hyperbole in the world of sex research has historically been the rule rather than the exception; in 1987 Shere Hite, for example, would claim that 98 percent of American women were dissatisfied in their relationships with men. Similarly, Masters and Johnson's overly optimistic picture of therapy outcomes appeared too good to be true. Considerable gaps in the data provided in *Human Sexual Inadequacy* opened them to criticism from therapists who could not match their results. As it turned out, their standards for success were rather lower than they implied. All this led to a rancorous debate in sexology, a field that blossomed in the wake of Masters and Johnson's work and that abides today.

In spite of criticisms, William Masters and Virginia Johnson became unrivalled authorities. They published widely for a mass audience over the course of two decades, beginning with *The Pleasure Bond* in 1975, which focused on the importance of communication and commitment for couples. Their *Homosexuality in Perspective,* from 1979, was more controversial. In that volume, Masters and Johnson adopted the viewpoint that homosexuality is a learned behavior, and they suggested that therapy could change sexual orientation. This position, today often viewed as anachronistic, brought them a hail of criticism. Similarly, in *Crisis: Heterosexual Behavior in the Age of AIDS*, written with their colleague Robert Kolodny, they suggested that experts "gravely underestimated" the number of heterosexual HIV carriers in the United States. This grim outlook proved unwarranted for most groups of Americans, although, if anything, the authors underestimated the worldwide scope of the pandemic. (For their view that the AIDS virus might be transmitted via handling in food preparation or similar contact they were widely reproved.) An overview of Masters and Johnson's life work is contained in *Heterosexuality*, also written with Robert Kolodny, published in 1994.

It seems fitting that William Masters had a complex marital life. As a young man, he married Elisabeth Ellis, and with her raised two children. They were divorced in 1971, the year in which he wed Virginia Johnson. Masters and Johnson remained married to each other until their amicable divorce in 1993. Masters's third marriage, the same year, was to Geraldine Baker Oliver, whom he had known in medical school.

With a rich voice and quiet demeanor, William Masters presented the very image of the authoritative doctor. His attitude toward sexuality, wrote Edward M. Brecher, evolved from "his ability to set aside, at least in his professional life, all of [the] common reactions to sexuality, and to substitute for them the kind of attitude that scientists customarily hold toward digestion, circulation, and other physiological phenomena." But this didn't work at parties. He found it difficult to socialize, Masters once said, because, "The conversation always drifted to sex, much to my frustration."

The Masters and Johnson Institute, unlike the Kinsey Institute, did not become an endowed research or therapeutic organization. Indeed, the St. Louis institute suffered from lack of funding as sex therapy mutated and expanded. In 1994 Masters shut the institute down. Although for many years he had worked seven days a week, including holidays, he was already semiretired, and as he explained, "I'm tired." Suffering from Parkinson's disease, Masters eventually moved to Tucson, Arizona. There he died on February 16, 2001.

# Gerald M. Edelman [b. 1929]

## The Chemistry of Immunity and the Biology of Neurology

Gerald M. Edelman has forged two broad paths in a career in which he moved from immunology to neuroscience. He won the Nobel Prize in 1972 for clarifying the chemistry behind the great diversity of antibodies by which the body recognizes invading organisms. Edelman went on to work in neuroscience, where he developed, over the course of decades, a general theory of brain function. His biological model remains controversial, and to what degree it turns out to be right remains to be seen. But Edelman's "neural Darwinism" represents a prominent effort to redefine conceptual analysis of the brain in the context of an ongoing revolution in neuroscience.

Gerald Maurice Edelman was born on July 1, 1929, in New York City, the son of Anna Freedman and Edward Edelman. His father was a general practitioner, and the family divided its time between a home in Queens, in the relatively poor neighborhood of Ozone Park, and another residence in more prosperous Long Beach, Long Island. His father was an amateur musician, and Gerald himself excelled on the violin and considered a musical career. Although an excellent student, Edelman was not accepted at the prestigious universities to which he applied, and so he attended Ursinus College, a small institution in rural Pennsylvania. There he majored in chemistry and graduated in 1950. He went on to attend medical school at the University of Pennsylvania, receiving his medical degree in 1954. He interned at Massachusetts General Hospital before being conscripted in 1955 in the wake of the Korean War.

Edelman's interest in the immune system developed during his service in the army, when he was posted to France and worked at the American Hospital in Paris. Advances in biochemistry had made available more detailed knowledge about antibodies, but their structure and design remained fairly indistinct. Returning to the United States in 1957, Edelman began working as a graduate fellow at the Rockefeller Institute. Known for research in immunology, the Rockefeller was where Karl Landsteiner, the Austrian-born chemist and physician, had first demonstrated the specificity of antibody reactions, about 1917. After receiving a doctorate in physical chemistry from the Rockefeller Institute in 1960, Edelman remained there as

assistant professor. He was named associate professor in 1963 and full professor in 1966.

Antibodies, as they were understood when Edelman began his research, mediate the specific immune response to antigens—that is, all substances the body regards as foreign. Like other researchers, Edelman was drawn to the theory of clonal selection proposed in the 1950s principally by Niels Jerne and Macfarlane Burnet (p. 280). This theory suggested that the specific immune reaction begins when an antigen—often a protein—is recognized by one among a huge number of different circulating antibodies. That particular antibody is thereby selected and subsequently reproduced in large numbers to tag invaders, which are then disabled or destroyed. Immune response via clonal selection had started to gain respect as experimental data to support it accumulated. But in terms of the system's basic chemistry, much remained to be learned.

Antibodies are blood proteins that belong to the group of large and complex molecules known as immunoglobulins. The various classes of immunoglobulins—today we count five—resemble one another in overall shape, but each has different functions and is activated by specific types of antigens. By the 1950s several classes of immunoglobulins had been discovered, but they could not be purified. A breakthrough came in 1958 when British chemist Rodney Porter found ways to cleave immunoglobulin G (IgG) molecules into three predictable fragments and to show that two of the fragments were antigen binding while the third was not. This functional difference formed the experimental basis of much research, and Edelman's own original work began at this juncture.

One common hypothesis concerning the structure of immunoglobulins suggested they were comprised of single long chains of polypeptides. Edelman challenged this concept in 1959 and went on to suggest that IgG might be comprised of several such chains. By 1961 he had succeeded in splitting IgG into separate chains that he labeled "heavy" and "light" in terms of molecular weight. Each chain might vary somewhat and so possess specific antigen-binding properties. This picture was further clarified in 1963, when Rodney Porter showed that the IgG molecule was actually comprised of a pair of identical heavy chains and a pair of identical light chains. This became understood as the basic structure for all classes of immunoglobulins.

Edelman's work contributed not only to defining the overall structure of immunoglobulins, but also to understanding how the body generates its great diversity of antibodies. Clonal selection theory demanded some genetic mechanism for creating a huge number of preexisting antibodies, each with some distinctive binding site, able to capture specific invading organisms. Macfarlane Burnet himself had suggested that mutating genes in the immunoglobulin-producing cells might be responsible. Some scientists hypothesized that as many as 6,000 genes might be involved—a large number, but not entirely implausible.

Edelman, however, had a different and more elegant answer that required detailed analysis of a single molecule. In 1965 he and his colleagues—"mad as we were," he later remarked—undertook to analyze the precise order of amino acids in an entire immunoglobulin molecule. The full sequence, about 1,300 amino acids, was elucidated by 1969. The most interesting of several results to emerge from this task was a way to understand the patterns of amino acid variation in the constant and variable regions of these proteins. The "internal periodicity" of the amino acid sequences was too great to be the result of chance mutations. This suggested to Edelman, and to other researchers about the same time, that the process involves an evolutionary development known as "gene duplication" that facilitates genetic recombination on a somatic level. Briefly, several genes are programmed to recombine, over and over, during somatic development; they produce by mutation the great array of variations that show up as variable regions on the light chains of immunoglobulin molecules. These regions serve as recognition sites for antigens. The genes for these light chains fuse with genes that code for the heavy polypeptide chains; together they manufacture an almost unlimited variety of antibody proteins. The process as Edelman envisioned and described it was in large measure correct, and today forms the foundation of the basic chemistry of antibody structure.

Historically, Edelman's work must be viewed as part of a larger restructuring of the concept of the immune system in the second half of the twentieth century. Originally, immune response was predominantly understood to be a means by which the body defends itself against invading microorganisms—and popularly, it often still is. But its complexity and multiple functions render that idea too simple. Edelman, like several other researchers, was struck by the ways in which the immune system is best viewed as a recognition system. As early as 1970 he suggested that the "special genetic mechanisms" that give rise to the immune system might also be found at the root of "other systems of pattern recognition"—most significantly, the central nervous system.

The potential significance of this concept was so great that Edelman eventually shifted the focus of his research from immunology to neurobiology. His work in cell-cell recognition and developmental neurobiology formed the bridge for this shift. Edelman isolated several types of cell adhesion molecules (CAMs) from tissue, including neuronal cell adhesion molecules (N-CAMs). He suggested that what he called substrate adhesion molecules (SAMs) link cells together to provide a matrix for neuronal networks.

Edelman eventually undertook to develop a general theory of brain function, and he persisted in this effort over the course of more than twenty years. Although his theory was rooted in the picture of the immune system that he himself had helped develop, Edelman also examined the philosophical and physiological models that had been proposed for the brain since the seventeenth century. He noted that much recent research failed to adequately take into account the theory of evolution, which he regarded as "a theory absolutely essential to understanding the matter of the mind." Rockefeller University—the Rockefeller Institute changed its name in 1965—accommodated Edelman's aspirations in neurobiology and provided him with his own Neurosciences Institute, which he served as director from 1981.

Edelman laid out the major elements of his theory in several books. *Neural Darwinism* appeared in 1987 and excited considerable debate. It was followed in 1988 by *Topobiology*, which presents his account of the development and morphology of the brain and nervous system. In *The Remembered Present*, published in 1989, Edelman outlines a theory of how perceptual categories arise and how these could lead to a higher order of consciousness and to capabilities such as generalization and self-reference. In addition to these technical works, Edelman also wrote *Bright Air, Brilliant Fire* in 1992 as a summary for a lay audience. Most recently, he has published *A Universe of Consciousness: How Matter Becomes Imagination*, in collaboration with Giulio Tononi.

In broad outline, Edelman views the brain as "a self-organizing system" and suggests that considerable individual variation in organization exists between any two brains. The basic structure of the brain is genetically determined, but its specific development is established through selection on a somatic level. Through what he calls "experiential selection," a process that takes place throughout life, neuronal groups "compete" and are constantly modified. Although Edelman's concepts of "maps" and "reentrant signaling" are not easy to understand, they delineate a dynamic process that could account for ordinary perception as well as for category building and higher forms of consciousness. "Learning by selection" helps explain the flexibility and adaptability of the brain, Edelman believes, as well as the individuality that is its hallmark, especially in complex species like human beings.

The theory of neuronal group selection (TNGS), as Edelman calls it, also involves a substantial critique of much speculation in neuroscience concerning the brain. In general, Edelman suggests that brain organization is fluid rather than rigid and should not be compared to a switchboard or computer. Edelman objects strenuously to the idea that neural processes represent "algorithms," and he points out the errors of what he calls "machine functionalism" when it comes to describing the brain. Edelman suggests that the dynamics of the brain are chemical and that the central nervous system is better envisioned as a jungle or rain forest than an abundant number of electrical switches activated by computer programs.

Edelman is not the first to apply Darwinian principles to thinking about the brain, but his major tenets are original in relying on the concept of somatic selection. And his expositions, although sometimes hard to follow, are consistently imaginative and account for the complex skein of human experience in ways that other, more reductionist theories do not.

With the perspective of more than a decade since his first major work in neuroscience, Edelman's theories have proved controversial but much discussed, durable but unproven. He has been criticized for obscurity of language and concept. Francis Crick, the molecular biologist turned neuroscientist, famously described the theory as "neural Edelmanism." He has also been taken to task for ignoring other biologically based theories in neuroscience and for using "out-of-date caricatures, so he ends up unwittingly reinventing the wheels that cognitive scientists have been considering, improving and replacing for years." But among those who found his ideas of great interest was Oliver Sacks, the eminent neurologist. Sacks called *Bright Air, Brilliant Fire* "strenuous and sometimes maddening, and one must struggle to understand it. . . ." He added, though, "If one struggles, if one reads and reads again the stubborn paragraphs finally yield their meaning and a brilliant and captivating new version of the mind emerges."

"One must be dazzled, even disoriented, upon meeting Gerald Edelman," wrote David Hellerstein in 1988. Edelman is famously possessed of a powerful and dominating personality, and is considered by detractors an "empire-building egomaniac," but by others a genius. In 1950 he married Maxine Morrison; they had three children. Edelman remained at Rockefeller University until 1991, when he moved his Neuroscience Institute to La Jolla, California, where he is chairman of the Department of Neurobiology at Scripps Institute.

# Harold Varmus  [b. 1939]

## Molecular Pathways to Cancer

A unified explanation of cancer, understood as uncontrolled cell proliferation, did not come easy to modern medicine. In 1909 Peyton
Rous (p. 261) demonstrated that an infectious "filterable virus" could
cause a type of sarcoma in poultry, but he was not believed, not least
because most cancers do not appear to be contagious or the result of
infection. Evidence long implicated environmental agents such as chimney
ash, but how this or other chemicals might cause malignant tumors
remained a mystery. Some cancers clearly had a hereditary component.
Through most of the twentieth century no comprehensive explanation of
cancer withstood scrutiny.

By the 1960s, however, molecular biology set a new agenda for cancer
research as discoveries clarified the mechanisms of cell metabolism and
the complex ways by which cells grow and divide. At the same time, better
tools and greater funding accelerated investigation and yielded results in
related domains, including medical genetics, tumor virology, and cell biology. The key to constructing a new basic theory of cancer—if one is to
choose among significant milestones—was quite possibly the discovery in
1976 of the cellular origin of cancer-causing genes. The "proto-oncogene
theory" of cancer causation, which shaped so much subsequent research,
is owed principally to Harold Varmus and Michael Bishop.

Harold Eliot Varmus was born in Oceanside, New York, on December
18, 1939. His father, Frank Varmus, was a physician; his mother, Beatrice
Barasch, was a psychiatric social worker. Harold spent most of his
childhood in Freeport, Long Island, and attended high school there. His
commitment to science came rather late. At Amherst College, although
he was considering medicine, he studied English and was editor of the
campus newspaper, and his undergraduate thesis concerned the novels of
Charles Dickens. He received his bachelor's degree magna cum laude in
1961. He went on to graduate school at Harvard University, where he studied Anglo-Saxon and metaphysical poetry for a year, receiving a master's
degree in 1962. Taking stock, he viewed his friends as "more engaged in the
real world," he once said. "That provoked a sort of jealousy, and I decided
to go to medical school after all." He entered Columbia University's College

of Physicians and Surgeons, received his medical degree in 1966, and took his internship and residency at Columbia's Presbyterian Hospital.

The dazzling developments in molecular biology coming to fruition during the 1960s led Varmus to abandon clinical medicine for research. In 1968 he received the opportunity to work at the National Institutes of Health, in part because he opposed the Vietnam War and did not want to serve in the military. The NIH would offer a working education in scientific method to physicians who wanted to do research. Varmus gained his scientific credentials through work in the laboratory of Ira Pastan, an endocrinologist studying the genetics of thyroid function. He took up one of the hot topics in molecular biology, namely, the way in which a "signaling molecule"—cyclic AMP—can regulate gene expression. He found this work to be "an aesthetic merger of genetics with molecular biology" and immensely gratifying.

By 1969 Varmus's own objective was clear. He wanted to study the possible genetic basis of cancer. He sought and found a congenial group on the West Coast and took a position as postdoctoral fellow and lecturer at the University of California in San Francisco. Here his significant research came on the heels of recent tantalizing hypotheses concerning the origin of cancer. He began his investigations in the laboratory of Michael Bishop, a virologist and biochemist; their relationship soon became one of coequals, and they would make their major discoveries as a team.

At center stage in much cancer research among virologists, as Bishop and Varmus began to work together, was the virus that infects poultry discovered by Peyton Rous in 1909. The Rous sarcoma virus (RSV), like some other tumor-causing viruses, was known to consist not of DNA, but of RNA—ribonucleic acid. As early as 1963 Howard Temin had suggested that this virus's modus operandi would involve inserting itself into a host's DNA, from which redoubt it could reproduce viral RNA. This idea, controversial and at first largely rejected, was confirmed about 1970 with the discovery of reverse transcriptase, an enzyme that directs just such an operation. Temin thereupon put forward what he called the "protovirus" model of tumor causation, suggesting that information from viral RNA is copied into a host cell's DNA, where it might remain until expressed as a cancer-causing, infectious agent.

Another, somewhat similar hypothesis about cancer causation that emerged about the same time was the "virogene-oncogene" model. This theory, associated with George Todaro and Robert Huebner, suggested that the mammalian genome had acquired viral gene fragments over the course of evolution. Ordinarily dormant, such genes might be activated by exogenous carcinogens such as radiation, various chemicals, or perhaps viruses. This theory gave rise to a series of questions concerning the operation and origin of cancer-causing genes that needed experimental confirmation.

To test the virogene-oncogene model, Varmus and Bishop from about 1971 took steps to demonstrate the presence in animal cells of specific DNA sequences that derived from viral RNA. This required techniques that allowed a single viral gene to be compared with the DNA of an animal that the virus was known to infect—not a simple matter at the time. Several years of work were required, and Varmus and Bishop operated in informal cooperation with several other laboratories. They continued to employ the Rous sarcoma virus as a model. From this virus the "src" gene (pronounced "sark," and named with reference to "sarcoma") was successfully isolated and used to develop a highly sensitive and reliable probe in 1974 by Dominique Stehelin, a French scientist in their laboratory.

But this effort had a surprising result. The src gene that Varmus and Bishop expected to find in infected chickens actually belonged to the animal's normal genome. In fact, it could be found in other birds and animals as well—indeed, in every species tested. "From these findings," wrote Varmus later, "we drew conclusions that seem even bolder in retrospect, knowing they are correct, than they did at the time."

In essence, Varmus and Bishop now argued for a new model that did not, as a general rule, involve an infective agent. Rather, the viral gene that caused Rous's chicken sarcoma probably originated in the genome of ordinary cells and was only later picked up by a retrovirus. In addition the src gene's conservation through evolution and its presence in most animal species indicate that it plays some central role in cell metabolism. When this ordinary gene malfunctions, it is transformed into an "oncogene" that can cause tumor formation. Moreover, if there were one such gene in normal DNA, there were likely to be other "proto-oncogenes"—genes that under certain circumstances will be expressed, most commonly as mutations, subverting ordinary metabolism and leading to cancer.

Although their theory was not without critics, its potential significance was apparent when Bishop and Varmus reported their results in 1976 in a paper published in *Nature*. "More than any other single experiment," writes Robert Weinberg, "this work defined a milestone in twentieth-century cancer research because it refocused thinking on the ultimate origins of cancer, directing attention to a site deep inside the cell." Neither the invading virus nor any of the multitude of environmental carcinogens, but rather specific lengths of DNA henceforth became the center of attention in cancer research. The work of Bishop and Varmus had produced a powerful, if preliminary, overview of how cancer develops.

Cancer, as this view evolved, represents a series of events at the level of the genome. Susceptibilities to some cancers are genetic and heritable, but cancer can also arise through chance, or, more often, when promoted by insults from without, such as the constant tissue wounding caused by cigarette smoking. This theory corresponds nicely, in general, with much research, both contemporary and historical. Environmental mutagens clearly played a role in many cancers, but the incriminating statistics of exposure vis-à-vis pathology had previously only underscored the fact that the mechanism of causation, at a cellular level, was unknown. Viruses had been implicated, but few could be harvested from patients or experimental animals. The new model that Varmus and Bishop proposed had a coherent fit with the results of older theories and experiments, and also took advantage of the most advanced developments in biochemistry and molecular biology. It became the basis of what Joan Fujimura describes as "the oncogene bandwagon" that won considerable funding and attracted researchers from diverse fields.

Varmus and Bishop were awarded the Nobel Prize in 1989, thirteen years after their major discovery. So fruitful was their work that the award was not unexpected, but so many of their findings had emerged from other significant discoveries that it did not please everyone. While Howard Temin had become a Nobel laureate for his work on RNA viruses (he would die prematurely in 1994), virologist Peter Duesberg, whose research had supported Temin's, was unhappy to be overlooked. Most displeased was Dominique Stehelin, the French researcher who had conducted some of the crucial laboratory experiments with Varmus and Bishop. Indeed, his loud complaints underscored a certain dissatisfaction with the dominance of American scientists in cancer research, due in part to their tremendous advantage in funding. Varmus's Nobel Prize acceptance speech was a model of attribution, as he cited more than forty other researchers whose work had led him and Bishop to their basic discoveries.

Still a laboratory scientist, by the 1980s Varmus was moving into the domain of scientific policy. He served on various panels and chaired the scientific advisory group that recommended the name *human immunodeficiency virus* (HIV) for the virus that causes AIDS. In 1993 he became the first Nobel laureate to head the National Institutes of Health, the government institution that funds biomedical research. He brought both prestige and a strong stance in support of basic research to the NIH and was well received by the biomedical community. He remained at the NIH until 2000, when he became president and chief executive officer of the Memorial Sloan-Kettering Cancer Center in New York.

In a number of ways—by background, accomplishment, and career path—Varmus's life and work epitomize the medical researcher in the United States at the end of the twentieth century. Like a great number of other brilliant scientists, he is of Jewish and Eastern European ancestry; he is also the son of a physician. He was trained by the National Institutes of Health and is, in sum, a product of the well-financed American scientific establishment. In 1969 Varmus married Constance Casey, an editor and writer, and they have two sons.

Varmus maintained his interest in literature, and in his Nobel Prize acceptance speech he compared cancer to Grendel in *Beowulf:* "In our adventures, we have only seen our monster more clearly and described his scales and fangs in new ways—ways that reveal a cancer cell to be, like Grendel, a distorted version of our normal selves."

# Raymond Damadian [b. 1936]

## Magnetic Resonance Imaging

Medicine owes most of its tools for imaging the human body to twentieth-century physics. Within weeks of their discovery in 1895, the mysterious X rays of Wilhelm Conrad Röntgen (p. 100) were used in diagnosis. Decades later, laser technology was a practical result of quantum mechanics. Ultrasonography emerged from problem solving in submarine detection, and CT scans capitalized on computer technology. Medicine's most significant recent technology, used for visualizing the interior of the human body in three-dimensional detail, is magnetic resonance imaging (MRI).

MRI makes use of nuclear magnetic resonance (NMR), the capacity of atomic nuclei to absorb and emit characteristic radio waves. Scans using MRI show high-contrast details of organs and muscles, and can detect the smallest plaques and tumors. They enable physicians to see through bone and visualize its marrow, and to distinguish blood vessels within flesh. Although NMR was proposed as early as the 1920s and was used in physics and chemistry research from the 1940s, not until the 1970s was its value for medicine apparent. The recognition of its potential and the development of a useful machine are owed in greatest measure to Raymond Damadian.

A physician trained in chemistry and biophysics, Damadian was the first to conceive of MRI as a diagnostic tool, one that held special promise for detecting tumors. He also built the first MRI machine for medical use. "No one else," writes Betty Ann Kevles, "had the imagination, or hubris to...jump to the construction of a whole-body machine." A visionary inventor with a background in medicine and biophysics, Raymond Damadian founded the FONAR Corporation, a major manufacturer of MRI scanners.

Raymond V. Damadian, an eldest son, was born in Manhattan, New York, on March 16, 1936. His father was an Armenian whose family had immigrated to the United States during the Turkish persecutions in the early twentieth century; his mother, Odette Yazedjian, was French-Armenian. Raymond was close to both his parents, as well as to his maternal grandmother, whose death from breast cancer when he was ten years old strongly affected him. But his intellectual outlook was influenced by growing up in the working-class section of Forest Hills, Queens. "Most of our neighbors were of Jewish descent," he remembers, "very much interested in traditional goals of scholarship and high achievement." From age eight Raymond also showed exceptional talent for music. He studied violin for eight years at the Juilliard School, the prestigious conservatory, and for a time hoped for a career as a musician. But he also did well academically and, under a Ford Foundation scholarship, entered the University of Wisconsin at age sixteen. He studied mathematics and chemistry, and after receiving his bachelor's degree in 1956, he decided to enter medical school. Damadian returned to New York to study at the Albert Einstein College of Medicine, and was awarded his medical degree in 1960.

Damadian's postgraduate education reflects his several talents. Attracted by such cutting-edge disciplines as immunology and transplantation, he chose to enter research rather than clinical medicine. During a year at Washington University School of Medicine he studied nephrology. He went on to Harvard University as a fellow in biophysics. Entering the Air Force Medical Corps in 1965, Damadian undertook research in physiological chemistry at the School of Aerospace Medicine at Brooks Air Force Base in Texas. In 1967 he took a faculty position with the State University of New York at the Downstate Medical Center in Brooklyn.

Damadian's work early in his career strongly foreshadowed his development of MRI. One of the first problems he tackled was the so-called sodium pump—the hypothetical mechanism that keeps sodium outside cells while retaining potassium within. A basic feature of cellular chemistry, the "pump" had been assumed since the 1940s to derive its energy from ATP molecules, the cell's basic energy source. But Damadian was intrigued by the absence of a specific known structure to accomplish this, and he investigated the problem with some thoroughness. He came to believe that the underlying concept of a sodium pump was mistaken. In this he followed physiologist Gilbert Ling, who had developed a controversial theory of the cell. Damadian eventually devised what could be described as an alternate theory of the cellular pump, the ion exchanger resin theory. Simply put, the theory holds that potassium, as a charged molecule, accumulates inside the cell by attaching to molecules of the opposite charge. The cell, sustained by water, prefers potassium ions to sodium ions because, when fully hydrated, sodium is a larger molecule that occupies more space than potassium.

Through this work Damadian became familiar with nuclear magnetic resonance. In 1969 he learned of experiments to measure sodium and

potassium concentrations in human organs that used a device known as a nuclear magnetic resonance spectrometer. This was interesting but not altogether surprising news. NMR was used frequently by organic chemists as a tool for analyzing compounds. A sufficiently strong magnetic field will cause the nuclei of elements to align in direct relation to it, like compass needles pointing north. Because they also possess "spin," the nuclei "wobble." Each element wobbles, or precesses, at a characteristic frequency that can be elicited as a signal.

The prospect of distinguishing different tissues using NMR led Damadian to consider the medical implications. He thought first of cancer. X rays could not visualize most tumors, especially in early stages, nor in many cases could the more recently developed CT scans. But if cancerous cells could be distinguished from normal cells on the basis of sodium or potassium composition, Damadian immediately saw the possibilities for a new machine using NMR. The characteristic resonances of soft tissues could be generated as a computerized scan. Cancerous cells, with different water composition, would resonate differently from normal cells. "Once I made the hit with cancer," he later said, "I began thinking of its applications in other diseases, such as kidney disease and mental disease."

Damadian's view of the potential for medical NMR was not shared by others, but experiments with mice followed, and Damadian published "Tumor Detection by Nuclear Magnetic Resonance" in *Science* on March 19, 1971. There Damadian wrote suggestively that, "In principle, nuclear magnetic resonance (NMR) techniques combine many of the desirable features of an external probe for the detection of internal cancers." The paper garnered skepticism.

Building a machine for human imaging involved resolving a great number of problems, not the least of which was scale. What Damadian envisioned many of his colleagues viewed as impractical. A full-body imaging machine was seen, writes Rodney Roemer, "as not only impossible but lunatic. This was like comparing a minnow to Moby Dick." Nevertheless, Damadian was not alone in thinking about the applications of

NMR to medicine. Paul Lauterbur in the United States and Peter Mansfield in England learned of Damadian's early demonstrations of NMR with mice. Each began work on a scanner.

The development of MRI for scanning the human body, from Damadian's first patent application until the first image was obtained, took over five years. In 1972 Damadian applied for a patent on a three-dimensional in vivo scan for an "Apparatus and Method for Detecting Cancer Tissue." The patent application included a technique for focusing the scan—a critical aspect of any such machine. This method he would call FONAR, an alternating acronym for *field focused nuclear magnetic resonance*. By the time the patent was granted in 1974, Damadian had demonstrated that NMR could be used to distinguish a wide variety of tumorous tissues. The rate of "relaxation time" for breast cancer tissue, for example, was much different from the rate for normal breast tissue.

The next step, constructing a prototype, was a huge undertaking. For human body scanning, Damadian decided he would need a powerful 5,000-gauss superconducting magnet. The coils of such magnets are comprised of material such as niobium-titanium, which when cooled to a temperature approaching absolute zero conducts electricity without resistance; they generate powerful magnetic fields for their size. By 1976 Damadian decided that, in addition, two thermoslike "Dewar" flasks were needed to contain the liquid helium used to cool the magnet. Each of these would weigh 2,500 pounds and stand ten feet tall and six feet wide. (Only one of these was ultimately used because the team was unable to develop a satisfactory vacuum in the other.) Together with graduate students Larry Minkoff and Michael Goldsmith, Damadian worked virtually nonstop for the next two years. He was in constant competition with Lauterbur, who made a number of original contributions for imaging NMR, but toward whom Damadian developed considerable antagonism.

Throughout development of the machine that Damadian named "Indomitable," he was hampered by lack of funding. In principle, the project might have benefited greatly from the United States government's "war on cancer" announced in 1971. But Damadian received just a small grant from the National Institutes of Health, and this only after appealing directly to President Richard Nixon. His own originality and his immodest scientific style hobbled Damadian in seeking support through grants. Damadian's search for funds, constant and idiosyncratic, is recounted in Sonny Kleinfield's popular account of MRI, *A Machine Called Indomitable*.

The completed MRI whole-body scanner was first tested in 1977. A dead turkey was the first patient, and Damadian himself stepped into the scanner on May 11, 1977. His bulk made this effort a failure, but there were no ill effects. Not until July was the machine's signal properly tuned to provide an image of Larry Minkoff, and Damadian recorded in his notebook:

4:45 AM FANTASTIC SUCCESS
First Human Image
Complete in Amazing Detail
Showing Heart
Lungs
Vertebra
Musculature

Rather than license the scanner for manufacture, Damadian decided to develop the product himself. FONAR was incorporated in 1978, and two years later the company offered the "QED 80" for sale. Imaging was repeatedly improved, and soon MRI became a much-desired medical tool used with great benefit in distinguishing between different types of soft tissue. MRI was a clear improvement over computerized tomography—the CT scan—for imaging features of the brain, and was a better diagnostic tool for a variety of tumors. It did not displace the CT scan, though, which by 1980 was available in most hospitals. Indeed, the latter prepared the way for MRI, in terms both of cost and of laying out new frontiers in terms of the potential uses.

Patent infringement suits are today a predictable part of introducing medical technology. By 1983, when a number of companies had entered the MRI marketplace, FONAR was ready to take them to court. Damadian had protected his machine with a solid group of patents. With some competitors he made financial settlements. General Electric continued litigation but lost its fight in court and eventually was compelled to pay FONAR over $100 million in 1991.

Raymond Damadian remains the head of FONAR. In 1988 he was awarded the National Medal of Technology, and the next year he was inducted into the National Inventors Hall of Fame. As a medical student he had married Donna Terry, and they had three children, two sons and a daughter. Damadian emerges in various profiles as brilliant but difficult, dedicated but self-absorbed, far-sighted but at times grandiose. "I was called a lunatic, a crackpot," he has recalled. "I was the madman."

# Bert Vogelstein [b. 1949]

## A Genetic Explanation for Cancer

Cancer arises, as matters are understood today, when key genes malfunction. Most types have some environmental trigger, while genetic components can render an individual susceptible or even virtually fated to develop certain tumors. This broad view derives largely from research that began in the 1960s amidst a host of advances in molecular biology. It was consolidated on a theoretical plane by such figures as Harold Varmus (p. 351), whose work connected cancer to genes associated with growth and communication between and within cells.

Applying this basic knowledge to treat human cancers—a leap from the laboratory to the patient—has been long desired and long promised. One important stream of research has its source in the model of colon cancer developed in the late 1980s and derived from correlations of clinical findings with genetic changes tracked over time. The principal figure in this work was a physician who turned to research at Johns Hopkins University: Bert Vogelstein.

Bert Vogelstein was born on June 2, 1949. He is the son of a lawyer and descendant of a long line of well-known rabbis. A legal career was also Bert's first choice before he became interested in science. He has described an unusual childhood in which he was close to his parents and excelled as a student, but had few fast friends. Some days he did not attend school but went to the public library to read. At the University of Pennsylvania he majored in mathematics, earning a bachelor's degree early, and spent a year as a graduate student, also in mathematics. But at last he applied to medical school, returning to Baltimore to attend Johns Hopkins and receiving his medical degree in 1974. Vogelstein took a residency in pediatrics at Johns Hopkins Hospital before working for two years, from 1976 to 1978, as a research associate at the National Cancer Institute. His subsequent decision to study cancer emerged from harrowing experiences with children suffering from the disease.

In coming to cancer research when he did in the late 1970s, Vogelstein benefited from a generation of advances in molecular biology. Genes were increasingly manipulable. They could be isolated and multiplied using recombinant techniques and studied in a variety of ways. From 1978 the

nucleotide sequences that comprise any particular stretch of DNA could be read, base by base. This advance soon led, on a technical level, to the development of restriction fragment length polymorphisms (known as RFLPs or "riflips"), which made it possible to recognize and map specific genes and their variant forms, or alleles. This technology—and more soon to follow—represented a long-desired bridge between the individual and the human genome.

Indeed, Vogelstein's achievement would derive from his insight into the evolving possibilities of investigating cancer using the tools of molecular biology. Most significantly, he began to work directly with human cancers. This was not then common in molecular biology, and Vogelstein had some trouble, in early years, funding this research. The ability to trace human genetic mutations to pathology, inherited or acquired, was both novel and of historic significance, as Vogelstein realized. The situation was in a sense analogous to the revolution in medicine in the early nineteenth century when Parisian doctors began linking specific diseases to physiological changes found at autopsy.

A direct influence on Vogelstein was the work of Alfred Knudson with the cancer known as retinoblastoma. In most cases, this childhood cancer—in which a malignant tumor arises on the retina of one or both eyes—was clearly inherited, but it could also arise spontaneously. Knudson's statistical analysis in 1971 suggested that two separate mutations on a single chromosome might be responsible. This hypothesis was ignored until experimental evidence validated it in 1982. Vogelstein, as well as other researchers, realized that this progressive "two-hit" theory might apply to other cancers as well. In 1982 Vogelstein decided to investigate colon cancer.

A major disease, colon cancer is exceptionally vicious because, like lung cancer, it often goes undetected until it metastasizes, or spreads to other sites in the body. Still, the disease was known to develop in stages, progressing from harmless polyp to malignant tumor. Vogelstein and his colleagues began harvesting tumor tissue at various stages from patients undergoing operations for colon cancer, and searching for genes gone awry. They were able to focus on genes found along chromosomes 5, 17, and 18. Vogelstein detected the presence of a mutated gene in cells taken from some twenty-two of thirty tumors—a spectacular finding. "Our results support a model," he wrote, "in which accumulated alterations affecting at least one dominant-acting [gene] and several tumor-suppressor genes are responsible for the development of colorectal cancer." The accumulation of mutant genes over time had a good prospective fit with puzzling clinical aspects of colon cancer—its stagewise development and the fact that it can take years to progress to malignancy.

What was true for colon cancer could be expected to apply to other cancers as well, and the success of Vogelstein's multifaceted approach created a prominent line of investigation that was widely imitated. In the stepwise model of colon cancer, several genes are affected over time. For colorectal cancer, Vogelstein and his colleagues showed that the first event was usually the mutation, in a single cell, of a specific tumor suppressor gene known as adenomatous polyposis coli (APC). This defect could be inherited or acquired and would lead to cell proliferation. Activation of the "K-ras oncogene" would be the next event and would result in development within the colon of a large benign polyp. Loss of the tumor suppressor genes on chromosome 18 and of the "p53" tumor suppressor gene on chromosome 17 ultimately made that cell erupt into a malignant cancer.

At the same time, Vogelstein's work continued to clarify the problem of inherited susceptibility to the various cancers. His discovery in 1990 of the overall significance of p53 had cast light on the power of the tumor suppressor genes. About three years later, Vogelstein isolated genes that appeared to belong to a completely different group, and they became known as the "mismatch-repair genes." He found that a small but signifi-cant percentage of cases of colon cancer are due to inheritance of mutant copies of such genes. Such mutations could be detected in potential vic-tims, at least in principle. As a consequence, the publication in *Science* on May 7, 1993, of "Genetic Mapping of a Locus Predisposing to Human Colorectal Cancer" represented a landmark in recent research, a robust link between laboratory and clinical medicine concerning a fatal and prominent form of cancer.

Put in broad terms, the work of Vogelstein (and, it should be acknowl-edged, many others) laid a foundation for greater advances not only in the theory of carcinogenesis, but also in the treatment and prevention of most of the major and minor cancers. "By the early 1990s," writes Michael Wald-holz, "Vogelstein's multistep model of cancer genesis, so rational, elegant and provable, was embraced by nearly every major basic cancer research lab in the United States and abroad." Vogelstein became the researcher most often cited in the biological sciences, and he was widely regarded as a can-didate for the Nobel Prize. He remained a central figure in cancer research through the rest of the decade and into the twenty-first century.

By 1999 Vogelstein held a joint appointment as professor of oncology and professor of pathology at the Johns Hopkins University School of Medicine and as an investigator with the Howard Hughes Medical Insti-tute. Considered highly competitive and often described as a workaholic, Vogelstein's personal style is, by contrast, subdued and even self-deprecat-ing. He married Ilene Cardin in 1971, and they have three children.

# Robert Gallo [b. 1937]

# Luc Montagnier [b. 1932]

## The Contentious Discovery of Human Immunodeficiency Virus (HIV)

In the early 1980s acquired immune deficiency syndrome (AIDS) emerged as a deadly pandemic and dimmed the unrealistic hope of forever conquering infectious disease. In the United States and Europe AIDS appeared first among homosexual men, while in Africa and elsewhere it developed as a heterosexual illness. The cause, as it turned out, is a virus, transmitted principally through exchange of body fluids. In several ways AIDS is an ideal example of a new contemporary disease: it is an artifact of imperialism, promulgated via international travel and trade, and spread primarily by specific kinds of compulsive drug use and sexual behavior.

Two virologists are most famously and closely associated with discovering the human immunodeficiency virus (HIV) that causes AIDS: the French scientist Luc Montagnier and the American Robert Gallo. Deadly or debilitating diseases—tuberculosis and polio come to mind—have often generated controversy in medical research. AIDS is no exception. Through the 1980s, Gallo and Montagnier were at the center of a maelstrom of heated debate, partisan rhetoric, and inculpatory investigative journalism. Chauvinism, the lure of revenues and funding, and politically inspired governmental oversight all played significant roles. When the dust settled, initial discovery of HIV was generally credited to Montagnier's work at the Institut Pasteur. Gallo's work, at the Laboratory of Tumor Cell Biology at the National Cancer Institute, helped to pave the way for, and confirmed and provided substantial evidence for, Montagnier's discovery.

Together the work of Gallo, Montagnier, and their colleagues led directly to the development of a diagnostic test and indirectly to a number of advances in pharmacological therapy for AIDS. With the use of combination therapies, the mid-1990s saw genuine but limited progress, and for those with money to treat it, AIDS could be a chronic disease that might eventually lead to a fatal loss of immune competence. But among the poor, especially in parts of Africa and elsewhere, AIDS burgeoned into a devastating epidemic that has claimed millions of lives. A cure or preventive

vaccine, announced as imminent in 1983, remained an elusive goal.

Because the historical perspective on AIDS is so short, it seems reasonable to profile Gallo and Montagnier together, briefly recounting the discovery of HIV, the controversy it generated, and the tentative reconciliation that followed.

Robert Gallo was born on March 23, 1937, in Waterbury, Connecticut. His father, Francis Anton Gallo, was a metallurgist who owned a welding company; his mother was Louise Mary Ciancuilli. Gallo, like a number of other scientists, had been impressed as a boy by *The Microbe Hunters* by Paul de Kruif (p. 401). The most formidable influence on his choice of a career, though, was the illness of his sister, Judy. When Robert was eleven and Judy was five, she fell ill with leukemia. Remission with the early antimetabolite therapy then in use was brief. "The jolly, plump, pretty sister I remembered," Gallo wrote in his autobiography, "was now emaciated, jaundiced, and covered with bruises. When she smiled I saw only the caked blood covering her teeth. This was the last time I would ever see Judy, and it remains the most powerful and frightening demon of my life."

After receiving a bachelor's degree from Providence College, where he majored in biology, Robert Gallo married a hometown girlfriend, Jane Hayes, in 1961; they would have two children. Gallo went on to attend Jefferson Medical College in Philadelphia, receiving his medical degree in 1963. He began his career in the field of cell biology and spent some time at the University of Chicago, where from 1963 to 1965 he undertook work on the biosynthesis of hemoglobin, the oxygen transport protein in the blood. For a time he was involved with clinical medicine, after receiving a prestigious appointment with the National Cancer Institute of the National Institutes of Health. But he found clinical work with hopeless cases of childhood cancer personally wrenching, and he disliked the depressing atmosphere of the cancer ward. While recognizing chemotherapy was sometimes effective, albeit often marginally, he was also disturbed by its toxic side effects. Gallo acknowledged his own inclination toward research, and from 1966 remained in the laboratory, initially involved in studies of leukemia.

In retrospect, the turning point of Gallo's career was the discovery of retroviruses, the study of which constituted an important field in cancer research from about 1970. Comprised essentially of RNA wrapped in a protein sheath, retroviruses adopt a strategy for reproduction that reverses the usual process of information transfer: They replicate by conversion to DNA (thanks to the enzyme "reverse transcriptase") and insertion into the genome of their host, by which ruse, as genes, they can be expressed—to the detriment of the cell and the living organism of which it is a part. The retroviral theory of the origin of cancer would be considerably modified, but it stimulated Gallo in his search for cancer viruses from the early 1970s, about the time he was appointed head of the Laboratory of Tumor Cell Biology at the National Cancer Institute.

Gallo's belief that some forms of leukemia might be caused by an infective retrovirus was a plausible idea that was, nevertheless, not at first popular. In 1975 Gallo and Robert E. Gallagher announced the isolation of a human leukemia virus. But HL23V-1, as it was called, turned out to be a laboratory contaminant—it was actually another virus, found in the woolly monkey, known as the simian sarcoma-associated virus. Gallo's error, although in some measure embarrassing, was only one of a number of similar gaffes in the recent history of cancer research.

Gallo rebounded, with efforts that would be both invaluable and treacherous for understanding AIDS several years later. His laboratory became deeply involved in immune system research and played a significant role in the discovery of T cell growth factor, known today as interleukin-2. The T cells are central to the immune response, and they are also the type of cells that become dysfunctional in leukemia. Now they could be cultivated in tissue—a significant advance. In addition, encouraged by the discovery of retroviruses that indisputably caused leukemia in cats and cattle, Gallo believed he could count on the existence of a carcinogenic human virus. In 1981 he was able to announce discovery of the human *T* cell leukemia *v*irus (HTLV-I or a variant, HTLV-II), associated with several forms of the disease.

In brief, Gallo's contributions to retroviral theory and his research in leukemia involving work with the immune system's T cells explain his subsequent prominence in the race to discover the AIDS virus.

Luc Montagnier's background was in certain respects similar to Gallo's. He was drawn early to science, and he also was touched by a family death from cancer. Five years older than his American counterpart, Montagnier was born on August 18, 1932, the only child of Marianne Rousselet and

Antoine Montagnier, an accountant who pursued his serious interest in science as an avocation in a basement laboratory. The death of Luc's grandfather from colon cancer affected him deeply. "The discovery of this mysterious, inexorable illness," Montagnier later wrote, "no doubt figured significantly in my choice of study." Montagnier received a degree in natural science in 1953, his *license* two years later, and, in 1960, his medical degree from the University of Paris. His marriage to Dorothy Ackerman in 1961 would bring them three children.

Montagnier's early career included several significant discoveries in and around retrovirus research. Working in Scotland from 1963 to 1965, he made important inroads in understanding how viral RNA reproduces in cells. Montagnier also helped develop a technique that showed how the polyoma virus—an exceptionally small DNA virus—could induce cancer in normal rodent cells. Returning to France, Montagnier expanded this research in various ways as laboratory director at the Institut du Radium (today the Institut Curie); in 1972 he also became chief of the viral oncology unit of the Institut Pasteur.

As was the case for Gallo, Montagnier's preoccupation with the new theory of retroviruses placed him in an ideal position to investigate the cellular pathology of AIDS when the epidemic arose.

Since the advent of penicillin during World War II and the Salk polio vaccine in the 1950s, medical pundits had been suggesting that infectious diseases of all sorts might one day be eradicated. By the late 1970s, however—just about the time that smallpox indeed seemed thoroughly defeated—such prophesies began to appear naive. A growing number of male homosexuals, in the United States and in Europe, began to develop clusters of symptoms and a variety of infectious diseases. The prognosis was invariably fatal. Within several years the underlying disease was recognized as a disorder of the immune system. The emergence of the disease in hemophiliacs and other recipients of blood transfusion strongly suggested a transmissible infectious agent, and, as it could not be filtered from the blood, it was thought to be a virus.

Robert Gallo was not initially drawn to study the new disease, but in 1982 he learned that one of its characteristics was T cell deficiency. Such an immune-system-related illness was close to his field of research in leukemia, a disease of the protective white blood cells, or lymphocytes. A year later, in February 1983, Gallo proposed that the cause of AIDS might well be a retrovirus. His specific suspicion was that the AIDS virus would be a variant of HTLV-I or HTLV-II, the leukemia viruses he had previously discovered.

Montagnier soon lent partial support to Gallo's suggestion. In January 1983 he cultured cells from a biopsy of a patient with enlarged lymph nodes, an early sign of AIDS. His laboratory demonstrated the presence of reverse transcriptase, the telltale enzyme that almost invariably indicates that a retrovirus is at work. Montagnier entertained the possibility that Gallo was right, and this retrovirus was closely related to HTLV-I and HTLV-II.

But laboratory results showed something strikingly different. Whereas the HTLV viruses would ultimately cause cells to proliferate, this was not the case with the virus Montagnier had discovered in his patients with lymph node disease. Rather, the lymphocytes died off. Montagnier began to call this virus lymphadenopathy-associated virus (LAV). Gallo, already unduly certain in early 1983 that HTLV was the AIDS virus, initially doubted Montagnier's results.

Gallo published three papers in a single issue of *Science* in May 1983. His laboratory had been able to produce HTLV-III, as he called the virus, in a permanent cell line. He believed that he had derived the virus from two AIDS patients and other sources. In the same issue of *Science,* Montagnier published a single paper on his work on LAV. While admitting the possibility that this virus was a version of Gallo's HTLV, Montagnier, on the basis of his own evidence, was explicitly not committed to it. Montagnier's paper appeared after Gallo's three papers in the magazine and received relatively little attention.

Gallo's conviction that the AIDS virus would be a variant of HTLV set the stage for a confrontation with Montagnier. At a meeting in Cold Spring Harbor in September 1983, Montagnier elaborated on his discovery of what might be the AIDS virus in a prominent presentation. In a strikingly undiplomatic and aggressive way that he later regretted, Gallo challenged Montagnier's results. "He treated Montagnier roughly," recalled Jacques Leibowitch, an early AIDS researcher, "just because he presented data that Gallo didn't want to recognize."

The scientific work on both sides of the Atlantic continued over the next six months. Montagnier, working at the Pasteur with an informal group, "Les

Dix," isolated the LAV virus he had drawn from AIDS patients of different backgrounds suffering various infections. He gradually became convinced that this virus was not the HTLV virus from Gallo's laboratory. Meanwhile, Gallo's conviction that HTLV was the AIDS virus seems to have created a situation ripe for error, not unlike the one committed by Robert Koch (p. 24) when he had announced a vaccine for tuberculosis in 1890. Although Gallo's laboratory had received samples of Montagnier's LAV in July and September 1983, he seems not to have specifically compared the French virus with the HTLV that his laboratory had begun to culture with such great success. This logical step might have saved much subsequent controversy.

In early 1984 dual and conflicting announcements inaugurated the public phase of the AIDS dispute. "I still retain..." wrote Montagnier later, "a feeling of bitterness about this period. We knew we were right, but we were the only ones." On April 24, 1984, Margaret Heckler, U.S. secretary of health and human welfare, announced that Gallo and his colleagues at the NIH had discovered and isolated the AIDS virus, which he was calling HTLV-III. In addition, Heckler was able to announce that a blood test for the disease would soon be available, and she went on to suggest that a vaccine was just a couple of years away. A series of articles followed, published prominently in *Science* on May 4, 1984.

On the day before the Heckler announcement, however, the *New York Times* reported that the Centers for Disease Control and Prevention (CDC) believed that the AIDS virus had been discovered—but through the work of Montagnier and his colleagues at the Institut Pasteur, not Gallo. Researchers at the CDC had become convinced, based on laboratory analysis, that the French virus LAV was the cause of AIDS.

The substantive issue in the conflict—whether LAV or HTLV-III was the cause of AIDS—was debated over the next two years. Eventually it became clear that the HTLV-III virus and Montagnier's LAV virus were identical. Probably the contamination that obscured this fact had taken place in Gallo's laboratory. In April 1986 Gallo admitted that in one of his 1983 articles a photo of what he had called HTLV-III was in fact LAV. According to Steven Epstein in his *Impure Science: AIDS, Activism and the Politics of Knowledge*, "[A]lthough Gallo continued to present the discovery of HTLV-III as a natural outgrowth of HTLV research, he was eventually forced to accept the prevailing view that, from a genetic standpoint, the new virus was not reasonably classifiable as an HTLV virus."

For a time the virus's nomenclature was an index of the scientific and political confusion that had come to plague the science surrounding AIDS. The World Health Organization used the name LAV/HTLV-III, recommended by the CDC, while the American government preferred

HTLV-III/LAV. In 1986 the matter was resolved when an International Committee on the Taxonomy of Viruses successfully proposed the name human immunodeficiency virus, or HIV.

Gallo would cede primacy of discovery of the AIDS virus to the French in April 1986, but an economic issue was at stake as well. Full discovery of the virus meant, finally, the ability to propagate it in culture, and this in turn quickly led to the development of a test for antibodies that would become the source of considerable revenue. Gallo's laboratory, on behalf of the National Institutes of Health, had applied for and received patents for such a test for the HTLV-III virus—which was, in fact, LAV. The French application for a U.S. patent for the same virus had been filed somewhat earlier. Thus, the Americans originally won a patent based on a virus actually discovered by the French. Not surprisingly, the French government sued.

In 1987 the dispute over the patent was officially concluded with a document signed by both U.S. President Ronald Reagan and French President Jacques Chirac, as well as by Montagnier and Gallo. The accord called for a joint declaration explaining how the virus was discovered. Royalties from the antibody test would be shared, and Montagnier's name was added to the patent. A bare-bones and unsatisfactory chronology of events was published by all parties in *Nature* on April 2, 1987.

Yet the conflict did not end there. In 1989 John Crewdson, an investigative journalist with the *Chicago Tribune,* published a long article, "The Great AIDS Quest," in which he all but charged Gallo with stealing the virus from Montagnier. This set off an investigation, initiated in 1990 by the National Institutes of Health. It concluded that Gallo had exercised poor judgment and found one of the scientists in his laboratory, Mikulas Popovic, guilty of a single charge of misconduct. These findings were both overturned on appeal. However, the Office of Research Integrity (ORI), a Congressional oversight committee of the Department of Health and Human Services, undertook a separate inquiry. The ORI, with an ideological and know-nothing attitude toward science, was disposed to find Gallo culpable of scientific misconduct. So it did. Gallo appealed and was finally vindicated in 1993.

Both Montagnier and Gallo continued to hold high profiles as research on HIV expanded in many directions and while AIDS developed into a global pandemic without precedent in the contemporary world. Both published scientific autobiographies that focused on their search for the AIDS virus. Gallo's *Virus Hunting* was published in 1991. Montagnier's *Virus: My Search for the Origin of AIDS* first appeared in France in 1995, and in English translation in 1999.

Gallo, after thirty years at the National Cancer Institute, became head of the Institute of Human Virology at the University of Maryland in 1997. As with some laboratories in the past—those founded for Robert Koch and Emil von Behring (p. 195), for example—this was built largely to Gallo's specifications. It included divisions for basic research, epidemiology, and clinical medicine, as well as a pharmaceutical marketing arm. Gallo twice received the Albert Lasker Award: in 1982 for his work on the viral origins of cancer, and again in 1986 for his work on AIDS. In 1987 he received the Gairdner Foundation Award.

Montagnier enjoyed a similar fate. His high profile at the Institut Pasteur and as director of research at the Centre Nationale de La Recherche Scientifique (CNRS), as well as in the international scientific community, made him the object of considerable attention in the French media. He was also the target of great scrutiny. He helped to found the World Foundation for AIDS Research and Prevention in 1993. In 1997 Montagnier stepped down as head of the AIDS and Retrovirus Research Department at the Institut Pasteur to accept a position created for him as director of the Center for Molecular and Cellular Biology at Queens College in New York. In 1998 Montagnier shared the Warren Alpert Foundation Award with Gallo—a measure of reconciliation on the ceremonial circuit.

Both Robert Gallo and Luc Montagnier straddled the fields of molecular biology and oncology, demonstrating an inclination for aggressive research programs when they began scientific work in the 1960s. They worked with retroviruses at a time when it was both tantalizing and unfashionable. Gallo, known for egoism and hyperbole, was described by Jon Cohen as "blunt, crass, frenetic, and competitive." Montagnier's view of the world was suffused with pugnacity and combativeness. "Like a roulette player at the table," he once said, "I'm addicted to getting results out of my laboratory."

# Part VI  Omnium-Gatherum

# Celsus [c. 25 B.C. – A.D. 50]

## Cicero of Medicine

Aurelius Cornelius Celsus, who lived during the first century of the common era, was an encyclopedist of the first rank. He was the author—by plausible conjecture—of a huge compendium that includes writings on philosophy, law, and rhetoric as well as military theory and agriculture. But all that survives of *De artibus,* as the whole work is called, is *De medicina*—a series of eight treatises on medicine. Rediscovered in the fifteenth century, it was published in 1478 and greatly pleased the humanists, whose intellectual quests would, within a century, stir the crucible of Renaissance medicine. Celsus wrote in Latin, and his vocabulary became the basis for medical nomenclature down to modern times.

Was Celsus a physician? Almost certainly not. Class considerations alone would make it unlikely, for his name clearly suggests he was patrician-born and prosperous. Some have suggested Celsus was only a compiler, perhaps general editor of the works that bear his name, or the translator of some unknown Greek text. *De medicina* is a masterpiece of Latin prose, however, and the beauty of its style argues against such an interpretation. Today, Celsus is more often regarded as having synthesized a work covering the whole of medicine. He obviously drew on both observation and written sources, and his own good sense shines throughout the work. "The judiciousness of his opinions," wrote medical historian Ralph Major, "the clarity of his descriptions, the striking lack of verbosity and pomposity in his explanations, combined with his pure and elegant Latin, make *De medicina* one of the greatest of medical texts."

Nothing is known about the life of Aurelius Cornelius Celsus except that his presence is on record in Rome for the year 25 B.C. He lived, then, about the same time as Jesus Christ, in the early years of the empire, in the wake of the republic. The composition of *De artibus* is usually dated at about A.D. 25 to 35, during the reign of Tiberius.

*De medicina* begins with a historical overview. Celsus is an exceptional source of knowledge about the various schools of Greek medicine from the time of Homer, and he discusses dozens of figures of antiquity. "I shall not hesitate to make use of the authority of ancient men," he writes, "and especially of Hippocrates [(p. 29)]." Among the others who also influenced

him was Asclepiades.* As he traces the history of the various schools, Celsus develops the broad organizational plan for the eight books of his encyclopedia. He writes that by the ancients "the Art of Medicine was divided into three parts: one being that which cures through diet, another through medicaments, and the third by the hand."

Celsus begins Book I with a discussion of diet and hygiene. He recommends exercise, considers sweating beneficial, and favors fresh fruit over dried. Book II is concerned extensively with the etiology of disease and with symptoms and prognosis. It depends heavily on Hippocrates, as might be imagined. Celsus notes, for example, that a sudden increase or decrease in body weight may signal the onset of a grave disease. Sweating and fatigue and fever are harbingers of serious trouble ahead. Celsus notes the importance of carefully monitoring the course of fevers and their accompanying manifestations.

Book III deals with treatment and generalized diseases such as the common cold and pneumonia. Here one finds Celsus's famous fourfold formula for inflammation: redness and swelling, heat and pain *(rubor, et tumor, cum calore et dolore).* It is interesting to note what, among his many examples, he says about dysentery. "Sometimes in the patients, this drags on," writes Celsus, "sometimes it hurries them off." This was indeed the case at the time and would remain so for nearly two thousand years. Not until the late nineteenth century would amoebic and bacillary dysentery be distinguished from each other and from other diseases that cause serious diarrhea, such as typhus and typhoid. A long time would also pass before there was a more effective way to treat the wasting diseases, including tuberculosis, for which Celsus recommends a long trip to Egypt, turpentine, and a dietary regimen of milk and honey. He also describes malaria, which was a serious cause of mortality during the empire and is sometimes thought to have contributed to Rome's decline.

---

*Asclepiades (c. 120–30 B.C.) was a controversial Greek physician who treated many wealthy Romans. He was an early example of the charismatic, bombastic healer with simple theories, snappy slogans, and gentle therapies. His actual works are lost.

Celsus's account of rabies was as comprehensive as anything else to appear before the nineteenth century, and used to be cited often. He suspected the saliva of the rabid animal contained "hydrophonia," as the Greeks called the poison. The disease in humans was "most wretched." The victim, writes Celsus, "is tormented at the same time with thirst and the fear of water, and in which there is but little hope." Therapy? For Celsus the only remedy was to throw the patient by surprise into a fish pond and insure that he swallow some water.

One always hears that life in Rome was not short on cruelty, and you could not gainsay as much by reading Celsus. He distinguishes several types of mental illness, and while soft music might work for mild melancholy, the treatments for serious cases were generally of last resort: torture, fetters, whipping if necessary, and starvation.

Book IV concerns anatomic description of certain diseases. The first twenty-three chapters of Book V list the medicines available to Celsus. He had opium as well as diuretics, purgatives, and laxatives. But most items on the long list are for external use only: tannin for local applications, and plasters and poultices. Skin diseases and ulcers of various kinds are the subject of Book VI. Celsus's descriptions of skin lesions are so precise that they are still found in the dermatological nomenclature.

Books VII and VIII deal with surgery, and Celsus's work reflects the greater attention paid to this craft in the centuries since Hippocrates. In Book VII he delineates classic operations, including a procedure for cataracts and lithotomy, or removal of a stone from the urinary tract. He has a section on plastic surgery showing how the skin might be repaired, concentrating on the nose and the head. In any event, Celsus advises the surgeon never to perform procedures too quickly, but to "do everything just as if the other's screams made no impression on him."

Finally, fractures and dislocations are treated in Book VIII. Celsus describes how to use splints and starched bandages on fractures. He provides descriptions for over one hundred surgical instruments, including hooks, scalpels, forceps, speculums, and amputation saws. Among these tools was one used for extracting the roots of teeth; another held open wounds for the removal of arrowheads. Many of the instruments described in De medicina have since been excavated from archaeological sites and can be found today in museums of medicine and antiquity.

In spite of his clarity and completeness, Celsus was not an authority for, nor was he discussed by, the Greek physicians such as Galen (p. 34) who dominated Roman medicine in the first century and again in the Middle Ages. De medicina was consequently lost to medicine for fourteen hundred years. But in the mid-fifteenth century Tommaso Parentucelli, an eminent priest whose father was a physician, discovered an ancient manuscript of Celsus's great work in the papal library at St. Ambrose in Milan. This was in 1443, and four years later Tommaso became Pope Nicholas V, patron of humanists. In 1478 *De medicina* was published at Florence, the first general text on medicine to come from a printing press.

# Ibn Sina (Avicenna) [980–1037]

## Prince of Physicians

The survival of the Western medical tradition, as rooted in Greco-Roman thought, depended upon the Arabic intellectuals of the Middle Ages. As the Roman Empire declined, scholars and intellectuals were driven from the Christian West and found refuge in Persia. They brought with them the medical classics of Hippocrates, Galen, and others, and these were translated first into Syriac and subsequently into Arabic. Using these works as a base of knowledge, Haly Abbas wrote a famous textbook of clinical medicine, and Muhammad ibn Zakariya' al-Razi became a distinguished physician as well as a scientist and philosopher. But the most influential of the great Arab physicians is Ibn Sina, or as the Christian scholars called him, Avicenna.

Ibn Sina is remembered as a philosopher, mathematician, and poet as well as a physician. He was the author of over two hundred fifty works, including a remarkable encyclopedia of science, and his poetry, written in Persian, is always highly praised. His compendium, the *Al-Qanun fi'l-Tibb (Canon of Medicine),* when translated into Latin in the Middle Ages, became part of the powerful Scholastic tradition. "It was so forceful and persuasive," writes historian Henry Sigerist, "that it dominated medicine in the East and the West for six hundred years." Although dogmatic in his approach, Ibn Sina is still eminently readable, and the *Canon* provides descriptions and diagnoses that have long intrigued physicians and made his work the subject of many commentaries. Indeed, Ibn Sina, who was trained as a jurist as well as a physician, well illustrates the importance of rhetoric to science and medicine. "The *Qanun* covered the various branches of medicine with a precision and thoroughness that gave it authoritative sway over the discipline for hundreds of years," writes Lawrence I. Conrad, "and it ranks as one of the most impressive and enduring achievements of medieval Islamic science."

A fair amount is known about Ibn Sina, largely because he himself dictated a memoir concerning his early life. Abu Ali al-Husayn ibn 'Abdallah ibn Sina was born about 980 near Bukhara, then an intellectual center of Islam and a powerful kingdom under the rule of the Samanids. (Today Bukhara is found in Uzbekistan.) Ibn Sina's father was a government employee, possibly a tax collector, and an intellectual who belonged to

a hashish cult. By his own account, Ibn Sina was a remarkable prodigy who had memorized the Koran by the age of ten. Under his father's guidance, he studied mathematics, astronomy, medicine, and philosophy. He also committed to memory Aristotle's *Metaphysics*—without, at first, understanding it.

"Medicine is not a difficult subject," wrote Ibn Sina, "and in a short space of time, of course, I excelled in it...." Indeed, at age seventeen Ibn Sina effected a cure of the Samanid ruler Nuh Ibn Mansur. This brought him into favor at court, and he gained access to the royal library. He must have made good use of it over several years as palace physician.

About the turn of the eleventh century, the Turks put an end to the Samanid regime, and a period of political unrest ensued. Ibn Sina began a period of wandering. He eventually was appointed to a high executive post, as vizier to Shama ad-Dawlah in Hamadan. Although the historical record is not clear, Ibn Sina seems to have angered elements of the military. For a time he was forced into hiding, and he was briefly imprisoned. He was later reinstated.

Ibn Sina's *Canon* is a systematic and comprehensive work consisting of five books. The first book, the most complex of all, gives the fundamentals of medicine, including basic theory concerning the causes and treatment of disease, and rules of hygiene and good health. It is a handbook of sorts, with instructions for bloodletting, cautery, and other procedures. Materia medica is the subject of Book Two, which lists and describes the various properties and uses of available drugs.

Book Three of the *Canon* discusses diseases "from head to toe," beginning with the brain and ending with pains of the joints and diseases of the nails. General pathology is the subject of Book Four, which deals with contagious diseases and such topics as fevers, pustules, wounds, and fractures. Book Five discusses all the various "compound drugs." These included theriacs (paste-like antidotes made from pulverized drugs mixed with honey), troches (tablet-like compounds, to be dissolved in the mouth), and other similar medications, such as electuaries and cathartics.

The great virtues of the *Canon* are its clarity and textbook completeness. It is free of the disorder that pervades Galen's writings, and while various hands created the Hippocratic corpus, the *Canon* is the product of one mind and covers the whole of medicine. Accordingly, its entry into Western medicine was an event of major importance. The *Canon* was translated into Latin in the twelfth century by Gerard de Cremona, of Toledo. An improved translation, among the first medical books printed, was published in 1526 in Venice and was reprinted time and again during the fifteenth and sixteenth centuries. Ibn Sina would be pleased to know that his work was taught in European universities well into the seventeenth century, until Scholasticism had fully run its course.

Ibn Sina spent the last period of his life, from 1024, at Isfahan as physician and scientific counselor to the ruler there. His schedule seems to have been at once demanding and laced with hedonism. He enjoyed tackling difficult problems with students, drank a good deal of wine, and enjoyed an extravagant sexual life. A recent biographer writes, "The master was vigorous in all his powers, the sexual being the most powerful and predominant of his concupiscent faculties, and he indulged it often."

Ibn Sina fell ill of colic, which was complicated by an ulcer, and died in 1037 — ironically, a victim of an overdose of purified opium, the rules for the dosage of which he had done much to improve. He did not marry and left no children. In his last days Ibn Sina is said to have freed his slaves and donated his possessions to the poor. Buried at Hamadan, his tomb became a place of pilgrimage. At the suggestion of William Osler (p. 181), Reuben Levy visited there in 1919, just after the First World War. He found the tomb guarded by learned men, who viewed it as a holy place. Indeed, Levy was told that if he poured water into a trough in the gravestone, "I should immediately be cured of any fever I might be suffering from." Levy adds sententiously, "I regretted that at the moment my health happened to be remarkably good, and that I therefore was unable to take advantage of the opportunity to put the matter to a scientific test." An architecturally impressive mausoleum has since been built on the site, together with a museum and a library.

Ibn Sina's influence first came into question in 1527, when Paracelsus (p. 50) burned a copy of the *Canon* during his inaugural lecture in Basel. But it persisted in Western medicine until the scientific revolution and today abides elsewhere. The *Canon* retains particular appeal for Yunani medicine, which is still widely practiced in India and is especially popular among rural populations. Books on Yunani are sometimes published in

English in the alternative medicine genre. In 1991 G. M. Chisti, an Indian hakim (physician), published *The Traditional Healer's Handbook*. It was, the author asserted, based on the work of Ibn Sina. His hope is that "a second millennium of students and practitioners will discover an immense reward in the special and extraordinary genius of Hakim Ibn Sina, the Prince of Physicians."

# Louise Bourgeois [c. 1563–1636]

## Persistence of the Midwife

A ssistance at childbirth has historically been the domain of women. Midwifery as an activity is as old as civilization, but its customs and practices have varied greatly by epoch, country, and region. In the Western tradition the role of midwives was significant in the Roman Empire and during the Middle Ages, when these women often had a range of duties, including verifying the identity of children and the state of the hymen. Midwives came under increased civil scrutiny and municipal regulation during the Renaissance and Reformation, and at times they had the distinction of being associated with witchcraft. Through history, educated midwives have occasionally documented their lives and views. One of the best examples is Louise Bourgeois. Midwife at the births of the children of Henry IV and Marie de Medici, she is the author of, among other works, the famous *Observations diverses.*

Louise Bourgeois was born outside Paris about 1563 in the well-heeled suburb of Saint-Germain. Nothing much is known of her childhood. She certainly learned to read and write, and like most young women of her class, she probably was taught needlework. In 1584 she married Martin Boursier, an established barber-surgeon who apparently had once lived in the house of, and seems to have been the assistant to, Ambroise Paré (p. 119). Bourgeois writes of having seen, in 1590, "the great surgeon Paré, lying on his deathbed, and, although at the age of eighty, with as unclouded an intellect as ever, and as anxious as ever to learn something from those who visited him." Bourgeois and her husband remained in Saint-Germain, and after several years were the parents of three children. Bourgeois speaks well of her husband, and they appear to have enjoyed considerable felicity.

A peculiar set of historic circumstances both disrupted Louise Bourgeois's private life and led to her becoming midwife to the French court. In 1589, Henry of Navarre, about to become Henry IV, first Bourbon king of France, laid siege to Paris, which was then in the hands of the Catholic League. This military operation did not spare the Faubourg Saint-Germain, and so directly affected Bourgeois and her husband. She later wrote of having "remained with no possessions but the few we had saved, on which we lived selling them off bit by bit every day." The wars probably played a role

in her decision to become a midwife, with its financial rewards. Whether she learned her craft from her husband or performed an informal apprenticeship is not clear, but she soon became busy, she later wrote, and in 1598 passed a civic examination to become a "sworn matron."

Exactly how Louise Bourgeois came to court is a complicated story. In 1600 Henry IV, having converted to Catholicism, took as his queen consort Marie de Medici, daughter of the grand duke of Tuscany. It appears that a friend introduced Bourgeois to Marie, who accepted her as midwife for her upcoming confinement. On September 26, 1601, Bourgeois was summoned to the royal chambers. The king himself greeted her, saying, "Come in midwife, come to my wife who is ailing, and see whether she be in travail." Once the little dauphin came into the world, Louise called for wine. She initially refrained from spurting it over the child's body, as was customary. But the king told her, "Do to it, as thou wouldst to any other child." Some of Henry's pleasure at having a son, rather than a daughter, seems to have been displaced on Bourgeois. She came into royal favor.

Over the next decade Bourgeois not only delivered the six children born to the queen, but also attended to other royal births. While keeping a private practice in the Latin Quarter, she would generally spend the queen's final month of pregnancy at court and remain another month after the delivery. She was well paid for her efforts, receiving some 900 livres per birth, when the usual fee was 50. She received what appears to have been a bonus of 6,000 livres in 1608. The assassination of Henry IV in 1610 put an end to Marie's childbearing, but Bourgeois remained midwife to nobles at court for some years to come.

Bourgeois would not command interest today were it not for her *Observations diverses,* published in several volumes between 1617 and 1626. Far more than a compilation of acquired knowledge, it is a practical manual with a rational approach and includes some forty-eight case histories. *Observations* is written in French, is direct if disorganized, and incorporates much medical knowledge and theory. Bourgeois's anatomical account of childbirth and theory is orthodox in its main lines, and her framework generally is rational, though not formal. She knew how to perform a manual extraction of a baby by podalic version, could deliver a child of a dying mother, and could successfully deliver twins after a long labor.

Bourgeois's relationships with physicians and surgeons were an outcome of her unique status as midwife to royalty. She is critical of them, sometimes acerbic in her comments, but also frequently diplomatic. In a recent biography, Wendy Perkins calls Bourgeois both "a conformist and a subversive, striving for acceptability and demanding recognition in her own right in a domain from which she would normally have been excluded." Thus, for example, Bourgeois avoids the strongly interventionist inclination sometimes found among doctors in the sixteenth century. She stresses the importance of a tranquil atmosphere in the birthing room—as midwives do today. At the same time, she retains traditional notions, such as placing the hide of a recently killed hare on the mother's abdomen just after birth and urging the woman to vomit in order to expel the afterbirth.

Indeed, Bourgeois belongs essentially to the Renaissance and in many ways strongly reminds one of Ambroise Paré—both a friend and critic of midwives—most particularly in her mingling of common sense and the fantastical. *Observations* contains some fine stories, of the kind Paré related in his *On Monsters and Marvels*. One of the best is the tale of a young lactating mother asleep in a vineyard. A serpent slithers across the woman's bosom, seizes a nipple and will not relinquish it. Nothing can make the snake let it go, and it grows like a natural child. The woman is forced to carry its body in a sling around her neck—until she comes across a snake charmer, and is unburdened. The tale, writes Bourgeois, shows "how very nutritious" is woman's milk.

Bourgeois's career among the aristocracy seems to have come to an end in 1627 with the death of Marie de Bourbon-Montpensier, sister-in-law of Louis XIII, during delivery of a daughter. Although the autopsy report does not directly blame Bourgeois, she was certainly embarrassed by it. She wrote a detailed account in reply that included a bitter denunciation. Her *Apologie* was not favorably received, and Bourgeois was no longer welcome at the royal court.

Bourgeois's final work is *Recueil des secrets (Collected Secrets)*, published in 1635. Like any number of similar works from the seventeenth century, it contains recipes for some two hundred eighty cures, potions, and other preparations. It was aimed at the homemaker as well as the midwife.

Today midwives still deliver two-thirds of the world's infants, if not more. The complex fact is that childbirth is not an illness, but it remains potentially fatal. Ordinarily it does not require a doctor; sometimes complications demand one. Today, midwives must contend with the challenge of obstetrical technology, which becomes ever more advanced. For them to shun such technology leads to the impression of their being anachronistic, but "if midwives adopt obstetric technology," write Raymond G. DeVries and Rebeca Barroso, "they set in motion a process that changes their profession so drastically that it becomes subsumed by, or indistinguishable from, obstetrics."

In the United States, midwives play a variety of supportive and useful roles, and perform normal deliveries in homes or homelike settings. But they survive and prosper by making appropriate arrangements with medical authorities. They do not themselves employ forceps or perform cesarean sections, and they generally do not attempt high-risk deliveries.

Not much is known of Louise Bourgeois's final years, but she was left a widow in 1632. By her own account, she was pleased with her offspring, who represented a small medical dynasty. Both her daughters married physicians. One son became a physician to Louis XIII; another became an apothecary. The image of Louise Bourgeois in the frontispiece to *Observations* is accompanied by a few lines of poetry:

> *The fault of this perfect portrait*
> *Today strikes our eyes clearly*
> *Because we only can see the corporeal face*
> *Not the spirit admired for its heavenly work*

Louise Bourgeois died in December 1636.

# Samuel Hahnemann [1755–1843]

## The Progress of Homeopathy

The first half of the nineteenth century was disappointing for doctors and their patients. With modern chemistry only in its infancy, medical therapeutics was in a period of false dawn. "Therapeutic skepticism" was popular in the highest echelons of medicine — a frank acknowledgment of the gap between scientific knowledge of the human body and the prospect for treating its ills. This distance would not begin to close until about 1880, with establishment of the germ theory of disease. Meanwhile, alternative theories and treatments proliferated. Perhaps the most significant of any number of systems — then as today — was homeopathy, developed by the German physician Samuel Hahnemann.

Samuel Christian Friedrich Hahnemann was born on April 10, 1755, in the historic town of Meissen, Germany. His father, Christian Gottfried Hahnemann, made his living by painting fine porcelain; his mother was Johanna Spiess. All biographical sketches of Hahnemann describe his childhood in idealized tones: he grew up in a loving home strongly infused with religious feelings. Samuel's father played a strong role in his early education, but opposed his entering the university for financial reasons. Nevertheless, Hahnemann undertook medical studies at Leipzig in 1775, and two years later continued them at Vienna. He received his medical degree from the University of Erlangen in 1779.

From early in his career, Hahnemann hoped to make original contributions to medicine. His first essay, from 1784, was "Directions for Curing Old Diseases," which stressed principles of hygiene that would become popular in hospital practice several decades later. As he investigated mainstream medicine, according to one of his biographers, Hahnemann "found it a shallow pool compared to the unfathomable gulf of erudition and mystery it was supposed to be." Hahnemann was by no means the only physician unhappy with contemporary therapies, but his sensitivity to patients' suffering and his intellectual bent were a potent combination. For a time Hahnemann stopped practicing in order to devote himself to writing and translating. In 1786 he published a significant work on arsenic poisoning. Beginning in 1787 he also wrote a number of papers on topics in chemistry. In 1789 he wrote a paper on syphilis that critically examined the mercury treatments. Hahnemann's work in chemistry is important because in his day the entire field was just emerging. Not for the better part of a century would scientists even agree on the nature of molecules.

Therapeutics remained the focus of Hahnemann's interest, and it is not surprising that he translated William Cullen's *Materia medica*. Discussing cinchona, used to treat malaria, Cullen—one of the most influential physicians of his day—was hard-pressed to explain how it worked. Hahnemann found unlikely Cullen's suggestion that it might strengthen the stomach, so as an experiment, he ingested cinchona himself while in a healthy (nonmalarial) state. Within a few days, he found that he developed anxiety and prostration, symptoms a bit like those of malaria. Cinchona worked to cure malaria, Hahnemann would decide, because in smaller doses, "like cures like": *similia similibus curantur*. This idea, in various forms, dated to the earliest days of rational medicine. It now became the basis of homeopathy. The famous "law of similars" came to Hahnemann as a sudden insight, and he published his "Essay on a New Principle for Ascertaining the Curative Powers of Drugs" in 1796, and coined the term "homeopathy." The same year, Edward Jenner (p. 152) introduced a preventive vaccine against smallpox, which Hahnemann took as confirmation of his theory.

If cinchona had this relationship to malaria, Hahnemann reasoned, other substances might work against other diseases. He set out to identify them, test them, and establish the proper potency for making them therapeutic. He would "prove" the drugs by using them on himself or on another healthy individual, carefully noting any symptomlike reactions. After discovering the substance's action in larger doses, Hahnemann would "potentize" it for therapeutic purposes. This essentially involved diluting it, often many times, to achieve the smallest effective dose. Although in terms of ordinary chemistry the original substance would be entirely lost through these methods, for homeopathy this was the remedy.

The two principal works of homeopathy are both written by Hahnemann. One may be described as philosophical and practical; the other was his pharmacopoeia. The latter, *Materia Medica Pura,* appeared between 1811 and 1821, in six volumes. It describes in detail the action of the various homeopathic remedies, their dosages, and their rationales. Characteristically, Hahnemann emphasizes the individualized case-by-case approach. "It is the duty of physicians to distinguish subtle variations of every *individual* case—that is to specialize and individualize in each personal case, instead of treating the disease."

In 1810 Hahnemann published his *Organon der rationellen Heilkunde (Organon of Rational Healing),* which set out his system in doctrinal form.

He would revise the work four times before his death. A final edition would appear in 1921, and the book remains in print today. The *Organon* is aphoristic, consisting of 291 comments. "The physician's highest calling," Hahnemann begins this memorable book, "his only calling, is to make sick people healthy—to heal, as it is termed." He takes the view, as many other critics of medicine have done, that the complex terminology of "theoretical" medicine is unintelligible and pretentious. It is high time, writes Hahnemann, to "*start acting* instead—that is, helping and healing."

Much of homeopathy's appeal lay in its combination of emphasis on the real concerns of individuals, both in sickness and in health, with what today would be called "lifestyle" issues. Hahnemann recommends exercise and calls into question "errors of living." Chronically ill patients should avoid damp rooms and strong-smelling flowers and perfume, not to mention long naps and masturbation or coitus interruptus. Hahnemann discusses—to some extent defends—"magnetic" healing and mesmerism. One of his treatises, from 1803, is titled "Coffee and Its Effects."

From the beginning, homeopathy was controversial and adopted a provocative stance toward mainstream medicine, or allopathy, as Hahnemann called it. His ideas won support at first, and in 1812 he began to teach at the University of Leipzig. But strong criticism of homeopathy was published in 1819, and Hahnemann incurred the wrath of the local apothecaries, who accused him of infringing on their rights. Hahnemann lost his case in court, and after further criticisms and protests by physicians, he left Leipzig in 1821. He moved to Köthhen at the invitation of the Grand Duke Ferdinand where, in 1828, he started to publish *Die chronischen Krankheiten, ihre eigenthümliche Natur und homöopathische Heilung (The Chronic Diseases, Their Nature and Homeopathic Cure)*. In this, his last book, Hahnemann developed his theory of the psora—an internal "itch" with all sorts of manifestations, including but not limited to warts, tumors, and bone disease—that he believed accounted for as much as seven-eighths of all chronic conditions. This concept exposed Hahnemann and homeopathy to considerable ridicule.

In spite of the controversy it provoked, homeopathy enjoyed considerable success during the first half of the nineteenth century. Compared to bleeding and purging, which were the standard practices of ordinary physicians, homeopathic remedies constituted "gentle medicine." Although intellectually suspect, its practitioners tended not to be purist or dogmatic, but moderate and eclectic in approach. Indeed, the durability of homeopathy, writes Norman Gevitz, "was due in large part to the intellectual accommodation that homeopathic physicians were able to make with Hahnemann's original doctrines and the external medical and social world."

Hahnemann was not happy with many of his followers in the United States, even while homeopathy began to flourish there when conventional medicine was at a nadir. Brought to the United States by German immigrants, homeopathy became, and would remain, the best known of several unorthodox medicines. It was the object of organized opposition as early as 1846, when the American Medical Association (AMA) was founded. In the years that followed, homeopaths were subject to what Robin Marantz Henig has called a "period of medical McCarthyism." Indeed, the AMA's battle against homeopathy was not based on the presumed therapeutic superiority of conventional medicine; it was a turf war. In 1856 the AMA banned any and all discussion of homeopathic theory. Some members were expelled from the organization simply because they were married to homeopaths.

But this antagonism did not kill homeopathy. As late as 1870 it is estimated that about one in eight American doctors was a sectarian, and homeopathy was the largest of the sects. In 1900 there were still some twenty-two homeopathic colleges. But with the sea change in American medical education after the turn of the century, homeopathy was marginalized, and its decline was augmented by factional strife. By 1940 all the homeopathic colleges in the United States had closed. But one significant aspect of homeopathy remained untouched. Senator Royal Copeland was the chief congressional sponsor of the Food, Drug, and Cosmetic Act of 1938 — and a homeopathic physician. When the bill was passed, he insured that medications listed in the *Homeopathic Pharmacopeia of the United States* would be exempt from regulation, on the basis that homeopathic remedies were so dilute that they could not represent a threat from a toxicity standpoint. In terms of its legal status, the law of infinitesimals worked to homeopathy's advantage.

Homeopathy has regained some of its lost ground in recent decades and has a growing number of adherents in the United States and Europe, South America, and India. National health insurance systems tend to reimburse homeopathic physicians, who employ little if any advanced technology. (Some homeopaths use X rays and have made other concessions to orthodox medicine.) Homeopaths tend to tailor their treatments carefully to individual patients and, unlike most conventional doctors, may spend considerable time taking histories and investigating the nuances of various symptoms. Today's homeopathic pharmacopoeia includes some powerful substances among about 1300 listed, but whether they are effective at homeopathic dosages cannot be easily ascertained by conventional research.

It comes as no surprise that Samuel Hahnemann married the stepdaughter of an apothecary, Henrietta Kuchlerine, in 1783. They had eight children. Their son Friedrich trained as a homeopath but appears to have died insane. In 1835, five years after Henrietta's death, an elderly but virile Hahnemann married a French woman, Melanie d'Hervilly, who was just about fifty years his junisor. At age eighty, Hahnemann moved with Melanie to Paris, where he spent his final years in private practice. Melanie was also an energetic publicist for homeopathy, and Hahnemann's practice quickly became renowned. "People from all walks of life flocked to his door," claims one of his recent biographers, "rich and poor alike, and none was turned away." Hahnemann died at the age of eighty-eight, on July 2, 1843. Originally buried in a public grave in Montmartre—for reasons that are obscure, because he was not a pauper—his remains were later moved to the famous Père Lachaise cemetery. Eventually an impressive granite monument was erected with the inscription *Non inutilis vixi*—"I have not lived in vain."

# Daniel David Palmer [1845–1913]
## Chiropractic

While stooped over in a cramped position one day, a janitor named Harvey Lillard heard a "pop" in his neck. This was in 1878, and Lillard was stone-deaf for the next seventeen years. He "could not hear the racket of a wagon on the street or the ticking of a watch." In 1895, however, he went to clean the offices of D. D. Palmer, a "magnetic healer" in the bustling Mississippi River city of Davenport, Iowa. Noticing that one of Lillard's vertebrae was "racked from its normal position," Palmer convinced Lillard—who could read lips—to allow him to "lever it back." When this was done, Lillard exulted, "I can hear, Doc, I can hear!" This marked the beginnings of a novel approach to understanding and treating disease, founded together with a philosophy of life—chiropractic.

Although controversial from the start, chiropractic flourished in the years before World War I. Palmer's system was continued by his son, B. J. Palmer, who developed chiropractic education and a central core of beliefs and practical knowledge. Medical authorities viewed it as the redoubt of quacks, but chiropractic resisted extinction and became widely considered "complementary" to conventional treatment. As a system of manipulation of the spinal column, it can be relatively inexpensive. Chiropractic has survived, prospered, and spread abroad, with about fifty thousand practitioners worldwide.

Daniel David Palmer was born on March 7, 1845, in a village known today as Port Perry, northeast of Toronto, Canada, on the shores of Lake Scugog. His mother was superstitious, while his father was "disposed to reason on the subjects pertaining to life." Daniel recalled that he was a sensitive child. According to a story that is probably apocryphal, he liked to search for skeletons of dead animals and to mend the broken bones of live ones. Daniel and his younger brother, Thomas, attended a country school for only a few years before hard times intervened. The failure of his father's business compelled Daniel at about age ten to take work in a local factory. He and his brother remained in Canada while their parents relocated to the United States. Only after a number of years, in 1865—the American Civil War probably did not dispose them to move earlier—did Daniel and Thomas make the long journey to join their parents in Iowa.

Although largely self-educated, Palmer began to teach in 1866 and worked in a number of schools over the next fifteen years. Historian J. Stuart Moore culled a sampling of Palmer's didactic remarks and aphorisms from his daybooks. "The best physicians," wrote Palmer, "are Dr. Diet, Dr. Quiet, and Dr. Merryman." Like most teachers at the time, he applied corporal punishment, but he reminded himself to give "time between the strokes."

While teaching in New Boston, Illinois, Palmer began keeping bees. This hobby apparently became lucrative, for he cultivated and sold a brand of honey, "Sweet Home Raspberry," nationwide. His apiarian enterprise came to an end in 1881, however. According to one account, his first wife died; by another version, a harsh winter froze his bees. In any event, Palmer returned to live with his family in What Cheer, Iowa. There he sold fish and operated a grocery before moving to Letts, Iowa, to teach once again. But a second marriage was not a success, and he was unsettled in his career.

Palmer's entry into medicine came through his pursuits in the healing and spirituality movements, both popular in the United States in the years after the Civil War. Friedrich Anton Mesmer's "animal magnetism" enjoyed a revival in the name of science, and "magnetic healing" became a popular, though suspect, form of treating illness. As a healer Palmer was largely an autodidact, acquiring his methods from such works as the handbook by E. D. Babbit, *Vital Magnetism, The Life Fountain*. Babbit suggested that by touching and rubbing different areas of the body the practitioner could relieve various ailments, from constipation to apoplexy. Babbit also recommended sleeping with the head pointing north, to align the body with the earth's magnetic currents, an idea that gained some popularity. Also according to Babbit, tobacco and alcohol were to be avoided, and one should bathe every day and eat fruits and vegetables. Babbit's work, fairly typical for the genre, was one of many that Palmer studied.

In 1887 Palmer opened his "Magnetic Cure and Infirmary" in Davenport, Iowa. With the benefits of advertising and a central location, his annual income of $700 increased almost sevenfold by 1895, the year in which he happened upon Harvey Lillard, the janitor, and sowed the seeds of chiropractic. One of Palmer's early patients, the Reverend Samuel Weed, gave the method its name, combining ancient Greek words for "done by hand."

Chiropractic developed while conventional medicine was moving rapidly toward scientific respectability. Palmer had been derided by establishment voices as a mountebank when he was a magnetic healer. Now he sought to present chiropractic as scientifically sound, claiming to have "systematized and correlated" the principle he had discovered. At the same time, he developed an underlying "philosophy of life"—in fact, a rough-and-ready metaphysics. "The human body represents the actions of three laws," he wrote, "spiritual, mechanical and chemical, united as one...." He invoked the ancient humoral concept of balance, in which "dis-ease" is due to a loss of harmony. If some bony structure in the body breaks down or becomes misaligned, for example, Palmer suggested that the body's balance of intellectual faculties—comprised of two forms of intelligence, "innate" and "educated"—will be disturbed. Illness will result. Chiropractic, Palmer maintained, can restore this balance. He made the remarkable claim that all diseases—or at least 95 percent of them—are due to dislocations of the spinal column.

Palmer emphasized the philosophical content of chiropractic and underplayed its debt to manipulation by hand, which had a long history, especially in folk medicine. He also denied that his methods owed anything to osteopathy, another therapy based on manipulation of the skeletal system that had been founded several years earlier.* "D. D. Palmer's general vision was not the vision of a lone crank," writes historian J. Stuart Moore in his *Chiropractic in America*. Nor was his claim to be "scientific" unusual for the time. "His chiropractic philosophy," adds Moore, "was part of the harmonial tradition, a search for the Grand Principle of life which, unlike the mechanical approach that also sought monistic answers, expressed a need to integrate Spirit with Nature."

Palmer's success was also due to the skills and dynamism of his son, Bartlett Joshua Palmer. Just fourteen years old when his father invented chiropractic, three years later B. J. became one of the first students to attend the Palmer Infirmary and Chiropractic School, graduating in 1902. The school was not a success when David Daniel ran it, but B. J. became an administrator in 1906, and in his hands it flourished. He trained practi-

---

*Osteopathy was founded in 1874 by Andrew Taylor Still, a bonesetter from Missouri. Therapeutically it was more eclectic and theoretically more flexible than chiropractic. As a consequence, osteopathy eventually made peace with regular medicine. Today osteopaths in the United States are trained physicians; some perform manipulations.

tioners, wrote a major textbook, and married a woman who had studied anatomy at Rush Medical College in Chicago. Against opposition from other chiropractors, he introduced the use of X rays about 1909 and made various other concessions to scientific discoveries. Chiropractic's distinctive identity is due to B. J. Palmer's strong leadership.

Chiropractic adapted and mutated over the course of one hundred years. After mainstream American medical education was revamped by about 1920, chiropractic schools seemed notably retrograde. In recent decades, however, their curriculums have been refurbished. Chiropractors still rely mainly on manipulation of the spine. Indeed, the "straight" chiropractors adhere to D. D. Palmer's original philosophy; they employ no drugs or surgery. Others are more eclectic "mixers" who learn naturopathy and other alternative healing methods, from which they derive their pharmacopoeia. Some chiropractors ally themselves rather closely to mainstream medicine, receiving referrals from orthodox physicians.

D. D. Palmer, from a psychological point of view, remains an intriguing figure. He was no stranger to grandiose thinking. He said that he had received a diploma "from no earthly school but from High Heaven." He wrote that the answer to the question that plagued medicine for centuries—why one person falls ill and another remains well—"was answered in September 1895." After his first, beloved wife's death, he next married a woman he claimed was an alcoholic. After liquor carried her away, he wed a drug addict. He had a marked tendency to narcissistic rage and was sometimes carted off to jail for physically abusing his wife and children. B. J. Palmer claimed that his own spinal curvature was due to his father's beatings.

It is not surprising, then, that when his son became a powerful force in chiropractic, D. D. Palmer could not get along with him. Embittered, he left the school he had founded in Iowa to found others in Oregon and Oklahoma. He finally settled in California. In his last days he authored a huge tome, *The Science, Art and Philosophy of Chiropractic*, before dying of typhoid fever in Los Angeles on October 20, 1913.

# Lydia Pinkham  [1819–1883]

## "A Sure Cure..."

**W**ith her intuitive grasp of the transformation of everyday life in the late nineteenth century, Lydia Pinkham penned, among many advertising appeals:

> *OVERWORKED WOMEN*
> *THE WORLD*
> *IS DAILY GROWING BETTER AS*
> *THE VIRTUES OF*
> *LYDIA E. PINKHAM'S VEGETABLE COMPOUND*
> *BECOME KNOWN TO WOMEN, FOR*
> *THE HEALTH OF WOMEN*
> *IS THE HOPE OF THE RACE!*

A feminist who had been an abolitionist, who approved of the temperance movement, and who adored phrenology, Lydia Pinkham became one of the best-known purveyors of patent medicines in late nineteenth-century America. The story of her Vegetable Compound, writes historian Sarah Stage, "speaks to…changing cultural attitudes toward female sexuality, and to the prolonged failure of the medical profession to provide adequate treatment for women's physiological and psychological complaints."

Although the patent medicine era represents an aspect of folk medicine, it also speaks powerfully to the marketing tactics for today's pharmaceuticals. "Lydia Pinkham was an advertising pioneer," writes Dan Yaeger, "a manufacturer becoming the symbol of the product." Her Vegetable Compound became omnipresent; her portrait graced not only drugstore displays but barns and fences in rural America. A similar kind of of exposure exists today for a wide variety of prescription and over-the-counter drugs, with television and print ads pitched to consumers and samples dispensed on street corners. Some of these drugs are more powerful, specific, and valuable than Lydia Pinkham's famous compound. But others—from "cures" for baldness to ineffective remedies for obesity—refurbish the appeal of old-time nostrums, whether by appealing to human vanity or by offering simplistic solutions to complex disorders.

The tenth of twelve children, Lydia Estes was born on February 19, 1819, in Lynn, Massachusetts. Her parents were Billy Estes, who had made enough money as a shoemaker to become a gentleman farmer, and Rebecca Chase. Both Lydia's parents were of Quaker background, and her mother was a follower of Emanuel Swedenborg, the famous scientist, theologian, and mystic. Lydia was raised in the abolitionist and reform-minded tradition of nineteenth-century New England. Her environment was strongly intellectual—Frederick Douglass was a friend of the family—and she was well educated. For several years after graduating from the Lynn Academy, she taught school.

Lydia Pinkham was a political activist as well as a wife and mother. In 1842, in her early twenties, she helped found the Freeman's Institute, an abolitionist organization for which, the following year, she became secretary. In this capacity she met leading abolitionists, including Wendell Philipps, and was a supporter of pacificist and antislavery agitator William Lloyd Garrison. She was also an advocate of women's rights, and became friendly with incipient feminists such as Abby Kelly and Lucretia Mott. In 1843 Lydia married Isaac Pinkham, who, like her father, was a shoemaker aiming at a career and fortune in real estate. Not particularly gifted in business, Isaac would try a variety of enterprises over the years. The couple eventually had five children.

As countless women had done across centuries, Lydia Pinkham collected medical lore and local recipes for medicines, and eventually she developed a personal pharmacopoeia. She became locally known for her curative potions, and she kept a notebook in which she wrote down folk remedies. To treat asthma, for example, she suggested splitting the spleen of a newly butchered hog in two and attaching the halves to the soles of the feet "until perfectly dry." She created her own botanicals and kept bottles on hand for neighbors. The birth of Pinkham's Vegetable Compound as a patent medicine came soon after her husband suffered a reversal of fortunes and a nervous breakdown in the wake of the 1873 financial panic. Presumably at the suggestion of her son Dan, "Lydia E. Pinkham's Vegetable Compound" was first manufactured in the Pinkham family cellar.

The Pinkham Vegetable Compound was developed to treat menstrual cramps and general complaints more euphemistically referred to as "women's ills." Most ingredients for Pinkham's medicine could be found in *The American Dispensary,* a popular guide to remedies made from plants, written by the botanic physician John King. Unicorn root, life root, pleurisy root, and black cohosh are all listed in this reference as useful agents for treating menstrual problems, preventing miscarriage, and ameliorating a variety of other ills. According to family lore, Pinkham received the recipe for her compound to settle a loan that her husband had paid on behalf of a neighbor. The first bottles were sold in 1875. This was the same year, incidentally, in which a Pinkham family neighbor, Mary Baker Eddy, published her famed *Science and Health with Key to the Scriptures.* The Lydia E. Pinkham Medicine Company was formally organized in 1876.

The Vegetable Compound had a pungent odor and a sharp aftertaste. For many years, physicians and skeptics assumed that the compound's efficacy was due to its high alcohol content—at one time this was thirty-eight proof. More recently, it has been suggested that another ingredient, black cohosh (roots and stem of a perennial herb), might ease symptoms associated with menstruation and menopause. Fenugreek seed, a kind of clover, seems to have been Pinkham's own contribution to the potion. It has a reputation as an aphrodisiac.

Promoted by her sons Dan and Will with the kind of diligent hard work prized in nineteenth-century America, Lydia Pinkham's Vegetable Compound was originally labeled "A Sure Cure" for not only "all FEMALE WEAKNESSES" but "All Weakness of the generative organs of either sex; [and is] second to no remedy that has ever been before the public; and for all the diseases of the Kidneys it is the Greatest Remedy in the World." In spite of, or because of, such exaggerations, "Pinkham's" gradually gained brand-name recognition and commercial momentum. In 1876, an elaborate newspaper ad on the front page of the *Boston Herald* proved profitable, and demonstrated to Pinkham the value of advertising. Another significant break came when Charles N. Crittendon, a major New York broker of patent remedies, began to carry the medicine. In 1879 the decision to place Lydia Pinkham's image on the medicine's label was a defining moment in Madison Avenue marketing. Her earnest grandmotherly features were appealing, and the picture was reprinted everywhere. Sometimes a small-town newspaper, with few engravings on hand, would use Pinkham's picture whenever the image of a famous woman was required. Her name and compound were so well known that by the 1880s the medicine, and its originator, became grist for college parody:

> Tell me, Lydia, of your secrets,
> And the wonders you perform,
> How you take the sick and ailing
> And restore them to the norm?

Lydia's celebrity was due in part to the way the Vegetable Compound was packaged to include personal advice and moral wisdom. She promoted fiscal reform, discussed corseting and other evils of fashion, and warned about the plight of the working woman. These ancillaries were an effective

form of advertising. The company also offered counsel by mail, and eventually issued over one hundred booklets that dispensed advice on cooking, beauty tips, and sketches of famous women. It also made use of glowing testimonials to sell its product. These essentially literate methods enabled the Pinkhams to reach both rural and growing urban populations, and to distinguish their label from a hundred others.

For all the success of the Vegetable Compound, Lydia Pinkham's own last years were painful. In 1881, just five years after the medicine was first marketed, Lydia lost two of her beloved sons, William and Tom, to tuberculosis. In the wake of this tragedy, she turned to spiritualism, then a national craze in the United States. Seances were held in the Pinkham home every week over the next year until, late in 1882, Lydia suffered a stroke. She felt she would rather be dead with her sons than alive without them, and her end came on May 17, 1883. She was buried in Pine Grove Cemetery. Husband Isaac died in 1889.

The Vegetable Compound long outlived Lydia Pinkham, in spite of a growing distrust of patent medicines in the early twentieth century, which was fueled first by muckrakers and subsequently by the American Medical Association. In 1904 the *Ladies' Home Journal* targeted the Vegetable Compound with articles such as "How the Private Confidences of Women Are Laughed At." The Pinkham company had neglected to inform customers that its founder had died twenty years earlier, or that their letters were actually answered by typists who filled out forms. The *Journal* published a photo of Lydia's tombstone side by side with one of the company's advertisements soliciting letters, and it disclosed how correspondence with Lydia Pinkham was actually done.

Despite these revelations, the company was not seriously harmed. It also survived introduction of the Pure Food and Drug Act, passed in 1906, mainly by modifying its claims. Neither this nor reduction of its alcohol content substantially hurt the product, which subsequently proclaimed itself "Recommended as a vegetable tonic in conditions for which this preparation is adapted."

Indeed, the Pinkham Vegetable Compound's heyday came during the boom times of the 1920s. The company expanded, and plants opened in Canada as well as in Mexico and Cuba. The company reached its apogee, with up to $3 million in annual sales. But this success could not last. Physicians had gained prestige from scientific advances and recent improvements in medical education, and they were antagonistic to patent remedies. The American Medical Association, which had been railing against nostrum makers since 1849, finally acquired the standing and resources to mount a significant campaign against them. Nevertheless, if Pinkham's did not have quite the staying power of a few compounds such as Geritol and Carter's Little Liver Pills, this was due to luck and poor management as much as to the pharmacological revolution in the wake of the Second World War.

Faulty administration and a family feud over the direction of the company, beginning in the mid-1920s, contributed to the compound's decline. The Pinkhams and the Goves, descendant families, clashed over policy in the business, which they jointly controlled after the death of Will Gove, Lydia's son-in-law. Lydia Pinkham Gove, granddaughter of the founder, was a dynamic and ambitious woman and a nationally known aviatrix. Her attempts to wrest control of the company led to a decline in advertising and sales. After she was removed from power in 1937, the business experienced a mild resurgence in the 1940s. But the company limped into the second half of the twentieth century. In 1968 it was sold to Cooper Laboratories, which manufactured the product for several years from Puerto Rico. It managed to gross about $700,000 in annual sales for a time but eventually shut down production.

But Lydia would not die. When Johnson and Johnson absorbed Cooper Laboratories in 1987, it sold the Lydia Pinkham name to Numark Laboratories. Numark made changes in the formula and decided to market it as a nutritional supplement. Black cohosh, eliminated by Cooper Laboratories, was returned to the formula, which now also includes vitamins C and E in addition to Jamaica dogwood, pleurisy root, licorice, dandelion, gentian, motherwort, and 10 percent alcohol, "solely as a solvent and a preservative." The compound, also sold in pill form, offers "Nutritional support to help you feel better during menstruation and menopause." And, no surprise: every package and every label include an approximate portrait of Lydia — the "knowledgeable, caring woman."

# Paul de Kruif   [1890–1971]

## The Microbe Hunters

Everybody read *The Microbe Hunters*. A perennial bestseller since its publication in 1926, it is still in print in the twenty-first century—a striking achievement for a book about popular science. Written in breathless prose which today sounds more like fiction than fact, *The Microbe Hunters* tells the triumphant stories of the men who contributed mightily to developing the germ theory of disease. Recounted in its pages are the stories of Louis Pasteur (p. 18) ("Microbes Are a Menace!"), Robert Koch (p. 24) ("The Death Fighter"), Elie Metchnikoff (p. 186) ("The Nice Phagocytes"), and eleven others.

In a recent assessment Edward S. Golub characterized *The Microbe Hunters* as "an incredibly popular and stunningly incorrect book." Its author was Paul de Kruif, a microbiologist by training who, in the words of novelist Sinclair Lewis, was also "a man with a knife-edge mind and an iconoclasm that really means something." Whatever de Kruif's faults, his prose impressed millions and influenced two generations of aspiring scientists. It might be excessive, but only scarcely so, to say that the impassioned prose in Paul de Kruif's books changed the world. He tried. "He was a natural enthusiast," wrote H. L. Mencken, "and embraced every new idea with roars."

Paul Henry de Kruif was born to a Dutch immigrant family on March 2, 1890, in Zeeland, Michigan. His mother, Hendrika J. Kremer, was devoted to her husband, Hendrik de Kruif. But Paul described his father, who sold farm implements, as a "tough, totally self-made man whose formal schooling had ended at the second grade." He recalled him as a gloomy individual who read a chapter of the Bible to his family after meals and, for minor infractions, "bared my back and had at me with a horsewhip with the abandon of a Captain Bligh." Paul attended the University of Michigan, receiving his bachelor of science degree in 1912. His father wanted him to become either a lawyer or a doctor, and he began medical school. But his first interest lay in laboratory research. He received his Ph.D. in 1916. During World War I de Kruif served as a captain with the U.S. Sanitary Corps in France. In experiments he had some success with an antitoxin for treating infection by the bacteria *Clostridium welchii*, a common cause of a gas gangrene in wounded soldiers.

After the war de Kruif returned to Michigan, where he worked as an assistant professor of biology. But in 1920 he moved to New York with dispatch when offered a position at the Rockefeller Institute—already a force in medical research since its founding in 1901. At the Rockefeller de Kruif became friendly with, among others, Alexis Carrel (p. 199) and Peyton Rous (p. 261). But he came to dislike Simon Flexner, the institute's director, whom he considered pompous. De Kruif was a promising researcher, but when one of his early projects failed, he soon became discouraged.

In addition to scientific curiosity, de Kruif possessed literary ambitions. Within months of his arrival in New York he met and became friends with playwright Clarence Day. His position at the prestigious Rockefeller made him welcome among a group of established literary figures. In part to augment his income, he soon began writing on medical topics for the popular press and found his calling. "But there was a missionary hidden in him," wrote H. L. Mencken, de Kruif's friend, in an astute portrait, "a heritage from his Dutch Calvinist ancestors, and he longed to take the gospel of science to the plain people."

Initially, de Kruif's moonlighting caused him no grief. But chapters of his first, irreverent book on contemporary medical research were published anonymously (signed "K——, MD") in *Century* magazine in 1922. *Our Medicine Men* was to be "a spoof of the exaggerated pretensions of a part of the medical profession." But when Simon Flexner learned the identity of the author, he was not amused. He objected that de Kruif's writing could upset the institute's harmony and sense of camaraderie. "I felt deep in my bones," wrote de Kruif later, "that a spirit of competition is what makes truly hot science and what is science if not hot?" In any event, de Kruif resigned from the Rockefeller in short order, and thereafter devoted himself to writing.

*Our Medicine Men* did not displease everyone and received a friendly review from Morris Fishbein, the famous physician and author who became known as the "voice of the AMA." De Kruif and Fishbein soon became the best of friends. Through Fishbein, de Kruif met the American novelist Sinclair Lewis and helped him create his best-selling account of the doctor-as-hero, *Arrowsmith*. Their collaboration was spirited and stormy. Lewis was notoriously difficult to work with, and the two became drinking partners as well as writing partners. (De Kruif could outdrink Lewis and almost anybody else.) Lewis, wrote de Kruif, "began to teach me to forget the stuffy, stilted prose of scientific reports from the Rockefeller Institute and to write all out—free style." A tremendous success when published in 1925, *Arrowsmith* won Lewis the Pulitzer Prize (which he refused) and brought de Kruif one-quarter of the book's considerable royalties.

De Kruif conceived *The Microbe Hunters* as a book that would render human the heroes of bacteriology. "In their adventures they are brave, sometimes; they are stupid, often; they have good hunches and a few brilliant intuitions; they are, above all, lucky." Aiming at a popular audience, de Kruif found the key to the book's success in his ability to turn out what Sinclair Lewis called "purple passages." The reader could not help being swept up in the prose, which dramatized historic events at the laboratory bench. "'Wait! here are whole bunches of them ... like cigarettes in a pack,'" writes de Kruif, inventing words for Robert Koch. "'Heh! here is one lone devil inside a lung cell ... I wonder ... have I found him — that tubercle bug, already?'" De Kruif wrote about Leeuwenhoek, the "janitor of Delft" who "had stolen upon and peeped into a fantastic sub-visible world of little things." Elie Metchnikoff was the scientist who discovered the "nice phagocytes."

The publisher of *The Microbe Hunters* had hoped the book would at least sell out its first printing of 2,800 copies, but it was an immediate bestseller, boosted by positive reviews by Mencken, William Allen White, and Heywood Broun. De Kruif, wrote Robert L. Duffus in the *New York Times*, "has brought his dead microbe hunters to warm and vigorous life, and it is impossible to avoid seeing that these were usually men of fanatical purposes and turbulent emotions." Sales soon topped 100,000 copies; eventually they would exceed 1,000,000. *The Microbe Hunters* continued to be popular through the 1930s, 1940s, and 1950s. Dozens of printings in the inexpensive paperback format continued through the 1960s. A seventieth anniversary edition was issued in 1996.

Paul de Kruif followed *The Microbe Hunters* with a number of books, most involving the success of individuals against high odds. *The Hunger Fighters* and *Seven Iron Men* were not great successes, but de Kruif bounced back in 1932 with *Men Against Death,* another medical bestseller that profiled notable figures, some of whom he knew personally. With Sidney Howard, de Kruif cowrote *Yellow-Jack!* in 1934, a play that told the story of Walter Reed's battle against yellow fever. In 1936 his *Why Keep Them Alive?* was born of the Great Depression and was filled with indignation over the economic disaster's toll on the health of children in a land still enormously wealthy. This book reflected de Kruif's infatuation (later hotly denied) with left-wing causes.

De Kruif's career evolved in a curious way. For many years his vivid prose had been found in popular magazines such as *Country Gentleman* and *Ladies' Home Journal.* He was, by and large, a chronicler of mainstream medicine with an interest in promising therapies. But in 1940, when de Kruif became a contributing editor for *Reader's Digest,* he began to turn out a steady stream of sensationalism. "A Working Cure for Athlete's Foot," which involved daubing the feet with camphor and phenol, proved worse than the disease, and aroused the ire of the American Medical Association. His 1945 book, *The Male Hormone,* trumpeted the masculinizing effects of methyltestosterone. De Kruif, according to John Heidenry, would "unearth miracle cures for just about everything, sometimes almost every month, on the slenderest of evidence."

Paul de Kruif had a fairly tumultuous personal life. He liked thinking of himself as a nihilist and Dostoyevskian character, filled with passion and an uncontrollable sensuality that he called "my inner enemy." Before he had worked at the Rockefeller, he had deserted his first wife, Mary Fisher, and their two sons. He had fallen in love with Rhea Elizabeth Barbarin, whom he eventually married in 1922. Their nearly divine union did not tame his desire for other women, and he felt monumentally guilty about his extramarital dalliances. Upon Rhea's death in 1957, de Kruif published a memoir, *The Sweeping Wind.* He soon married his third and last wife, Eleanor Lappage, who would outlive him.

*The Microbe Hunters,* although by no means profound, inspired a great number of medical researchers and Nobelists. It enthralled Gertude Belle Elion, who was awarded the prize for her discoveries in pharmacology, and James Watson, who grew up to codiscover the structure of DNA. As a boy Carleton Gajdusek (p. 302) went so far as to stencil the names of the book's biographees on the steps leading to his attic laboratory. The list could go on.

Like many of his generation, de Kruif viewed himself—and medicine—through a hypermasculine lens. Sensitive but psychologically naive, he had little patience for what he jokingly called "the analism promulgated by Sigmund Freud." He loved to box, chop wood, and swim in the waters of Lake Michigan. Sometimes he stayed up all night listening to the symphonies of Beethoven. Often, "when life got scrambled as a result of my turbulence," wrote de Kruif, "violent activity in the outdoors calmed me down, dragged my ashes, let me start over with a clean cortex and hypothalamus."

That ploy ceased to work shortly after he turned eighty-one. On April 3, 1971, Paul de Kruif died of a heart attack in Holland, Michigan.

# Henri Dunant  [1828–1910]

## Founding the Red Cross

By the mid-nineteenth century, the Industrial Revolution had tendered new technics for warfare. Weapons for the common soldier were more accurate and deadly, and machined bullets and shrapnel could tear through the body as never before. The military merits of such firepower clashed with the changing values of an expanding middle class, many of whom were increasingly able to empathize with pain and suffering. Nothing illustrates this conflict better than the outcome of the Battle of Solferino on June 24, 1859. More than 300,000 troops from the Austrian, French, and Sardinian armies were involved. At day's end, some 30,000 lay dead, and thousands more were wounded and dying. Witnessing the battle and giving aid in its aftermath was a young Swiss bourgeois, Henri Dunant.

"Bodies of men and horses covered the battlefield; corpses were strewn over roads, ditches, ravines, thickets and fields," wrote Dunant. "[T]he approaches of Solferino were literally thick with dead."

In *A Memory of Solferino,* Dunant recounted the dreadful agony of the wounded. He told of the lack of provisions for treating them. After his book had become a bestseller, he proposed and went on to organize an international convention from which would emerge an organization of volunteers. Decades later, toward the end of a long life by turns productive and tragic, Dunant told a journalist, "It is I who founded the Red Cross."

Jean Henri Dunant was born on May 8, 1828, the eldest child of prosperous Genevans. His father, Jean Jacques, was a prosperous merchant and town councilman. His mother, Anne-Antoinette Calladon, was a descendant of a famous family. In his memoirs, Dunant wrote of his mother's profound influence on him. She was, as she had leisure to be, devoted to philanthropic charitable work. Evangelism was a strong force in Geneva at the time, and Henri was religious as a youth. For a time he worked for the League of Alms, a devout youth group. Dunant also became an enthusiastic letter writer early in his life, and had an international array of correspondents. He wrote in his memoirs that he always had "the liveliest interest in the unfortunate, the disinherited of this world, the humble and oppressed and indigent, embracing their causes with enthusiasm, and with passion...." When novelist Harriet Beecher Stowe, author of *Uncle Tom's*

*Cabin,* came through Geneva, Henri introduced himself. A little later, he was also strongly influenced by the work of Florence Nightingale (p. 88).

After finishing his studies in 1853, Dunant entered the business world, where he wanted both to make money and to help the disadvantaged. As cashier for a company seeking to develop investments in Algeria, Dunant visited the expanding French colony. For a time he became dazzled with the prospect of earning a fortune, fancied himself an entrepreneur, and assiduously sought to develop a business venture in growing and milling corn. But in 1855 he also helped establish the World Alliance of the Young Men's Christian Association. Three years later, he took time off from business in Algeria to visit neighboring Tunisia and wrote a book, *Notice sur la régence de Tunis (Notes on the Regency of Tunis)*. It included an intriguing twenty-page chapter comparing slavery in Muslim countries with that in the United States.

In 1859 Dunant went to Solferino on business. Bureaucratic obstacles had impeded his agricultural project in spite of considerable financial backing. He needed to obtain water rights for his Algerian land. He conceived the idea of asking permission of none other than the emperor of France. Louis Napoleon was then at war in Italy, and that is where Dunant went to find him. It is characteristic of Dunant's intellect and sometimes misplaced opportunism that he composed a brief book for the occasion entitled *The Empire of Charlemagne Reestablished*. This extravagance, Dunant somehow thought, would appeal to the emperor. When Louis Napoleon finally saw it, he asked Dunant to suspend publication because of possible political embarrassment.

Meanwhile, however, Dunant witnessed Solferino. Nothing had prepared him for the carnage as French and Sardinian forces attacked the Austrians, who occupied the high ground around the small town. The battle raged all day. As Dunant graphically described it later, the hand-to-hand combat was "indescribably hideous. Austrians and Allied troops trampled on one another, slaughtering one another over the bleeding corpses, felling their adversaries with rifle butts, and smashing in their skulls, or disemboweling them with saber or bayonet. There was no question of quarter: it was butchery, a battle of wild beasts, maddened with rage and drunk with blood." In the afternoon came a thunderstorm. "The skies became black and a violent storm broke over the contending armies." The Austrians fell back and the battle ended.

Relief preparation was not even remotely adequate, on either side. During the battle and for eight days after, Dunant tried to help. He had no medical training, and in some cases the best he could do was to hand out cigars to wounded soldiers. (Tobacco was thought to be an antiseptic, and

its fragrance was preferable to putrefying flesh.) But he also organized groups of women to help him, and even put a couple of tourists to work. He had fresh fruit brought in, as well as bandages and clothing.

Thus there emerged the concept of organized volunteers to help the wounded, on and off the battlefield. It was embodied in *Un souvenir de Solferino,* published in 1862. The small book created a sensation. The brothers Goncourt, in France, called it "a thousand times more beautiful than Homer." Charles Dickens warmly endorsed it, and Victor Hugo was moved. It was soon widely translated, and Dunant became a famous man.

*Un souvenir de Solferino* is comprised of two parts. Dunant first skillfully describes the battle and its aftermath in unsparing detail. In the second part Dunant outlines the prospect of "an inviolable Convention" as "a basis for Societies for the relief of wounded in the various countries of Europe." He asks: "Would it not be possible in time of peace and quiet to form relief societies for the purpose of having care given to the wounded in wartime by zealous, devoted, and thoroughly qualified volunteers?" This was the idea that gave birth to the Red Cross.

Dunant became a force for benevolence over the next two years as he traveled throughout Europe gathering support for an international aid society. Dunant used his eminence to visit heads and representatives of state, encouraging their participation. In February 1863 the Geneva Society for Public Welfare was founded with the express purpose of promulgating Dunant's plan.

The Geneva Convention, as it became known, was held in August 1864, with representatives of sixteen countries. From its work emerged a document that in ten articles embodies the basic principles of international first aid in wartime. These include respect for the wounded, the concept that military hospitals will be treated as neutral territory, and the idea that enemy soldiers deserve care. Medical personnel, identified by a white armband, were to be considered neutral and protected from harm. Their standard was to be a red cross on a white background—the Swiss flag with colors reversed. Twelve nations signed the treaty on August 22, 1864. The United States, together with Great Britain, and Sweden initially declined to sign.

Although some nations were cautious and others decidedly reluctant, the Red Cross was a powerful idea whose time had come. As was the case when Florence Nightingale brought a nursing staff to the Crimean War front, the revolution in communications and improved transportation inflicted responsibility on nations at war. As armies grew larger and arms more deadly, the conventions of the Red Cross represented what it called "correlative refinements of mercy." The brief war between Prussia and Austria in 1866 provided an early and successful test, and nine more nations had signed the Geneva accords by 1867.

Dunant, however, was not rewarded in the years after the first Geneva Convention. In 1866 he published "Universal and International Society for the Revival of the Orient," a pamphlet in which he suggested developing a "neutral colony" in Palestine. By the next year, though, he was bankrupt. Dunant had never won the water rights for Algeria, and his creditors lost confidence. Improvidence was not a virtue in Swiss society, and Dunant found himself ostracized. His resignation from the International Committee of the Red Cross was accepted with alacrity by Gustave Moynier, an early supporter who had become his rival in the organization. For decades afterward, Moynier would downplay Dunant's significance in founding the Red Cross.

Humiliated by his financial embarrassment, Dunant was ultimately forced to leave Geneva altogether. Emotionally, he was devastated. "I lost that elasticity, that energy," he later wrote, "that confidence that I had until then, and I fell into a black depression." As Dunant wrote later, in the years that followed there were days when he ate little more than a crust of bread, slept outdoors, and kept his collar clean with chalk. If he did not suffer from clinical depression, Dunant's excess of poverty clearly suggests there was a psychopathological dimension to his loss of verve.

In spite of these difficulties, Dunant was still occasionally in the public eye until the mid-1870s. Notably, he was in Paris during the Franco-Prussian War of 1871, which ended the regime of Louis Napoleon. The work of the newly formed Red Cross in this conflict was not fully effective, but it represented an important series of lessons in organization. Dunant participated in Red Cross activities, seeing to the administration of ambulances, passing out clothing and first-aid kits, and negotiating on behalf of French prisoners in Prussian hands. During the insurrectionist Commune that followed, when the people of Paris refused to accept French capitulation to the Germans, Dunant was suspected by both sides of being a spy. The next year he brought together a conference that was to be the foundation for the "universal alliance" to deal with the treatment of war prisoners and to arbitrate international disputes through the courts. These ideas were ahead of their time and did not then come to fruition.

The rediscovery of Henri Dunant, after years of obscurity, is a tale in itself. He disappeared from public view in 1875. Twelve years later, in 1887, he arrived in the Swiss village of Heiden, a parachutist without baggage. His health was poor, his beard was white, and he was suffering from eczema. He had turned against organized religion and believed that people should emancipate themselves from its shackles. "I am a disciple of Christ, as in the first century: simply that," wrote Dunant. In 1895 Georges Baumberger, a journalist, published word of his whereabouts, and created a sensation. Dunant, by then living in a hospice, was described as "a deserted and poor but not a broken and embittered man … demanding nothing of the world for himself."

In 1901 Henri Dunant was awarded the first Nobel Prize for peace, which he shared with Frédéric Passy (1822–1912), a French economist and founder, in 1867, of the International Peace League. Dunant was in poor health and unable to travel to collect the award, and the prize money was placed in accounts out of the reach of Dunant's creditors, who still harassed him. Dunant would live for almost ten more years, dying on October 30, 1910. His final years were fairly peaceful and in his cottage in Heiden he was a remote eminence, visited by royalty. His last words are said to have been, "How dark it is."

Today, the doctrine of the International Red Cross, derived from Dunant's early conceptions, still promotes the ideals of bringing relief to human suffering. Its volunteers are deployed in cases of natural and other disaster as well as in war. Neutrality and impartiality are still its watchwords, but this has become a complex stance in the present context of international humanitarian law. In recent years the Red Cross has flourished, funded privately for the most part; it has a presence in 169 countries and millions of members. Other conventions updated the original Geneva accords, the last time in 1949. They still represent an international standard. Henri Dunant would be pleased, writes Caroline Moorehead, "to see his great machine so efficiently at work … [and] gratified that his fundamental question — how to protect people in the hands of the enemy — continues to fly like a flag over the entire organization."

But Dunant would have been saddened to learn that, in the century after he witnessed the Battle of Solferino, warfare grew deadlier and bloodier. He had predicted "that future battles will only become more and more murderous." But Dunant did not envision wholesale genocide,

and during World War II, in fact, the International Red Cross's unwillingness to speak out against the Nazi Holocaust cost it credibility. The need
for the Red Cross was all the greater, however, in the last half of the twentieth century, both during and after the Cold War. The twenty-first
century opened with renewed ethnic conflicts and brushfire wars, proliferation of small arms in the hands of guerillas and terrorists, and "ethnic
cleansing" on the part of governments. The Red Cross had an enduring
role to play in a world filled with events that challenge humanity.

# Envoy

A collective biography is hard to end without expressing regret for any number of individuals not included for lack of space and time. But it is worth pointing out that not since the nineteenth century could one hope to provide a reasonably complete set of profiles, whether in medicine or the history of any living and evolving discipline. Today, when 300 individuals have been known to sign a single scientific paper, apologies for exclusion begin to sound precious.

One inexcusable omission who might count for all is Alexandre Yersin, a Swiss-born French bacteriologist who may be considered one of the heroes of modern medicine. He isolated the bacillus that causes diphtheria and investigated syphilis as well as a host of diseases that affect humans and animals. Most famously he discovered the germ, now called *Yersinia pestis,* responsible for bubonic plague. We know the date: June 23, 1894, a few days before the Japanese researcher, Shibasaburo Kitasato, discovered the same thing. The inevitable priority dispute was resolved with less rancor than many.

For years Yersin lived and worked in an old barracks that he had painted stark white. Locals called it the "Ivory Tower." A high school named after him still operates, and artifacts from his life and laboratory can be found in his office, now a museum at the Institut Pasteur—in Nha Trang, Vietnam. Yersin himself founded the institute in 1895 and designed its building, erected in 1904.

When he died, on March 1, 1943, Alexandre Yersin was buried on a hill in the Dien Khanh District, in sight of the beautiful coastline on the South China Sea, with its crisp clear water and sandy white beaches. To reach the site of his tomb one follows an earthen staircase that winds up from the old Mandarin highway. A stone and cement obelisk looks out across the Bay of Cam Ranh. The inscription reads: "Benefactor and Humanist—Venerated by the Vietnamese People."

For us, Yersin's resting place—in a part of the world long colonized, exploited, and devastated—might best be a reminder that Western medicine is part and parcel of Western culture. For all its works and wonders, that civilization, like others before and concurrent, tends to be domineering if not

*Alexandre Yersin outside his straw hut in Hong Kong, about 1895.*

omnipotent, imperious if not imperialist—and the purveyor, to be simple and frank, of much of the misery it laments. One can imagine Yersin's memorial in years past, writes Jean-Claude Guillebaud, recalling the Vietnam War, "often surrounded by smoke from explosions, skirted by patrols, flown over by squadrons, perhaps licked by flames."

At a time when medicine has become powerful as never before, at the dawn of what many think will be a revolution in diagnosis and treatment, it is worth underscoring the dynamics and complexity of nature, and the fragility of human ecology. Nothing could be more impressive than discovering, as Alexandre Yersin did, the microbe that provoked bubonic plague, widely identified as the Black Death—the disease that over centuries carried away literally millions of people and caused untold misery. Yet such an achievement, and feats  still more spectacular to come, should not inspire an excess admiration that fuels hubris rather than self-reflection, or impassioned triumphalism instead of compassion. Far preferable to fantasies of immortality are the enduring words of Hippocrates: *Ars longa, vita brevis.*

# Source Notes

See Bibliography (p. 437) for complete citations for these frequently cited works: C. Gillispie, *Dictionary of Scientific Biography* and C. Moritz et al, *Current Biography Yearbook.*

## Introduction

xvii "You will do my post-mortem?...": Quoted in R. B. Vaughan, "The Romantic Rationalist," *Medical History* 10 (1965): 215.

xviii "Grandma was gone...": Quoted in S. Kleinfeld, *A Machine Called Indomitable* (Times Books, 1985), p. 46.

xviii "that one old gentleman...": L. King, *Medical Thinking* (Princeton University Press, 1982), p. 13.

xix "to resuscitate what was...": H. Sigerist, "Developments and Trends in Dentistry" in *On the Sociology of Medicine,* ed. M. Roemer (MD Publications, 1960), p. 327.

xxii "has become the prisoner...": R. Porter, *The Greatest Benefit to Mankind* (W. W. Norton, 1997), p. 717.

xxiii "We must strive...": G. Rosen, *A History of Public Health* (Johns Hopkins University Press, 1993), p. 471.

## Charles Darwin

3 "The passion for collecting...": C. Darwin, *The Autobiography of Charles Darwin, 1809–1882* (Norton, 1958), p. 23.

6 "man is descended...": C. Darwin, *The Descent of Man* (Appleton, 1877), pp. 368–69.

6 "mutually indispensable...": A. Flew, *Darwinian Evolution,* 2d ed. (Transition Publishers, 1997), p. 23.

7 "What have the doctors...": W. F. Bynum, "Darwin and the Doctors: Evolution, Diathesis, and Germs in 19th-Century Britain," *Gesnerus* 40, no. 1/2 (1983): 45.

7 "as Darwin studied...": Ibid., p. 48.

7 "a little explored...": Quoted in A. Bearn and E. Miller, "Archibald Garrod and the Development of the Concept of Inborn Errors of Metabolism," *Bulletin of the History of Medicine* 53 (1979): 324.

7 "conviction, based on...": H. Krebs, *Reminiscences and Reflections* (Clarendon Press, 1981), p. 118.

## Rudolf Virchow

8 "has made the whole...": L. C. Lane, "Rudolf Virchow" in *Occidental Medical Times,* August (1893): 9.

8  "Are the triumphs...": Quoted in H. E. Sigerist, *The Great Doctors: A Biographical History of Medicine* (W. W. Norton, 1933), p. 339.

10  "natural attorneys for the poor": J. and E. Bendiner, *Biographical Dictionary of Medicine* (Facts on File, 1990), p. 248.

11  "that the independent...": Quoted in W. Coleman, *Biology in the Nineteenth Century* (John Wiley & Sons, 1971), p. 46.

11  "Throughout the range...": Quoted in E. A. Carlsson, ed., *Modern Biology: Its Conceptual Foundations* (George Braziller, 1967), p. 25.

11  "caused a revolution...": R. H. Major, *A History of Medicine*, vol. 2 (Charles C. Thomas, 1954), p. 808.

13  "more than a medical...": E. H. Ackerknecht, *Rudolf Virchow: Doctor, Statesman, Anthropologist* (University of Wisconsin Press, 1953), p. 123.

## Claude Bernard

14  "His philosophy...": Preface to H. Parvez and S. Parvez, eds., *Advances in Experimental Medicine: A Centenary Tribute to Claude Bernard* (Elsevier, 1980), p. 1.

14  "Bernard shaped...": H. LaFollette and N. Shanks, "Animal Experimentation: The Legacy of Claude Bernard," *International Studies in the Philosophy of Science* 8, no. 3 (1994): 203.

17  "conquer living nature...": Quoted in W. Coleman, "The Cognitive Basis of the Discipline: Claude Bernard on Physiology," *ISIS* 76 (1985): 56.

17  "constant conditions of temperature...": J. Olmsted and E. Olmsted, *Claude Bernard and the Experimental Method in Medicine* (Henry Schuman, 1952), p. 108.

17  "religious and very beautiful": Ibid., p. 245.

17  "The costs of researchers'...": LaFollette and Shanks, "Animal Experimentation," p. 207.

17  "as others breathe...": Quoted in E. D. Robin, ed., *Claude Bernard and the Internal Environment* (Marcel Dekker, 1979), p. 14.

## Louis Pasteur

18  "He made happiness...": R. Vallery-Radot, *The Life of Pasteur* (Doubleday, 1928), p. 296.

20  "And I wait...": Ibid., p. 109.

21  "merely communicates...": Ibid., p. 311.

22  "I have perfected...": J. Nicolle, *Louis Pasteur: The Story of His Major Discoveries* (Basic Books, 1961), p. 197.

22  "looked around him...": Vallery-Radot, *The Life of Pasteur*, p. 464.

22  "warm, effusive, personal...": W. Clark, *At War Within: The Double-Edged Sword of Immunity* (Oxford University Press, 1995), p. 32.

## Robert Koch

24  "Bacteriology's consolidation...": R. Porter, *The Greatest Benefit to Mankind* (W W. Norton, 1997), p. 436.

26  "all locations where...": R. Koch, "The Etiology of Tuberculosis" *Review of Infectious Diseases* 4 (1982): 1271.

27  "red letter day...": *Dictionary of Scientific Biography,* vol. 7, p. 423.

28  "utterances were carefully...": T. Brock, Robert Koch: *A Life in Medicine and Bacteriology* (American Society of MM, 1998), p. 292.

## Hippocrates

30  "Examining the body...": *Dictionary of Scientific Biography*, vol. 6, p. 424.
31  "Spongy, porous parts...": Hippocrates, "Ancient Medicine" in *Hippocrates*, vol. 1 (Harvard University Press, 1923), p. 59.
32  "If I fulfill...": Ibid., p. 3.
33  "the autonomy of medicine...": O. Temkin, *Hippocrates in a World of Pagans and Christians* (Johns Hopkins University Press, 1991), p. 256.

## Galen

34  "climax and flower...": C. Singer, "Galen as a Modern" in *Toward Modern Science*, ed. R. M. Palter (E. P. Dutton, 1969), p. 120.
34  "sometimes bites her maids...": S. Nuland, *Doctors: The Biography of Medicine* (Alfred A. Knopf, 1988), p. 37.
35  "has not gone as far...": Quoted in A. J. Brock, *Greek Medicine* (J. M. Dent & Sons, 1929), p. 133.
36  "We have, then,...": Galen, *On the Natural Faculties* (Harvard University Press, 1916), p. 31.
37  "The pulse is...": Quoted in O. Temkin, *Galenism* (Cornell University Press, 1973), p. 103.
38  "He is the upholder...": V. Nutton, "Roman Medicine, 250 B.C. to A.D. 200" in *The Western Medical Tradition*, ed. L. I. Conrad et al (Cambridge University Press, 1995), p. 70.

## Andreas Vesalius

42  "After I had brought...": Quoted in C. D. O'Malley, *Andreas Vesalius of Brussels* (University of California Press, 1964), p. 14.
44  "I could have done nothing...": Ibid., p. 222.

## William Harvey

45  "I do not profess...": W. Harvey, *The Works of William Harvey*, M.D. (Sydenham Society, 1847), p. 7.
46  "It is certain...": Quoted in A. Wear, "The Heart and Blood from Vesalius to Harvey" in *Companion to the History of Modern Science*, ed. R. C. Olby et al (Routledge, 1990), p. 575.
47  "incongruous and mutually subversive...": Harvey, *The Works*, p. 11.
47  "For it is the heart...": Harvey, *The Works*, p. 47.
48  "It is absolutely necessary...": Quoted in R. Porter, *The Greatest Benefit to Mankind* (W. W. Norton, 1997), p. 214.
48  "completely refashioned...": R. G. Frank, Jr., *Harvey and the Oxford Physiologists* (University of California Press, 1980), p. xii.

## Paracelsus

50  "tramps, butchers, and barbers": Quoted in R. Porter, *The Greatest Benefit to Mankind* (W. W. Norton, 1997), p. 201.

50  "No one requires...": G. Feder, "Paradigm Lost," *Lancet* 341 (1993): 1397.

50  "It is difficult...": *Dictionary of Scientific Biography,* vol. 10, p. 311.

51  "The patients are your...": Quoted in B. Aubrey, "Paracelsus" in *Great Scientists,* vol. 9 (Grolier, 1989), p. 152.

52  "Come then, and listen...": Quoted in W. H. Brock, *The Norton History of Chemistry* (W. W. Norton, 1993), pp. 43–44.

52  "For the sun...": Paracelsus, *Selected Writings* (Princeton University Press, 1973), p. 21.

53  "has a special...": A. G. Debus, *Man and Nature in the Renaissance* (Cambridge University Press, 1978), p. 23.

54  "lived like a pig...": Brock, *Chemistry,* p. 44.

54  "But after,...": R. Browning, "Paracelsus" in B. Jaffe, *Crucibles: The Story of Chemistry* (Dover, 1976), p. 20.

## Giovanni Morgagni

55  "It was Morgagni...": R. Porter, "The Eighteenth Century" in *The Western Medical Tradition,* ed. L. I. Conrad et al (Cambridge University Press, 1995), p. 410.

55  "I have passed my life...": Quoted in S. Nuland, *Doctors: The Biography of Medicine* (Alfred A. Knopf, 1988), p. 168.

57  "his work remains...": R. Margotta, *The Story of Medicine* (Golden Press, 1968), p. 232.

57  "the new medicine...": Quoted in Nuland, *Doctors,* p. 152.

57  "yet reads without spectacles...": Ibid., p. 169.

## Xavier Bichat

58  "His works have become...": Quoted in J. E. Lesch, *Science and Medicine in France: The Emergence of Experimental Physiology,* 1790–1815 (Harvard University Press, 1984), p. 80.

58  "he had fulfilled...": Ibid., p. 68.

59  "are themselves composed...": Quoted in C. G. Cumston, *An Introduction to the History of Medicine,* (Alfred A. Knopf, 1926), p. 363.

60  "a starting point...": Lesch, *The Emergence of Experimental Physiology,* p. 79.

61  "this audacious young man...": N. Dobo and A. Role, *Bichat: la vie fulgurante d'un genie* (Perrin, 1989), p. 7.

## René Laennec

62  "is like a set of chains...": Quoted in S. Nuland, *Doctors: The Biography of Medicine* (Alfred A. Knopf, 1988), p. 209.

63  "His character pleases me so little...": J. Duffin, *To See with a Better Eye: A Life of R. T. H. Laennec* (Princeton University Press, 1998), p. 37.

63  "Laennec had established...": Ibid., p. 76.

63  "extraordinary beauty...": M. Foucault, *The Birth of the Clinic* (Random House, 1973), p. 169.

63  "reduced to a third...": Quoted in Nuland, *Doctors,* p. 220.

64  "I rolled a quire...": Ibid.

64  "a cylinder which...": L. Acierno, *History of Cardiology* (Parthenon, 1994), p. 469.

65  "great and wonderful discovery...": R. Kervan, *Laennec* (Pergamon Press, 1960), p. 154.
65  "Stethoscope Song": Quoted in S. Reiser, *Medicine and the Reign of Technology* (Cambridge University Press, 1978), p. 34.
65  "I believe that you...": G. Eliot, *Middlemarch* (Penguin, 1965), pp. 460–61.
66  "a vigorous if challenging...": Duffin, *To See with a Better Eye,* p. 8.

## Johannes Müller

67  "with full hearts...": V. Robinson, *Pathfinders in Medicine* (Medical Life Press, 1929), p. 385.
67  "So magnetic was...": Ibid.
67  "How can a single tongue...": Quoted in J. Walsh, *Makers of Modern Medicine* (Books for Libraries, 1907), p. 221.
69  "With the exception of...": Quoted in Robinson, *Pathfinders,* p. 384.
69  "It contains such...": W. Haberling, *German Medicine* (Paul B. Hoeber, 1934), p. 80.
69  "more widespread in the organism...": *Dictionary of Scientific Biography,* vol. 9, p. 572.

## François Magendie

71  "I compare myself...": *Dictionary of Scientific Biography,* vol. 9, p. 7.
71  "Medicine is a science...: Quoted in R. Porter and W. F. Bynum, "The Art and Science of Medicine" in *Companion Encyclopedia of the History of Medicine* (Routledge, 1993), p. 7.
71  "He found some value...": H. de Balzac, *La peau de chagrin* ("The Wild Ass's Skin") (Penguin, 1977), pt. 3, "The Death Agony," pp. 245–46.
72  "It would be more advantageous...": L. Deloyers, *François Magendie: Précurseur de la médicine expérimentale* (Presses Universitaires de Bruxelles, 1970), p 79.
73  "exerted a very profound influence...": *Dictionary of Scientific Biography,* vol. 9, p. 7.
74  "In reference to all these phenomena...": Quoted in I. Bloch, *The Sexual Life of Our Time* (1908; reprint, Allied Book Company, 1928), p. 49.

## Pierre Louis

75  "indispensable to count": Quoted in S. J. Reiser, *Medicine and the Reign of Technolog* (Cambridge University Press, 1978), p. 33.
75  "to appreciate the value...": Ibid.
75  "He consecrated the whole...": Quoted in W. Osler, "The Influence of Louis on American Medicine" in *An Alabama Student and Other Biographical Essays* (Oxford University Press, 1908), p. 193.
77  "a new era...: Quoted in A. Bollet, "Medical History: Pierre Louis," *American Journal of the Medical Sciences* 266, no. 2 (1973): 98.
77  "all establish narrow limits...": Quoted in A. Morabia, "P. C. A. Louis and the Birth of Clinical Epidemiology," *Journal of Clinical Epidemiology* 49, no. 12 (1996): 1330.
78  "the object of our reverence...": Quoted in R. H. Major, *A History of Medicine,* vol. 2 (Charles C. Thomas, 1954), p. 671.

78  "With Louis…": Reiser, *Medicine and the Reign of Technology,* p. 32.
78  "knew no distinction…": Quoted in Osler, *The Influence of Louis,* p. 198.

## Carl Ludwig

80  "the great inaugurator…": K. Rothschuh, *History of Physiology* (Robert E. Krieger, 1973), p. 211.
80  "When the history…": Quoted in G. Rosen, "Carl Ludwig and His American Students," *Bulletin of the Institute of the History of Medicine* **4,** no. 8 (1936): 617.
81  "veritable turning point": K. Rothschuh, *History of Physiology* (Robert E. Krieger, 1973), p. 205.
81  "first modern textbook…": Rosen, "Carl Ludwig," p. 615.
81  "The task of a scientific…": Ibid.
82  "Destiny has conferred…": Ibid., p. 617.
83  "is nothing other than…": T. Lenoir, "Science for the Clinic: Science Policy and the Formation of Carl Ludwig's Institute in Leipzig" in *The Investigate Enterprise: Experimental Physiology in Nineteenth-Century Medicine,* ed. W. Coleman and F L. Holmes (University of California Press, 1988), p. 157.
83  "I hope that you…": Quoted in Lenoir, "Science for the Clinic," p. 155.
83  "in such superlative terms…": L. Acierno, *The History of Cardiology* (Parthenon, 1994), p. 218.
83  "formal but very kindly…": Quoted in S. Flexner and J. Flexner, *William Henry Welch* (Viking, 1941), p. 84.

## Jacob Henle

85  "with isolated steps…": B. Bracegirdle, *History of Microtechnique,* 2d ed. (Science Heritage, 1986), p. 310.
85  "All free surfaces…": Quoted in V. Robinson, *Pathfinders in Medicine* (Medical Life Press, 1929), p. 483.
85  "the most systematic…": H. Harris, *The Birth of the Cell* (Yale University Press, 1999), p. 107.
85  "a landmark in the history…": G. Rosen, *A History of Public Health,* expanded ed. (Johns Hopkins University Press, 1993), p. 274.
86  "The material of contagions…": R. H. Major, *A History of Medicine,* vol. 2 (Charles C. Thomas, 1954), p. 798.
86  "understand the processes…": *Dictionary of Scientific Biography,* vol. 6, p. 270.
86  "contained the first real…": Quoted in Robinson, *Pathfinders in Medicine,* pp. 487–88.
87  "A hypothesis which…": Ibid., p. 491.
87  "The physiology of the sick…": Ibid.

## Florence Nightingale

88  "Much of what now…": I. B. Cohen, "Florence Nightingale," *Scientific American* 250, no. 3 (1984): 128.
89  "If I should determine…": Quoted in L. R. Seymer, *A General History of Nursing* (Macmillan, 1933), p. 80.
90  "Why have we…": Ibid., p. 83.
90  "a prejudice will have been broken…": Ibid., p. 84.
91  "I use the word…": F. Nightingale, *Notes on Nursing* (Harrison, 1859), p. 6.

92   "an ambiguous combination...": C. Hobbs, *Florence Nightingale* (Twayne, 1997), p. 93.
92   "a lost lamb bleating...": Quoted in Hobbs, *Florence Nightingale*, p. 31.
93   "I am an egg full...": F. Nightingale, *Ever Yours, Florence Nightingale: Selected Letters* (Harvard University Press, 1990), p. 418.
93   "Thousands of soldiers wept...": B. Dossey, *Florence Nightingale* (Springhouse, 1999), p. 415.

## Joseph Lister

94   "This Yankee dodge...": R. Fisher, *Joseph Lister* (Stein and Day, 1977), p. 37
96   "[I]t occurred to me...": *Dictionary of Scientific Biography*, vol. 8, p. 403.
97   "next to the promulgation...": Ibid., p. 406.
98   "to that later life...": Fisher, *Joseph Lister*, p. 325.
98   "the rare nobility of...": *Dictionary of Scientific Biography*, vol. 8, p. 409.
98   "was positively afraid...": Fisher, *Joseph Lister*, p. 297.
99   "Only those who lived...": Quoted in H. Cushing, *The Life of Sir William Osler* (Oxford University Press, 1940), p. 995.

## Wilhelm Conrad Röntgen

100   "Her noseless, eyeless face...": Quoted in O. Glasser, *Dr. W. C. Röntgen* (Charles C. Thomas, 1958), p. 81.
102   "are not identical...": *Glasser, Röntgen*, p. 50.
102   "constitutes an epoch-making result...": Quoted in Glasser, *Röntgen*, p. 56.
103   "will be very much interested...": Ibid., p. 57.
103   "not only changed medical practice...": R. G. Evens, "Röntgen Retrospective: One Hundred Years of a Revolutionary Technology," *Journal of the American Medical Association* 274, no. 11 (1995): 913.
103   "robust, erect, vigorous,...": W. Woglom, *Discoverers for Medicine* (Yale University Press, 1949), p. 60.

## Theodor Boveri

105   "There is no doubt...": E. Mayr, *Growth of Biological Thought* (Harvard University Press, 1982), p. 748.
105   "the characters dealt with...": Quoted in F. Balter, "Theodore Boveri," *Science* 144 (1964): 812.
106   "are independent individuals...": Quoted in F. Balter, *Theodore Boveri* (University of California Press, 1967), p. 66.
107   "I regard the chromosomes...": Quoted in Balter, "Theodore Boveri," p. 811.
107   "We may identify every...": Mayr, *Biological Thought*, p. 748.
107   "completed the shift of emphasis...": *Dictionary of Scientific Biography*, vol. 2, p. 363.
107   "specific assortment of chromosomes...": Ibid., p. 364.
107   "the basis for the cytological...": Ibid.
108   "I have gradually grown.": Balter, "Theodor Boveri," p. 815.

## Santiago Ramón y Cajal

110   "my greatest year...": S. Ramón y Cajal, *Recollections of My Life* (MIT Press, 1989), p. 321.

111  "I began to explain...": Ibid., pp. 356–57.

111  "doctrine of dynamic...": T. Wasson, ed., *Nobel Prize Winners* (H. W. Wilson, 1988), p. 854.

112  "classic of medical science...": *Dictionary of Scientific Biography,* vol. 11, p. 274.

112  "direct, mordant and uncompromising.": F. Garrison, "Ramon y Cajal" in *Contributions to the History of Medicine* (Hafner, 1966), p. 956.

## Oswald Avery

113  "marked the opening...": J. Lederberg, "The Transformation of Genetics by DNA: An Anniversary Celebration of Avery, Macleod and McCarty," *Genetics* 136 (1994): 423.

115  "What is the substance...": H. Judson, *The Eighth Day of Creation: The Makers of the Revolution in Biology* (Simon & Schuster, 1979), p. 36.

116  "it is possible...": Ibid., p. 39.

116  "nothing less than...": C. Sexton, *Burnet: A Life* (Oxford University Press, 1999), p. 104.

116  "a possible copying mechanism...": Quoted in Judson, *The Eighth Day of Creation,* p. 198.

## Ambroise Paré

119  "Chyurgery is an Art...": L. Zimmerman and I. Veith, *Great Ideas in the History of Surgery,* 2d rev. ed. (Dover, 1967), p. 179.

119  "one of those great...": H. Ellis, "Surgery and Manipulation" in *Medicine: A History of Healing* ed. R. Porter (Marlowe Press, 1997), p. 128.

119  "I had the meanes...": Zimmerman and Veith, *Great Ideas,* pp. 180–81.

120  "I could not sleep...": L. Clendening, ed., *Source Book of Medical History* (Henry Schuman, 1942), p. 193.

121  "to repair or supply...": Zimmerman and Veith, *Great Ideas,* p. 184.

122  "We can see many...": A. Paré, *On Monsters and Marvels* (University of Chicago Press, 1982), p. xv.

## Bernardino Ramazzini

123  "how speedily men...": Lucretius, *On the Nature of the Universe,* trans. R. E. Latham (Penguin, 1951), p. 242.

124  "I asked the poor...": Quoted in H. Sigerist, *On the History of Medicine* (MD Publications, 1936), p. 52.

124  "[O]ut of these Places...": Ibid.

125  "could have been written...": C. Tedeschi, "Bernardino Ramazzini (1633–1714): De Morbis Artificum," *Human Pathology* 1, no. 2 (1970): 319.

125  "will always be...": Quoted in Tedeschi, "Bernardino Ramazzini," p. 319.

125  "On visiting a poor home...": R. Margotta, *The Story of Medicine* (Golden Press, 1968), p. 224.

126  "his singular Learning...": Quoted in J. Talbott, *A Biographical History of Medicine* (Grune & Stratton, 1970), p. 136.

## Girolamo Fracastoro

128  "decist fra thar...": M. Hudson and R. Morton, "Fracastor and Syphilis: 500 Years On," *Lancet* 348 (1996): 1495.

128  "I sing of that…": L. Clendening, ed., *Source Book of Medical History* (Henry Schuman, 1942), p.110.

128  "the foul sores…": Ibid., p. 121.

129  "which foster the…": Ibid., p. 105.

129  "The affinities of…": Ibid., p. 108.

129  "generate and propagate…": Quoted in T. Rosebury, *Microbes and Morals: The Strange Story of Venereal Disease* (Viking Press, 1971), p. 40.

129  "worked out a clear…": Quoted in L. Wilkinson, "Epidemiology" in *Companion Encyclopedia of the History of Medicine,* ed. W. F. Bynum and R. Porter (Routledge, 1993), p. 1265.

## Thomas Sydenham

132  "It is a very…": K. Dewhurst, *Dr. Thomas Sydenham (1624–1689)* (University of California Press, 1966), p. 49.

132  "His plain dogmatic…": G. Meynell, *Materials for a Biography of Dr. Thomas Sydenham (1624–1689)* (Winterdown, 1988), p. 44.

132  "that shining light…": Quoted in G. A. Lindeboom, *Hermann Boerhaave* (Methuen, 1968), p. 54.

134  "the usual pomp of…": R. R. Trail "Sydenham's Impact on English Medicine," *Medical History* 9, no. 4 (1965): 358–59.

134  "a plump hot lad…": Dewhurst, *Dr. Thomas Sydenham,* p. 55.

135  "in its vagueness,…": E. Ackerknecht, *A Short History of Medicine,* rev. ed. (Johns Hopkins University Press, 1982), p. 123.

135  "in order to…": Meynell, *Materials for a Biography,* p. 78.

135  "I am in dispaire…": Dewhurst, *Dr. Thomas Sydenham,* p. 45.

## Hermann Boerhaave

136  "undisputed master": H. Sigerist, "Boerhaave's Influence Upon American Medicine," in H. Sigerist, *On the History of Medicine* (MD Publications, 1960), p. 202.

136  "is to understand…": Quoted in D. Breo, "MDs of the Millennium—The Dozen Who Made a Difference," *Journal of the American Medical Association* 263, no. 1 (1990): 112.

136  "molded my character…": G. A. Lindeboom, *Hermann Boerhaave* (Methuen, 1968), p. 16.

138  "Perhaps it is…": Ibid., pp. 353–54.

138  "builds for himself…": H. Boerhaave, "Institutiones Medicae" in *Source Book of Medical History,* ed. L. Clendening (Henry Schuman, 1942), p. 281.

138  "Boerhaave, celebrated…": B. Jaffe, *Crucibles: The Story of Chemistry* (Dover, 1976), p. 61.

139  "passing light…": C. G. Cumston, *An Introduction to the History of Medicine* (Alfred A. Knopf, 1926), p. 333.

139  "probably the most…": E. A. Underwood, *Boerhaave's Men at Leyden and After* (Edinburgh University Press, 1977), p. 188.

## John Hunter

140  "excited the greatest…": Quoted in J. Kobler, *The Reluctant Surgeon: A Biography of John Hunter* (Doubleday, 1960), p. 271.

140  "mark the rise of surgery...": R. Porter, *Western Medical Tradition,* ed. L. I. Conrad (Cambridge University Press, 1995), p. 399.
141  "When I was a boy...": Quoted in H. Sigerist, *The Great Doctors: A Biographical History of Medicine* (W. W. Norton & Company, 1933), p. 220.
142  "It was hardly necessary...": Quoted in Kobler, *The Reluctant Surgeon,* p. 114.
143  "the mind is subject...": Ibid., p. 273.
144  "I am fearful...": Ibid., p. 206.
144  "My life is in...": Ibid., p. 209.
144  "admiration of his...": Ibid., p. 327.

## Pierre Fauchard

145  "He found the dental art...": Quoted in B. Weinberger, *Pierre Fauchard: Surgeon-Dentist* (Pierre Fauchard Academy, 1941), p. 3.
145  "From my youth...": Ibid., p. 13.
146  "Fauchard used the...": R. King, *The Making of the Dentiste, 1650–1760* (Ashgate, 1998), p. 7.
146  "Even today it is a...": Weinberger, *Pierre Fauchard,* p. 94.
146  "cutting through the gums...": J. Wynbrandt, *The Excruciating History of Dentistry* (St. Martin's Press, 1998), p. 67.
147  "brought a great deal...": Weinberger, *Pierre Fauchard,* p. 65.
147  "But what will one...": Ibid.

## Philippe Pinel

148  "Ah, ça! citoyen...": Quoted in H. W. Haggard, *The Doctor in History* (Yale University Press, 1934), p. 356.
149  "everything presented to me...": P. Pinel, "Treatise on Insanity," excerpted in *Medicine and Western Civilization,* ed. D. Rothman, S. Marcus and S. Kiceluk (Rutgers University Press, 1995), p. 166.
149  "represented the first attempt...": *Dictionary of Scientific Biography,* vol. 10, p. 613.
150  "adopted the...": J. Goldstein, "Psychiatry" in *Companion Encyclopedia of the History of Medicine,* ed. W. F. Bynum and R. Porter (Routledge, 1993), p. 1355.
150  "He wanted, as practical-minded...": H. Sigerist, *The Great Doctors: A Biographical History of Medicine* (W. W. Norton & Company, 1933), p. 279.
151  "irrelevant philanthropist...": D. Weider, "Philippe Pinel (1745–1826)" in *Doctors, Nurses, and Medical Practitioners* (Greenwood Press, 1997), p. 219.
151  "Almost imperturbable...": G. Zilboorg, *A History of Medical Psychology* (W. W. Norton & Company, 1941), p. 320.
151  "Please come to...": Ibid.

## Edward Jenner

152  "the most terrible...": Quoted in W. Woglom, *Discoverers for Medicine* (Yale University Press, 1949), p. 61.
154  "a member of the elite...": A. Crosby, "Smallpox" in *Cambridge World History of Human Disease,* ed. K. Kiple (Cambridge University Press, 1993), p. 1012.
155  "the merit and...": E. S. Golub, *The Limits of Medicine* (Times Books, 1994), p. 126.
155  "the Great Spirit...": Quoted in J. Kobler, *The Reluctant Surgeon: A Biography of John Hunter* (Doubleday, 1960), p. 183.
156  "gilded butt...": Ibid., p. 182.

## William Thomas Green Morton

157 "can be seen...": U. Trohler, "Surgery (Modern)" in *Companion Encyclopedia of the History of Medicine*, ed. W. F. Bynum and R. Porter (Routledge, 1993), p. 985.

158 "A new era...": Quoted in S. Nuland, Doctors: *The Biography of Medicine* (Alfred A. Knopf, 1988), p. 282.

158 "possessed by the...": Quoted in J. Fenster, *Ether Day: The Strange Tale of America's Greatest Medical Discovery and the Haunted Men Who Made It* (Harper-Collins, 2001), p. 69.

159 "Your patient is...": Quoted in Nuland, *Doctors*, p. 282.

159 "Unrestrained and free...": Ibid., p. 290.

159 "I am not able...": B. Duncan, *The Development of Inhalation Anaesthesia* (Oxford University Press, 1947), p. 82.

161 "the patient should...": W. T. G. Morton, "Remarks on the Proper Mode of Administering Ether by Inhalation" in *Source Book of Medical History*, ed. L. Clendening (1942; reprint Dover, 1960), p. 371.

161 "thinking opportunist": Fenster, *Ether Day*, p. 68.

161 "not a great man...": Ibid., p. 229.

161 Epitaph. Quoted in L. Ludovici, *The Discovery of Anaesthesia* (Thomas Y. Crowell, 1961), p. 219.

## John Snow

163 "the most terrible outbreak...": J. Snow, "On the Mode of Communication of Cholera" in *Source Book of Medical History*, ed. L. Clendening (Henry Schuman, 1942), p. 468.

## Ignaz Semmelweis

165 "[Y]ou are a murderer...": Quoted in S. Nuland, *Doctors: The Biography of Medicine* (Alfred A. Knopf, 1988), p. 258.

166 "One has to watch...": Quoted in H. S. Glasscheib, *The March of Medicine: The Emergence and Triumph of Modern Medicine* (G. P. Putnam's Sons, 1964), p. 101.

166 "I could not understand...": I. Semmelweis, *The Etiology, Concept, and Prophylaxis of Childbed Fever* (University of Wisconsin Press, 1983), p. 71.

167 "I myself will say...": W. Broad and N. Wade, *Betrayers of the Truth* (Simon & Schuster, 1982), p. 137.

168 "This murder must...": Quoted in Nuland, *Doctors*, p. 257.

168 "It is always...": Glasscheib, *The March of Medicine*, p. 105.

168 "contributed importantly...": K. C. Carter, "Ignaz Semmelweis, Carl Mayrhofer, and the Rise of Germ Theory," *Medical History* 29 (1985): 53.

168 "his own faulty nature...": Nuland, *Doctors*, p. 239.

## Theodor Billroth

170 "Criticism is the principal need...": Quoted in H. Sigerist, *The Great Doctors: A Biographical History of Medicine* (W. W. Norton & Company, 1933), p 381.

171 "the greatest joy...": Quoted in R. Rutledge, "Theodor Billroth: A Century Later," Surgery 118 (1995): 42.

172 "one of the most congenial characters...": H. Sigerist, *The Great Doctors*, p. 380.

172  "intuitive, sensitive, humane…": M. Allgower and U. Tröhler, "Biographical Note on Theodor Billroth," *British Journal of Surgery* 68 (1981): 678.

172  "was a center of social activity…": L. Zimmerman and I. Vieth, *Great Ideas in the History of Surgery,* 2d rev. ed. (Dover, 1967), p. 491.

## Sigmund Freud

174  "possibility that there…": F. Sulloway, *Freud: Biologist of the Mind* (Basic Books, 1983), p. 121.

174  "talking cure": Ibid., p. 55.

176  "The greatest legacy…": R. T. Fancher, *Cultures of Healing: Correcting the Image of American Mental Health Care* (W. H. Freeman, 1995), p. 139.

177  "medieval (spirit-possession)…": Quoted in J. Forrester, *Dispatches from the Freud Wars* (Harvard University Press, 1995), p. 10.

178  "odd bunch": R. Porter, *The Greatest Benefit to Mankind* (W. W. Norton, 1997), p. 205.

## William Osler

181  "'magic spell'…": J. M. T. Finney, *A Surgeon's Life* (G. P. Putnam's Sons, 1940), p. 276.

182  "loose, slipshod way…": E. G. Reid, *The Great Physician: A Short Life of Sir William Osler* (Oxford University Press, 1931), p. 76.

183  "radiated cultural as well as…": P. Starr, *The Social Transformation of American Medicine* (Basic Books, 1982), p. 116.

183  "Haste! Haste!…": Finney, *A Surgeon's Life,* p. 278.

184  "Better go in…": C. S. Bryan, *Osler* (Oxford University Press, 1997), p. 149.

184  "an aeroplane flight…": R. Major, *A History of Medicine,* vol. 2 (Charles C. Thomas, 1954), p. 910.

184  "Soap and water…": Bryan, *Osler,* p. 164.

184  "Man should go…": Ibid.

184  "Osler's aphorisms…": Ibid.

184  "To write the modern history…": M. Bliss, *William Osler: a Life in Medicine* (Oxford University Press, 1999), p. 497.

185  "may never be surpassed…": Ibid., p. 499.

## Elie Metchnikoff

187  "one day, when the whole family…": Quoted in W. W. Woglom, *Discoverers for Medicine* (Yale University Press, 1949), p. 49.

187  "A zoologist until then…": *Dictionary of Scientific Biography,* vol. 9, p. 333.

187  "defines organismal identity…": A. I. Tauber, *The Immune Self: Theory or Metaphor* (Cambridge University Press, 1994), p. 5.

189  "most visible adornment…": W. F. Bynum, *Science and the Practice of Medicine in the Nineteenth Century* (Cambridge University Press, 1994), pp. 159–60.

189  "hysterical character out of…": P. de Kruif, *The Microbe Hunters* (Harcourt Brace & Company, 1926), p. 207.

189  "who was as clay…": R. B. Vaughan, "The Romantic Rationalist: A Study of Elie Metchnikoff," *Medical History* 10 (1965): 204.

190  "You will do…": Quoted in R. B. Vaughan, "The Romantic Rationalist," *Medical History* 10 (1965): 215.

## Willem Einthoven

192 "one of the most...": Quoted in R. G. Frank, Jr., "The Telltale Heart: Physiological Instruments, Graphic Methods, and Clinical Hopes," in *The Investigative Enterprise: Experimental Physiology in Nineteenth-Century Medicine*, ed. W. Coleman and F. L. Holmes (University of California Press, 1988), p. 251.

193 "From the nature...": Quoted in M. Duke, *The Development of Medical Techniques and Treatments* (International Universities Press, 1990) p. 60.

194 "every form of...": Ibid., p. 61.

194 "a man of regular...": Frank, "The Telltale Heart," p. 262.

194 "can provide diagnostic...": J. S. Borer, "Current Status of Noninvasive Testing: An Overview," *Cardiology* 71 (1984): 66.

## Emil von Behring

195 "To the extent that...": E. Shorter, *Bedside Manners: The Troubled History of Doctors and Patients* (Simon & Schuster, 1985), p. 131.

195 "the dogma that...": A. M. Silverstein, *A History of Immunology* (Academic Press, 1989), p. 55.

197 "The foundation was thus laid...": G. Rosen, *A History of Public Health*, expanded ed. (Johns Hopkins University Press, 1993), p. 306.

197 "placed in the hands...": Quoted in T. Sourkes, *Nobel Prize Winners in Medicine and Physiology* (Abelard-Schuman, 1967), p. 28.

198 "If we have...": Quoted in A. Chase, *Magic Shots* (William Morrow, 1982), p. 179.

## Alexis Carrel

199 "Between 1901 and 1910...": J. H. Comroe, Jr., *Exploring the Heart* (W. W. Norton & Company, 1983), p. 180.

199 "on vascular suture...": Quoted in Comroe, *Exploring the Heart*, p. 181.

199 "scientist and mystic...": W. S. Edwards and P. D. Edwards, *Alexis Carrel: Visionary Surgeon* (Charles C. Thomas, 1974), p. v.

201 "no certain diagnosis...": Quoted in T. Malinin, *Surgery and Life: The Extraordinary Career of Alexis Carrel* (Harcourt Brace Jovanovich, 1979), p. 14.

201 "If your heart...": Ibid., p. 25.

201 "Cells are specific...": A. Carrel, *Man, the Unknown* (Harper and Brothers, 1935), p. 319.

203 "worthwhile features...": Edwards and Edwards, *Alexis Carrel: Visionary Surgeon* (Charles C. Thomas, 1974), p. 104.

203 "despoiled the poor...": Carrel, *Man, the Unknown*, p. 319.

## Frederick Banting

205 "a melting down of flesh...": E. Ackerknecht, *A Short History of Medicine*, rev. ed. (Johns Hopkins University Press, 1982), p. 711.

206 "Ligate pancreatic...": Quoted in M. Bliss, *The Discovery of Insulin* (University of Chicago Press, 1982), p. 50.

208 "a much more intricate...": Ibid., p. 19.

208 "the greatest advance...": R. B. Welbourn, "Endocrine Diseases" in *Companion Encyclopedia of the History of Medicine*, ed. W. F. Bynum and R. Porter (Routledge, 1993), p. 502.

209 "Next person who...": Quoted in Bliss, *The Discovery of Insulin*, p. 236.

## Walter B. Cannon

210  "to a tradition…": H. Dale, "Walter Bradford Cannon" in *Obituary Notices of Fellows of the Royal Society of London*, vol. 5 (Royal Society, 1947), p. 407.

210  "every change in the outer…": D. Fleming, "Walter B. Cannon and Homeostasis," *Social Research* 51, no. 3 (1984): 629.

210  "That wish was most natural…": W. B. Cannon, *The Way of an Investigator* (Hafner, 1945), p. 15.

211  "Don't do it…": Ibid., p. 19.

212  "We do not 'feel…": S. Benison et al., *Walter B. Cannon: The Life and Times of a Young Scientist* (Harvard University Press, 1987), p. 315.

212  "cease to be a…": Cannon, *The Way of an Investigator*, p. 130.

213  "Further research…": Ibid., pp. 113–14.

## Archibald Garrod

214  "the great pioneer…": C. Booth, "Clinical Research" in *Companion Encyclopedia of the History of Medicine*, ed. W. F. Bynum and R. Porter (Routledge, 1993), p. 217.

215  "can hardly be ascribed…": Quoted in A. Bearn, "Archibald Edward Garrod, the Reluctant Geneticist," *Genetics* 137 (1994): 2.

216  "I do not see…": Ibid.

216  "Both alkaptonuria and cystinuria…": A. Bearn and E. Miller, "Archibald Garrod and the Development of the Concept of Inborn Errors of Metabolism," *Bulletin of the History of Medicine* 53 (1979): 324.

216  "not only appreciated…": Ibid.

216  "I believe that no two…": Ibid.

## Otto Warburg

219  "If the combustible substances…": Quoted in T. Sourkes, *Nobel Prize Winners in Medicine and Physiology* (Abelard-Schuman, 1966), pp. 155–56.

219  "The significance of Warburg's…": G. Allen, *Life Science in the Twentieth Century* (John Wiley & Sons, 1975), p. 178.

220  "for his discovery…": T. Wasson, ed., *Nobel Prize Winners* (H. W. Wilson, 1988), p. 1104.

220  "like the world…" Quoted in R. Govindjee, "On the requirement of minimum number of four versus eight quanta of light for the evolution of one molecule of oxygen in photosynthesis: A historical note." *Photosynthetic Research* 59 (1999): 251.

221  "Cancer, above all other diseases…": *Dictionary of Scientific Biography*, vol. 14, p. 176.

221  "detested his style…": R. Weinberg, *Racing to the Beginning of the Road* (Harmony Books, 1996), p. 13.

221  "There is really no reason…": H. Krebs, *Reminiscences and Reflections* (Clarendon Press, 1981), p. 151.

## Abraham Flexner

223  "That is precisely…": H. Berliner, *A System of Scientific Medicine* (Tavistock, 1985), p. 103.

223  "adapted to American…": Ibid., p. 106.

224  "In half an hour or less...": A. Flexner, *An Autobiography* (Simon & Schuster, 1960), p. 79.

224  "the worst of things...": K. Ludmerer, *Learning to Heal* (Basic Books, 1985), p. 186.

225  "Schools collapsed...": Ibid., p. 187.

225  "potential source of...": Quoted in Berliner, *A System of Scientific Medicine,* p. 115.

225  "Flexner is the worst...": Quoted in *Current Biography Yearbook* 1941, p. 289.

226  "prize academic snob...": H. Perkin, quoted in T. N. Bonner, "The Historical Reputation of Abraham Flexner," *Academic Medicine* 64, no. 1 (1989): 17.

226  "No other American...": Quoted in Bonner, "The Historical Reputation of Abraham Flexner," p. 17.

226  "probably the most...": Ibid., p. 18.

226  "While not entirely...": S. Lawrence, "Medical Education" in *Companion Encyclopedia of the History of Medicine,* ed. W. F. Bynum and R. Porter (Routledge, 1993), p. 1170.

## Harvey Cushing

227  "developed many...": I. Rutkow, *Surgery: An Illustrated History* (Mosby-Year Book, 1993), p. 503.

227  "He would emerge...": W. B. Cannon, "Harvey (Williams) Cushing" in *Obituary Notices of Fellows of the Royal Society of London,* vol. 3 (Royal Society, 1941), p. 290.

227  "a personality of...": Ibid.

228  "Dr. Röntgen may...": E. Thomson, *Harvey Cushing* (H. Schuman, 1950), p. 68.

229  "You must not...": S. Lehrer, *Explorers of the Body* (Doubleday, 1979), p. 153.

230  "the most inaccessible...": Cannon, "Harvey (Williams) Cushing," p. 279.

231  "No eminent and inspiring...": Ibid., p. 290.

## Hans Spemann

233  "I found here...": Quoted in V. Hamburger, *The Heritage of Experimental Embryology: Hans Spemann and the Organizer* (Oxford University Press, 1988), p. 9.

234  "the crowning achievement...": Ibid., p. vii.

234  "What so far...": Ibid., p. 99.

235  "creates an organization field...": Quoted in *Dictionary of Scientific Biography,* vol. 12, p. 569.

## Henry Dale

237  "I was, frankly...": H. Dale, *Adventures in Physiology: A Selection of Scientific Papers* (Pergamon Press, 1953), p. xvi.

239  "Elucidation of impulse transmission...": R. Porter, *The Greatest Benefit to Mankind* (W. W. Norton & Company, 1997), p. 572.

## Hans Krebs

243  "likely to be connected...": H. Krebs, *Reminiscences and Reflections* (Clarendon Press, 1981), p. 112.

244  "Because I have had...": Ibid., p. 232.

## Howard Florey

246 "a very well known phenomenon.": Quoted in G. Macfarlane, *Howard Florey: The Making of a Great Scientist* (Oxford University Press, 1970), p. 182.

## Wilder Penfield

251 "This is a startling...": W. Penfield and H. Jasper, *Epilepsy and the Functional Anatomy of the Human Brain* (Little, Brown, 1954), p. 143.
252 "I looked through...": Quoted in Penfield, *No Man Alone*, p. 36.
253 "to make a...": Ibid., p. 110.
253 "It called for true...": Ibid., p. 238.
253 "understanding the brain...": Ibid., p. 329.
253 "the relief of sickness...": Ibid., p. 316.

## Selman Waksman

256 "I have measured the growth...": S. Waksman, *My Life with the Microbes* (Simon & Schuster, 1954), p. 3.
256 "loved me dearly, with...": F. Ryan, *The Forgotten Plague* (Little, Brown, 1992), p. 33.
257 "protozoan theory of soil fertility...": Waksman, *My Life*, p. 113.
258 "relatively easy to isolate...": Ibid., p. 225.
259 "a very important message...": Ryan, *The Forgotten Plague*, pp. 240–41.
259 "As I look back...": Waksman, *My Life*, p. 285.

## Peyton Rous

262 "by means of a cell-free...": Quoted in T. Wasson, ed., *Nobel Prize Winners* (H. W. Wilson, 1988), p. 889.
262 "These revolutionary findings...": Quoted in *Current Biography Yearbook* 1967, p. 355.
262 "especially interesting": E. Jordan, *Text-Book of General Bacteriology* (W. B. Saunders, 1916), p. 527.
264 "Refined, gentle, exquisitely cultured": P. de Kruif, *The Sweeping Wind* (Harcourt, Brace & World, 1962), p. 15.
264 "Later, when the new...": A. Hodgkin, *Chance and Design: Reminiscences of Science in Peace and War* (Cambridge University Press, 1992), p. 239.

## John Franklin Enders

266 "transformed virus...": J. S. Smith, *Patenting the Sun: Polio and the Salk Vaccine* (William Morrow, 1990), p. 126.
268 "close at hand in...": Quoted in T. Sourkes, *Nobel Prize Winners in Medicine and Physiology* (Abelard-Schuman, 1966), p. 319.
268 "It was in the...": A. Chase, *Magic Shots* (William Morrow, 1982), p. 322.
269 "Enders, in his...": F. Robbins, "Reminiscences of a Virologist" in *Polio*, ed. T. Daniel and F. Robbins (University of Rochester Press, 1997), p. 130.

## Ernst Ruska

272 "We succeeded...": E. Ruska, *The Early Development of Electron Lenses and Electron Microscopy* (S. Hirzel, 1990), p. 24.
272 "The psychological hurdles...": Ibid., p. 108.

273  "Ruska could always...": T. Mulvey, "Forty Years of Electron Microscopy," *Physics Bulletin* 24 (1973): 153.

## Willem J. Kolff

275  "If man can grow...": *Current Biography Yearbook* 1983, p. 211.
275  "I am going to...": A. B. Weisse, *Conversations in Medicine* (New York University Press, 1984), p. 354.
275  "For me, there was...": *Current Biography Yearbook* 1983, p. 211.
275  "because I could not...": *Weisse, Conversations,* p. 349.
275  "He would agonize...": Ibid.
276  "I found that in...": Ibid., p. 350.
277  "I did not for one...": Quoted in C. Gottschalk and S. Fellner, "History of the Science of Dialysis," *American Journal of Nephrology* 17 (1997): 296.
279  "These are honest...": Weisse, *Conversations,* p. 372.

## Macfarlane Burnet

280  "overpowering in its...": W. Clark, *At War Within: The Double-Edged Sword of Immunity* (Oxford University Press, 1995), p. 256.
283  "would make real sense...": F. M. Burnet, "The Impact of Ideas on Immunology," Cold Spring Harbor Symposia on Quantitative Biology 32 (1967): 2.
283  "Immunology after clonal...": Clark, *At War Within,* p. 259.
284  "that I have the...": M. Burnet, *Dominant Mammal: the Biology of Human Destiny* (St. Martin's Press, 1971), p. 1.

## Rosalyn Sussman Yalow

287  "hanging from the...": S. McGrayne, *Nobel Prize Women in Science* (Birch Lane, 1993), p. 337.
288  "wanted to be...": Quoted in O. Opfell, *The Lady Laureates* (Scarecrow Press, 1986), p. 260.

## Benjamin Spock

291  "Feed'em whenever...": Quoted in T. Maier, *Dr. Spock: An American Life* (Harcourt Brace, 1998), p. 321.
291  "The political message...": Ibid., p. 458.
292  "But having discovered...": B. Spock and M. Morgan, *Spock on Spock* (Pantheon, 1989), p. 110.
292  "cover the emotional...": B. Spock, "Autobiography of Benjamin McLane Spock." Unpublished manuscript.
293  "My purpose was not...": Spock and Morgan, *Spock on Spock,* p. 135.
293  "They never sneered...": Ibid., p. 137.
293  "part of a sustained...": M. Zuckerman, "Dr. Spock: The Confidence Man" in *The Family in History,* ed. C. Rosenberg (University of Pennsylvania Press, 1975), p. 207.
293  "sick, mentally disordered...": W. Graebner, "The Unstable World of Benjamin Spock: Social Engineering in a Democratic Culture, 1917–1950," *Journal of American History* 67 (1980): 615.
293  "Spock was nothing...": Ibid.
294  "not impressive, but...": Spock and Morgan, *Spock on Spock,* p. 219.

## Arthur Kornberg

296 "High adventures in...": "The Biologic Synthesis of Deoxyribonucleic Acid" in *Nobel Lectures in Physiology or Medicine, 1942–1962* (Elsevier, 1964), p. 668.

297 "It was clear...": A. Kornberg, *The Golden Helix: Inside Biotech Ventures* (University Science Books, 1995) p. 23.

297 "Instead of waiting...": A. B. Weisse, *Conversations in Medicine* (New York University Press, 1984), p. 388.

297 "What is the chemical...": Kornberg, "The Biologic Synthesis of Deoxyribonucleic Acid," p. 668.

298 "unique in present...": Ibid., p. 672.

299 "by the 'polymerase'...": A. Kornberg, *For the Love of Enzymes* (Harvard University Press, 1989), p. 159.

300 " The way was open...": Ibid., p. 199.

300 "In a very small way...": Ibid., pp. 199–200.

301 "as faceless as...": Weisse, *Conversations*, p. 393.

301 "the true molecular...": Kornberg, *For the Love of Enzymes*, p. 6.

## Carleton Gajdusek

302 "at the hub of what...": R. Bingham, "Outrageous Ardor" in *A Passion to Know*, ed. A. L. Hammond (Charles Scribner's Sons, 1984), p. 18.

302 "new class of...": T. Wasson, ed., *Nobel Prize Winners* (H. W. Wilson, 1988), p. 362.

305 "an intelligence quotient...": Quoted in R. Rhodes, *Deadly Feasts* (Simon & Schuster, 1997), p. 32.

306 "However troubling...": Rhodes, *Deadly Feasts*, p. 216

## Ernst Wynder

307 "the patient has...": F. E. Tylecote, quoted in R. Kluger, *Ashes to Ashes: America's Hundred-Year Cigarette War, the Public Health, and the Unabashed Triumph of Philip Morris* (Alfred A. Knopf, 1997), p. 70.

307 "chain of evidence...": E. Wynder, "Tobacco and Health: A Review of the History and Suggestions for Public Health Policy," *Public Health Reports* 103, no. 1 (1988): 10.

308 "[S]moking...": Ibid., p. 9.

310 "Scientists and physicians...": R. Weinberg, *Race for the Beginning of the Road* (Harmony Books, 1996), p. 27.

311 "very versatility...": Kluger, *Ashes to Ashes*, p. 423.

311 "the human body is...": Wynder, "Tobacco and Health," p. 8.

311 "help us to die...": Ibid., p. 16.

## Melanie Klein

312 "The influence of...": H. Segal, *Melanie Klein* (Penguin, 1981), p. 175.

312 "the language of...": P. H. M. King, "The Life and Work of Melanie Klein in the British Psych-Analytical Society," *International Journal of Psychoanalysis* 64 (1983): 254.

314 "Freud acquainted us...": Quoted in J. Sayers, *Mothers of Psychoanalysis* (W. W. Norton, 1991), p. 219.

## Godfrey Hounsfield

318  "I think at the start...": Personal communication, 20 May 1999.

319  "mathematically reconstruct...": Ibid.

319  "Once I realized...": Quoted in C. Susskind, "The Invention of Computed Tomography" in *History of Technology,* vol. 6, ed. A. R. Hall and N. Smith (Mansell Publishing, 1981), p. 49.

319  "The diagnostic implications...": Susskind, "The Invention of Computed Tomography," p. 54.

320  "sitting at his usual...": Ibid., p. 75.

## Jean Dausset

322  "If there existed...": J. Dausset, "Je sais tout... sur presque rien," *Libération,* 14 March 1995, 6.

322  "With the naked eye...": Ibid.

324  "Disguising ourselves...": Quoted in Current Biography Yearbook 1981, p. 110.

325  "will be tailored...": J. Dausset, "Je sais tout... sur presque rien," p. 6.

325  "There are no longer...": Ibid.

## James Black

326  "I found the way patients...": Quoted in W.M. Davis, "James White Black," in *Nobel Prize Winners,* vol. 3, ed. F. N. Magill (Salem Publishing, 1990), p. 1532.

329  "Are you trying to...": Quoted in T. Bass, *Reinventing the Future* (Addison-Wesley, 1994), p. 51.

329  "I have absolutely...": Ibid., p. 52.

329  "The most creative...": Ibid.

## Walter Gilbert

331  "There's something...": S. S. Hall, *Invisible Frontiers* (Atlantic Monthly Press, 1987), p. 33.

332  "The problems...": Quoted in W. Gilbert and M. Ptashne, "Genetic Repressors," *Scientific American* 265, no. 2 (1991): 30.

332  "In light of...": Hall, *Invisible Frontiers,* pp. 34–35.

334  "an intellectual self-confidence...": Quoted in *Current Biography Yearbook* 1992, p. 235.

## Solomon Snyder

336  "Research in a laboratory...": Quoted in E. J. McMurray and D. Olendorf, eds., *Notable Twentieth-Century Scientists* (Gale Research, 1995), p. 430.

336  "the powerful feeling of...": S. Snyder, *Drugs and the Brain* (Scientific American Library, 1986), p. 181.

339  "some of the finest...": Quoted in M. Holloway, "The Reward of Ideas That Are Wrong," *Scientific American* 265, no. 2 (1991): 30.

339  "There is warmth about...": Quoted in *Current Biography Yearbook* 1996, p. 527.

339  "I am still unable... ": S. Snyder, *Brainstorming* (Harvard University Press, 1989), p. 190.

## William Masters

340  "By making the study...": John Heidenry, *What Wild Ecstasy* (Simon & Schuster, 1997), p. 167.

342  "a massive state...": W. Masters and V. Johnson, *Human Sexual Response* (Little, Brown, 1966), p. vii.

343  "lambasted and...": E. Nemy, "Divorced, Yes, But Not Split," *New York Times,* 24 March 1994: C1.

343  " a little, not very...": Quoted in Heidenry, *What Wild Ecstasy,* p. 34.

344  "gravely underestimated": W. Masters, V. Johnson, and R. Kolodny, *Crisis: Heterosexual Behavior in the Age of AIDS* (Grove Press, 1988), p. 4.

344  "his ability to...": E. Brecher, The *Sex Researchers* (Little, Brown, 1969), p. 287.

344  "The conversation...": Nemy, "Divorced," p. C6.

## Gerald M. Edelman

347  "mad as we were": Quoted in E. J. McMurray and D. Olendorf, eds., *Notable Twentieth-Century Scientists* (Gale Research, 1995), p. 551.

348  "special genetic...": G. Edelman, "The Structure and Function of Antibodies," *Scientific American* 223, no. 12 (1970): 42.

348  "a theory absolutely...": G. Edelman, *Bright Air, Brilliant Fire* (Basic Books, 1992), pp. 39–40.

348  "a self-organizing...": Ibid., p. 25.

349  "out-of-date caricatures...": D. Dennett, "Revolution on the Mind," *New Scientist,* 13 June 1992, 48.

349  "If one struggles...": O. Sacks, "Making up the Mind," *New York Review of Books* 40, no. 7 (1993): 50.

349  "One must be...": D. Hellerstein, "Plotting a Theory of the Brain," *New York Times Magazine,* 22 May 1988, 28.

## Harold Varmus

351  "more engaged in...": Quoted in *Current Biography Yearbook* 1996, p. 603.

352  "an aesthetic merger...": H. Varmus, "Retroviruses and Oncogenes I (Nobel Lecture)," *Angewandte Chemie* 29, no. 7 (1990): 708.

353  "From these findings...": Ibid., p. 710

353  "More than any other...": R. Weinberg, *Racing to the Beginning of the Road* (Harmony Books, 1996), p. 110.

355  "In our adventures...": H. Varmus, "Retroviruses and Oncogenes," in *Les Prix Nobels* (Almqvist & Wiksell, 1989), p. 28.

## Raymond Damadian

356  "No one else had...": B. A. Kevles, *Naked to the Bone* (Rutgers University Press, 1997), p. 179.

357  "Most of our neighbors...": S. Kleinfield, *A Machine Called Indomitable* (Times Books, 1985), pp. 40–41.

358  "Once I made the hit...": Personal communication, 6 August 1999.

358  "as not only impossible...": R. Roemer, "Nuclear Magnetic Resonance: A Historical Perspective" in *MRI for Technologists,* ed. P. Woodward and R. D. Freimark (McGraw-Hill, 1995), p. 5.

360  "4:45 AM FANTASTIC...": J. Mattson and M. Simon, *The Story of MRI* (Bar-Ilan University Press, 1990), p. 681.

360  "I was called a...": Kleinfield, *A Machine Called Indomitable,* p. 6.

## Bert Vogelstein

363  "Our results support...": Quoted in J. Bishop and M. Waldholz, *Genome* (Simon & Schuster, 1990), p. 172.

364  "By the early 1990s...": M. Waldholz, *Curing Cancer* (Simon & Schuster, 1997), p. 132.

## Robert Gallo
## Luc Montagnier

366  "The jolly, plump...": R. Gallo, *Virus Hunting: AIDS, Cancer, and the Human Retrovirus* (Basic Books, 1991), p. 18.

368  "The Discovery of...": L. Montagnier, *Virus: The Co-Discoverer HIV Tracks Its Rampage and Charts the Future* (W. W. Norton, 2000), p. 16.

369  "He treated Montagnier...": P. Radetsky, *The Invisible Invaders* (Little, Brown, 1991), p. 330.

370  "I still retain...": Montagnier, Virus, p. 65.

370  "[A]lthough Gallo...": S. Epstein, *Impure Science: AIDS, Activism and the Politics of Knowledge* (University of California Press, 1996), p. 77.

372  "blunt, crass, frenetic...": J. Cohen, *Shots in the Dark: The Wayward Search for the AIDS Vaccine* (W. W. Norton, 2001), p. 17.

372  "Like a roulette...": Quoted in T. Bass, *Reinventing the Future* (Addison-Wesley, 1994), p. 33.

## Celsus

375  "The judiciousness of his opinions...": R. Major, *A History of Medicine,* vol. 1 (Charles C. Thomas, 1954), p. 172.

375  "I shall not...": Celsus, *De medicina,* vol. 1, trans. W. G. Spencer (Loeb Classical Library, 1961), p. 85.

376  "the Art of Medicine...": Ibid., p. 7.

376  "Sometimes in the...": Ibid., p. 435.

377  "is tormented at...": Celsus, *De medicina,* vol. 2, p. 113.

377  "do everything just...": B. L. Gordon, *Medicine Throughout Antiquity.* (F. A. Davis, 1949), p. 667.

## Ibn Sina (Avicenna)

379  "It was so forceful...": H. Sigerist, "Medieval Medicine" in H. Sigerist, *On the History of Medicine* (MD Publications, 1960), p. 129.

379  "The Qanun covered...": L. I. Conrad, "Arab-Islamic Medicine" in *Companion Encyclopedia of the History of Medicine,* ed. W. F. Bynum and R. Porter (Routledge, 1993), p. 701.

380  "Medicine is not...": Quoted in R. Levy, "Avicenna—His Life and Times" in *Toward Modern Science,* ed. R. P. Palter (E. P. Dutton, 1969), p. 205.

381  "The master was vigorous...": L. E. Goodman, *Avicenna* (Routledge, 1992), pp. 43–44.

381  "I should immediately...": Levy, *Avicenna,* p. 208.

382  "a second millennium...": G. M. Chisti, *The Traditional Healer's Handbook* (Healing Arts Press, 1991), p. 1.

## Louise Bourgeois

383  "the great surgeon...": Quoted in W. Goodell, *A Sketch of the Life and Writings of Louyse Bourgeois* (Collins, 1876), p. 6.

383  "remained with no...": Quoted in W. Perkins, *Midwifery and Medicine in Modern France: Louise Bourgeois* (University of Exeter Press, 1996), p. 16.

384  "Come in midwife...": Goodell, *A Sketch*, p. 20.

384  "Do to it...": Ibid., p. 23.

385  "a conformist and...": Perkins, *Midwifery and Medicine*, p. 51.

385  "how very nutritious": Quoted in Goodell, *A Sketch*, p. 46.

386  "if midwives adopt...": R. G. DeVries and R. Barroso, "Midwives Among the Machines" in *Midwives, Society and Childbirth*, ed. H. Marland and A. M. Rafferty, (Routledge, 1997), p. 268.

## Samuel Hahnemann

387  "found it a shallow...": H. P. Holmes, *Samuel Hahnemann: A Lecture* (The Homeopathic Physician, 1984), p. 5.

388  "It is the duty...": Quoted in T. Cook, *Homeopathic Medicine Today: A Modern Course of Study* (Keats Publishing, 1989), p. 11.

389  "The physician's highest calling...": S. Hahnemann, *Organon der rationellen Heilkunde* (Cooper, 1982), p. 9.

389  "*start acting* instead...": Ibid.

389  "was due in large...": N. Gevitz, "Unorthodox Medical Theories" in *Companion Encyclopedia of the History of Medicine*, ed. W. F. Bynum and R. Porter (Routledge, 1993), p. 611.

390  "period of medical...": R. Marantz-Henig, "Medicine's New Age," *Civilization* (Apr.-May, 1997): 48.

391  "People from all...": Cook, *Homeopathic Medicine Today*, p. 15.

391  "*Non inutilis vixi*": Ibid., p.17.

## Daniel David Palmer

392  "could not hear...": Quoted in N. Altman, *The Chiropractic Alternative* (J. P. Tarcher, 1981), p. 46.

392  "I can hear, Doc,...": F. P. DeGiacomo, *Man's Greatest Gift to Man... Chiropractic* (LSR Learning Associates, 1987), p. 39.

392  "disposed to reason...": Quoted in J. S. Moore, *Chiropractic in America* (Johns Hopkins University Press, 1993), p. 5.

393  "The best physicians...": Ibid., p. 7.

394  "The human body...": Quoted in Altman, *The Chiropractic Alternative*, p. 48.

394  "D. D. Palmer's....": Moore, *Chiropractic in America*, p. 21.

395  "from no earthly...": Ibid., p. 5.

395  "was answered...": Ibid., p. 4.

## Lydia Pinkham

396  "*OVERWORKED WOMEN/THE WORLD*...": J. Burton, *Lydia Pinkham Is Her Name* (Farrar, Straus, 1949), p. 181.

396 "speaks to…changing…": S. Stage, *Female Complaints: Lydia Pinkham and the Business of Women's Medicine* (W. W. Norton, 1979), p. 11.

396 "Lydia Pinkham was…": D. Yaeger, "The Lady Who Helped Ladies," *Yankee,* September 1989, 64.

398 "A Sure Cure…": Ibid., p. 67.

398 *"Tell me, Lydia…":* Quoted in Burton, *Lydia Pinkham,* p. 278.

399 "Recommended as a…": Yaeger, "The Lady Who Helped Ladies," p. 114.

400 "solely as a…": Product packaging, Lydia Pinkham Herbal Remedy.

## Paul de Kruif

401 "an incredibly popular…": E. S. Golub, *The Limits of Medicine* (Times Books, 1994), p. 4.

401 "a man with a…": M. Schorer, *Sinclair Lewis: An American Life* (McGraw-Hill, 1961), p. 365.

401 "He was a natural…": H. L. Mencken, *My Life as Author and Editor* (Alfred A. Knopf, 1993), p. 276.

401 "tough, totally…": P. de Kruif, *The Sweeping Wind* (Harcourt Brace & World, 1962), p. 51.

401 "bared my back…": Ibid., p. 65.

402 "But there was a…": Mencken, *My Life,* p. 277.

402 "a spoof of the…": Quoted in "Dr. Paul de Kruif, Popularizer of Medical Exploits, Is Dead," *New York Times,* 2 March 1971: 38.

402 "I felt deep in…": de Kruif, *The Sweeping Wind,* p. 51.

402 "began to teach me…": Ibid., p. 83.

403 "In their adventures…": Ibid., p. 106.

403 "'Wait! here are whole…'": P. de Kruif, *The Microbe Hunters* (Harcourt Brace & Company, 1926), p. 130.

403 "had stolen upon…": de Kruif, *The Sweeping Wind,* p. 115.

403 "has brought his dead…": R. Duffus, review of *The Microbe Hunters,* by Paul de Kruif, *New York Times,* 29 February 1926, sec. 3, p. 10.

404 "unearth miracle cures…": J. Heidenry, *Theirs Was the Kingdom* (W. W. Norton, 1993), p. 137.

404 "my inner enemy": de Kruif, *The Sweeping Wind,* p. 23.

404 "the analism promulgated…": Ibid., p. 110.

404 "when life got…": Ibid., p. 8.

## Henri Dunant

405 "Bodies of men and…": C. Rothkopf, *Jean-Henri Dunant* (Franklin Watts, 1969), p. 45.

405 "It is I who…": E. Hart, *Man Born to Live: Life and Work of Henry Dunant* (Victor Gollancz, 1953), p. 17.

405 "the liveliest interest…": H. Babel, *Les quatres hommes qui ont fait Genève* (Tribune Editions, 1981), p. 102.

406 "indescribably hideous…": Quoted in Hart, *Man Born to Live,* pp. 70–71.

407 "a thousand times…": Quoted in R. Major, *A History of Medicine* (Charles C. Thomas, 1954), p. 870.

407 "a basis for Societies…": Quoted in Rothkopf, *Jean-Henri Dunant,* p. 63.

407 "Would it not be…": Ibid., p. 61.

408  "correlative refinements...": Quoted in C. Moorehead, *Dunant's Dream* (Carroll & Graf, 1999), pp. 50–51.

408  "I lost that elasticity...": Ibid., p. 110.

409  "I am a disciple...": Hart, *Man Born to Live*, p. 339.

409  "a deserted and poor...": Quoted in Major, *A History of Medicine*, pp. 870–71.

409  "to see his great...": Moorehead, *Dunant's Dream*, p. 716.

410  "future battles...": Quoted in Rothkopf, *Jean-Henri C. Moorchead Dunant*, p. 64.

## Envoy

412  "often surrounded by...": J.-C. Guillebaud, *Return to Vietnam* (Verso, 1994), p. 77.

# Bibliography

Absolon, Karel B. *The Belle Epoque of Surgery: The Life and Times of Theodor Billroth.* Rockville, MD: Kabel Publishers, 1995.

Acierno, Louis J. *The History of Cardiology.* London: Parthenon, 1994.

Ackerknecht, Erwin H. *Rudolf Virchow: Doctor, Statesman, Anthropologist.* Madison: University of Wisconsin Press, 1953.

———. *A Short History of Psychiatry.* 2d rev. ed. New York: Hafner, 1968.

———. *A Short History of Medicine.* Rev. ed. Baltimore: Johns Hopkins University Press, 1982.

Alexander, Franz G., and Sheldon T. Selesnick. *The History of Psychiatry.* New York: Harper & Row, 1966.

Allen, Garland. *Life Science in the Twentieth Century.* New York: John Wiley & Sons, 1975.

Allgower, M., and U. Tröhler. "Biographical Note on Theodor Billroth." *British Journal of Surgery* 68 (1981): 678–79.

Altman, Nathaniel. *The Chiropractic Alternative.* Los Angeles: J. P. Tarcher, 1981.

Arrizabalaga, John, John Henderson, and Roger French. *The Great Pox: The French Disease in Renaissance Europe.* New Haven, CT: Yale University Press, 1997.

Babel, Henry. *Les Quatres Hommes qui ont fait Geneve.* Geneva: Tribune Editions, 1981.

Baldry, P. E. *The Battle Against Bacteria.* London: Cambridge University Press, 1965.

Balter, Fritz. "Theodor Boveri." *Science* 144 (1964): 809–15.

———. *Theodor Boveri: Life and Work of a Great Biologist: 1862–1915.* Berkeley: University of California Press, 1967.

Balzac, Honore de. *The Wild Ass's Skin [La Peau de Chagrin].* Translated by Herbert J. Hunt. London: Penguin, 1977.

Bass, Thomas A. *Reinventing the Future.* Reading, MA: Addison-Wesley, 1994.

Bearn, Alexander G. *Archibald Garrod and the Individuality of Man.* Oxford: Clarendon Press, 1993.

———. "Archibald Edward Garrod, the Reluctant Geneticist." *Genetics* 137 (1994): 1–4.

Bearn, Alexander G., an.d Elizabeth D. Miller. "Archibald Garrod and the Development of the Concept of Inborn Errors of Metabolism." *Bulletin of the History of Medicine* 53 (1979): 315–28.

Bendiner, Jessica, and Elmer Bendiner. *Biographical Dictionary of Medicine.* New York: Facts on File, 1990.

Benison, Saul, A. Clifford Barger, and Elin L. Wolfe. *Walter B. Cannon: The Life and Times of a Young Scientist.* Cambridge: Harvard University Press, 1987.

Berliner, Howard S. *A System of Scientific Medicine.* New York: Tavistock, 1985.

Bichat, Xavier. *Physiological Researches in Life and Death.* Boston: Richardson and Lord, 1827.

Biddle, Wayne. *A Field Guide to Germs.* New York: Doubleday, 1995.

Bingham, Roger. "Outrageous Ardor." In *A Passion to Know,* edited by Allen L. Hammond, 11–22. New York: Charles Scribner's Sons, 1984.

Bishop, Jerry E., and Michael Waldholz. *Genome.* New York: Simon & Schuster, 1990.

Bliss, Michael. *The Discovery of Insulin.* Chicago: University of Chicago Press, 1982.

———. *William Osler: A Life in Medicine.* New York: Oxford University Press, 1999.

Bloch, Iwan. *The Sexual Life of Our Time.* 1908. Reprint, New York: Allied Book Company, 1928.

Bollet, Alfred J. "Pierre Charles Alexander Louis." *American Journal of the Medical Sciences* 266, no. 2 (1973): 93–101.

Bonner, Thomas Neville. "The Historical Reputation of Abraham Flexner." *Academic Medicine* 64, no. 1 (1989): 17–18.

———. "Searching for Abraham Flexner." *Academic Medicine* 73, no. 2 (1998): 160–66.

Booth, Christopher C. "Clinical Research." In *Companion Encyclopedia of the History of Medicine,* edited by W. F. Bynum and Roy Porter, 205–29. London: Routledge, 1993.

Borek, Ernest. *The Atoms Within Us.* New York: Columbia University Press, 1961.

Borer, Jeffrey S. "Current Status of Noninvasive Testing: An Overview." *Cardiology* 71 (1984): 65–68.

Bracegirdle, Brian. *A History of Microtechnique.* 2d ed. Lincolnwood, IL: Science Heritage, 1986.

Brecher, Edward M. *The Sex Researchers.* Boston: Little, Brown, 1969.

Breger, Louis. *Freud: Darkness in the Midst of Vision.* New York: John Wiley & Sons, 2000.

Breo, Dennis L. "MDs of the Millennium—The Dozen Who Made a Difference." *Journal of the American Medical Association* 263, no. 1 (1990): 108–112.

Broad, William, and Nicholas Wade. *Betrayers of the Truth.* New York: Simon & Schuster, 1982.

Brock, A. J. *Greek Medicine.* New York: J. M. Dent & Sons, 1929

Brock, Thomas. *Robert Koch: A Life in Medicine and Bacteriology.* Washington, DC: American Society of Microbiology, 1999.

Brock, William H. *The Norton History of Chemistry.* New York: W. W. Norton, 1993.

Brody, Howard et al. "John Snow Revisited: Getting a Handle on the Broad Street Pump." *Pharos* 62 (1999): 2–8.

Browning, C. H. "Emil Behring and Paul Ehrlich: Their Contributions to Science." *Nature* 175 (1955): 570–75.

Bryan, Charles S. "What Is the Oslerian Tradition?" *Annals of Internal Medicine* 120, no. 8 (1994): 682–87.

———. *Osler: Inspirations from a Great Physician.* New York: Oxford University Press, 1997.

Bullough, Vern. *Science in the Bedroom.* New York: Basic Books, 1994.

Bullough, Vern, and Bonnie Bullough. *The Emergence of Modern Nursing.* New York: Prodist, 1978.

Burnet, F. M. "The Impact of Ideas on Immunology." *Cold Spring Harbor Symposia on Quantitative Biology* 32: 1–8. 1967.

———. *Dominant Mammal: The Biology of Human Destiny.* New York: St. Martin's Press, 1971.

Burton, Jean. *Lydia Pinkham Is Her Name.* New York: Farrar, Straus, 1949.

Bynum, W. F. "Darwin and the Doctors: Evolution, Diathesis, and Germs in 19th-Century Britain." *Gesnerus* 40, no. 1/2 (1983): 43–53.

———. "Nosology." In *Companion Encyclopedia of the History of Medicine,* edited by W. F. Bynum and Roy Porter, 335–56. London: Routledge, 1993.

———. *Science and the Practice of Medicine in the Nineteenth Century.* Cambridge: Cambridge University Press, 1994.

Bynum, W. F., and Roy Porter, eds. *Companion Encyclopedia of the History of Medicine.* London: Routledge, 1993.

Cannon, Walter B. "Harvey (Williams) Cushing." In *Obituary Notices of Fellows of the Royal Society,* vol. 3, 277–90. London: Royal Society, 1941.

———. *The Way of an Investigator.* New York: Hafner, 1945.

Carlson, Elof Axel, ed. *Modern Biology: Its Conceptual Foundations.* New York: George Braziller, 1967.

Carrel, Alexis. *Man, the Unknown.* New York: Harper and Brothers, 1935.

Carter, K. Coddell. "Ignaz Semmelweis, Carl Mayrhofer, and the Rise of Germ Theory." *Medical History* 29 (1985): 33–53.

Carter, K. Codell, and Barbara R. Carter. *Childbed Fever: A Scientific Biography of Ignaz Semmelweis.* Westport, CT: Greenwood Press, 1994.

Celsus, Aulus Cornelius. *De medicina.* 3 vols. Translated by W. G. Spencer. Cambridge, MA: Loeb Classical Library, 1961.

Chase, Allan. *Magic Shots.* New York: William Morrow, 1982.

Chisti, G. M. *The Traditional Healer's Handbook: A Classic Guide to the Medicine of Avicenna.* Rochester,s VT: Healing Arts Press, 1991.

Clark, Ronald. *Freud: The Man and His Cause.* New York: Random House, 1980.

Clark, William. *At War Within: The Double-Edged Sword of Immunity.* New York: Oxford University Press, 1995.

Clendening, Logan, ed. *Source Book of Medical History.* New York: Henry Schuman, 1942.

Cohen, I. Bernard. "Florence Nightingale." *Scientific American* 250, no. 3 (1984): 128–37.

Cohen, Jon. *Shots in the Dark: The Wayward Search for an AIDS Vaccine.* New York: W. W. Norton, 2001.

Coleman, William. *Biology in the Nineteenth Century: Problems of Form, Function, and Transformation.* New York: John Wiley & Sons, 1971.

———. "The Cognitive Basis of the Discipline: Claude Bernard on Physiology." *ISIS* 76 (1985): 49–70.

Comroe, Julius H., Jr. *Exploring the Heart.* New York: W. W. Norton, 1983.

Conrad, Lawrence I. "Arab-Islamic Medicine." In *Companion Encyclopedia of the History of Medicine,* edited by W. F. Bynum and Roy Porter, 676–727. London: Routledge, 1993.

Conrad, Lawrence I., et al. *The Western Medical Tradition.* Cambridge: Cambridge University Press, 1995.

Cook, Trevor M. *Homeopathic Medicine Today: A Modern Course of Study.* New Canaan, CT: Keats Publishing, 1989.

Crosby, Alfred. A. "Smallpox." In *Cambridge World History of Human Disease,* edited by Kenneth F. Kiple, 1008–13. Cambridge: Cambridge University Press, 1993.

Cumston, Charles Greene. *An Introduction to the History of Medicine.* New York: Alfred A. Knopf, 1926.

Cziko, Gary. *Without Miracles.* Cambridge: MIT Press, 1995.

Dale, Henry. "Walter Bradford Cannon: 1871–1945." In *Obituary Notices of Fellows of the Royal Society of London*, vol. 5, 406–19. London: Royal Society, 1947.

———. *Adventures in Physiology: A Selection of Scientific Papers.* London: Pergamon Press, 1953.

———. "Some Fifty Years in British Medical Science." In *A Dozen Doctors*, edited by Dwight J. Ingle, 1–13. Chicago: University of Chicago Press, 1963.

Darwin, Charles. *On the Origin of Species by Means of Natural Selection, or the Preservation of Favoured Races in the Struggle for Life.* London: John Murray, 1859.

———. *The Descent of Man, and Selection in Relation to Sex.* New York: D. Appleton, 1872.

———. *The Autobiography of Charles Darwin, 1809–1882.* Edited by Nora Barlow. New York: W. W. Norton, 1958.

Dausset, Jean, and Jean Bernard. *La mosaïque humaine: entretiens sur les révolutions de la médecine et le devenir de l'homme.* Paris: Calmann-Lévy, 2000.

Davis, W. Marvin. "James Whyte Black." In *Nobel Prize Winners*, vol. 3, edited by Frank N. Magill, 1529–37. Pasadena, California: Salem Press, 1990.

Debre, Patrice. *Louis Pasteur.* Baltimore: Johns Hopkins University Press, 1998.

Debus, Allen G. *Man and Nature in the Renaissance.* Cambridge: Cambridge University Press, 1978.

DeGiacomo, Frank P. *Man's Greatest Gift to Man…Chiropractic.* Old Bethpage, NY: LSR Learning Associates, 1987.

de Kruif, Paul. *The Microbe Hunters.* New York: Harcourt Brace & Company, 1926.

———. *Men Against Death.* New York: Harcourt Brace & Company, 1932.

———. *The Sweeping Wind.* New York: Harcourt Brace & World, 1962.

Deloyers, Lucien. *François Magendie: Précurseur de la médecine expérimentale.* Brussels: Presses Universitaires de Bruxelles, 1970.

Dennett, Daniel C. "Review of Varela et al. & Edelman." *New Scientist* 134 (1992): 48–49.

Desmond, Adrian, and James Moore. *Darwin.* New York: W. W. Norton, 1991.

DeVries, Raymond, and Rebeca Barroso. "Midwives Among the Machines." In *Midwives, Society and Childbirth*, edited by Hilary Marland and Anne Marie Rafferty, 248–72. London: Routledge, 1997.

Dewhurst, Kenneth. *Dr. Thomas Sydenham, 1624–1689.* Berkeley: University of California Press, 1966.

Dobo, Nicolas, and Andre Role. *Bichat: la vie fulgurante d'un genie.* Paris: Perrin, 1989.

Dossey, Barbara. *Florence Nightingale: Mystic, Visionary, Healer.* Springhouse, PA: Springhouse, 1999.

Dubos, René. *Man, Medicine, and Environment.* New York: Frederick A. Praeger, 1968.

Duffin, Jacalyn. *To See with a Better Eye: A Life of R. T. H. Laennec.* Princeton, NJ: Princeton University Press, 1998.

Duncan, Barbara. *The Development of Inhalation Anaesthesia.* London: Oxford University Press, 1947.

Edelman, Gerald. "The Structure and Function of Antibodies." *Scientific American* 223, no. 12 (1970): 34–42.

———. *Bright Air, Brilliant Fire.* New York: Basic Books, 1992.

Edelstein, Ludwig. *The Hippocratic Oath: Text, Translation, and Interpretation.* Baltimore: Johns Hopkins Press, 1943.

Edwards, W. Sterling, and Peter D. Edwards. *Alexis Carrel: Visionary Surgeon.* Springfield, IL: Charles C. Thomas, 1974.

Eliot, Georsge. *Middlemarch*. Middlesex: Penguin, 1965.

Ellis, Harold. "Surgery and Manipulation." In *Medicine: A History of Healing*, edited by Roy Porter, 118–43. New York: Marlowe Press, 1997.

Epstein, Steven. *Impure Science: AIDS, Activism and the Politics of Knowledge*. Berkeley: University of California Press, 1996.

Evens, Ronald G. "Röntgen Retrospective: One Hundred Years of a Revolutionary Technology." *Journal of the American Medical Association* 274, no. 11 (1995): 912–16.

Fancher, Robert T. *Cultures of Healing: Correcting the Image of American Mental Health Care*. New York: W. H. Freeman, 1995.

Feder, Gene. "Paradigm Lost: A Celebration of Paracelsus on His Quincentenary." *Lancet* 341 (1993): 1396–98.

Feindel, W. "The Contributions of Wilder Penfield to the Functional Anatomy of the Human Brain." *Human Neurobiology* 1 (1982): 231–34.

Feldberg, Wilhelm. "Henry Hallett Dale." *British Journal of Pharmacology* 35, no. 1 (1969): 1–9.

Fenster, Julie M. *Ether Day: The Strange Tale of America's Greatest Medical Discovery and the Haunted Men Who Made It*. New York: HarperCollins, 2001.

Finger, Stanley. *Origins of Neuroscience*. New York: Oxford University Press, 1994.

Finney, John Miller Turpin. *A Surgeon's Life*. New York: G. P. Putnam's Sons, 1940.

Fishbein, Morris. *The New Medical Follies*. New York: Boni and Liveright, 1927.

Fisher, Richard. *Joseph Lister*. New York: Stein and Day, 1977.

Fleming, Donald. "Walter B. Cannon and Homeostasis." *Social Research* 51, no. 3 (1984): 609–40.

Flew, Anthony. *Darwinian Evolution*. 2d ed. New Brunswick, NJ: Transaction Publishers, 1997.

Flexner, Abraham. *An Autobiography*. New York: Simon & Schuster, 1960.

Flexner, James Thomas. *An American Saga: The Story of Helen Thomas and Simon Flexner*. Boston: Little, Brown, 1984.

Flexner, Simon, and James Thomas Flexner. *William Henry Welch*. New York: Viking, 1941.

Forrester, John. *Dispatches from the Freud Wars*. Cambridge: Harvard University Press, 1997.

Foss, Laurence, and Kenneth Rothenberg. *The Second Medical Revolution*. Boston: Shambhala, 1987.

Foucault, Michel. *The Birth of the Clinic*. New York: Random House, 1973.

Frank, Robert G., Jr. *Harvey and the Oxford Physiologists*. Berkeley: University of California Press, 1980.

———. "The Telltale Heart: Physiological Instruments, Graphic Methods, and Clinical Hopes, 1854–1914." In *The Investigative Enterprise: Experimental Physiology in Nineteenth-Century Medicine*, edited by William Coleman and Frederic L. Holmes, 211–90. Berkeley: University of California Press, 1988.

Fruton, Joseph S. "Claude Bernard the Scientist." In *Claude Bernard and the Internal Environment*, edited by Eugene Debs Robin, 36–40. New York: Marcel Dekker, 1979.

Fujimura, Joan. *Crafting Science: A Sociohistory of the Quest for the Genetics of Cancer*. Cambridge: Harvard University Press, 1996.

Fye, W. Bruce. "Carl Ludwig." *Clinical Cardiology* 14 (1991): 361–63.

Gallo, Robert. *Virus Hunting: AIDS, Cancer, and the Human Retrovirus.* New York: Basic Books, 1991.

Ganellin, C. Robin. "Cimetidine." In *Chronicles of Drug Discovery,* vol. 1, edited by J. S. Bindra and D. Lednicer, 1–38. New York: John Wiley & Sons, 1982.

Garrison, Fielding. History of Medicine. 4th ed. Philadelphia: W. B. Saunders, 1929.

———. "Laennec." In *Contributions to the History of Medicine,* 899–903. New York: Hafner, 1960.

———. "Ramon y Cajal." In *Contributions to the History of Medicine,* 939–64. New York: Hafner, 1966.

Gay, Peter. *Freud: A Life for Our Time.* New York: Basic Books, 1988.

Geison, Gerald L. *The Private Science of Louis Pasteur.* Princeton, NJ: Princeton University Press, 1995.

Gevitz, Norman. "Unorthodox Medical Theories." In *Companion Encyclopedia of the History of Medicine,* edited by W. F. Bynum and Roy Porter, 603–33. London: Routledge, 1993.

Gilbert, Walter, and Mark Ptashne. "Genetic Repressors." *Scientific American* 222, no. 6 (1970): 36–44.

Gillispie, Charles, ed. *Dictionary of Scientific Biography.* 14 vols. New York: Charles Scribner's Sons, 1970.

Glasscheib, H. S. *The March of Medicine: The Emergence and Triumph of Modern Medicine.* New York: G. P. Putnam's Sons, 1964.

Glasser, Otto. *Dr. W. C. Rontgen.* Springfield, IL: Charles C. Thomas, 1958.

Goldstein, Jan. "Psychiatry." In *Companion Encyclopedia of the History of Medicine,* edited by W. F. Bynum and Roy Porter, 1350–72. London: Routledge, 1993.

Golub, Edward S. *The Limits of Medicine.* New York: Times Books, 1994.

Goodell, William. *A Sketch of the Life and Writings of Louyse Bourgeois.* Philadelphia: Collins, 1876.

Goodman, Lenn E. *Avicenna.* London: Routledge, 1992.

Gordon, Benjamin Lee. *Medicine Throughout Antiquity.* Philadelphia: F. A. Davis, 1949.

Gottschalk, Carl W., and Susan K. Fellner. "History of the Science of Dialysis." *American Journal of Nephrology* 17 (1997): 289–98.

Govindjee, Rajni. "On the requirement of minimum number of four versus eight quanta of light for the evolution of one molecule of oxygen in photosynthesis: A historical note." *Photosynthetic Research* 59 (1999): 249–254.

Graebner, William. "The Unstable World of Benjamin Spock: Social Engineering in a Democratic Culture, 1917–1950." *Journal of American History* 67 (1980): 612–29.

Grant, Linda. *Sexing the Millennium: Women and the Sexual Revolution.* New York: Grove Press, 1994.

Grosskurth, Phyllis. *Melanie Klein: Her World and Her Work.* New York: Knopf, 1986.

Guillebaud, Jean-Claude. *Return to Vietnam.* London: Verso, 1994.

Gumpert, Martin. *Hahnemann.* New York: L. B. Fischer, 1946.

Haberling, W. *German Medicine.* New York: Paul B. Hoeber, 1934.

Haggard, Howard W. *The Doctor in History.* New Haven: Yale University Press, 1934.

Hahnemann, Samuel. *Organon of Medicine.* Blaine, WA: Cooper, 1982.

Hall, A. Rupert. *The Revolution in Science, 1500–1750.* London: Longman, 1983.

Hall, Stephen S. *Invisible Frontiers.* New York: Atlantic Monthly Press, 1987.

———. *A Commotion in the Blood.* New York: Henry Holt, 1997.

Hamburger, Viktor. *The Heritage of Experimental Embryology: Hans Spemann and the Organizer.* New York: Oxford University Press, 1988.

Harris, Henry. *The Birth of the Cell.* New Haven: Yale University Press, 1999.

Hart, Ellen. *Man Born to Live: Life and Work of Henry Dunant.* London: Victor Gollancz, 1953.

Harvey, William. *The Works of William Harvey, M.D.* Translated by Robert Willis. London: Sydenham Society, 1847.

Hawkes, Peter J. "Ernst Ruska." *Physics Today* 43, no. 7 (1990): 84–85.

Heidenry, John. *Theirs Was the Kingdom.* New York: W. W. Norton, 1993.

———. *What Wild Ecstasy.* New York: Simon & Schuster, 1997.

Hellerstein, David. "Plotting a Theory of the Brain." *New York Times Magazine,* 22 May 1988.

Henig, Robin Marantz. "Medicine's New Age." *Civilization,* April/May 1997, 42–49.

Hertzler, Arthur. *The Horse and Buggy Doctor.* New York: Harper & Brothers, 1938.

Hippocrates. *[Works]* Cambridge: Harvard University Press, 1923.

Hobbs, Colleen. *Florence Nightingale.* New York: Twayne, 1997.

Hodgkin, Alan. *Chance and Design: Reminiscences of Science in Peace and War.* Cambridge: Cambridge University Press, 1992.

Holloway, Marguerite. "The Reward of Ideas That Are Wrong." *Scientific American* 265, no. 2 (1991): 29–30.

Holmes, H. P. *Samuel Hahnemann: A Lecture.* Philadelphia: The Homeopathic Physician, 1894.

Hudson, Margaret M., and Robert S. Morton. "Fracastoro and Syphilis: 500 Years On." *Lancet* 348 (1996): 1495–96.

Jaffe, Bernard. *Crucibles: The Story of Chemistry.* New York: Dover, 1976.

Jarcho, Saul. "Morgagni and Auenbrugger in the Retrospect of Two Hundred Years." *Bulletin of the History of Medicine* 35, no. 6 (1961): 489–96.

Jordan, Edwin Oakes. *A Text-Book of General Bacteriology.* Philadelphia: W. B. Saunders, 1916.

Jouanna, Jacques. *Hippocrates.* Baltimore: Johns Hopkins University Press, 1998.

Judson, Horace Freeland. *The Eighth Day of Creation: The Makers of the Revolution in Biology.* New York: Simon & Schuster, 1979.

Kervran, Roger. *Laennec: His Life and Times.* Oxford: Pergamon Press, 1960.

Kevles, Bettyann. *Naked to the Bone.* New Brunswick, NJ: Rutgers University Press, 1997.

King, Lester S. *The Road to Medical Enlightenment, 1650–1695.* New York: American Elsevier, 1970.

———. *The Philosophy of Medicine: The Early Eighteenth Century.* Cambridge: Harvard University Press, 1978.

———. *Medical Thinking: A Historical Preface.* Princeton, NJ: Princeton University Press, 1982.

King, Pearl H. M. "The Life and Work of Melanie Klein in the British Psycho-analytical Society." *International Journal of Psychoanalysis* 64 (1983): 250–60.

King, Roger. *The Making of the Dentiste, 1650–1760.* Brookfield, VT: Ashgate, 1998.

Kleinfield, Sonny. *A Machine Called Indomitable.* New York: Times Books, 1985.

Kluger, Richard. *Ashes to Ashes: America's Hundred-Year Cigarette War, the Public Health, and the Unabashed Triumph of Philip Morris.* New York: Alfred A. Knopf, 1997.

Kobler, John. *The Reluctant Surgeon: A Biography of John Hunter.* Garden City, NY: Doubleday, 1960.

Kornberg, Arthur. *For the Love of Enzymes.* Cambridge: Harvard University Press, 1989.

———. "The Biologic Synthesis of Deoxyribonucleic Acid." In *Nobel Lectures in Physiology or Medicine, 1942–1962,* 664–80. Amsterdam: Elsevier, 1964.

———. *The Golden Helix: Inside Biotech Ventures.* Sausalito, CA: University Science Books, 1995.

Krebs, Albin. "Dr. Paul de Kruif, Popularizer of Medical Exploits, Is Dead." *New York Times,* 3 April 1971, 38.

Krebs, Hans. *Reminiscences and Reflections.* Oxford: Clarendon Press, 1981.

LaFollette, Hugh, and Niall Shanks. "Animal Experimentation: The Legacy of Claude Bernard." *International Studies in the Philosophy of Science* 8, no. 3 (1994): 195–210.

Lambert, L. "Some Anecdotes Around and with Colonel Ernst August Ruska." *Ultramicroscopy* 20 (1986): 337–40.

Lambert, L., and T. Mulvey. "Ernst Ruska (1906–1988), Designer Extraordinaire of the Electron Microscope: A Memoir." *Advances in Imaging and Electron Physics* 95 (1996): 3–62.

Lane, Levi C. "Rudolf Virchow." Reprint of *Occidental Medical Times,* August 1893.

Lawrence, Susan. "Medical Education." In *Companion Encyclopedia of the History of Medicine,* edited by W. F. Bynum and Roy Porter, 1151–79. London: Routledge, 1993.

Lederberg, Joshua. "The Transformation of Genetics by DNA: An Anniversary Celebration of Avery, Macleod and McCarty." *Genetics* 136 (1994): 423–26.

Lehrer, Steven. *Explorers of the Body.* Garden City, NY: Doubleday, 1979.

Lenoir, Timothy. "Science for the Clinic: Science Policy and the Formation of Carl Ludwig's Institute in Leipzig." In *The Investigative Enterprise: Experimental Physiology in Nineteenth-Century Medicine,* edited by William Coleman and Fredric L. Holmes, 139–78. Berkeley: University of California Press, 1988.

Lesch, John E. *Science and Medicine in France: The Emergence of Experimental Physiology, 1790–1815.* Cambridge: Harvard University Press, 1984.

Levy, Reuben. "Avicenna—His Life and Times." In *Toward Modern Science,* edited by Robert P. Palter, 202–19. New York: E. P. Dutton, 1969.

Levy, Steven. "Dr. Edelman's Brain." *New Yorker* 70, no. 11 (1994): 62–73.

Lewis, Jefferson. *Something Hidden: A Biography of Wilder Penfield.* New York: Doubleday, 1981.

Lindeboom, G. A. *Hermann Boerhaave.* London: Methuen, 1968.

Lister, Joseph. "On the Antiseptic Principle of the Practice of Surgery." In *The Collected Papers of Joseph Baron Lister,* vol. 2, 9–21. Oxford: Clarendon Press, 1909.

Louis, Pierre Charles Alexander. *Pathological Researches on Phthisis.* Boston: Hilliard, Gray, 1836.

———. *Anatomical, Pathological and Therapeutic Researches upon the Disease Known by the Name of Gastroenteritis, Putrid, Adynamic, Ataxic, Typhoid Fever, &c., Compared with the Most Common Acute Diseases.* Boston: I. R. Butts, 1836.

———. *Research on the Effects of Bloodletting in Some Inflammatory Diseases, and on the Influence of Tartarized Antimony and Vesication in Pneumonitis.* Boston: Hilliard, Gray, 1836.

Lucretius. *On the Nature of the Universe.* Translated by R. E. Latham. London: Penguin, 1951.

Ludmerer, Kenneth M. *Learning to Heal.* New York: Basic Books, 1985.

———. *Time to Heal.* New York: Oxford University Press, 1999.

Ludovici, L. J. *The Discovery of Anaesthesia.* New York: Thomas Y. Crowell, 1961.

Macfarlane, Gwyn. *Howard Florey: The Making of a Great Scientist.* London: Oxford University Press, 1979.

———. *Alexander Fleming: The Man and the Myth.* Cambridge: Harvard University Press, 1984.

Maier, Thomas. *Dr. Spock: An American Life.* New York: Harcourt Brace, 1998.

Major, Ralph H. *A History of Medicine.* 2 vols. Springfield, IL: Charles C. Thomas, 1954.

Malinin, Theodore. *Surgery and Life: The Extraordinary Career of Alexis Carrel.* New York: Harcourt Brace Jovanovich, 1979.

Margotta, Roberto. *The Story of Medicine.* New York: Golden Press, 1968.

Masters, William H., and Virginia E. Johnson. *Human Sexual Response.* Boston: Little, Brown, 1966.

Masters, William H., Virginia E. Johnson, and Robert C. Kolodny. *Crisis: Heterosexual Behavior in the Age of AIDS.* New York: Grove Press, 1988.

Mattson, James, and Simon Merrill. *The Story of MRI.* Ramat Gan, Israel: Bar-Ilan University Press, 1990.

McGrayne, Sharon Bertsch. *Nobel Prize Women in Science.* New York: Birch Lane, 1993.

McKenzie, A. E. E. *The Major Achievements of Science.* New York: Simon & Schuster, 1973.

McMurray, Emily J., and Donna Olendorf, eds. *Notable Twentieth-Century Scientists.* 4 vols. Detroit: Gale Research, 1995.

Mayr, Ernst. *The Growth of Biological Thought: Diversity, Evolution, and Inheritance.* Cambridge: Harvard University Press, 1982.

Medawar, P. B., and J. S. Medawar. *The Life Science: Current Ideas of Biology.* New York: Harper & Row, 1977.

Mencken, H. L. *My Life as Author and Editor.* New York: Alfred A. Knopf, 1993.

Meynell, Geoffrey. *Materials for a Biography of Dr. Thomas Sydenham, 1624–1689.* Folkestone, England: Winterdown, 1988.

Montagnier, Luc. *Virus: The Co-Discoverer of HIV Tracks Its Rampage and Charts the Future.* New York: W. W. Norton, 2000.

Moore, J. Stuart. *Chiropractic in America.* Baltimore: Johns Hopkins University Press, 1993.

Moorehead, Caroline. *Dunant's Dream: War, Switzerland, and the History of the Red Cross.* London: HarperCollins, 1998.

Mora, George. "Historiographic and Cultural Trends in Psychiatry: A Survey." *Bulletin of the History of Medicine* 35 (1961): 26–36.

Morabia, Alfredo. "P. C. A. Louis and the Birth of Clinical Epidemiology." *Journal of Clinical Epidemiology* 49, no. 12 (1996): 1327–33.

Morgan, Neil. "From Physiology to Biochemistry." In *Companion to the History of Modern Science,* edited by R. C. Olby, 494–502. London: Routledge, 1990.

Moritz, Charles, ed. and others. *Current Biography Yearbook.* New York: H. W. Wilson, 1940–2000.

Morton, Leslie, and Robert Moore. *A Bibliography of Medical and Biomedical Biography.* 2d ed. Brookfield, VT: Gower Publishing, 1994.

Morton, William T. G. "Remarks on the Proper Mode of Administering Ether by Inhalation." 1847. Reprinted in *Source Book of Medical History,* edited by L. Clendening, 366–72. New York: Dover, 1960.

Mulvey, Thomas. "Forty Years of Electron Microscopy." *Physics Bulletin* 24 (1973): 147–54.

Newton, James D. *Uncommon Friends.* New York: Harcourt Brace Jovanovich, 1987.

Nicolle, Jacques. *Louis Pasteur: The Story of His Major Discoveries.* New York: Basic Books, 1961.

Nightingale, Florence. *Notes on Nursing.* London: Harrison, 1859.

———. *Ever Yours, Florence Nightingale: Selected Letters.* Edited by Martha Vicinus and Bea Nergaard. Cambridge: Harvard University Press, 1990.

Nitske, W. Robert. *The Life of Wilhelm Conrad Rontgen.* Tucson: University of Arizona Press, 1971.

Nuland, Sherwin B. *Doctors: The Biography of Medicine.* New York: Alfred A. Knopf, 1988.

Nutton, Vivian. "Roman Medicine, 250 B.C. to A.D. 200." In *The Western Medical Tradition,* edited by Lawrence I. Conrad et al., 39–70. Cambridge: Cambridge University Press, 1995.

O'Malley, C. D. *Andreas Vesalius of Brussels.* Berkeley: University of California Press, 1964.

Oldstone, Michael B. A. *Viruses, Plagues, and History.* New York: Oxford University Press, 1998.

Olmsted, J. M. D., and E. Harris Olmsted. *Claude Bernard and the Experimental Method in Medicine.* New York: Henry Schuman, 1952.

Osler, William. "The Influence of Louis on American Medicine." In *An Alabama Student and Other Biographical Essays,* 190–210. New York: Oxford University Press, 1908.

Pachter, Henry M. *Paracelsus: Magic into Science.* New York: Henry Schuman, 1951.

Paracelsus. *Selected Writings.* Edited by Norbert Guterman. Princeton, N.J.: Princeton University Press, 1973.

Paré, Ambroise. *On Monsters and Marvels.* Chicago: University of Chicago Press, 1982.

Parry, Albert. *The Russian Scientist.* New York: Macmillan, 1973.

Parvez, H., and S. Parvez, eds. *Advances in Experimental Medicine: A Centenary Tribute to Claude Bernard.* Amsterdam: Elsevier, 1980.

Pelling, Margaret. *Cholera, Fever, and English Medicine, 1825–1865.* New York: Oxford University Press, 1978.

Penfield, Wilder. *No Man Alone.* Boston: Little, Brown, 1977.

Penfield, Wilder, and Herbert Jasper. *Epilepsy and the Functional Anatomy of the Human Brain.* Boston: Little, Brown, 1954.

Perkins, Wendy. *Midwifery and Medicine in Modern France: Louise Bourgeois.* Exeter: University of Exeter Press, 1996.

Perutz, M. F. "The Pioneer Defended." *New York Review of Books,* 21 December 1995, 54–58.

Pickstone, John V. "Physiology and Experimental Medicine." In *Companion to the History of Modern Science,* edited by R. C. Olby et al., 728–42. London: Routledge, 1990.

Pinel, Philippe. *Nosographie philosophique, ou, La Méthode de l'analyse appliquée a la médecine.* Paris: Chez Richard, Caille et Ravier, an 7 [1798].

Porter, Roy. *The Greatest Benefit to Mankind.* New York: W. W. Norton, 1997.

Porter, Roy, ed. *Biographical Dictionary of Scientists.* 2d ed. New York: Oxford University Press, 1994.

Porter, Roy, and W. F. Bynum. "The Art and Science of Medicine." In *Companion Encyclopedia of the History of Medicine,* edited by W. F. Bynum and Roy Porter, 3–11. London: Routledge, 1993.

Radetsky, Peter. *The Invisible Invaders: Viruses and the Scientists Who Pursue Them.* Boston: Little, Brown, 1994.

Ramón y Cajal, Santiago. *Recollections of My Life.* Cambridge: MIT Press, 1989.

Reid, Edith Gittings. *The Great Physician: A Short Life of Sir William Osler.* New York: Oxford University Press, 1931.

Reiser, Stanley Joel. *Medicine and the Reign of Technology.* Cambridge: Cambridge University Press, 1978.

Rhodes, Richard. *Deadly Feasts.* New York: Simon & Schuster, 1997.

Ring, Malvin E. *Dentistry: An Illustrated History.* New York: Abrams/C. V. Mosby, 1985.

Roazen, Paul. *Freud and His Followers.* New York: Alfred A. Knopf, 1975.

Robbins, Frederick C. "Reminiscences of a Virologist." In *Polio,* edited by Thomas M. Daniel and Frederick C. Robbins, 121–34. Rochester, NY: University of Rochester Press, 1997.

Robin, Eugene Debs, ed. *Claude Bernard and the Internal Environment.* New York: Marcel Dekker, 1979.

Robinson, Paul. *The Modernization of Sex.* New York: Harper & Row, 1976.

Robinson, Victor. *Pathfinders in Medicine.* New York: Medical Life Press, 1929.

———. "Robert Koch." *Medical Life,* n.s., 39, no. 3 (1932): 129–67.

Roemer, Rodney. "Nuclear Magnetic Resonance: A Historical Perspective." In *MRI for Technologists,* edited by Peggy Woodward and Roger D. Freimarck, 3–10. New York: McGraw-Hill, 1995.

Rosebury, Theodore. *Microbes and Morals: The Strange Story of Venereal Disease.* New York: Viking Press, 1971.

Rosen, George. "Carl Ludwig and His American Students." *Bulletin of the Institute of the History of Medicine* 4, no. 8 (1936): 609–50.

———. *A History of Public Health.* 1958. Reprint (expanded edition), Baltimore: Johns Hopkins University Press, 1993.

Rothkopf, Carol. *Jean-Henri Dunant.* New York: Franklin Watts, 1969.

Rothman, David. J., Steven Marcus, and Stephanie Kiceluk, eds. *Medicine and Western Civilization.* New Brunswick, NJ: Rutgers University Press, 1995.

Rothschuh, Karl. *History of Physiology.* Huntington, NY: Robert E. Krieger, 1973.

Ruska, Ernst. *The Early Development of Electron Lenses and Electron Microscopy.* Stuttgart: S. Hirzel, 1980.

Russell, Nicholas. "Oswald Avery and the Origin of Molecular Biology." *British Journal of the History of Science* 21 (1988): 393–400.

Rutkow, Ira. *Surgery: An Illustrated History.* St. Louis: Mosby-Year Book, 1993.

Rutledge, Robb H. "Theodor Billroth: A Century Later." *Surgery* 118 (1995): 36–43.

Ryan, Frank. *The Forgotten Plague.* Boston: Little, Brown, 1992.

Sacks, Oliver. "Making up the Mind." *New York Review of Books,* 8 April 1993, 42–50.

Salinsky, Michael. "Early Chapters in the Stethoscope's Evolution." *Journal of the American Medical Association* 264, no. 21 (1990): 2817.

Sayers, Janet. *Mothers of Psychoanalysis.* New York: W. W. Norton, 1991.

Schafer, Roy. "One Perspective on the Freud-Klein Controversies, 1941–45." *International Journal of Psycho-Analysis* 75 (1994): 359–65.

Schild, H. O. "Dale and the Development of Pharmacology." *British Journal of Pharmacology* 56 (1976): 3–7.

Schorer, Mark. *Sinclair Lewis: An American Life.* New York: McGraw-Hill, 1961.

Segal, Hanna. *Melanie Klein.* New York: Penguin, 1981.

Semmelweis, Ignaz. *The Etiology, Concept, and Prophylaxis of Childbed Fever.* Translated and edited by K. Codell Carter. Madison: University of Wisconsin Press, 1983.

Sexton, Christopher. *Burnet: A Life.* New York: Oxford University Press, 1999.

Seymer, Lucy Ridgley. *A General History of Nursing.* New York: Macmillan, 1933.

Shorter, Edward. *Bedside Manners: The Troubled History of Doctors and Patients.* New York: Simon & Schuster, 1985.

———. *A History of Psychiatry.* New York: John Wiley & Sons, 1997.

Sigerist, Henry E. *The Great Doctors: A Biographical History of Medicine.* New York: W. W. Norton, 1933.

———. *Henry E. Sigerist on the History of Medicine.* Edited by Felix Marti-Ibañez. New York: MD Publications, 1936.

———. *Primitive and Archaic Medicine.* Vol. 1 of *A History of Medicine.* New York: Oxford University Press, 1951.

———. "Developments and Trends in Dentistry." In *Henry E. Sigerist on the Sociology of Medicine,* edited by Milton I. Roemer, 327–36. New York: MD Publications, 1960.

Silverstein, Arthur M. *A History of Immunology.* San Diego: Academic Press, 1988.

Singer, Charles. "Galen as a Modern." In *Toward Modern Science,* edited by Robert M. Palter, 108–22. New York: E. P. Dutton, 1969.

Small, Hugh. *Florence Nightingale: Avenging Angel.* London: Constable, 1998.

Smith, Jane S. *Patenting the Sun: Polio and the Salk Vaccine.* New York: William Morrow, 1990.

Smith, Roger. *The Human Sciences.* New York: W. W. Norton, 1997.

Snow, John. "On the Mode of Communication of Cholera." 1854. Excerpted in *Source Book of Medical History,* edited by L. Clendening, 468–73. New York: Henry Schuman, 1942.

Snyder, Solomon. *Biological Aspects of Mental Disorder.* New York: Oxford University Press, 1980.

———. *Drugs and the Brain.* New York: Scientific American Library, 1986.

———. *Brainstorming: The Science and Politics of Opiate Research.* Cambridge: Harvard University Press, 1989.

Sourkes, Theodore. *Nobel Prize Winners in Medicine and Physiology, 1901–1965.* New York: Abelard-Schuman, 1966.

Spemann, Hans. *Embryonic Development and Induction.* New Haven, CT: Yale University Press, 1938.

Spemann, Hans, and Hilde Mangold. "Induction of Embryonic Primordia by Implantation of Organizers from a Different Species." In *Foundations of Experimental Embryology,* edited by Benjamin H. Willier and Jane M. Oppenheimer, 144–84. New York: Hafner Press, 1974.

Spock, Benjamin. *The Common Sense Book of Baby and Child Care.* New York: Duell, Sloan & Pearce, 1946.

Spock, Benjamin, and Mary Morgan. *Spock on Spock.* New York: Pantheon, 1989.

Stage, Sarah. *Female Complaints: Lydia Pinkham and the Business of Women's Medicine.* New York: W. W. Norton, 1979.

Stanley, Autumn. *Mothers and Daughters of Invention: Notes for a Revised History of Technology.* New Brunswick, NJ: Rutgers University Press, 1995.

Starr, Paul. *The Social Transformation of American Medicine.* New York: Basic Books, 1982.

Stone, Michael H. *Healing the Mind.* New York: W. W. Norton, 1997.

Strachey, Lytton. *Eminent Victorians.* London: Chatto & Windus, 1918.

Straus, Eugene. *Rosalyn Yalow, Nobel Laureate: Her Life and Work in Medicine.* New York: Plenum, 1998.

Sulloway, Frank J. *Freud: Biologist of the Mind.* New York: Basic Books, 1983.

Susskind, Charles. "The Invention of Computed Tomography." In History of Technology, vol. 6, edited by A. Rupert Hall and Norman Smith, 39–79. London: Mansell Publishing, 1981.

Talbott, John H. *A Biographical History of Medicine.* New York: Grune & Stratton, 1970.

Tauber, Alfred I. *The Immune Self: Theory or Metaphor.* Cambridge: Cambridge University Press, 1994.

Tedeschi, Cesare G. "Bernardino Ramazzini (1633–1714): *De morbis artificum.*" *Human Pathology* 1, no. 2 (1970): 315–20.

Temkin, Oswei. *Galenism.* Ithaca, NY: Cornell University Press, 1973.

———. *Hippocrates in a World of Pagans and Christians.* Baltimore: Johns Hopkins University Press, 1991.

Thomson, Elizabeth H. *Harvey Cushing: Surgeon, Author, Artist.* New York: Henry Schuman, 1950.

Trail, R. R. "Sydenham's Impact on English Medicine." *Medical History* 9 (1965): 356–64.

Tröhler, Ulrich. "Surgery (Modern)." In *Companion Encyclopedia of the History of Medicine,* edited by W. F. Bynum and Roy Porter, 984–1028. London: Routledge, 1993.

Underwood, E. Ashworth. *Boerhaave's Men at Leyden and After.* Edinburgh: Edinburgh University Press, 1977.

Vallery-Radot, René. *The Life of Pasteur.* New York: Doubleday, Doran, 1928.

Varmus, Harold. "Retroviruses and Oncogenes I (Nobel Lecture)." *Angewandte Chemie* 29, no. 7 (1990): 707–822.

Vaughan, R. B. "The Romantic Rationalist: A Study of Elie Metchnikoff." *Medical History* 10 (1965): 201–15.

Venzmer, Gerhard. *5000 Years of Medicine.* New York: Taplinger, 1968.

Wainwright, Milton. Miracle Cure: *The Story of Penicillin and the Golden Age of Antibiotics.* Oxford: Basil Blackwell, 1990.

Waksman, Selman. *My Life with the Microbes.* New York: Simon & Schuster, 1954.

———. *The Actinomycetes: A Summary of Current Knowledge.* New York: Ronald Press, 1967.

Waldholz, Michael. *Curing Cancer.* New York: Simon & Schuster, 1997.

Wangensteen, O., and S. Wangensteen. *The Rise of Surgery.* Minneapolis: University of Minnesota Press, 1978.

Wasson, Tyler, ed. *Nobel Prize Winners.* New York: H. W. Wilson, 1988.

Wear, Andrew. "The Heart and Blood from Vesalius to Harvey." In *Companion to the History of Modern Science,* edited by R. C. Olby et al., 568–82. London: Routledge, 1990.

Weinberg, Robert A. *Racing to the Beginning of the Road.* New York: Harmony Books, 1996.

———. *One Renegade Cell: How Cancer Begins.* New York: Basic Books, 1998.

Weinberger, Bernhard W. *Pierre Fauchard: Surgeon-Dentist.* Minneapolis: Pierre Fauchard Academy, 1941.

Weiner, Doris B. "Philippe Pinel." In *Doctors, Nurses, and Medical Practitioners: A Bio-Bibliographical Sourcebook,* edited by Lois N. Magner, 216–21. Westport, CT: Greenwood Press, 1997.

Weisse, Allen B. *Conversations in Medicine.* New York: New York University Press, 1984.

———. *Medical Odysseys.* New Brunswick, NJ: Rutgers University Press, 1991.

Welbourn, R. B. "Endocrine Diseases." In *Companion Encyclopedia of the History of Medicine,* edited by W. F. Bynum and Roy Porter, 484–511. London: Routledge, 1993.

Wilkinson, Lise. "Epidemiology." In *Companion Encyclopedia of the History of Medicine,* edited by W. F. Bynum and Roy Porter, 1262–82. London: Routledge, 1993.

Williams, Greer. *Virus Hunters.* New York: Alfred A. Knopf, 1967.

Williams, Trevor. *Howard Florey: Penicillin and After.* London: Oxford University Press, 1984.

Willius, Frederick Arthur, and Thomas Keys, eds. *Classics of Cardiology.* New York: Dover, 1961. Reprint of *Cardiac Classics,* St. Louis: C. V. Mosby, 1941.

Woglom, William H. *Discoverers for Medicine.* New Haven, CT: Yale University Press, 1949.

Wynbrandt, James. *The Excruciating History of Dentistry.* New York: St. Martin's Press, 1998.

Wynder, Ernst. "Tobacco and Health: A Review of the History and Suggestions for Public Health Policy." *Public Health Reports* 103, no. 1 (1988): 8–18.

Yaeger, Dan. "The Lady Who Helped Ladies." *Yankee,* September 1989, 64–67, 112–18.

Young, D. A. B. "Florence Nightingale's Fever." *British Medical Journal* 311 (1995): 1697–701.

Young, James Harvey. *The Toadstool Millionaires.* Princeton, NJ: Princeton University Press, 1961.

Zilboorg, Gregory. *A History of Medical Psychology.* New York: W. W. Norton, 1941.

Zimmerman, Leo M., and Ilza Veith. *Great Ideas in the History of Surgery.* 2d rev. ed. New York: Dover, 1967.

Zuckerman, Michael. "Dr. Spock: The Confidence Man." In *The Family in History,* edited by Charles Rosenberg, 179–207. Philadelphia: University of Pennsylvania Press, 1975.

# Index

*Page references to full profiles are printed in boldface type.*

# Picture Credits